An Introduction to Quantum
Computing

An Introduction to Quantum Computing

Phillip Kaye
Raymond Laflamme
Michele Mosca

OXFORD
UNIVERSITY PRESS

OXFORD
UNIVERSITY PRESS

Great Clarendon Street, Oxford OX2 6DP

Oxford University Press is a department of the University of Oxford.
It furthers the University's objective of excellence in research, scholarship,
and education by publishing worldwide in

Oxford New York

Auckland Cape Town Dar es Salaam Hong Kong Karachi
Kuala Lumpur Madrid Melbourne Mexico City Nairobi
New Delhi Shanghai Taipei Toronto
With offices in
Argentina Austria Brazil Chile Czech Republic France Greece
Guatemala Hungary Italy Japan South Korea Poland Portugal
Singapore Switzerland Thailand Turkey Ukraine Vietnam

ISBN 978-0-19-857049-3

Printed in the United Kingdom by
Lightning Source UK Ltd., Milton Keynes

Contents

Preface   x

Acknowledgements   xi

1   INTRODUCTION AND BACKGROUND   1

   1.1   Overview   1

   1.2   Computers and the Strong Church–Turing Thesis   2

   1.3   The Circuit Model of Computation   6

   1.4   A Linear Algebra Formulation of the Circuit Model   8

   1.5   Reversible Computation   12

   1.6   A Preview of Quantum Physics   15

   1.7   Quantum Physics and Computation   19

2   LINEAR ALGEBRA AND THE DIRAC NOTATION   21

   2.1   The Dirac Notation and Hilbert Spaces   21

   2.2   Dual Vectors   23

   2.3   Operators   27

   2.4   The Spectral Theorem   30

   2.5   Functions of Operators   32

   2.6   Tensor Products   33

   2.7   The Schmidt Decomposition Theorem   35

   2.8   Some Comments on the Dirac Notation   37

3   QUBITS AND THE FRAMEWORK OF QUANTUM MECHANICS   38

   3.1   The State of a Quantum System   38

   3.2   Time-Evolution of a Closed System   43

   3.3   Composite Systems   45

   3.4   Measurement   48

	3.5	Mixed States and General Quantum Operations	53
		3.5.1 Mixed States	53
		3.5.2 Partial Trace	56
		3.5.3 General Quantum Operations	59
4	**A QUANTUM MODEL OF COMPUTATION**		61
	4.1	The Quantum Circuit Model	61
	4.2	Quantum Gates	63
		4.2.1 1-Qubit Gates	63
		4.2.2 Controlled-U Gates	66
	4.3	Universal Sets of Quantum Gates	68
	4.4	Efficiency of Approximating Unitary Transformations	71
	4.5	Implementing Measurements with Quantum Circuits	73
5	**SUPERDENSE CODING AND QUANTUM TELEPORTATION**		78
	5.1	Superdense Coding	79
	5.2	Quantum Teleportation	80
	5.3	An Application of Quantum Teleportation	82
6	**INTRODUCTORY QUANTUM ALGORITHMS**		86
	6.1	Probabilistic Versus Quantum Algorithms	86
	6.2	Phase Kick-Back	91
	6.3	The Deutsch Algorithm	94
	6.4	The Deutsch–Jozsa Algorithm	99
	6.5	Simon's Algorithm	103
7	**ALGORITHMS WITH SUPERPOLYNOMIAL SPEED-UP**		110
	7.1	Quantum Phase Estimation and the Quantum Fourier Transform	110
		7.1.1 Error Analysis for Estimating Arbitrary Phases	117
		7.1.2 Periodic States	120
		7.1.3 GCD, LCM, the Extended Euclidean Algorithm	124
	7.2	Eigenvalue Estimation	125

7.3   Finding-Orders   130

       7.3.1   The Order-Finding Problem   130

       7.3.2   Some Mathematical Preliminaries   131

       7.3.3   The Eigenvalue Estimation Approach to Order Find-
               ing   134

       7.3.4   Shor's Approach to Order Finding   139

7.4   Finding Discrete Logarithms   142

7.5   Hidden Subgroups   146

       7.5.1   More on Quantum Fourier Transforms   147

       7.5.2   Algorithm for the Finite Abelian Hidden Subgroup
               Problem   149

7.6   Related Algorithms and Techniques   151

8   ALGORITHMS BASED ON AMPLITUDE
    AMPLIFICATION   152

8.1   Grover's Quantum Search Algorithm   152

8.2   Amplitude Amplification   163

8.3   Quantum Amplitude Estimation and Quantum Counting   170

8.4   Searching Without Knowing the Success Probability   175

8.5   Related Algorithms and Techniques   178

9   QUANTUM COMPUTATIONAL COMPLEXITY THEORY
    AND LOWER BOUNDS   179

9.1   Computational Complexity   180

       9.1.1   Language Recognition Problems and Complexity
               Classes   181

9.2   The Black-Box Model   185

       9.2.1   State Distinguishability   187

9.3   Lower Bounds for Searching in the Black-Box Model: Hybrid
       Method   188

9.4   General Black-Box Lower Bounds   191

9.5   Polynomial Method   193

       9.5.1   Applications to Lower Bounds   194

       9.5.2   Examples of Polynomial Method Lower Bounds   196

9.6   Block Sensitivity   197

    9.6.1 Examples of Block Sensitivity Lower Bounds   197

9.7   Adversary Methods   198

    9.7.1 Examples of Adversary Lower Bounds   200

    9.7.2 Generalizations   203

10 QUANTUM ERROR CORRECTION   204

10.1 Classical Error Correction   204

    10.1.1 The Error Model   205

    10.1.2 Encoding   206

    10.1.3 Error Recovery   207

10.2 The Classical Three-Bit Code   207

10.3 Fault Tolerance   211

10.4 Quantum Error Correction   212

    10.4.1 Error Models for Quantum Computing   213

    10.4.2 Encoding   216

    10.4.3 Error Recovery   217

10.5 Three- and Nine-Qubit Quantum Codes   223

    10.5.1 The Three-Qubit Code for Bit-Flip Errors   223

    10.5.2 The Three-Qubit Code for Phase-Flip Errors   225

    10.5.3 Quantum Error Correction Without Decoding   226

    10.5.4 The Nine-Qubit Shor Code   230

10.6 Fault-Tolerant Quantum Computation   234

    10.6.1 Concatenation of Codes and the Threshold Theorem   237

APPENDIX A   241

A.1 Tools for Analysing Probabilistic Algorithms   241

A.2 Solving the Discrete Logarithm Problem When the Order of
a Is Composite   243

A.3 How Many Random Samples Are Needed to Generate
a Group?   245

A.4 Finding r Given $\frac{k}{r}$ for Random k 247

A.5 Adversary Method Lemma   248

A.6 Black-Boxes for Group Computations   250

A.7 Computing Schmidt Decompositions   253

A.8 General Measurements   255

A.9 Optimal Distinguishing of Two States   258

    A.9.1 A Simple Procedure   258

    A.9.2 Optimality of This Simple Procedure   258

Bibliography   260

Index   270

Preface

We have offered a course at the University of Waterloo in quantum computing since 1999. We have had students from a variety of backgrounds take the course, including students in mathematics, computer science, physics, and engineering. While there is an abundance of very good introductory papers, surveys and books, many of these are geared towards students already having a strong background in a particular area of physics or mathematics.

With this in mind, we have designed this book for the following reader. The reader has an undergraduate education in some scientific field, and should particularly have a solid background in linear algebra, including vector spaces and inner products. Prior familiarity with topics such as tensor products and spectral decomposition is not required, but may be helpful. We review all the necessary material, in any case. In some places we have not been able to avoid using notions from group theory. We clearly indicate this at the beginning of the relevant sections, and have kept these sections self-contained so that they may be skipped by the reader unacquainted with group theory. We have attempted to give a gentle and digestible introduction of a difficult subject, while at the same time keeping it reasonably complete and technically detailed.

We integrated exercises into the body of the text. Each exercise is designed to illustrate a particular concept, fill in the details of a calculation or proof, or to show how concepts in the text can be generalized or extended. To get the most out of the text, we encourage the student to attempt most of the exercises.

We have avoided the temptation to include many of the interesting and important advanced or peripheral topics, such as the mathematical formalism of quantum information theory and quantum cryptography. Our intent is not to provide a comprehensive reference book for the field, but rather to provide students and instructors of the subject with a reasonably brief, and very accessible introductory graduate or senior undergraduate textbook.

Acknowledgements

The authors would like to extend thanks to the many colleagues and scientists around the world that have helped with the writing of this textbook, including Andris Ambainis, Paul Busch, Lawrence Ioannou, David Kribs, Ashwin Nayak, Mark Saaltink, and many other members of the Institute for Quantum Computing and students at the University of Waterloo, who have taken our introductory quantum computing course over the past few years.

Phillip Kaye would like to thank his wife Janine for her patience and support, and his father Ron for his keen interest in the project and for his helpful comments.

Raymond Laflamme would like to thank Janice Gregson, Patrick and Jocelyne Laflamme for their patience, love, and insights on the intuitive approach to error correction.

Michele Mosca would like to thank his wife Nelia for her love and encouragement and his parents for their support.

1

INTRODUCTION AND BACKGROUND

1.1 Overview

A computer is a physical device that helps us process information by executing algorithms. An algorithm is a well-defined procedure, with finite description, for realizing an information-processing task. An information-processing task can always be translated into a physical task.

When designing complex algorithms and protocols for various information-processing tasks, it is very helpful, perhaps essential, to work with some idealized computing model. However, when studying the true limitations of a computing device, especially for some practical reason, it is important not to forget the relationship between computing and physics. Real computing devices are embodied in a larger and often richer physical reality than is represented by the idealized computing model.

Quantum information processing is the result of using the physical reality that quantum theory tells us about for the purposes of performing tasks that were previously thought impossible or infeasible. Devices that perform quantum information processing are known as *quantum computers*. In this book we examine how quantum computers can be used to solve certain problems more efficiently than can be done with classical computers, and also how this can be done reliably even when there is a possibility for errors to occur.

In this first chapter we present some fundamental notions of computation theory and quantum physics that will form the basis for much of what follows. After this brief introduction, we will review the necessary tools from linear algebra in Chapter 2, and detail the framework of quantum mechanics, as relevant to our model of quantum computation, in Chapter 3. In the remainder of the book we examine quantum teleportation, quantum algorithms and quantum error correction in detail.

1

1.2 Computers and the Strong Church–Turing Thesis

We are often interested in the amount of *resources* used by a computer to solve a problem, and we refer to this as the *complexity* of the computation. An important resource for a computer is *time*. Another resource is *space*, which refers to the amount of memory used by the computer in performing the computation. We measure the amount of a resource used in a computation for solving a given problem as a function of the length of the input of an instance of that problem. For example, if the problem is to multiply two n bit numbers, a computer might solve this problem using up to $2n^2+3$ units of time (where the unit of time may be seconds, or the length of time required for the computer to perform a basic step).

Of course, the exact amount of resources used by a computer executing an algorithm depends on the physical architecture of the computer. A different computer multiplying the same numbers mentioned above might use up to time $4n^3+n+5$ to execute the same basic algorithm. This fact seems to present a problem if we are interested in studying the complexity of algorithms themselves, abstracted from the details of the machines that might be used to execute them. To avoid this problem we use a more coarse measure of complexity. One coarser measure is to consider only the highest-order terms in the expressions quantifying resource requirements, and to ignore constant multiplicative factors. For example, consider the two computers mentioned above that run a searching algorithm in times $2n^2 + 3$ and $4n^3 + n + 7$, respectively. The highest-order terms are n^2 and n^3, respectively (suppressing the constant multiplicative factors 2 and 4, respectively). We say that the running time of that algorithm for those computers is in $O(n^2)$ and $O(n^3)$, respectively.

We should note that $O\left(f(n)\right)$ denotes an *upper* bound on the running time of the algorithm. For example, if a running time complexity is in $O(n^2)$ or in $O(\log n)$, then it is also in $O(n^3)$. In this way, expressing the resource requirements using the O notation gives a hierarchy of complexities. If we wish to describe *lower* bounds, then we use the Ω notation.

It often is very convenient to go a step further and use an even more coarse description of resources used. As we describe in Section 9.1, in theoretical computer science, an algorithm is considered to be *efficient* with respect to some resource if the amount of that resource used in the algorithm is in $O(n^k)$ for some k. In this case we say that the algorithm is *polynomial* with respect to the resource. If an algorithm's running time is in $O(n)$, we say that it is *linear*, and if the running time is in $O(\log n)$ we say that it is *logarithmic*. Since linear and logarithmic functions do not grow faster than polynomial functions, these algorithms are also efficient. Algorithms that use $\Omega(c^n)$ resources, for some constant c, are said to be *exponential*, and are considered not to be efficient. If the running time of an algorithm cannot be bounded above by any polynomial, we say its running time is *superpolynomial*. The term 'exponential' is often used loosely to mean superpolynomial.

One advantage of this coarse measure of complexity, which we will elaborate on, is that it appears to be robust against reasonable changes to the computing model and how resources are counted. For example, one cost that is often ignored when measuring the complexity of a computing model is the time it takes to move information around. For example, if the physical bits are arranged along a line, then to bring together two bits that are n-units apart will take time proportional to n (due to special relativity, if nothing else). Ignoring this cost is in general justifiable, since in modern computers, for an n of practical size, this transportation time is negligible. Furthermore, properly accounting for this time only changes the complexity by a linear factor (and thus does not affect the polynomial versus superpolynomial dichotomy).

Computers are used so extensively to solve such a wide variety of problems, that questions of their power and efficiency are of enormous practical importance, aside from being of theoretical interest. At first glance, the goal of characterizing the problems that can be solved on a computer, and to quantify the efficiency with which problems can be solved, seems a daunting one. The range of sizes and architectures of modern computers encompasses devices as simple as a single programmable logic chip in a household appliance, and as complex as the enormously powerful supercomputers used by NASA. So it appears that we would be faced with addressing the questions of computability and efficiency for computers in each of a vast number of categories.

The development of the mathematical theories of computability and computational complexity theory has shown us, however, that the situation is much better. The *Church–Turing Thesis* says that a computing problem can be solved on *any* computer that we could hope to build, if and only if it can be solved on a very simple 'machine', named a *Turing machine* (after the mathematician Alan Turing who conceived it). It should be emphasized that the Turing 'machine' is a mathematical abstraction (and not a physical device). A Turing machine is a computing model consisting of a finite set of states, an infinite 'tape' which symbols from a finite alphabet can be written to and read from using a moving head, and a transition function that specifies the next state in terms of the current state and symbol currently pointed to by the head.

If we believe the Church–Turing Thesis, then a function is computable by a Turing machine if and only if it is computable by some realistic computing device. In fact, the technical term *computable* corresponds to what can be computed by a Turing machine.

To understand the intuition behind the Church–Turing Thesis, consider some other computing device, A, which has some finite description, accepts input strings x, and has access to an arbitrary amount of workspace. We can write a computer program for our universal Turing machine that will *simulate* the evolution of A on input x. One could either simulate the logical evolution of A (much like one computer operating system can simulate another), or even more naively, given the complete physical description of the finite system A, and the laws of physics governing it, our universal Turing machine could alternatively simulate it at a physical level.

The original Church–Turing Thesis says nothing about the efficiency of computation. When one computer simulates another, there is usually some sort of 'overhead' cost associated with the simulation. For example, consider two types of computer, A and B. Suppose we want to write a program for A so that it simulates the behaviour of B. Suppose that in order to simulate a single step of the evolution of B, computer A requires 5 steps. Then a problem that is solved by B in time $O(n^3)$ is solved by A in time in $5 \cdot O(n^3) = O(n^3)$. This simulation is efficient. Simulations of one computer by another can also involve a trade-off between resources of different kinds, such as time and space. As an example, consider computer A simulating another computer C. Suppose that when computer C uses S units of space and T units of space, the simulation requires that A use up to $O(ST2^S)$ units of time. If C can solve a problem in time $O(n^2)$ using $O(n)$ space, then A uses up to $O(n^3 2^n)$ time to simulate C.

We say that a simulation of one computer by another is *efficient* if the 'overhead' in resources used by the simulation is *polynomial* (i.e. simulating an $O(f(n))$ algorithm uses $O(f(n)^k)$ resources for some fixed integer k). So in our above example, A can simulate B efficiently but not necessarily C (the running times listed are only upper bounds, so we do not know for sure if the exponential overhead is necessary).

One alternative computing model that is more closely related to how one typically describes algorithms and writes computer programs is the random access machine (RAM) model. A RAM machine can perform elementary computational operations including writing inputs into its memory (whose units are assumed to store integers), elementary arithmetic operations on values stored in its memory, and an operation conditioned on some value in memory. The classical algorithms we describe and analyse in this textbook implicitly are described in log-RAM model, where operations involving n-bit numbers take time n.

In order to extend the Church–Turing Thesis to say something useful about the efficiency of computation, it is useful to generalize the definition of a Turing machine slightly. A *probabilistic Turing machine* is one capable of making a random binary choice at each step, where the state transition rules are expanded to account for these random bits. We can say that a probabilistic Turing machine is a Turing machine with a built-in 'coin-flipper'. There are some important problems that we know how to solve efficiently using a probabilistic Turing machine, but do not know how to solve efficiently using a conventional Turing machine (without a coin-flipper). An example of such a problem is that of finding square roots modulo a prime.

It may seem strange that the addition of a source of randomness (the coin-flipper) could add power to a Turing machine. In fact, some results in computational complexity theory give reason to suspect that every problem (including the "square root modulo a prime" problem above) for which probabilistic Turing machine can efficiently guess the correct answer with high probability, can be solved efficiently by a deterministic Turing machine. However, since we do not have proof of this equivalence between Turing machines and probabilistic Turing machines, and problems such as the square root modulo a prime problem above are evidence that a coin-flipper may offer additional power, we will state the following thesis in terms of probabilistic Turing machines. This thesis will be very important in motivating the importance of quantum computing.

(Classical) Strong Church–Turing Thesis: *A probabilistic Turing machine can efficiently simulate any realistic model of computation.*

Accepting the Strong Church–Turing Thesis allows us to discuss the notion of the intrinsic complexity of a problem, independent of the details of the computing model.

The Strong Church–Turing Thesis has survived so many attempts to violate it that before the advent of quantum computing the thesis had come to be widely accepted. To understand its importance, consider again the problem of determining the computational resources required to solve computational problems. In light of the strong Church–Turing Thesis, the problem is vastly simplified. It will suffice to restrict our investigations to the capabilities of a probabilistic Turing machine (or any equivalent model of computation, such as a modern personal computer with access to an arbitrarily large amount of memory), since any realistic computing model will be roughly equivalent in power to it. You might wonder why the word 'realistic' appears in the statement of the strong Church–Turing Thesis. It is possible to describe special-purpose (classical) machines for solving certain problems in such a way that a probabilistic Turing machine simulation may require an exponential overhead in time or space. At first glance, such proposals seem to challenge the strong Church–Turing Thesis. However, these machines invariably 'cheat' by not accounting for all the resources they use. While it seems that the special-purpose machine uses exponentially less time and space than a probabilistic Turing machine solving the problem, the special-purpose machine needs to perform some physical task that implicitly requires superpolynomial resources. The term *realistic model of computation* in the statement of the strong Church–Turing Thesis refers to a model of computation which is consistent with the laws of physics and in which we explicitly account for *all* the physical resources used by that model.

It is important to note that in order to actually implement a Turing machine or something equivalent it, one must find a way to deal with realistic errors. Error-correcting codes were developed early in the history of computation in order to deal with the faults inherent with any practical implementation of a computer. However, the error-correcting procedures are also not perfect, and could introduce additional errors themselves. Thus, the error correction needs to be done in a *fault-tolerant* way. Fortunately for classical computation, efficient fault-tolerant error-correcting techniques have been found to deal with realistic error models.

The fundamental problem with the classical strong Church–Turing Thesis is that it appears that classical physics is not powerful enough to efficiently simulate quantum physics. The basic principle is still believed to be true; however, we need a computing model capable of simulating arbitrary 'realistic' physical devices, including quantum devices. The answer may be a quantum version of the strong Church–Turing Thesis, where we replace the probabilistic Turing machine with some reasonable type of *quantum* computing model. We describe a quantum model of computing in Chapter 4 that is equivalent in power to what is known as a quantum Turing machine.

Quantum Strong Church–Turing Thesis: *A quantum Turing machine can efficiently simulate any realistic model of computation.*

1.3   The Circuit Model of Computation

In Section 1.2, we discussed a prototypical computer (or *model of computation*) known as the probabilistic Turing machine. Another useful model of computation is that of a *uniform families of reversible circuits*. (We will see in Section 1.5 why we can restrict attention to reversible gates and circuits.) Circuits are networks composed of *wires* that carry bit values to *gates* that perform elementary operations on the bits. The circuits we consider will all be *acyclic*, meaning that the bits move through the circuit in a linear fashion, and the wires never feed back to a prior location in the circuit. A circuit C_n has n wires, and can be described by a circuit diagram similar to that shown in Figure 1.1 for $n = 4$. The input bits are written onto the wires entering the circuit from the left side of the diagram. At every time step t each wire can enter at most one gate G. The output bits are read-off the wires leaving the circuit at the right side of the diagram.

A circuit is an array or network of gates, which is the terminology often used in the quantum setting. The gates come from some finite family, and they take

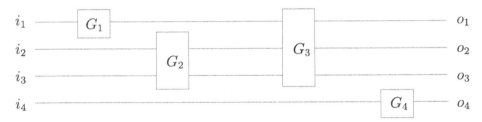

Fig. 1.1 A circuit diagram. The horizontal lines represent 'wires' carrying the bits, and the blocks represent gates. Bits propagate through the circuit from left to right. The input bits i_1, i_2, i_3, i_4 are written on the wires at the far left edge of the circuit, and the output bits o_1, o_2, o_3, o_4 are read-off the far right edge of the circuit.

information from input wires and deliver information along some output wires. A *family* of circuits is a set of circuits $\{C_n | n \in \mathbb{Z}^+\}$, one circuit for each input size n. The family is *uniform* if we can easily construct each C_n (say by an appropriately resource-bounded Turing machine). The point of uniformity is so that one cannot 'sneak' computational power into the definitions of the circuits themselves. For the purposes of this textbook, it suffices that the circuits can be generated by a Turing machine (or an equivalent model, like the log-RAM) in time in $O(n^k |C_n|)$, for some non-negative constant k, where $|C_n|$ denotes the number of gates in C_n.

An important notion is that of *universality*. It is convenient to show that a finite set of different gates is all we need to be able to construct a circuit for performing any computation we want. This is captured by the following definition.

Definition 1.3.1 *A set of gates is* universal *for classical computation if, for any positive integers n, m, and function $f : \{0, 1\}^n \rightarrow \{0, 1\}^m$, a circuit can be constructed for computing f using only gates from that set.*

A well-known example of a set of gates that is universal for classical computation is $\{\text{NAND}, \text{FANOUT}\}$.[1] If we restrict ourselves to reversible gates, we cannot achieve universality with only one- and two-bit gates. The *Toffoli* gate is a reversible three-bit gate that has the effect of flipping the third bit, if and only if the first two bits are both in state 1 (and does nothing otherwise). The set consisting of just the Toffoli gate is universal for classical computation.[2]

In Section 1.2, we extended the definition of the Turing machine and defined the probabilistic Turing machine. The probabilistic Turing machine is obtained by equipping the Turing machine with a 'coin-flipper' capable of generating a random binary value in a single time-step. (There are other equivalent ways of formally defining a probabilistic Turing machine.) We mentioned that it is an open question whether a probabilistic Turing machine is more powerful than a deterministic Turing machine; there are some problems that we do not know how to solve on a deterministic Turing machine but we know how to solve efficiently on a probabilistic Turing machine. We can define a model of *probabilistic circuits* similarly by allowing our circuits to use a 'coin-flipping gate', which is a gate that acts on a single bit, and outputs a random binary value for that bit (independent of the value of the input bit).

When we considered Turing machines in Section 1.2, we saw that the complexity of a computation could be specified in terms of the amount of *time* or *space* the machine uses to complete the computation. For the circuit model of computation one natural measure of complexity is the number of gates used in the circuit C_n. Another is the *depth* of the circuit. If we visualize the circuit as being divided

---

[1] The NAND gate computes the negation of the logical AND function, and the FANOUT gate outputs two copies of a single input wire.

[2] For the Toffoli gate to be universal we need the ability to add ancillary bits to the circuit that can be initialized to either 0 or 1 as required.

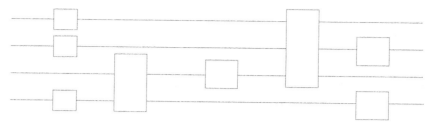

Fig. 1.2 A circuit of depth 5, space (width) 4, and having a total of 8 gates.

into a sequence of discrete time-slices, where the application of a single gate requires a single time-slice, the depth of a circuit is its total number of time-slices. Note that this is not necessarily the same as the total number of gates in the circuit, since gates that act on disjoint bits can often be applied in *parallel* (e.g. a pair of gates could be applied to the bits on two different wires during the same time-slice). A third measure of complexity for a circuit is analogous to space for a Turing machine. This is the total number of bits, or 'wires' in the circuit, sometimes called the *width* or *space* of the circuit. These measures of circuit complexity are illustrated in Figure 1.2.

1.4   A Linear Algebra Formulation of the Circuit Model

In this section we formulate the circuit model of computation in terms of vectors and matrices. This is not a common approach taken for classical computer science, but it does make the transition to the standard formulation of quantum computers much more direct. It will also help distinguish the new notations used in quantum information from the new concepts. The ideas and terminology presented here will be generalized and recur throughout this book.

Suppose you are given a description of a circuit (e.g. in a diagram like Figure 1.1), and a specification of some input bit values. If you were asked to predict the output of the circuit, the approach you would likely take would be to trace through the circuit from left to right, updating the values of the bits stored on each of the wires after each gate. In other words, you are following the 'state' of the bits on the wires as they progress through the circuit. For a given point in the circuit, we will often refer to the state of the bits on the wires at that point in the circuit simply as the 'state of the computer' at that point.

The state associated with a given point in a *deterministic* (non-probabilistic) circuit can be specified by listing the values of the bits on each of the wires in the circuit. The 'state' of any particular wire at a given point in a circuit, of course, is just the value of the bit on that wire (0 or 1). For a probabilistic circuit, however, this simple description is not enough.

Consider a single bit that is in state 0 with probability p_0 and in state 1 with probability p_1. We can summarize this information by a 2-dimensional *vector* of probabilities

$$\begin{pmatrix} p_0 \\ p_1 \end{pmatrix}. \tag{1.4.1}$$

Note that this description can also be used for deterministic circuits. A wire in a deterministic circuit whose state is 0 could be specified by the probabilities $p_0 = 1$ and $p_1 = 0$, and the corresponding vector

$$\begin{pmatrix} 1 \\ 0 \end{pmatrix}. \tag{1.4.2}$$

Similarly, a wire in state 1 could be represented by the probabilities $p_0 = 0$, $p_1 = 1$, and the vector

$$\begin{pmatrix} 0 \\ 1 \end{pmatrix}. \tag{1.4.3}$$

Since we have chosen to represent the states of wires (and collections of wires) in a circuit by vectors, we would like to be able to represent *gates* in the circuit by *operators* that act on the state vectors appropriately. The operators are conveniently described by matrices. Consider the logical NOT gate. We would like to define an operator (matrix) that behaves on state vectors in a manner consistent with the behaviour of the NOT gate. If we know a wire is in state 0 (so $p_0 = 1$), the NOT gate maps it to state 1 (so $p_1 = 1$), and vice versa. In terms of the vector representations of these states, we have

$$\text{NOT} \begin{pmatrix} 1 \\ 0 \end{pmatrix} = \begin{pmatrix} 0 \\ 1 \end{pmatrix}, \qquad \text{NOT} \begin{pmatrix} 0 \\ 1 \end{pmatrix} = \begin{pmatrix} 1 \\ 0 \end{pmatrix}. \tag{1.4.4}$$

This implies that we can represent the NOT vector by the matrix

$$\text{NOT} \equiv \begin{bmatrix} 0 & 1 \\ 1 & 0 \end{bmatrix}. \tag{1.4.5}$$

To 'apply' the gate to a wire in a given state, we multiply the corresponding state vector on the left by the matrix representation of the gate:

$$\text{NOT} \begin{pmatrix} p_0 \\ p_1 \end{pmatrix} = \begin{bmatrix} 0 & 1 \\ 1 & 0 \end{bmatrix} \begin{pmatrix} p_1 \\ p_0 \end{pmatrix}. \tag{1.4.6}$$

Suppose we want to describe the state associated with a given point in a probabilistic circuit having *two* wires. Suppose the state of the first wire at the given point is 0 with probability p_0 and 1 with probability p_1. Suppose the state of the second wire at the given point is 0 with probability q_0 and 1 with probability q_1. The four possibilities for the combined state of both wires at the given point are $\{00,01,10,11\}$ (where the binary string ij indicates that the first wire is in state i and the second wire in state j). The probabilities associated with each of these four states are obtained by multiplying the corresponding probabilities for each of the four states:

$$\text{prob}(ij) = p_i q_j. \tag{1.4.7}$$

This means that the combined state of both wires can be described by the 4-dimensional vector of probabilities

$$\begin{pmatrix} p_0 q_0 \\ p_0 q_1 \\ p_1 q_0 \\ p_1 q_1 \end{pmatrix}. \tag{1.4.8}$$

As we will see in Section 2.6, this vector is the *tensor product* of the 2-dimensional vectors for the states of the first and second wires separately:

$$\begin{pmatrix} p_0 q_0 \\ p_0 q_1 \\ p_1 q_0 \\ p_1 q_1 \end{pmatrix} = \begin{pmatrix} p_0 \\ p_1 \end{pmatrix} \otimes \begin{pmatrix} q_0 \\ q_1 \end{pmatrix}. \tag{1.4.9}$$

Tensor products (which will be defined more generally in Section 2.6) arise naturally when we consider probabilistic systems composed of two or more subsystems.

We can also represent gates acting on more than one wire. For example, the controlled-NOT gate, denoted CNOT. This is a gate that acts on two bits, labelled the *control* bit and the *target bit*. The action of the gate is to apply the NOT operation to the target if the control bit is 0, and do nothing otherwise (the control bit is always unaffected by the CNOT gate). Equivalently, if the state of the control bit is c, and the target bit is in state t the CNOT gate maps the target bit to $t \oplus c$ (where '$\oplus$' represents the logical exclusive-OR operation, or addition modulo 2). The CNOT gate is illustrated in Figure 1.3.

The CNOT gate can be represented by the matrix

$$\text{CNOT} \equiv \begin{bmatrix} 1 & 0 & 0 & 0 \\ 0 & 1 & 0 & 0 \\ 0 & 0 & 0 & 1 \\ 0 & 0 & 1 & 0 \end{bmatrix}. \tag{1.4.10}$$

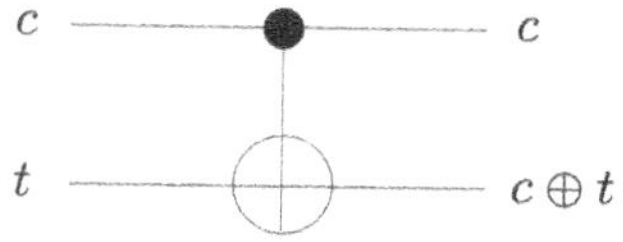

Fig. 1.3 The reversible CNOT gate flips the value of the target bit t if and only if the control bit c has value 1.

Consider, for example, a pair of wires such that the first wire is in state 1 and the second in state 0. This means that the 4-dimensional vector describing the combined state of the pair of wires is

$$\begin{pmatrix} 0 \\ 0 \\ 1 \\ 0 \end{pmatrix}. \tag{1.4.11}$$

Suppose we apply to the CNOT gate to this pair of wires, with the first wire as the control bit, and the second as the target bit. From the description of the CNOT gate, we expect the result should be that the control bit (first wire) remains in state 1, and the target bit (second wire) flips to state 1. That is, we expect the resulting state vector to be

$$\begin{pmatrix} 0 \\ 0 \\ 0 \\ 1 \end{pmatrix}. \tag{1.4.12}$$

We can check that the matrix defined above for CNOT does what we expect:

$$\text{CNOT} \begin{pmatrix} 0 \\ 0 \\ 1 \\ 0 \end{pmatrix} \equiv \begin{bmatrix} 1 & 0 & 0 & 0 \\ 0 & 1 & 0 & 0 \\ 0 & 0 & 0 & 1 \\ 0 & 0 & 1 & 0 \end{bmatrix} \begin{pmatrix} 0 \\ 0 \\ 1 \\ 0 \end{pmatrix} = \begin{pmatrix} 0 \\ 0 \\ 0 \\ 1 \end{pmatrix}. \tag{1.4.13}$$

It is also interesting to note that if the first bit is in the state

$$\begin{pmatrix} \dfrac{1}{2} \\ \dfrac{1}{2} \end{pmatrix}$$

and the second bit is in the state

$$\begin{pmatrix} 1 \\ 0 \end{pmatrix}$$

then applying the CNOT will create the state

$$\begin{pmatrix} \dfrac{1}{2} \\ 0 \\ 0 \\ \dfrac{1}{2} \end{pmatrix}.$$

This state cannot be factorized into the tensor product of two independent probabilistic bits. The states of two such bits are *correlated*.

We have given a brief overview of the circuit model of computation, and presented a convenient formulation for it in terms of matrices and vectors. The circuit model and its formulation in terms of linear algebra will be generalized to describe quantum computers in Chapter 4.

1.5   Reversible Computation

The theory of quantum computing is related to a theory of *reversible computing*. A computation is *reversible* if it is always possible to uniquely recover the input, given the output. For example, the NOT operation is reversible, because if the output bit is 0, you know the input bit must have been 1, and vice versa. On the other hand, the AND operation is not reversible (see Figure 1.4).

As we now describe, any (generally irreversible) computation can be transformed into a reversible computation. This is easy to see for the circuit model of computation. Each gate in a finite family of gates can be made reversible by adding some additional input and output wires if necessary. For example, the AND gate can be made reversible by adding an additional input wire and two additional output wires (see Figure 1.5). Note that additional information necessary to reverse the operation is now kept and accounted for. Whereas in any physical implementation of a logically irreversible computation, the information that would allow one to reverse it is somehow discarded or absorbed into the environment.

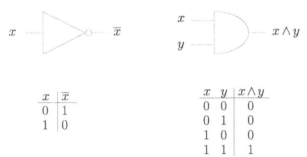

x	$\overline{x}$
0	1
1	0

x	y	$x \wedge y$
0	0	0
0	1	0
1	0	0
1	1	1

Fig. 1.4 The NOT and AND gates. Note that the NOT gate is reversible while the AND gate is not.

$$x_0 \longrightarrow \boxed{\text{AND}} \longrightarrow x_0$$
$$x_1 \longrightarrow \quad\quad \longrightarrow x_1$$
$$x_2 \longrightarrow \quad\quad \longrightarrow x_2 \oplus (x_0 \wedge x_1)$$

Fig. 1.5 The reversible AND gate keeps a copy of the inputs and adds the AND of x_0 and x_1 (denoted $x_1 \wedge x_2$) to the value in the additional input bit. Note that by fixing the additional input bit to 0 and discarding the copies of the x_0 and x_1 we can simulate the non-reversible AND gate.

Note that the reversible AND gate which is in fact the Toffoli gate defined in the previous section, is a generalization of the CNOT gate (the CNOT gate is reversible), where there are two bits controlling whether the NOT is applied to the third bit.

By simply replacing all the irreversible components with their reversible counterparts, we get a reversible version of the circuit. If we start with the output, and run the circuit backwards (replacing each gate by its inverse), we obtain the input again. The reversible version might introduce some constant number of additional wires for each gate. Thus, if we have an irreversible circuit with depth T and space S, we can easily construct a reversible version that uses a total of $O(S + ST)$ space and depth T. Furthermore, the additional 'junk' information generated by making each gate reversible can also be erased at the end of the computation by first copying the output, and then running the reversible circuit in reverse to obtain the starting state again. Of course, the copying has to be done in a reversible manner, which means that we cannot simply overwrite the value initially in the copy register. The reversible copying can be achieved by a sequence of CNOT gates, which XOR the value being copied with the value initially in the copy register. By setting the bits in the copy register initially to 0, we achieved the desired effect. This reversible scheme[3] for computing a function f is illustrated in Figure 1.6.

Exercise 1.5.1 A sequence of n CNOT gates with the target bits all initialized to 0 is the simplest way to copy an n-bit string y stored in the control bits. However, more sophisticated copy operations are also possible, such as a circuit that treats a string y as the binary representation of the integer $y_1 + 2y_2 + 4y_3 + \cdots 2^{n-1}y_n$ and adds y modulo 2^n to the copy register (modular arithmetic is defined in Section 7.3.2).

Describe a reversible 4-bit circuit that adds modulo 4 the integer $y \in \{0, 1, 2, 3\}$ represented in binary in the first two bits to the integer z represented in binary in the last two bits.

If we suppress the 'temporary' registers that are 0 both before and after the computation, the reversible circuit effectively computes

$$(x_1, x_2, x_3), (c_1, c_2, c_3) \longmapsto (x_1, x_2, x_3), (c_1 \oplus y_1, c_2 \oplus y_2, c_3 \oplus y_3), \qquad (1.5.1)$$

where $f(x_1, x_2, x_3) = (y_1, y_2, y_3)$. In general, given an implementation (not necessarily reversible) of a function f, we can easily describe a reversible implementation of the form

$$(x, c) \longmapsto (x, c \oplus f(x))$$

---

[3] In general, reversible circuits for computing a function f do not need to be of this form, and might require much fewer than twice the number of gates as a non-reversible circuit for implementing f.

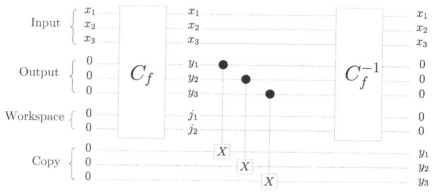

Fig. 1.6 A circuit for reversibly computing $f(x)$. Start with the input. Compute $f(x)$ using reversible logic, possibly generating some extra 'junk' bits j_1 and j_2. The block labelled C_f represents a circuit composed of reversible gates. Then copy the output $y = f(x)$ to another register. Finally run the circuit for C_f backwards (replacing each gate by its inverse gate) to erase the contents of the output and workspace registers. Note we write the operation of the backwards circuit by C_f^{-1}.

with modest overhead. There are more sophisticated techniques that can often be applied to achieve reversible circuits with different time and space bounds than described above. The approach we have described is intended to demonstrate that in principle we can *always* find some reversible circuit for any given computation.

In classical computation, one could choose to be more environmentally friendly and *uncompute* redundant or junk information, and reuse the cleared-up memory for another computation. However, simply discarding the redundant information does not actually affect the outcome of the computation. In quantum computation however, discarding information that is correlated to the bits you keep can drastically change the outcome of a computation. For this reason, the theory of reversible computation plays an important role in the development of quantum algorithms. In a manner very similar to the classical case, reversible quantum operations can efficiently simulate non-reversible quantum operations (and sometimes vice versa) so we generally focus attention on reversible quantum gates. However, for the purposes of implementation or algorithm design, this is not always necessary (e.g. one can cleverly configure special families of non-reversible gates to efficiently simulate reversible ones).

Example 1.5.1 As pointed out in Section 1.3, the computing model corresponding to uniform families of acyclic reversible circuits can efficiently simulate any standard model of classical computation. This section shows how any function that we know how to efficiently compute on a classical computer has a uniform family of acyclic reversible circuits that implements the function reversibly as illustrated in Equation 1.5.1.

Consider, for example, the arcsin function which maps $[0,1] \mapsto [0, \frac{\pi}{2}]$ so that $\sin(\arcsin(x)) = x$ for any $x \in [0,1]$. Since one can efficiently compute n-bit

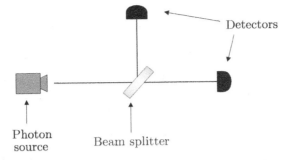

Fig. 1.7 Experimental setup with one beam splitter.

approximations of the arcsin function on a classical computer (e.g., using its Taylor expansion), then there is a uniform family of acyclic reversible circuits, $\text{ARCSIN}_{n,m}$, of size polynomial in n and m, that implement the function $\text{arcsin}_{n,m} : \{0,1\}^n \longmapsto \{0,1\}^m$ which approximately computes the arcsin function in the following way. If $y = \text{arcsin}_{n,m}(x)$, then

$$\left| \arcsin\left(\frac{x}{2^n}\right) - \frac{\pi y}{2^{m+1}} \right| < \frac{1}{2^m}.$$

The reversible circuit effectively computes

$$(x_1, x_2, \ldots, x_n), (c_1, c_2, c_3, \ldots, c_m) \longmapsto (x_1, x_2, \ldots, x_n), (c_1 \oplus y_1, c_2 \oplus y_2, \ldots, c_m \oplus y_m)$$
$$(1.5.2)$$

where $y = y_1 y_2 \ldots y_n$.

1.6 A Preview of Quantum Physics

Here we describe an experimental set-up that cannot be described in a natural way by classical physics, but has a simple quantum explanation. The point we wish to make through this example is that the description of the universe given by quantum mechanics differs in *fundamental* ways from the classical description. Further, the quantum description is often at odds with our intuition, which has evolved according to observations of macroscopic phenomena which are, to an extremely good approximation, classical.

Suppose we have an experimental set-up consisting of a photon source, a beam splitter (which was once implemented using a half-silvered mirror), and a pair of photon detectors. The set-up is illustrated in Figure 1.7.

Suppose we send a series of individual photons[4] along a path from the photon source towards the beam splitter. We observe the photon arriving at the detector on the right on the beam splitter half of the time, and arriving at the detector above the beam splitter half of the time, as illustrated in Figure 1.8. The simplest way to explain this behaviour in a theory of physics is to model the beam splitter as effectively flipping a fair coin, and choosing whether to transmit or reflect the

---

[4]When we reduce the intensity of a light source we observe that it actualy comes out in discrete "chunks", much like a faint beam of matter comes out one atom at a time. These discrete quanta of light are called "photons".

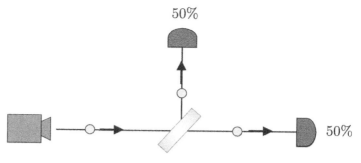

Fig. 1.8 Measurement statistics with one beam splitter.

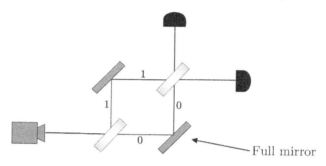

Fig. 1.9 Setup with two beam splitters.

photon based on the result of the coin-flip, whose outcome determines whether the photon is transmitted or reflected.

Now consider a modification of the set-up, shown in Figure 1.9, involving a pair of beam splitters, and fully reflecting mirrors to direct the photons along either of two paths. The paths are labelled 0 and 1 in Figure 1.9. It is important to note that the length of paths 0 and 1 are equal, so the photons arrive at the same time, regardless of which path is taken.

By treating the beam splitters as independently deciding at random whether to transmit or reflect incident photons, classical physics predicts that each of the detectors will register photons arriving 50 per cent of the time, on average. Here, however, the results of experiments reveal an entirely different behaviour. The photons are found arriving at only one of the detectors, 100 per cent of the time! This is shown in Figure 1.10.

The result of the modified experiment is startling, because it does not agree with our classical intuition. Quantum physics models the experiment in a way that correctly predicts the observed outcomes. The non-intuitive behaviour results from features of quantum mechanics called *superposition* and *interference*. We will give a preview of the new framework introduced to explain this interference.

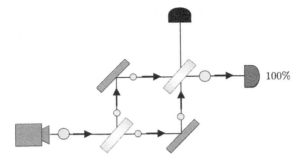

Fig. 1.10 Measurement statistics with two beam splitters.

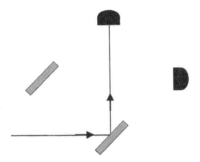

Fig. 1.11 The '0' path.

Suppose for the moment that the second beam splitter were not present in the apparatus. Then the photon follows one of two paths (according to classical physics), depending on whether it is reflected or transmitted by the first beam splitter. If it is transmitted through the first beam splitter, the photon arrives at the top detector, and if it is reflected, the photon arrives at the detector on the right. We can consider a photon in the apparatus as a 2-state system, letting the presence of the photon in one path represent a '0' and letting the presence of the photon in the other path represent a '1'. The '0' and '1' paths are illustrated in Figures 1.11 and 1.12, respectively.

For reasons that will become clear later, we denote the state of a photon in path '0' by the vector

$$\begin{pmatrix} 1 \\ 0 \end{pmatrix}$$ (1.6.1)

and of a photon in path '1' by the vector

$$\begin{pmatrix} 0 \\ 1 \end{pmatrix}.$$ (1.6.2)

The photon leaving the source starts out in the '0' path. In a classical description, we model the beam splitter as randomly selecting whether the photon will

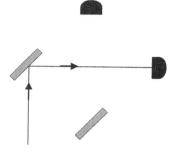

Fig. 1.12 The '1' path.

continue along the '0' path, or be reflected into the '1' path. According to the quantum mechanical description, the beam splitter causes the photon to go into a *superposition* of taking *both* the '0' and '1' paths. Mathematically, we describe such a superposition by taking a linear combination of the state vectors for the '0' and '1' paths, so the general path state will be described by a vector

$$\alpha_0 \begin{pmatrix} 1 \\ 0 \end{pmatrix} + \alpha_1 \begin{pmatrix} 0 \\ 1 \end{pmatrix} = \begin{pmatrix} \alpha_0 \\ \alpha_1 \end{pmatrix}. \tag{1.6.3}$$

If we were to physically measure the photon to see which path it is in, we will find it in path '0' with probability $|\alpha_0|^2$, and in path '1' with probability $|\alpha_1|^2$. Since we should find the photon in exactly one path, we must have $|\alpha_0|^2 + |\alpha_1|^2 = 1$.

When the photon passes through the beam splitter, we multiply its 'state vector' by the matrix

$$\frac{1}{\sqrt{2}} \begin{bmatrix} 1 & i \\ i & 1 \end{bmatrix}. \tag{1.6.4}$$

So for the photon starting out in path '0', after passing through the first beam splitter it comes out in state

$$\frac{1}{\sqrt{2}} \begin{bmatrix} 1 & i \\ i & 1 \end{bmatrix} \begin{pmatrix} 1 \\ 0 \end{pmatrix} = \frac{1}{\sqrt{2}} \begin{pmatrix} 1 \\ i \end{pmatrix} \tag{1.6.5}$$

$$= \frac{1}{\sqrt{2}} \begin{pmatrix} 1 \\ 0 \end{pmatrix} + \frac{i}{\sqrt{2}} \begin{pmatrix} 0 \\ 1 \end{pmatrix}. \tag{1.6.6}$$

This result corresponds with the observed behaviour that, after going through the first beam splitter, we would measure the photon in path '0' with probability $|\frac{1}{\sqrt{2}}|^2 = \frac{1}{2}$, and in path '1' with probability $|\frac{i}{\sqrt{2}}|^2 = \frac{1}{2}$.

If we do not measure which path the photon is in, immediately after it passes through the first beam splitter, then its state remains

$$\frac{1}{\sqrt{2}} \begin{bmatrix} 1 \\ i \end{bmatrix}. \tag{1.6.7}$$

Now if the photon is allowed to pass through the second beam splitter (before making any measurement of the photon's path), its new state vector is

$$\left(\frac{1}{\sqrt{2}} \begin{bmatrix} 1 & i \\ i & 1 \end{bmatrix} \right) \left(\frac{1}{\sqrt{2}} \begin{bmatrix} 1 \\ i \end{bmatrix} \right) = \begin{bmatrix} 0 \\ i \end{bmatrix}. \tag{1.6.8}$$

If we measure the path of the photon *after* the second beam splitter (e.g. by the detectors shown in Figure 1.9), we find it coming out in the '1' path with probability $|i|^2 = 1$. Thus after the second beam splitter the photon is entirely in the '1' path, which is what is observed in experiments (as illustrated in Figure 1.10). In the language of quantum mechanics, the second beam splitter has caused the two paths (in superposition) to *interfere*, resulting in cancelation of the '0' path. We see many more examples of quantum interference throughout this text.

It is not clear what it really 'means' for the photon to be in the state described by a vector like

$$\frac{1}{\sqrt{2}} \begin{pmatrix} 1 \\ i \end{pmatrix}, \tag{1.6.9}$$

but this unusual mathematical infrastructure does allow us to explain how these surprising interference patterns work and to make reliable predictions about the outcomes of measurements.

This new mathematical framework is called *quantum mechanics*, and we describe its postulates in more detail in Section 3.

1.7 Quantum Physics and Computation

We often think of *information* in terms of an abstract mathematical concept. To get into the theory of what information is, and how it is quantified, would easily take a whole course in itself. For now, we fall back on an intuitive understanding of the concept of information. Whatever information is, to be useful it must be stored in some physical medium and manipulated by some physical process. This implies that the laws of physics ultimately dictate the capabilities of any information-processing machine. So it is only reasonable to consider the laws of physics when we study the theory of information processing and in particular the theory of computation.

Up until the turn of the twentieth century, the laws of physics were thought to be what we now call *classical*. Newton's equations of motion and Maxwell's equations of electromagnetism predicted experimentally observed phenomena with remarkable accuracy and precision.

At the beginning of the last century, as scientists were examining phenomena on increasingly *smaller* scales, it was discovered that some experiments did not agree with the predictions of the classical laws of nature. These experiments involved observations of phenomena on the atomic scale, that had not been accessible in the days of Newton or Maxwell. The work of Planck, Bohr, de Broglie, Schrödinger, Heisenberg and others lead to the development of a new theory of physics that came to be known as 'quantum physics'. Newton's and Maxwell's laws were found to be an approximation to this more general theory of quantum physics. The classical approximation of quantum mechanics holds up very well on the macroscopic scale of objects like planets, airplanes, footballs, or even molecules. But on the 'quantum scale' of individual atoms, electrons, and photons, the classical approximation becomes very inaccurate, and the theory of quantum physics must be taken in to account.

A probabilistic Turing machine (described in Section 1.2) is implicitly a *classical* machine. We could build such a machine out of relatively large physical components, and all the aspects of its behaviour relevant to its performing a computation could be accurately predicted by the laws of classical physics.

One of the important classes of tasks that computers are used for is to simulate the evolution of physical systems. When we attempt to use computers to simulate systems whose behaviour is explicitly quantum mechanical, many physicists (including Richard Feynman) observed that we do not seem to be able to do so efficiently. Any attempt to simulate the evolution of a generic quantum–physical system on a probabilistic Turing machine seems to require an exponential overhead in resources.

Feynman suggested that a computer could be designed to exploit the laws of quantum physics, that is, a computer whose evolution is explicitly quantum mechanical. In light of the above observation, it would seem that we would be unable to simulate such a computer with a probabilistic Turing machine. If we believe that such a quantum computer is 'realistic' then it seems to violate the strong Church–Turing Thesis! The first formal model of a quantum computer was given by David Deutsch, who proposed a model for a quantum Turing machine as well as the quantum circuit model.

That it is possible to design a model of computation based explicitly on the principles of quantum mechanics is very interesting in itself. What is truly extraordinary is that important problems have been found that can be solved efficiently on a quantum computer, but *no* efficient solution is known on a probabilistic Turing machine! This implies that the theory of *quantum computing* is potentially of enormous practical importance, as well as of deep theoretical interest.

2

LINEAR ALGEBRA AND THE DIRAC NOTATION

We assume the reader has a strong background in elementary linear algebra. In this section we familiarize the reader with the algebraic notation used in quantum mechanics, remind the reader of some basic facts about complex vector spaces, and introduce some notions that might not have been covered in an elementary linear algebra course.

2.1   The Dirac Notation and Hilbert Spaces

The linear algebra notation used in quantum computing will likely be familiar to the student of physics, but may be alien to a student of mathematics or computer science. It is the *Dirac* notation, which was invented by Paul Dirac and which is used often in quantum mechanics. In mathematics and physics textbooks, vectors are often distinguished from scalars by writing an arrow over the identifying symbol: e.g. $\vec{a}$. Sometimes boldface is used for this purpose: e.g. **a**. In the Dirac notation, the symbol identifying a vector is written inside a 'ket', and looks like $|a\rangle$. We denote the dual vector for a (defined later) with a 'bra', written as $\langle a|$. Then inner products will be written as 'bra-kets' (e.g. $\langle a|b\rangle$). We now carefully review the definitions of the main algebraic objects of interest, using the Dirac notation.

The vector spaces we consider will be over the complex numbers, and are finite-dimensional, which significantly simplifies the mathematics we need. Such vector spaces are members of a class of vector spaces called *Hilbert* spaces. Nothing substantial is gained at this point by defining rigorously what a Hilbert space is, but virtually all the quantum computing literature refers to a finite-dimensional complex vector space by the name 'Hilbert space', and so we will follow this convention. We will use $\mathcal{H}$ to denote such a space.

Since $\mathcal{H}$ is finite-dimensional, we can choose a basis and alternatively represent vectors (kets) in this basis as finite column vectors, and represent operators with finite matrices. As you see in Section 3, the Hilbert spaces of interest for quantum computing will typically have dimension 2^n, for some positive integer n. This is because, as with classical information, we will construct larger state spaces by concatenating a string of smaller systems, usually of size two.

We will often choose to fix a convenient basis and refer to it as the *computational basis*. In this basis, we will label the 2^n basis vectors in the Dirac notation using the binary strings of length n:

$$\underbrace{|00\ldots00\rangle}_{n}\ ,\ |00\ldots01\rangle\ ,\ \ldots\ ,\ |11\ldots10\rangle\ ,\ |11\ldots11\rangle. \tag{2.1.1}$$

The standard way to associate column vectors corresponding to these basis vectors is as follows:

$$|00\ldots00\rangle \iff \left.\begin{pmatrix} 1 \\ 0 \\ 0 \\ \vdots \\ 0 \\ 0 \end{pmatrix}\right\}2^n,\quad |00\ldots01\rangle \iff \begin{pmatrix} 0 \\ 1 \\ 0 \\ \vdots \\ 0 \\ 0 \end{pmatrix},\quad \ldots$$

$$\ldots\ ,\quad |11\ldots10\rangle \iff \begin{pmatrix} 0 \\ 0 \\ 0 \\ \vdots \\ 1 \\ 0 \end{pmatrix},\quad |11\ldots11\rangle \iff \begin{pmatrix} 0 \\ 0 \\ 0 \\ \vdots \\ 0 \\ 1 \end{pmatrix}. \tag{2.1.2}$$

An arbitrary vector in $\mathcal{H}$ can be written either as a weighted sum of the basis vectors in the Dirac notation, or as a single column matrix.

Example 2.1.1 In $\mathcal{H}$ of dimension 4, the vector

$$\sqrt{\tfrac{2}{3}}|01\rangle + \tfrac{i}{\sqrt{3}}|11\rangle = \sqrt{\tfrac{2}{3}}|0\rangle \otimes |1\rangle + \tfrac{i}{\sqrt{3}}|1\rangle \otimes |1\rangle \tag{2.1.3}$$

in Dirac notation can be alternatively written as the column matrix

$$\begin{pmatrix} 0 \\ \sqrt{\tfrac{2}{3}} \\ 0 \\ \tfrac{i}{\sqrt{3}} \end{pmatrix}. \tag{2.1.4}$$

It is important to realize that these are simply alternative expressions for the same vector, both with respect to the same basis (the computational basis).

You might wonder why one should go to the trouble of learning a strange-looking new notation for vectors, when we could just as well use a column vector representation. One answer is that writing vectors using the Dirac notation often saves space. Particularly when writing sparse vectors (having few non-zero components), the Dirac notation is very compact. An n-qubit basis state is described by a 2^n-dimensional vector. In the Dirac notation, we represent this vector by a binary string of length n, but the column vector representation would have 2^n components. For states on 2 or 3 qubits this is not terribly significant, but imagine writing an 8-qubit state using column vectors. The column vectors would have $2^8 = 256$ components, which could be somewhat cumbersome to write out. The Dirac notation has other advantages, and these will begin to become apparent once you start working with things like operators, and various types of vector products.

2.2 Dual Vectors

Recall from linear algebra the definition of *inner product*. For the moment we will not use the Dirac notation, and write vectors in boldface. For vectors over the complex numbers, an inner product is a function which takes two vectors from the same space and evaluates to a single complex number. We write the inner product of vector $\mathbf{v}$ with $\mathbf{w}$ as $\langle \mathbf{v}, \mathbf{w} \rangle$. An inner product is such a function having the following properties.

1. Linearity in the second argument

$$\langle \mathbf{v}, \sum_i \lambda_i \mathbf{w}_i \rangle = \sum_i \lambda_i \langle \mathbf{v}, \mathbf{w}_i \rangle \tag{2.2.1}$$

2. Conjugate-commutativity

$$\langle \mathbf{v}, \mathbf{w} \rangle = \langle \mathbf{w}, \mathbf{v} \rangle^* \tag{2.2.2}$$

3. Non-negativity

$$\langle \mathbf{v}, \mathbf{v} \rangle \geq 0 \tag{2.2.3}$$

with equality if and only if $\mathbf{v} = \mathbf{0}$.

Note that in Equation (2.2.2), we use the notation c^* to denote the complex conjugate[1] of a complex number c, as will be our convention throughout this book.

A familiar example of an inner product is the *dot product* for column vectors. The dot product of $\mathbf{v}$ with $\mathbf{w}$ is written $\mathbf{v} \cdot \mathbf{w}$ and is defined as follows.

$$\begin{pmatrix} v_1 \\ v_2 \\ \vdots \\ v_n \end{pmatrix} \cdot \begin{pmatrix} w_1 \\ w_2 \\ \vdots \\ w_n \end{pmatrix} = \begin{pmatrix} v_1^* & v_2^* & \cdots & v_n^* \end{pmatrix} \begin{pmatrix} w_1 \\ w_2 \\ \vdots \\ w_n \end{pmatrix} = \sum_{i=1}^n v_i^* w_i \tag{2.2.4}$$

---

[1]The *complex conjugate* of $c = a + bi$ (where a and b are real) is $c^* = a - bi$.

We now return to the Dirac notation, and define the *dual vector space* and *dual vectors*.

Definition 2.2.1 *Let* $\mathcal{H}$ *be a Hilbert space. The Hilbert space* $\mathcal{H}^*$ *is defined as the set of linear maps* $\mathcal{H} \to \mathbb{C}$.

We denote elements of $\mathcal{H}^*$ by $\langle \chi |$, where the action of $\langle \chi |$ is:

$$\langle \chi | : |\psi\rangle \mapsto \langle \chi | \psi \rangle \in \mathbb{C}, \tag{2.2.5}$$

where $\langle \chi | \psi \rangle$ is the inner-product of the vector $|\chi\rangle \in \mathcal{H}$ with the vector $|\psi\rangle \in \mathcal{H}$.

The set of maps $\mathcal{H}^*$ is a complex vector space itself, and is called the *dual* vector space associated with $\mathcal{H}$. The vector $\langle \chi |$ is called the *dual* of $|\chi\rangle$. In terms of the matrix representation, $\langle \chi |$ is obtained from $|\chi\rangle$ by taking the corresponding row matrix, and then taking the complex conjugate of every element (i.e. the 'Hermitean conjugate' of the column matrix for $|\chi\rangle$). Then the inner product of $|\psi\rangle$ with $|\varphi\rangle$ is $\langle \psi | \varphi \rangle$, which in the matrix representation is computed as the single element of the matrix product of the row matrix representing $\langle \psi |$ with the column matrix representing $|\varphi\rangle$. This is equivalent to taking the dot product of the column vector associated with $|\psi\rangle$ with the column vector associated with $|\varphi\rangle$.

Example 2.2.2 Using the standard basis we defined earlier, consider two vectors

$$|\psi\rangle = \sqrt{\tfrac{2}{3}}|01\rangle + \tfrac{i}{\sqrt{3}}|11\rangle \tag{2.2.6}$$

and

$$|\varphi\rangle = \sqrt{\tfrac{1}{2}}|10\rangle + \sqrt{\tfrac{1}{2}}|11\rangle. \tag{2.2.7}$$

These are represented as column vectors

$$\begin{pmatrix} 0 \\ \sqrt{\tfrac{2}{3}} \\ 0 \\ \tfrac{i}{\sqrt{3}} \end{pmatrix}, \quad \begin{pmatrix} 0 \\ 0 \\ \sqrt{\tfrac{1}{2}} \\ \sqrt{\tfrac{1}{2}} \end{pmatrix} \tag{2.2.8}$$

respectively. The dot product of these two column vectors is

$$\begin{pmatrix} 0 \\ \sqrt{\tfrac{2}{3}} \\ 0 \\ \tfrac{i}{\sqrt{3}} \end{pmatrix} \cdot \begin{pmatrix} 0 \\ 0 \\ \sqrt{\tfrac{1}{2}} \\ \sqrt{\tfrac{1}{2}} \end{pmatrix} = \begin{pmatrix} 0 & \sqrt{\tfrac{2}{3}} & 0 & \tfrac{-i}{\sqrt{3}} \end{pmatrix} \begin{pmatrix} 0 \\ 0 \\ \sqrt{\tfrac{1}{2}} \\ \sqrt{\tfrac{1}{2}} \end{pmatrix}$$

$$= 0 \cdot 0 + \sqrt{\tfrac{2}{3}} \cdot 0 + 0 \cdot \sqrt{\tfrac{1}{2}} + \tfrac{-i}{\sqrt{3}}\sqrt{\tfrac{1}{2}}$$

$$= \frac{-i}{\sqrt{6}} \tag{2.2.9}$$

and so the inner product of $|\psi\rangle$ with $|\varphi\rangle$ is

$$\langle\psi|\varphi\rangle = \frac{-i}{\sqrt{6}}. \tag{2.2.10}$$

Two vectors are said to be *orthogonal* if their inner product is zero. The *norm* of a vector $|\psi\rangle$, denoted $\||\psi\rangle\|$, is the square root of the inner product of $|\psi\rangle$ with itself. That is,

$$\||\psi\rangle\| \equiv \sqrt{\langle\psi|\psi\rangle}. \tag{2.2.11}$$

The quantity $\||\psi\rangle\|$ is called the *Euclidean norm* of $|\psi\rangle$. A vector is called a *unit vector* if it has norm 1. A set of unit vectors that are mutually orthogonal is called an *orthonormal* set.

The *Kronecker delta function*, $\delta_{i,j}$, is defined to be equal to 1 whenever $i = j$, and 0 otherwise. We use the Kronecker delta function in our definition of an orthonormal basis.

Definition 2.2.3 *Consider a Hilbert space $\mathcal{H}$ of dimension 2^n. A set of 2^n vectors $B = \{|b_m\rangle\} \subseteq \mathcal{H}$ is called an orthonormal basis for $\mathcal{H}$ if*

$$\langle b_n|b_m\rangle = \delta_{n,m} \qquad \forall b_m, b_n \in B \tag{2.2.12}$$

and every $|\psi\rangle \in \mathcal{H}$ can be written as

$$|\psi\rangle = \sum_{b_n \in B} \psi_n|b_n\rangle, \text{ for some } \psi_n \in \mathbb{C}. \tag{2.2.13}$$

The values of ψ_n satisfy $\psi_n = \langle b_n|\psi\rangle$, and are called the 'coefficients of $|\psi\rangle$ with respect to basis $\{|b_n\rangle\}$'.

Example 2.2.4 Consider $\mathcal{H}$ of dimension 4. One example of an orthonormal basis for $\mathcal{H}$ is the computational basis which we saw earlier. The basis vectors are

$$|00\rangle, |01\rangle, |10\rangle \text{ and } |11\rangle. \tag{2.2.14}$$

These basis vectors are represented by the following column vectors.

$$\begin{pmatrix}1\\0\\0\\0\end{pmatrix}, \begin{pmatrix}0\\1\\0\\0\end{pmatrix}, \begin{pmatrix}0\\0\\1\\0\end{pmatrix}, \begin{pmatrix}0\\0\\0\\1\end{pmatrix}. \tag{2.2.15}$$

It is easy to check that the inner product of any two of these vectors is 0, and that the norm of each of these vectors is 1. In other words

$$\langle b_n | b_m \rangle = \delta_{n,m} \qquad (2.2.16)$$

for b_n and b_m from the set of 4 computational basis vectors above.

Example 2.2.5 The inner product calculated using the matrix representation in Example 2.2.2 can also be calculated directly using the Dirac notation. We use the fact that the computational basis is an orthonormal basis (see Example 2.2.4).

$$\langle \psi | \varphi \rangle = \left(\sqrt{\tfrac{2}{3}} \langle 01| + \tfrac{-i}{\sqrt{3}} \langle 11| \right) \left(\sqrt{\tfrac{1}{2}} |10\rangle + \sqrt{\tfrac{1}{2}} |11\rangle \right)$$

$$= \left(\sqrt{\tfrac{2}{3}} \right) \left(\sqrt{\tfrac{1}{2}} \right) \underbrace{\langle 01|10 \rangle}_{=0} + \left(\sqrt{\tfrac{2}{3}} \right) \left(\sqrt{\tfrac{1}{2}} \right) \underbrace{\langle 01|11 \rangle}_{=0}$$

$$+ \left(\tfrac{-i}{\sqrt{3}} \right) \left(\sqrt{\tfrac{1}{2}} \right) \underbrace{\langle 11|10 \rangle}_{=0} + \left(\tfrac{-i}{\sqrt{3}} \right) \left(\sqrt{\tfrac{1}{2}} \right) \underbrace{\langle 11|11 \rangle}_{=1}$$

$$= \tfrac{-i}{\sqrt{6}} \ .$$

Example 2.2.6 This time consider $\mathcal{H}$ of dimension 2. The computational basis is not the only orthonormal basis for $\mathcal{H}$ (there are infinitely many). An important example is the so-called *Hadamard basis*. We denote the basis vectors of the Hadamard basis as $|+\rangle$ and $|-\rangle$. We can express these basis vectors in terms of the familiar computational basis as follows.

$$|+\rangle = \tfrac{1}{\sqrt{2}} (|0\rangle + |1\rangle)$$
$$|-\rangle = \tfrac{1}{\sqrt{2}} (|0\rangle - |1\rangle). \qquad (2.2.17)$$

It is easy to check the normality and orthogonality of these basis vectors by doing the computation with the column vector representation in terms of the computational basis. For example,

$$\langle +|- \rangle = \tfrac{1}{2} (\langle 0| + \langle 1|)(|0\rangle - |1\rangle)$$
$$= \tfrac{1}{2} \begin{pmatrix} 1 \\ 1 \end{pmatrix} \cdot \begin{pmatrix} 1 \\ -1 \end{pmatrix}$$
$$= 0 \qquad (2.2.18)$$

and

$$\||+\rangle\|^2 = \langle +|+ \rangle$$
$$= \tfrac{1}{2} (\langle 0| + \langle 1|)(|0\rangle + |1\rangle)$$
$$= \tfrac{1}{2} \begin{pmatrix} 1 \\ 1 \end{pmatrix} \cdot \begin{pmatrix} 1 \\ 1 \end{pmatrix}$$
$$= 1$$
$$\implies \||+\rangle\| = 1. \qquad (2.2.19)$$

Note that if we express $|\psi\rangle = \sum_i \alpha_i |\phi_i\rangle$ with respect to any orthonormal basis $\{|\phi_i\rangle\}$, then $\||\psi\rangle\| = \sum_i |\alpha_i|^2$.

We state the following useful result, without proof.

Theorem 2.2.7 *The set $\{\langle b_n|\}$ is an orthonormal basis for $\mathcal{H}^*$ called the dual basis.*

2.3 Operators

Recall from linear algebra the following definition.

Definition 2.3.1 *A linear operator on a vector space $\mathcal{H}$ is a linear transformation $T : \mathcal{H} \to \mathcal{H}$ of the vector space to itself (i.e. it is a linear transformation which maps vectors in $\mathcal{H}$ to vectors in $\mathcal{H}$).*

Just as the inner product of two vectors $|\psi\rangle$ and $|\varphi\rangle$ is obtained by multiplying $|\psi\rangle$ on the left by the dual vector $\langle\varphi|$, an *outer product* is obtained by multiplying $|\psi\rangle$ *on the right* by $\langle\varphi|$. The meaning of such an outer product $|\psi\rangle\langle\varphi|$ is that it is an operator which, when applied to $|\gamma\rangle$, acts as follows.

$$\big(|\psi\rangle\langle\varphi|\big)|\gamma\rangle = |\psi\rangle\big(\langle\varphi|\gamma\rangle\big)$$
$$= \big(\langle\varphi|\gamma\rangle\big)|\psi\rangle. \qquad (2.3.1)$$

The outer product of a vector $|\psi\rangle$ with itself is written $|\psi\rangle\langle\psi|$ and defines a linear operator that maps

$$|\psi\rangle\langle\psi||\varphi\rangle \mapsto |\psi\rangle\langle\psi|\varphi\rangle = \langle\psi|\varphi\rangle|\psi\rangle. \qquad (2.3.2)$$

That is, the operator $|\psi\rangle\langle\psi|$ projects a vector $|\varphi\rangle$ in $\mathcal{H}$ to the 1-dimensional subspace of $\mathcal{H}$ spanned by $|\psi\rangle$. Such an operator is called an *orthogonal projector* (Definition 2.3.7). You will see operators of this form when we examine *density operators* in Section 3.5, and measurements in Section 3.4.

Theorem 2.3.2 *Let $B = \{|b_n\rangle\}$ be an orthonormal basis for a vector space $\mathcal{H}$. Then every linear operator T on $\mathcal{H}$ can be written as*

$$T = \sum_{b_n, b_m \in B} T_{n,m} |b_n\rangle\langle b_m| \qquad (2.3.3)$$

where $T_{n,m} = \langle b_n|T|b_m\rangle$.

We know that the set of all linear operators on a vector space $\mathcal{H}$ forms a new complex vector space $\mathcal{L}(\mathcal{H})$ ('vectors' in $\mathcal{L}(\mathcal{H})$ are the linear operators on $\mathcal{H}$). Notice that Theorem 2.3.2 essentially constructs a basis for $\mathcal{L}(\mathcal{H})$ out of the given basis for $\mathcal{H}$. The basis vectors for $\mathcal{L}(\mathcal{H})$ are all the possible outer products of pairs of basis vectors from B, that is $\{|b_n\rangle\langle b_m|\}$.

The action of T is then

$$T : |\psi\rangle \mapsto \sum_{b_n, b_m \in B} T_{n,m} |b_n\rangle \langle b_m |\psi\rangle = \sum_{b_n, b_m \in B} T_{n,m} \langle b_m |\psi\rangle |b_n\rangle. \qquad (2.3.4)$$

In terms of the matrix representation of T, $T_{n,m}$ is the matrix entry in the nth row and m^{th} column.

Example 2.3.3 Consider the operator Z that maps the computational basis states as follows:

$$|0\rangle \mapsto |0\rangle \qquad (2.3.5)$$
$$|1\rangle \mapsto -|1\rangle. \qquad (2.3.6)$$

This operator can be written as

$$|0\rangle\langle 0| - |1\rangle\langle 1| \qquad (2.3.7)$$

and has the following matrix representation with respect to the basis $\{|0\rangle, |1\rangle\}$:

$$\begin{bmatrix} 1 & 0 \\ 0 & -1 \end{bmatrix}. \qquad (2.3.8)$$

For any orthonormal basis $B = \{|b_n\rangle\}$, the identity operator can be written as

$$\mathbf{1} = \sum_{b_n \in B} |b_n\rangle\langle b_n|. \qquad (2.3.9)$$

Equation (2.3.9) is called the *resolution of the identity in the basis B*.

Notice that, for an operator T on $\mathcal{H}$, and $|\psi\rangle \in \mathcal{H}$, the map

$$|\psi\rangle \mapsto \langle\varphi|(T|\psi\rangle) \qquad (2.3.10)$$

is a linear map from $\mathcal{H}$ to $\mathbb{C}$, and thus belongs to $\mathcal{H}^*$. Each map in $\mathcal{H}^*$ corresponds to some vector $\langle\varphi'|$. The *adjoint* of the operator T, denoted $T^\dagger$, is defined as the linear map that sends $|\varphi\rangle \mapsto |\varphi'\rangle$, where $\langle\phi|(T|\psi\rangle) = \langle\phi'|\psi\rangle$ for all $|\psi\rangle$. The adjoint is captured in the following definition.

Definition 2.3.4 *Suppose T is an operator on $\mathcal{H}$. Then the* adjoint *of T, denoted $T^\dagger$, is defined as that linear operator on $\mathcal{H}^*$ that satisfies*

$$\left(\langle\psi|T^\dagger|\varphi\rangle\right)^* = \langle\varphi|T|\psi\rangle \ , \ \ \forall|\psi\rangle, |\varphi\rangle \in \mathcal{H}. \qquad (2.3.11)$$

In the standard matrix representation, the matrix for $T^\dagger$ is the complex conjugate transpose (also called the 'Hermitean conjugate', or 'adjoint') of the matrix for T.

The following definition is important, because (as we see in Section 3) it gives the class of operators which describe the time-evolution of the quantum states of closed systems.

Definition 2.3.5 *An operator U is called* unitary *if $U^\dagger = U^{-1}$, where U^{-1} is the inverse of U.*

Note that $U^\dagger = U^{-1}$ implies $U^\dagger U = I$, where I is the identity operator. The unitary operators preserve inner products between vectors, and in particular, preserve the norm of vectors.

We also define a class of operators that describes the *Hamiltonian* of a system as well as the *observables*, which correspond to an important type of measurement in quantum mechanics (see Section 3.4).

Definition 2.3.6 *An operator T in a Hilbert space $\mathcal{H}$ is called* Hermitean *(or self-adjoint) if*

$$T^\dagger = T \tag{2.3.12}$$

(i.e. it is equal to its own Hermitean conjugate).

Definition 2.3.7 *A* projector *on a vector space $\mathcal{H}$ is a linear operator P that satisfies $P^2 = P$. An* orthogonal projector *is a projector that also satisfies $P^\dagger = P$.*

Recall the following definition from basic linear algebra.

Definition 2.3.8 *A vector $|\psi\rangle$ is called an* eigenvector *of an operator T if*

$$T|\psi\rangle = c|\psi\rangle \tag{2.3.13}$$

for some constant c. The constant c is called the eigenvalue *of T corresponding to the eigenvector $|\psi\rangle$.*

The following result is relevant to measurements in quantum mechanics.

Theorem 2.3.9 *If $T = T^\dagger$ and if $T|\psi\rangle = \lambda|\psi\rangle$ then $\lambda \in \mathbb{R}$. In other words, the eigenvalues of a Hermitean operator are real.*

In linear algebra one learns that the *trace* of a square matrix is obtained by adding the elements on the main diagonal. We give a more abstract definition of trace.

Definition 2.3.10 *The* trace *of an operator A acting on a Hilbert space $\mathcal{H}$ is*

$$\text{Tr}(A) = \sum_{b_n} \langle b_n|A|b_n\rangle \tag{2.3.14}$$

where $\{|b_n\rangle\}$ is any orthonormal basis for $\mathcal{H}$.

Exercise 2.3.2 shows that indeed $\mathrm{Tr}(A)$ does not depend on the choice of orthonormal basis, and thus is well defined.

Exercise 2.3.1 Prove that the trace has the cyclic property $\mathrm{Tr}(ABC) = \mathrm{Tr}(BCA)$.

Exercise 2.3.2 Using the result of the previous exercise, together with the fact that a change of orthonormal basis can be written as a unitary operator, show that $\mathrm{Tr}(A)$ is independent of the basis in which it is expressed. Notice that in the matrix representation, $\mathrm{Tr}(A)$ equals the sum of the diagonal entries of the square matrix representing A.

2.4   The Spectral Theorem

The *spectral theorem* is a central result in linear algebra, because it is often very convenient to be able to specify a basis in which a given operator is diagonal (i.e. to *diagonalize* the operator). The spectral theorem applies to a wide class of operators which we now define.

Definition 2.4.1 *A* normal *operator A is a linear operator that satifies*

$$AA^\dagger = A^\dagger A. \tag{2.4.1}$$

Notice that both unitary and Hermitean operators are normal. So most of the operators that are important for quantum mechanics, and quantum computing, are normal. Since in this book we are only interested in Hilbert spaces having finite dimensions, we will only consider the spectral theorem in this special case (where it is slightly simpler).

Theorem 2.4.2 *(Spectral Theorem) For every normal operator T acting on a finite-dimensional Hilbert space $\mathcal{H}$, there is an orthonormal basis of $\mathcal{H}$ consisting of eigenvectors $|T_i\rangle$ of T.*

Note that T is diagonal in its own eigenbasis: $T = \sum_i T_i |T_i\rangle\langle T_i|$, where T_i are the eigenvalues corresponding to the eigenvectors $|T_i\rangle$. We sometimes refer to T written in its own eigenbasis as the *spectral decomposition* of T. The set of eigenvalues of T is called the *spectrum* of T.

The Spectral Theorem tells us that we can always diagonalize normal operators (in finite dimensions). Recall from linear algebra that the diagonalization can be accomplished by a change of basis (to the basis consisting of eigenvectors). The change of basis is accomplished by conjugating the operator T with a unitary operator P. With respect to the matrix representation for the operator T, we can restate the Spectral Theorem in a form which may be more familiar.

Theorem 2.4.3 *(Spectral Theorem) For every finite-dimensional normal matrix T, there is a unitary matrix P such that $T = P\Lambda P^\dagger$, where Λ is a diagonal matrix.*

The diagonal entries of Λ are the eigenvalues of T, and the columns of P encode the eigenvectors of T.

Example 2.4.4 Consider the operator X which acts as follows on the computational basis states.

$$X|0\rangle = |1\rangle \tag{2.4.2}$$
$$X|1\rangle = |0\rangle \tag{2.4.3}$$

The matrix representation for this operator is

$$X \equiv \begin{bmatrix} 0 & 1 \\ 1 & 0 \end{bmatrix}. \tag{2.4.4}$$

We have the following diagonalization of X.

$$\begin{bmatrix} 0 & 1 \\ 1 & 0 \end{bmatrix} = \begin{bmatrix} \frac{1}{\sqrt{2}} & \frac{1}{\sqrt{2}} \\ \frac{1}{\sqrt{2}} & -\frac{1}{\sqrt{2}} \end{bmatrix} \begin{bmatrix} 1 & 0 \\ 0 & -1 \end{bmatrix} \begin{bmatrix} \frac{1}{\sqrt{2}} & \frac{1}{\sqrt{2}} \\ \frac{1}{\sqrt{2}} & -\frac{1}{\sqrt{2}} \end{bmatrix} \tag{2.4.5}$$

So we have

$$P = \begin{bmatrix} \frac{1}{\sqrt{2}} & \frac{1}{\sqrt{2}} \\ \frac{1}{\sqrt{2}} & -\frac{1}{\sqrt{2}} \end{bmatrix} \tag{2.4.6}$$

and

$$\Lambda = \begin{bmatrix} 1 & 0 \\ 0 & -1 \end{bmatrix}. \tag{2.4.7}$$

Thus the eigenvalues of X are 1 and -1, and the corresponding eigenvectors of X are

$$\begin{pmatrix} \frac{1}{\sqrt{2}} \\ \frac{1}{\sqrt{2}} \end{pmatrix} \tag{2.4.8}$$

and

$$\begin{pmatrix} \frac{1}{\sqrt{2}} \\ -\frac{1}{\sqrt{2}} \end{pmatrix}. \tag{2.4.9}$$

In the Dirac notation, we have

$$X = |0\rangle\langle 1| + |1\rangle\langle 0| \tag{2.4.10}$$
$$P = |+\rangle\langle 0| + |-\rangle\langle 1| \tag{2.4.11}$$
$$= \tfrac{1}{\sqrt{2}}|0\rangle\langle 0| + \tfrac{1}{\sqrt{2}}|0\rangle\langle 1| + \tfrac{1}{\sqrt{2}}|1\rangle\langle 0| - \tfrac{1}{\sqrt{2}}|1\rangle\langle 1| \tag{2.4.12}$$
$$\Lambda = |0\rangle\langle 0| - |1\rangle\langle 1| \tag{2.4.13}$$

and the eigenvectors are

$$|+\rangle \equiv \tfrac{1}{\sqrt{2}}|0\rangle + \tfrac{1}{\sqrt{2}}|1\rangle \tag{2.4.14}$$

and

$$|-\rangle \equiv \tfrac{1}{\sqrt{2}}|0\rangle - \tfrac{1}{\sqrt{2}}|1\rangle. \qquad (2.4.15)$$

Note that these eigenvectors are the basis vectors $|+\rangle$ and $|-\rangle$ of the Hadamard basis described in Example 2.2.6.

2.5   Functions of Operators

One of the reasons why the Spectral Theorem is important is that it allows us to simplify the expressions for functions of operators. By the Spectral Theorem, we can write every normal operator T in the diagonal form

$$T = \sum_i T_i |T_i\rangle\langle T_i|. \qquad (2.5.1)$$

First, note that since each $|T_i\rangle\langle T_i|$ is a projector,

$$\left(|T_i\rangle\langle T_i|\right)^m = |T_i\rangle\langle T_i| \qquad (2.5.2)$$

for any integer m. Also noting that the eigenvectors are orthonormal, we have

$$\langle T_i|T_j\rangle = \delta_{i,j}, \qquad (2.5.3)$$

where $\delta_{i,j}$ is the Dirac delta function which equals 1 if $i = j$, and equals 0 otherwise.

So this means that computing a power of T (in diagonal form) is equivalent to computing the powers of the diagonal entries of T:

$$\left(\sum_i T_i |T_i\rangle\langle T_i|\right)^m = \sum_i T_i^m |T_i\rangle\langle T_i|. \qquad (2.5.4)$$

The Taylor series for a function $f : \mathbb{C} \to \mathbb{C}$, has the form

$$f(x) = \sum_{m=0}^{\infty} a_m x^m. \qquad (2.5.5)$$

For example, the Taylor series for e^x is $\sum_{m=0}^{\infty} \frac{1}{m!}x^m$. The range of values of x for which the Taylor series converges is called the *interval of convergence*. For any point x in the interval of convergence, the Taylor series of a function f converges to the value of $f(x)$.

Using the Taylor series for a function f, we can define the action of f on *operators* over $\mathbb{C}$ (provided the relevant Taylor series converges). For example, we would define the exponential function so that, for an operator T, we have

$$e^T = \sum_m \frac{1}{m!}T^m. \qquad (2.5.6)$$

In general, the Taylor series for any function f acting on an operator T will have the form

$$f(T) = \sum_m a_m T^m. \qquad (2.5.7)$$

If T is written in diagonal form, then the expression simplifies:

$$f(T) = \sum_m a_m T^m$$

$$= \sum_m a_m \left(\sum_i T_i |T_i\rangle\langle T_i| \right)^m$$

$$= \sum_m a_m \sum_i T_i^m |T_i\rangle\langle T_i|$$

$$= \sum_i \left(\sum_m a_m T_i^m \right) |T_i\rangle\langle T_i|$$

$$= \sum_i f(T_i) |T_i\rangle\langle T_i|. \qquad (2.5.8)$$

So when T is written in diagonal form, $f(T)$ is computed by applying f separately to the diagonal entries of T. In general, the procedure for computing a function f of an operator T is to first diagonalize T (the Spectral Theorem tells us we can do this for most of the operators that will be important to us), and then compute f individually on the diagonal entries.

2.6   Tensor Products

The *tensor product* is a way of combining spaces, vectors, or operators together. Suppose $\mathcal{H}_1$ and $\mathcal{H}_2$ are Hilbert spaces of dimension n and m respectively. Then the tensor product space $\mathcal{H}_1 \otimes \mathcal{H}_2$ is a new, larger Hilbert space of dimension $n \times m$. Suppose $\{|b_i\rangle\}_{i\in\{1,...,n\}}$ is an orthonormal basis for $\mathcal{H}_1$ and $\{|c_j\rangle\}_{j\in\{1,...,m\}}$ is an orthonormal basis for $\mathcal{H}_2$. Then

$$\{|b_i\rangle \otimes |c_j\rangle\}_{i\in\{1,...,n\},j\in\{1,...,m\}} \qquad (2.6.1)$$

is an orthonormal basis for the space $\mathcal{H}_1 \otimes \mathcal{H}_2$. The tensor product of two vectors $|\psi_1\rangle$ and $|\psi_2\rangle$ from spaces $\mathcal{H}_1$ and $\mathcal{H}_2$, respectively, is a vector in $\mathcal{H}_1 \otimes \mathcal{H}_2$, and is written $|\psi_1\rangle \otimes |\psi_2\rangle$. The tensor product is characterized by the following axioms:

1. For any $c \in \mathbb{C}$, $|\psi_1\rangle \in \mathcal{H}_1$, and $|\psi_2\rangle \in \mathcal{H}_2$,

$$c\big(|\psi_1\rangle \otimes |\psi_2\rangle\big) = \big(c|\psi_1\rangle\big) \otimes |\psi_2\rangle = |\psi_1\rangle \otimes \big(c|\psi_2\rangle\big). \qquad (2.6.2)$$

2. For any $|\psi_1\rangle, |\varphi_1\rangle \in \mathcal{H}_1$, and $|\psi_2\rangle \in \mathcal{H}_2$,

$$\big(|\psi_1\rangle + |\varphi_1\rangle\big) \otimes |\psi_2\rangle = |\psi_1\rangle \otimes |\psi_2\rangle + |\varphi_1\rangle \otimes |\psi_2\rangle. \qquad (2.6.3)$$

3. For any $|\psi_1\rangle \in \mathcal{H}_1$, and $|\psi_2\rangle, |\varphi_2\rangle \in \mathcal{H}_2$,

$$|\psi_1\rangle \otimes \big(|\psi_2\rangle + |\varphi_2\rangle\big) = |\psi_1\rangle \otimes |\psi_2\rangle + |\psi_1\rangle \otimes |\varphi_2\rangle. \qquad (2.6.4)$$

Suppose A and B are linear operators on $\mathcal{H}_1$ and $\mathcal{H}_2$ respectively. Then $A \otimes B$ is the linear operator on $\mathcal{H}_1 \otimes \mathcal{H}_2$ defined by

$$(A \otimes B)\big(|\psi_1\rangle \otimes |\psi_2\rangle\big) \equiv A|\psi_1\rangle \otimes B|\psi_2\rangle. \qquad (2.6.5)$$

This definition extends linearly over the elements of $\mathcal{H}_1 \otimes \mathcal{H}_2$:

$$(A \otimes B)\left(\sum_{ij} \lambda_{ij} |b_i\rangle \otimes |c_j\rangle\right) \equiv \sum_{ij} \lambda_{ij} A|b_i\rangle \otimes B|c_j\rangle. \qquad (2.6.6)$$

We have presented the tensor product using the Dirac notation. In the matrix representation, this translates as follows. Suppose A is an $m \times n$ matrix and B a $p \times q$ matrix, then the *left Kronecker product* of A with B is the $mp \times nq$ matrix

$$A \otimes B = \begin{bmatrix} A_{11}B_{11} & \cdots & A_{11}B_{1q} & \cdots\cdots & A_{1n}B_{11} & \cdots & A_{1n}B_{1q} \\ \vdots & \vdots & \vdots & \vdots \; \vdots & \vdots & \vdots & \vdots \\ A_{11}B_{p1} & \cdots & A_{11}B_{pq} & \cdots\cdots & A_{1n}B_{p1} & \cdots & A_{1n}B_{pq} \\ \vdots & \vdots & \vdots & \vdots \; \vdots & \vdots & \vdots & \vdots \\ \vdots & \vdots & \vdots & \vdots \; \vdots & \vdots & \vdots & \vdots \\ A_{m1}B_{11} & \cdots & A_{m1}B_{1q} & \cdots\cdots & A_{mn}B_{11} & \cdots & A_{mn}B_{1q} \\ \vdots & \vdots & \vdots & \vdots \; \vdots & \vdots & \vdots & \vdots \\ A_{m1}B_{p1} & \cdots & A_{m1}B_{pq} & \cdots\cdots & A_{mn}B_{p1} & \cdots & A_{mn}B_{pq} \end{bmatrix}. \qquad (2.6.7)$$

This matrix is sometimes written more compactly in 'block form' as

$$A \otimes B = \begin{bmatrix} A_{11}[B] & A_{12}[B] & \cdots & A_{1n}[B] \\ A_{21}[B] & A_{22}[B] & \cdots & A_{2n}[B] \\ \vdots & \vdots & \vdots & \vdots \\ A_{m1}[B] & A_{m2}[B] & \cdots & A_{mn}[B] \end{bmatrix}. \qquad (2.6.8)$$

Here, $[B]$ represents the $p \times q$ submatrix B. Then each block entry $A_{ij}[B]$ above is the matrix $[B]$ multiplied by the single entry in row i, column j, of matrix A.

$$A_{ij}[B] = \begin{bmatrix} A_{ij}B_{11} & A_{ij}B_{12} & \cdots & A_{ij}B_{1q} \\ A_{ij}B_{21} & A_{ij}B_{22} & \cdots & A_{ij}B_{2q} \\ \vdots & \vdots & \vdots & \vdots \\ A_{ij}B_{p1} & A_{ij}B_{p2} & \cdots & A_{ij}B_{pq} \end{bmatrix}. \qquad (2.6.9)$$

The matrix representation for the tensor product of two vectors, or two operators, is the left Kronecker product of the matrix representation of the two vectors or operators being 'tensored' together. For example, the matrix representation of $(\alpha_0|0\rangle + \alpha_1|1\rangle) \otimes (\beta_0|0\rangle + \beta_1|1\rangle)$ is

$$\begin{pmatrix} \alpha_0 \\ \alpha_1 \end{pmatrix} \otimes \begin{pmatrix} \beta_0 \\ \beta_1 \end{pmatrix} = \begin{pmatrix} \alpha_0\beta_0 \\ \alpha_0\beta_1 \\ \alpha_1\beta_0 \\ \alpha_1\beta_1 \end{pmatrix}. \tag{2.6.10}$$

A final important word about notation. We often leave the $\otimes$ symbol out of expressions, and thus $|\psi\rangle \otimes |\varphi\rangle$ is often written as just $|\psi\rangle|\varphi\rangle$, or sometimes even $|\psi\varphi\rangle$.

2.7 The Schmidt Decomposition Theorem

Here we present an important result for quantum information: the *Schmidt decomposition theorem*. We begin by stating the theorem, and then provide some examples illustrating it. Then we will describe an application of the theorem.

Theorem 2.7.1 *(Schmidt decomposition) If $|\psi\rangle$ is a vector in a tensor product space $\mathcal{H}_A \otimes \mathcal{H}_B$, then there exists an orthonormal basis $\{|\varphi_i^A\rangle\}$ for $\mathcal{H}_A$, and an orthonormal basis $\{|\varphi_i^B\rangle\}$ for $\mathcal{H}_B$, and non-negative real numbers $\{p_i\}$ so that*

$$|\psi\rangle = \sum_i \sqrt{p_i}|\varphi_i^A\rangle|\varphi_i^B\rangle. \tag{2.7.1}$$

The coefficients $\sqrt{p_i}$ are called *Schmidt coefficients*. To understand what this theorem is saying, suppose $\{|\varphi_i^A\rangle\}$ and $\{|\varphi_i^B\rangle\}$ were chosen to be any arbitrary orthonormal bases for $\mathcal{H}_A$ and $\mathcal{H}_B$ respectively. Then, as we saw in Section 2.6, the basis states for the space $\mathcal{H}_A \otimes \mathcal{H}_B$ are $|\varphi_i^A\rangle \otimes |\varphi_j^B\rangle$ (often written $|\varphi_i^A\rangle|\varphi_j^B\rangle$). The general vector $|\psi\rangle$ in $\mathcal{H}_A \otimes \mathcal{H}_B$ is then

$$|\psi\rangle = \sum_{i,j} \alpha_{i,j}|\varphi_i^A\rangle|\varphi_j^B\rangle \tag{2.7.2}$$

where the coefficients $\alpha_{i,j} = e^{i\phi_{i,j}}\sqrt{p_{i,j}}$ are in general complex numbers. Note that we have had to use different indices on the two sets of basis vectors to account for all the 'cross-terms'. If $\mathcal{H}_A$ has dimension m and $\mathcal{H}_B$ has dimension n, this general vector is a superposition of mn basis vectors. The Schmidt decomposition tells us that we can always find *some* pair of bases $\{|\varphi_i^A\rangle\}$ and $\{|\varphi_i^B\rangle\}$ such that all the 'cross terms' vanish, and the general vector simplifies to a sum over one set of indices

$$|\psi\rangle = \sum_i \sqrt{p_i}|\varphi_i^A\rangle|\varphi_i^B\rangle \tag{2.7.3}$$

and the coefficients can be assumed to be real (since any phase factors can be absorbed into the definitions of the basis elements). The number of terms in this sum will be (at most) the minimum of m and n.

Example 2.7.2 As a trivial example of the Schmidt decomposition theorem, consider the following vector in a 4-dimensional Hilbert space $\mathcal{H}_A \otimes \mathcal{H}_B$ where $\mathcal{H}_A$ and $\mathcal{H}_B$ each have dimension 2:

$$|\psi\rangle = |11\rangle. \tag{2.7.4}$$

This vector is already written in terms of Schmidt bases (for each of $\mathcal{H}_A$ and $\mathcal{H}_B$ the Schmidt basis is the computational basis). That is,

$$\{|\varphi_0^A\rangle = |0\rangle, \qquad |\varphi_1^A\rangle = |1\rangle\}, \tag{2.7.5}$$

$$\{|\varphi_0^B\rangle = |0\rangle, \qquad |\varphi_1^B\rangle = |1\rangle\}. \tag{2.7.6}$$

The Schmidt coefficients are $p_0 = 0$, $p_1 = 1$.

Example 2.7.3 As a slightly less trivial example, consider the following state on the same 4-dimensional space $\mathcal{H}_A \otimes \mathcal{H}_B$ as in the previous example:

$$|\psi\rangle = \tfrac{1}{2}|00\rangle + \tfrac{1}{2}|01\rangle + \tfrac{1}{2}|10\rangle + \tfrac{1}{2}|11\rangle. \tag{2.7.7}$$

In this example, the computational basis is not a Schmidt basis for either $\mathcal{H}_A$ or $\mathcal{H}_B$. Notice that we can rewrite the vector as

$$|\psi\rangle = \left(\tfrac{1}{\sqrt{2}}|0\rangle + \tfrac{1}{\sqrt{2}}|1\rangle\right)\left(\tfrac{1}{\sqrt{2}}|0\rangle + \tfrac{1}{\sqrt{2}}|1\rangle\right). \tag{2.7.8}$$

So we choose Schmidt bases to be

$$\{|\varphi_0^A\rangle = \tfrac{1}{\sqrt{2}}|0\rangle + \tfrac{1}{\sqrt{2}}|1\rangle, \qquad |\varphi_1^A\rangle = \tfrac{1}{\sqrt{2}}|0\rangle - \tfrac{1}{\sqrt{2}}|1\rangle\}, \tag{2.7.9}$$

$$\{|\varphi_0^B\rangle = \tfrac{1}{\sqrt{2}}|0\rangle + \tfrac{1}{\sqrt{2}}|1\rangle, \qquad |\varphi_1^B\rangle = \tfrac{1}{\sqrt{2}}|0\rangle - \tfrac{1}{\sqrt{2}}|1\rangle\} \tag{2.7.10}$$

and the Schmidt coefficients are $p_0 = 1$, $p_1 = 0$.

The Schmidt bases for the two parts of the composite space will not always be the same. Consider the following example.

Example 2.7.4

$$|\psi\rangle = \tfrac{1+\sqrt{6}}{2\sqrt{6}}|00\rangle + \tfrac{1-\sqrt{6}}{2\sqrt{6}}|01\rangle + \tfrac{\sqrt{2}-\sqrt{3}}{2\sqrt{6}}|10\rangle + \tfrac{\sqrt{2}+\sqrt{3}}{2\sqrt{6}}|11\rangle. \tag{2.7.11}$$

For this vector Schmidt bases are

$$\{|\varphi_0^A\rangle = \tfrac{1}{\sqrt{3}}|0\rangle + \tfrac{\sqrt{2}}{\sqrt{3}}|1\rangle, \qquad |\varphi_1^A\rangle = \tfrac{\sqrt{2}}{\sqrt{3}}|0\rangle - \tfrac{1}{\sqrt{3}}|1\rangle\}, \tag{2.7.12}$$

$$\{|\varphi_0^B\rangle = \tfrac{1}{\sqrt{2}}|0\rangle + \tfrac{1}{\sqrt{2}}|1\rangle, \qquad |\varphi_1^B\rangle = \tfrac{1}{\sqrt{2}}|0\rangle - \tfrac{1}{\sqrt{2}}|1\rangle\} \tag{2.7.13}$$

and the Schmidt coefficients are $p_0 = \tfrac{1}{4}$, $p_1 = \tfrac{3}{4}$.

In all the above examples, the bipartite space was one in which each subspace had dimension 2. The Schmidt decomposition theorem can be applied to more complicated bipartite vector space, even in cases where the two subspaces have different dimensions. We will examine a method for computing Schmidt decompositions in Section 3.5.2.

2.8 Some Comments on the Dirac Notation

Juggling bras and kets can be somewhat confusing if you are not familiar with working in the Dirac notation. Now we discuss a convention that potentially adds to this confusion. When we write tensor products of subsystems, we usually identify which vectors correspond to which subsystems by the order in which the respective tensor factors appear. For example, if system 1 is in state $|i\rangle$ and system 2 in state $|j\rangle$, we would write $|i\rangle \otimes |j\rangle$, or more simply $|i\rangle |j\rangle$, or even $|ij\rangle$. If we wanted to be completely unambiguous we could label the states with subscripts indexing the systems, and would write the above state as $|i\rangle_1 |j\rangle_2$. When computing the conjugate transpose, following the standard matrix convention we would write

$$\left(|i\rangle_1 |j\rangle_2\right)^\dagger = \langle i|_1 \langle j|_2. \tag{2.8.1}$$

Physicists more commonly order this differently, and write

$$\left(|i\rangle_1 |j\rangle_2\right)^\dagger = \langle j|_2 \langle i|_1. \tag{2.8.2}$$

According to this convention, we can compute inner products in the following way (now omitting the subscripts):

$$
\begin{aligned}
\left(|i\rangle |j\rangle\right)^\dagger |k\rangle |l\rangle &= \langle j|\langle i||k\rangle |l\rangle \\
&= \langle j|\langle i|k\rangle |l\rangle \\
&= \langle i|k\rangle \langle j||l\rangle \\
&= \langle i|k\rangle \langle j|l\rangle.
\end{aligned}
\tag{2.8.3}
$$

Now we derive a useful identity involving tensor products of operators written in outer-product form. This is a useful exercise to gain practice and confidence in working with the Dirac notation. In what follows, we will *not* be using the convention described in Equation (2.8.2).

Identity:

$$\left(|i\rangle_1 \otimes |j\rangle_2\right)\left(\langle k|_1 \otimes \langle l|_2\right) \equiv |i\rangle_1 \langle k|_1 \otimes |j\rangle_2 \langle l|_2. \tag{2.8.4}$$

In the above, we have written the $\otimes$ symbol everywhere, for clarity. However, in practice we often leave this symbol out, and sometimes write the labels of the factors inside a single ket (or bra). So the above identity could be more concisely written

$$|ij\rangle \langle kl| = |i\rangle \langle k| \otimes |j\rangle \langle l|. \tag{2.8.5}$$

3

QUBITS AND THE FRAMEWORK OF QUANTUM MECHANICS

In this section we introduce the framework of quantum mechanics as it pertains to the types of systems we will consider for quantum computing. Here we also introduce the notion of a quantum bit or 'qubit', which is a fundamental concept for quantum computing.

At the beginning of the twentieth century, it was believed by most that the laws of Newton and Maxwell were the correct laws of physics. By the 1930s, however, it had become apparent that these classical theories faced serious problems in trying to account for the observed results of certain experiments. As a result, a new mathematical framework for physics called *quantum mechanics* was formulated, and new theories of physics called *quantum physics* were developed in this framework. Quantum physics includes the physical theories of quantum electrodynamics and quantum field theory, but we do not need to know these physical theories in order to learn about quantum information. Quantum information is the result of reformulating information theory in this quantum framework.[1]

3.1 The State of a Quantum System

We saw in Section 1.6 an example of a two-state quantum system: a photon that is constrained to follow one of two distinguishable paths. We identified the two distinguishable paths with the 2-dimensional basis vectors

$$\begin{pmatrix} 1 \\ 0 \end{pmatrix} \text{ and } \begin{pmatrix} 0 \\ 1 \end{pmatrix} \qquad (3.1.1)$$

and then noted that a general 'path state' of the photon can be described by a complex vector

$$\begin{pmatrix} \alpha_0 \\ \alpha_1 \end{pmatrix} \qquad (3.1.2)$$

---

[1] It is worth noting that the term *quantum mechanics* is also often used to refer to that part of quantum physics that deals with a special limit of quantum field theory.

with $|\alpha_0|^2 + |\alpha_1|^2 = 1$. This simple example captures the essence of the first postulate, which tells us how physical states are represented in quantum mechanics.

State Space Postulate

The state of a system is described by a unit vector in a Hilbert space $\mathcal{H}$.

Depending on the degree of freedom (i.e. the type of state) of the system being considered, $\mathcal{H}$ may be infinite-dimensional. For example, if the state refers to the position of a particle that is free to occupy any point in some region of space, the associated Hilbert space is usually taken to be a continuous (and thus infinite-dimensional) space. It is worth noting that in practice, with finite resources, we cannot distinguish a continuous state space from one with a discrete state space having a sufficiently small minimum spacing between adjacent locations. For describing realistic models of quantum computation, we will typically only be interested in degrees of freedom for which the state is described by a vector in a finite-dimensional (complex) Hilbert space.[2] In particular, we will primarily be interested in composite systems composed of individual *two-level* systems. The state of each two-level system is described by a vector in a 2-dimensional Hilbert space. We can encode a *qubit* in such a two-level system. We would choose a basis for the corresponding 2-dimensional space. We would label one of the basis vectors with $|0\rangle$ and the other basis vector with $|1\rangle$. This is analogous to what is done for classical computation. For a classical computer, the two-level system may be the voltage level on a wire, which could be zero, or some positive value (say $+5\,\text{mV}$). We might encode a classical bit in such a system by assigning the binary value '0' to the state in which the voltage on the wire is 0, and the value '1' to the state in which the voltage on the wire is $+5\,\text{mV}$. The $\{|0\rangle, |1\rangle\}$ basis for the state of a qubit is commonly referred to as the *computational basis*.

A quantum mechanical two-level system might be a single photon that can be found in one of two distinct paths, as we saw in the introduction. Another example of a quantum two-level system is the presence or absence of a photon in a particular location or path.

The state of this system is described by a vector in a 2-dimensional Hilbert space. A convenient basis for this space consists of a unit vector for the state in which a photon is not present, and an orthogonal unit vector for the state in which a photon is present. We can label these states with $|0\rangle$ and $|1\rangle$, respectively. Then the general state of the system is expressed by the vector

$$\alpha_0|0\rangle + \alpha_1|1\rangle \tag{3.1.3}$$

where α_0 and α_1 are complex coefficients, often called the *amplitudes* of the basis states $|0\rangle$ and $|1\rangle$, respectively. Note that a complex amplitude α can be

---

[2]However, it is common to use infinite dimensional state spaces to model the physical systems used to implement quantum (as well as classical) information processing.

decomposed unique as a product $e^{i\theta}|\alpha|$ where $|\alpha|$ is the non-negative real number corresponding to the magnitude of α, and $e^{i\theta} = \frac{\alpha}{|\alpha|}$ has norm 1. The value θ is known as the 'phase', and we refer to the value $e^{i\theta}$ as a 'phase factor'.

The condition that the state is described by a *unit* vector means that $|\alpha_0|^2 + |\alpha_1|^2 = 1$. This condition is sometimes called the *normalization constraint*, and it is necessary for consistency with the way quantum measurements behave, as we will see in the Measurement Postulate. The general state of the system is a superposition of a photon being present, and a photon not being present.

Another example of a two-level quantum mechanical system is the spin state of certain types of particles. According to quantum physics, particles have a degree of freedom called *spin*, which does not exist in a classical description. Many particles fall into the category of so-called *spin-$\frac{1}{2}$* particles. For these, the *spin state* is indeed described by a vector in a 2-dimensional Hilbert space $\mathcal{H}$. A convenient basis for this space consists of a unit vector for the 'spin-up' state of the particle, and an orthogonal unit vector for the 'spin-down' state of the particle. We can label these basis vectors by $|0\rangle$ and $|1\rangle$, respectively. The general *spin state* of a spin-$\frac{1}{2}$ particle is a superposition of spin-up and spin-down.

As another example of a physical system whose state can be described by a vector in a 2-dimensional Hilbert space, consider an electron orbiting a nucleus. Suppose we choose energy as the degree of freedom of interest. There is a theoretically infinite number of possible energy levels for the electron, and so the Hilbert space would have infinite dimension. From quantum mechanics we know that these energy levels are *quantized.* That is, instead of a continuous range of possible energies, the electron is restricted to have energies from a discrete set. It is possible to have such a system for which the electron can easily be found in the *ground state* (lowest energy level), or the first excited state, but the amount of energy required to excite the system to higher energy levels is so high we are almost certain never to find energy levels higher than the first two. In such cases we can choose to ignore the subspace spanned by all energies higher than the first excited state, and for all practical purposes we have a two-level system described by a 2-dimensional vector in the space spanned by the lowest two energy levels.

An important point about state vectors is the following. The state described by the vector $e^{i\theta}|\psi\rangle$ is equivalent to the state described by the vector $|\psi\rangle$, where $e^{i\theta}$ is any complex number of unit norm. For example, the state

$$|0\rangle + |1\rangle \tag{3.1.4}$$

is equivalent to the state described by the vector

$$e^{i\theta}|0\rangle + e^{i\theta}|1\rangle. \tag{3.1.5}$$

On the other hand, *relative phase factors* between two orthogonal states in superposition *are* physically significant, and the state described by the vector

$$|0\rangle + |1\rangle \tag{3.1.6}$$

is physically different from the state described by the vector

$$|0\rangle + e^{i\theta}|1\rangle. \tag{3.1.7}$$

Technically we could describe quantum states by equivalence classes of unit vectors, but we will simply specify a unit vector, with the understanding that any two vectors that are related by a global phase are equivalent. We will motivate the fact that $|\psi\rangle$ and $e^{i\theta}|\psi\rangle$ are equivalent after we have introduced the Measurement Postulate.

So the State Space Postulate, together with the observation of the previous paragraph, tells us that we can describe the most general state $|\psi\rangle$ of a single qubit by a vector of the form

$$|\psi\rangle = \cos\left(\tfrac{\theta}{2}\right)|0\rangle + e^{i\varphi}\sin\left(\tfrac{\theta}{2}\right)|1\rangle \tag{3.1.8}$$

(we take $\tfrac{\theta}{2}$ instead of just θ to be consistent with the angle θ appearing in Figure 3.3, which will be discussed shortly). Consider the analogous situation for a deterministic classical bit. The state of a classical bit can be described by a single binary value ψ, which can be equal to either 0 or 1. This description could be expressed in terms of the diagram shown in Figure 3.1. In this figure, the state can be indicated by a point in one of two positions, indicated by the two points labelled 0 and 1.

Next consider the slightly more complicated situation of a classical bit whose value is not known exactly, but is known to be either 0 or 1 with corresponding probabilities p_0 and p_1. We might call this a *probabilistic classical bit*. The state of such a probabilistic bit is described by the probabilities p_0 and p_1, which satisfy $p_0 + p_1 = 1$ (reflecting the fact that we know the bit has to be either 0 or 1). As we saw in Section 1.4, we can represent these two probabilities by the 2-dimensional unit vector

$$\begin{pmatrix} p_0 \\ p_1 \end{pmatrix} \tag{3.1.9}$$

whose entries are restricted to be real and non-negative. This description could be expressed in terms of the diagram shown in Figure 3.2. In this figure, the

0

•

•

1

Fig. 3.1 The state of a deterministic classical bit can be represented as one of two points, labelled '0' and '1'.

Fig. 3.2 A probabilistic classical bit. Here the probabilities p_0 and p_1 of the bit being 0 and 1, respectively, are represented by the position of a point on the line segment between the points representing 0 and 1.

state could be drawn as a point on the line between the positions 0 and 1. We suppose this line has unit length, and the position of the point on the line is determined by the probabilities p_0 and p_1.

Note that with only one copy of such a probabilistic bit, we cannot determine p_0 and p_1 exactly. If we are given a means to obtain several independent copies of the probabilistic bit (where each copy independently outputs 0 with probability p_0 and 1 with probability p_1), then we could accumulate statistics about the values p_0 and p_1. Otherwise, we cannot in general 'clone' this bit and get two or more independent copies that would allow us to obtain arbitrarily good estimates of p_0 and p_1.

Now return to the state of a quantum bit, which is described by a complex unit vector $|\psi\rangle$ in a 2-dimensional Hilbert space. Up to a (physically insignificant) global phase factor, such a vector can always be written in the form

$$|\psi\rangle = \cos\left(\tfrac{\theta}{2}\right)|0\rangle + e^{i\varphi}\sin\left(\tfrac{\theta}{2}\right)|1\rangle. \qquad (3.1.10)$$

Such a state vector is often depicted as a point on the surface of a 3-dimensional sphere, known as the *Bloch sphere*, as shown in Figure 3.3. Two real parameters θ and φ are sufficient to describe a state vector, since state vectors are constrained to have norm 1 and are equivalent up to global phase. Points on the surface of the Bloch sphere can also be expressed in Cartesian coordinates as

$$(x, y, z) = (\sin\theta\cos\varphi, \sin\theta\sin\varphi, \cos\theta). \qquad (3.1.11)$$

We will also explain the meaning of points within the Bloch sphere when we consider density matrices in Section 3.5.

Figure 3.4 summarizes the graphical representations of the states of a classical bit, a probabilistic classical bit, and a quantum bit.

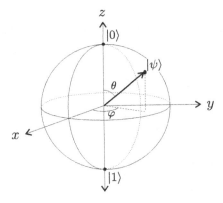

Fig. 3.3 State of a qubit on the Bloch sphere.

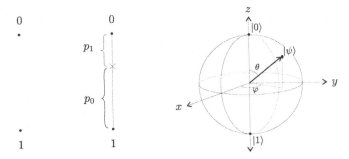

Fig. 3.4 States of deterministic classical, probabilistic classical, and quantum bits.

3.2 Time-Evolution of a Closed System

A physical system changes in time, and so the state vector $|\psi\rangle$ of a system will actually be a function of time, $|\psi(t)\rangle$. Quantum theory postulates that the evolution of the state vector of a closed quantum system is linear. In other words, if we know that some fixed transformation, let us call it U, maps $|\psi_i\rangle$ to $U|\psi_i\rangle$ then

$$U \sum_i \alpha_i |\psi_i\rangle = \sum_i \alpha_i U |\psi_i\rangle. \qquad (3.2.1)$$

For example, as we saw in the introduction, if $|0\rangle$ evolves to $\frac{1}{\sqrt{2}}|0\rangle + \frac{i}{\sqrt{2}}|1\rangle$, and $|1\rangle$ evolves to $\frac{i}{\sqrt{2}}|0\rangle + \frac{1}{\sqrt{2}}|1\rangle$, then $\alpha_0|0\rangle + \alpha_1|1\rangle$ evolves to

$$\alpha_0 \left(\frac{1}{\sqrt{2}}|0\rangle + \frac{i}{\sqrt{2}}|1\rangle \right) + \alpha_1 \left(\frac{i}{\sqrt{2}}|0\rangle + \frac{1}{\sqrt{2}}|1\rangle \right) \qquad (3.2.2)$$

$$= \frac{\alpha_0 + i\alpha_1}{\sqrt{2}}|0\rangle + \frac{i\alpha_0 + \alpha_1}{\sqrt{2}}|1\rangle. \qquad (3.2.3)$$

As we have mentioned briefly already, and will elaborate on in Section 3.4, the coefficients α_i of a state vector satisfy $\sum_i |\alpha_i|^2 = 1$. The only linear operators that preserve such norms of vectors are the *unitary* operators (see Section 2.3). This brings us to the Evolution Postulate.

Evolution Postulate

The time-evolution of the state of a *closed* quantum system is described by a unitary operator. That is, for any evolution of the closed system there exists a unitary operator U such that if the initial state of the system is $|\psi_1\rangle$, then after the evolution the state of the system will be

$$|\psi_2\rangle = U|\psi_1\rangle. \tag{3.2.4}$$

In quantum computing, we refer to a unitary operator U acting on a single-qubit as a *1-qubit (unitary) gate*. We can represent operators on the 2-dimensional Hilbert space of a single qubit as 2×2 matrices. A linear operator is specified completely by its action on a basis. For example, consider the quantum NOT gate which is a unitary operator mapping $|0\rangle$ to $|1\rangle$, and mapping $|1\rangle$ to $|0\rangle$. Being a linear operator, it will map a linear combination of inputs to the corresponding linear combination of outputs, and so the NOT gate maps the general state

$$\alpha_0|0\rangle + \alpha_1|1\rangle \tag{3.2.5}$$

to the state

$$\alpha_0|1\rangle + \alpha_1|0\rangle. \tag{3.2.6}$$

Recall that the basis vectors have a representation as column matrices. In terms of this matrix representation, the action of the NOT gate on the basis vectors is

$$\text{NOT}: \quad \begin{pmatrix} 1 \\ 0 \end{pmatrix} \mapsto \begin{pmatrix} 0 \\ 1 \end{pmatrix}, \quad \begin{pmatrix} 0 \\ 1 \end{pmatrix} \mapsto \begin{pmatrix} 1 \\ 0 \end{pmatrix}. \tag{3.2.7}$$

From this information, we can construct the matrix for the NOT gate (in the computational basis):

$$\begin{bmatrix} 0 & 1 \\ 1 & 0 \end{bmatrix}. \tag{3.2.8}$$

The gate acts on the state of a qubit by matrix multiplication from the left:

$$\text{NOT}|0\rangle \equiv \begin{bmatrix} 0 & 1 \\ 1 & 0 \end{bmatrix} \begin{pmatrix} 1 \\ 0 \end{pmatrix} = \begin{pmatrix} 0 \\ 1 \end{pmatrix} \equiv |1\rangle. \tag{3.2.9}$$

The NOT gate is often identified with the symbol X, and is one of the four *Pauli gates*:

$$\sigma_0 \equiv I \equiv \begin{bmatrix} 1 & 0 \\ 0 & 1 \end{bmatrix} \qquad \sigma_1 \equiv \sigma_x \equiv X \equiv \begin{bmatrix} 0 & 1 \\ 1 & 0 \end{bmatrix}$$

$$\sigma_2 \equiv \sigma_y \equiv Y \equiv \begin{bmatrix} 0 & -i \\ i & 0 \end{bmatrix} \qquad \sigma_3 \equiv \sigma_z \equiv Z \equiv \begin{bmatrix} 1 & 0 \\ 0 & -1 \end{bmatrix}. \tag{3.2.10}$$

As we will see in Chapter 4, the Pauli gates X, Y, and Z correspond to rotations about the x-, y- and z-axes of the Bloch sphere, respectively. One reason why the Pauli gates are important for quantum computing is that they span the vector space formed by all 1-qubit operators. In particular, this means that any 1-qubit unitary operator can be expressed as a linear combination of the Pauli gates.

It is worth noting that the unitarity of quantum evolution implies *reversibility*. This reversibility is a consequence of restricting attention to closed systems. We saw in Section 1.5 that any irreversible classical computation can be efficiently simulated by a reversible classical computation. The same holds for quantum computation (this is described in more detail in Section 3.5.3).

In a typical first course in quantum physics, one learns that the continuous time-evolution of a closed quantum mechanical system (ignoring special relativity) follows the *Schrödinger equation*

$$i\hbar \frac{d|\psi(t)\rangle}{dt} = H(t)|\psi(t)\rangle \qquad (3.2.11)$$

where $\hbar$ is a physical constant known as *Planck's constant* and $H(t)$ is a Hermitean operator known as the *Hamiltonian* of the system. The Hamiltonian is an operator which represents the total energy function for the system. It may in general be a function of time, but for convenience, let us consider Hamiltonians that are constant. In this case the solution to the Schrödinger equation for fixed times t_1 and t_2 is

$$|\psi(t_2)\rangle = e^{-i\hbar H(t_2 - t_1)}|\psi(t_1)\rangle. \qquad (3.2.12)$$

Exercise 3.2.1 Show that (3.2.12) is a solution of the time-independent Schrödinger equation.

For Hermitean operators H, the operator $e^{-iH(t_2 - t_1)}$ is a unitary operator. So for the case of (non-relativistic and continuous time) constant Hamiltonians, one can easily show that the Evolution Postulate follows from the Schrödinger equation.

3.3 Composite Systems

So far we have discussed the postulates for the case of a single system only, in particular a qubit. If all we ever needed to know was how isolated qubits behave when they are never allowed to interact with each other, then this would be sufficient. If we want to study potentially useful quantum computations we will need to understand how quantum mechanics works for systems composed of several qubits *interacting* with each other. That is, we would like to know how to describe the state of a closed system of n qubits, how such a state evolves in time, and what happens when we measure it. Treating a larger system as a composition of subsystems (of bounded size) allows for an exponentially more efficient description of operations acting on a small number of subsystems.

The way we represent composite quantum systems is in fact analogous to the way we treated composite classical probabilistic systems in Section 1.4. This brings us to our third postulate.

Composition of Systems Postulate

When two physical systems are treated as one combined system, the state space of the combined physical system is the tensor product space $\mathcal{H}_1 \otimes \mathcal{H}_2$ of the state spaces $\mathcal{H}_1, \mathcal{H}_2$ of the component subsystems. If the first system is in the state $|\psi_1\rangle$ and the second system in the state $|\psi_2\rangle$, then the state of the combined system is

$$|\psi_1\rangle \otimes |\psi_2\rangle. \tag{3.3.1}$$

As mentioned in Section 2.6, we often omit the '$\otimes$' symbol and write the joint state like $|\psi_1\rangle|\psi_2\rangle$, or sometimes even more compactly as $|\psi_1\psi_2\rangle$.

One can apply the Composition of Systems Postulate inductively to show that the state space of system composed of n distinct subsystems is the tensor product space of the state spaces of the n subsystems. For convenience, we will consider the subsystems to be of dimension 2, but it is straightforward to generalize to larger dimensional subsystems.

It is important to note that the state of a 2-qubit composite system cannot always be written in the product form $|\psi_1\rangle \otimes |\psi_2\rangle$. If the 2 qubits are prepared independently, and kept isolated, then each qubit forms a closed system, and the state *can* be written in the product form. However, if the qubits are allowed to interact, then the closed system includes both qubits together, and it may *not* be possible to write the state in the product form. When this is the case, we say that the qubits are *entangled*. From an algebraic point of view, the state of the composite system is a vector in the 4-dimensional tensor-product space of the 2 constituent qubits. The 4-dimensional state vectors that are formed by taking the tensor product of two 2-dimension state vectors form a sparse subset of all the 4-dimensional state vectors. In this sense, 'most' 2-qubit states are entangled.

Exercise 3.3.1 Consider the 2-qubit state

$$|\psi\rangle = \tfrac{1}{\sqrt{2}}|0\rangle|0\rangle + \tfrac{1}{\sqrt{2}}|1\rangle|1\rangle. \tag{3.3.2}$$

Show that this state is entangled by proving that there are no possible values $\alpha_0, \alpha_1, \beta_0, \beta_1$ such that

$$|\psi\rangle = (\alpha_0|0\rangle + \alpha_1|1\rangle)(\beta_0|0\rangle + \beta_1|1\rangle). \tag{3.3.3}$$

(Note, the state $|\psi\rangle$ above is called an *EPR pair*, named for Einstein, Podolsky, and Rosen, who considered such states in their investigations of quantum mechanics.)

Suppose we have a 2-qubit composite system, and we apply the NOT gate X to the first qubit. We implicitly apply the identity operator I to the second qubit at the same time. Thus the 2-qubit input $|\psi_1\rangle \otimes |\psi_2\rangle$ gets mapped to $X|\psi_1\rangle \otimes I|\psi_2\rangle = (X \otimes I)(|\psi_1\rangle \otimes |\psi_2\rangle)$. That is, the linear operator describing this operation on the composite system is

$$X \otimes I \tag{3.3.4}$$

which has the matrix representation

$$\begin{bmatrix} 0 & 1 \\ 1 & 0 \end{bmatrix} \otimes \begin{bmatrix} 1 & 0 \\ 0 & 1 \end{bmatrix} = \begin{bmatrix} 0 & 0 & 1 & 0 \\ 0 & 0 & 0 & 1 \\ 1 & 0 & 0 & 0 \\ 0 & 1 & 0 & 0 \end{bmatrix}. \tag{3.3.5}$$

Although it acts on the composite 2-qubit system, since it acts non-trivially on only one of the qubits, a gate such as this one is really a *1-qubit gate*.

If our system was the composition of n qubits, then applying the X gate to the first qubit corresponds to applying the operation $X \otimes I \otimes I \otimes \cdots \otimes I$ (with I repeated $n-1$ times) to the entire system. Note that if we ignore the subsystem structure and just treat the n-qubit system as a 2^n-dimensional system, we would need a $2^n \times 2^n$ dimensional matrix to describe this simple operation.

Just as there are 2-qubit states that cannot be written as the product of two 1-qubit states, there are 2-qubit gates (acting non-trivially on both qubits) that cannot be written as a tensor product of two 1-qubit gates. An important example is the quantum controlled-NOT, or CNOT gate (recall the classical version of this gate defined in Section 1.4). In terms of its action on the basis states of the 2-qubit system, the CNOT gate behaves as follows:

$$|00\rangle \mapsto |00\rangle, \quad |01\rangle \mapsto |01\rangle, \quad |10\rangle \mapsto |11\rangle, \quad |11\rangle \mapsto |10\rangle. \tag{3.3.6}$$

(recall $|00\rangle \equiv |0\rangle \otimes |0\rangle$). In the computational basis, the CNOT gate flips the state of the second qubit if the first qubit is in state $|1\rangle$, and does nothing otherwise. As with all unitary operators, the CNOT gate acts linearly over superpositions. The matrix representation for the CNOT gate is

$$\begin{bmatrix} 1 & 0 & 0 & 0 \\ 0 & 1 & 0 & 0 \\ 0 & 0 & 0 & 1 \\ 0 & 0 & 1 & 0 \end{bmatrix}. \tag{3.3.7}$$

Recall in Section 1.4, we saw that the tensor product is the mathematical tool to get a single description for a composite system composed of two or more subsystems. The Composition of Systems Postulate tells us that the same approach can be used to describe composite quantum mechanical systems.

3.4   Measurement

We have seen how the state of a single-qubit system is represented in quantum mechanics as a vector in a Hilbert space, and we have seen how such a state evolves according to a unitary operator. Notice that the Evolution Postulate assumes that the quantum system is *closed*, meaning that it is not allowed to interact with its environment. Ultimately we will be interested in measuring some properties of a system, and so at some point we must allow the system to interact with the measurement apparatus of some observer. When this happens the original system is no longer closed, and the Evolution Postulate is no longer appropriate for describing its evolution. It is possible to combine the system and any other part of the environment interacting with the system, including the measurement apparatus, into a larger closed quantum system. Such a fully quantum treatment of the interaction between observer and system would take us into controversial territory and distract from the main point of this text. It is convenient, conventional, and sufficient to introduce a measurement postulate and rely on more familiar notions of classical probability theory. The evolution of the state of a system during a measurement process is *not* unitary, and we add this additional postulate to describe such processes.

Suppose we have a system with N distinguishable states $|0\rangle, |1\rangle, \ldots, |N-1\rangle$, and some apparatus that will reliably distinguish these N states. Without loss of generality, let us say the apparatus will output the (classical) label 'i' together with the observed state $|i\rangle$ when $|i\rangle$ is provided as input. In other words, the measurement apparatus provides a classical description of the measurement outcome (which we simply denote as i where we indexed the possible measurement outcomes using the indices i; the values i do not need to be integers), along with some quantum state. Traditionally, the classical description or label is often described as a needle pointing to some value on a dial. But if we assume only finite resolution we can just as well assume a digital display with sufficiently many digits.

Quantum mechanics tells us that if the state $\sum_i \alpha_i |i\rangle$ is provided as input to this apparatus, it will output label i with probability $|\alpha_i|^2$ and leave the system in state $|i\rangle$. This is the essence of the Measurement Postulate. However, we will state a slightly more general version that can be derived from the above simple version together with the Evolution Postulate. Then we will discuss other common formulations of the measurement postulate and some of their well-known features.

Measurement Postulate

For a given orthonormal basis $B = \{|\varphi_i\rangle\}$ of a state space $\mathcal{H}_A$ for a system A, it is possible to perform a *Von Neumann measurement* on system $\mathcal{H}_A$ with respect to the basis B that, given a state

$$|\psi\rangle = \sum_i \alpha_i |\varphi_i\rangle, \tag{3.4.1}$$

outputs a label i with probability $|\alpha_i|^2$ and leaves the system in state $|\varphi_i\rangle$. Furthermore, given a state $|\psi\rangle = \sum_i \alpha_i |\varphi_i\rangle |\gamma_i\rangle$ from a bipartite state space $\mathcal{H}_A \otimes \mathcal{H}_B$ (the $|\varphi_i\rangle$ are orthonormal; the $|\gamma_i\rangle$ have unit norm but are not necessarily orthogonal), then performing a Von Neumann measurement on system A will yield outcome i with probability $|\alpha_i|^2$ and leave the bipartite system in state $|\varphi_i\rangle |\gamma_i\rangle$.

For the state $|\psi\rangle = \sum_i \alpha_i |\varphi_i\rangle$, note that $\alpha_i = \langle \varphi_i | |\psi\rangle = \langle \varphi_i |\psi\rangle$, and thus

$$|\alpha_i|^2 = \alpha_i^* \alpha_i = \langle \psi | \varphi_i \rangle \langle \varphi_i | \psi \rangle. \tag{3.4.2}$$

We can see that two states $|\psi\rangle$ and $e^{i\theta}|\psi\rangle$ (differing only by a global phase) are equivalent. Consider the state $e^{i\theta}|\psi\rangle = \sum_i \alpha_i e^{i\theta} |\varphi_i\rangle$ immediately before a measurement. The result i will occur with probability

$$p(i) = \alpha_i^* e^{-i\theta} \alpha_i e^{i\theta} = \alpha_i^* \alpha_i = |\alpha_i|^2 \tag{3.4.3}$$

and thus the resulting probability is the same as it would be for the state $|\psi\rangle$. The statistics of any measurements we could perform on the state $e^{i\theta}|\psi\rangle$ are exactly the same as they would be for the state $|\psi\rangle$. This explains our earlier claim that global phases have no physical significance.

Suppose we measure both qubits of a composite system in state

$$|\psi\rangle = \sqrt{\tfrac{1}{11}}|0\rangle|0\rangle + \sqrt{\tfrac{5}{11}}|0\rangle|1\rangle + \sqrt{\tfrac{2}{11}}|1\rangle|0\rangle + \sqrt{\tfrac{3}{11}}|1\rangle|1\rangle. \tag{3.4.4}$$

When we measure the two qubits in the computational basis, the probability of getting the result 00 is $\frac{1}{11}$, the probability of getting 01 is $\frac{5}{11}$, the probability of getting 10 is $\frac{2}{11}$, and the probability of getting 11 is $\frac{3}{11}$. Thus the probability of measuring 0 in the first qubit is thus $\frac{1}{11} + \frac{5}{11} = \frac{6}{11}$. To see what happens if we just measure the first qubit, it is convenient to rewrite $|\psi\rangle$ as

---

[2]Notice that here we use subscripts (e.g. $|\varphi_i\rangle$) to index different terms in a superposition of states on a single system. This is different from our usage in Section 3.3 where we used subscripts on $|\psi_1\rangle$ and $|\psi_2\rangle$ to index states on different subsystems of a bipartite system (factors in a tensor product). Both conventions are commonly used, and the meaning should always be clear from the context.

$$|\psi\rangle = \sqrt{\tfrac{6}{11}}|0\rangle \left(\sqrt{\tfrac{1}{6}}|0\rangle + \sqrt{\tfrac{5}{6}}|1\rangle \right) + \sqrt{\tfrac{5}{11}}|1\rangle \left(\sqrt{\tfrac{2}{5}}|0\rangle + \sqrt{\tfrac{3}{5}}|1\rangle \right). \qquad (3.4.5)$$

The measurement of just the first qubit gives 0 with probability $\tfrac{6}{11}$, and in this case the state of the second qubit is left in the superposition $\left(\sqrt{\tfrac{1}{6}}|0\rangle + \sqrt{\tfrac{5}{6}}|1\rangle \right)$.

One will find a variety of formulations of the Measurement Postulate in textbooks. They can all be derived from the simple postulates that have been outlined.

In Section 4.5, we will see how to implement a Von Neumann measurement with respect to an arbitrary basis $\{|\psi_i\rangle\}$ given the means to perform a Von Neumann measurement in the computational basis $\{|i\rangle\}$ and the ability to perform unitary transformations.

Combining the Measurement Postulate above with the other postulates, we can derive more general notions of measurement. In particular, if one wishes to measure a pure state $|\psi\rangle$ one can add an ancillary register[3] of arbitrary size initialized to some fixed state, say $|00\ldots0\rangle$. One can then perform a unitary operation on the joint system, followed by a Von Neumann measurement on some subsystem of the joint system to obtain a label i. Depending on what is done with the rest of the system (i.e. the part of the system that was not measured), one can derive a variety of generalized notions of quantum measurement (see Appendix A.8). In this section, we will only discuss one slight generalization of the Von Neumann measurements that can be derived in this way.

A Von Neumann measurement is a special kind of *projective measurement*.[4] Recall that an orthogonal projection is an operator P with the property that $P^\dagger = P$ and $P^2 = P$. For any decomposition of the identity operator $I = \sum_i P_i$ into orthogonal projectors P_i, there exists a projective measurement that outputs outcome i with probability $p(i) = \langle \psi | P_i | \psi \rangle$ and leaves the system in the renormalized state $\frac{P_i|\psi\rangle}{\sqrt{p(i)}}$. In other words, this measurement projects the input state $|\psi\rangle$ into one of the orthogonal subspaces corresponding to the projection operators P_i, with probability equal to the square of the size of the amplitude of the component of $|\psi\rangle$ in that subspace.

Exercise 3.4.1

(a) Prove that if the operators P_i satisfy $P_i^\dagger = P_i$ and $P_i^2 = P_i$, then $P_i P_j = 0$ for all $i \neq j$.

(b) Prove that any pure state $|\psi\rangle$ can be decomposed as $|\psi\rangle = \sum_i \alpha_i |\psi_i\rangle$ where $\alpha_i = \sqrt{p(i)}$, $p(i) = \langle \psi | P_i | \psi \rangle$, and $|\psi_i\rangle = \frac{P_i|\psi\rangle}{\sqrt{p(i)}}$.

---

[3]We will often refer to a register of ancillary qubits as simply an 'ancilla'.

[4]Also known as a Lüders measurement. The term 'Von Neumann measurement' is also often used to denote this more general notion of projective measurement.

Also prove that $\langle \psi_i | \psi_j \rangle = \delta_{i,j}$.

(c) Prove that any decomposition $I = \sum_i P_i$ of the identity operator on a Hilbert space of dimension N into a sum of nonzero projectors P_i can have at most N terms in the sum.

Note that the Von Neumann measurement as described in the Measurement Postulate (which can be described as a 'complete' or 'maximal' measurement) is the special case of a projective measurement where all the projectors P_i have rank one (in other words, are of the form $|\psi_i\rangle\langle\psi_i|$ for a normalized state $|\psi_i\rangle$).

The simplest example of a complete Von Neumann measurement is a complete measurement in the computational basis. This can be viewed as a projective measurement with respect to the following decomposition of the identity

$$I = \sum_{i \in \{0,1\}^n} P_i$$

where $P_i = |i\rangle\langle i|$.

A simple example of an incomplete projective measurement is a 'parity' measurement, where $P_0 = \sum_{\text{parity}(x)=0} |x\rangle\langle x|$ and $P_1 = \sum_{\text{parity}(x)=1} |x\rangle\langle x|$, where P_0 sums over all strings with an even number of 1s and P_1 with an odd number of 1s (Section 4.5 shows how to implement this projective measurement).

Projective measurements are often described in terms of an *observable*. An observable is a Hermitean operator M acting on the state space of the system. Since M is Hermitean, it has a spectral decomposition

$$M = \sum_i m_i P_i \tag{3.4.6}$$

where P_i is the orthogonal projector on the eigenspace of M with real eigenvalue m_i. Measuring the observable corresponds to performing a projective measurement with respect to the decomposition $I = \sum_i P_i$ where the measurement outcome i corresponds to the eigenvalue m_i.

Example 3.4.1 Consider the *Pauli observable Z*. Recall from Section 3.2 that the Pauli operator Z is defined by

$$Z \equiv \begin{bmatrix} 1 & 0 \\ 0 & -1 \end{bmatrix}. \tag{3.4.7}$$

In that section, we interpreted Z as a quantum gate. But it is easy to see that Z is a Hermitean operator, and so can be interpreted as an observable. The spectral decomposition for Z is

$$Z = |0\rangle\langle 0| - |1\rangle\langle 1|, \tag{3.4.8}$$

and so the eigenvalues of Z are 1 and -1, corresponding to eigenvectors $|0\rangle$ and $|1\rangle$ respectively. So the measurement operators are the projectors $|0\rangle\langle0|$ and $|1\rangle\langle1|$, and thus a measurement of the Pauli observable Z is a measurement in the computational basis, with eigenvalue $+1$ corresponding to $|0\rangle$ and eigenvalue -1 corresponding to $|1\rangle$.

Exercise 3.4.2 Show that measuring the observable $|1\rangle\langle1|$ is equivalent to measuring the observable Z up to a relabelling of the measurement outcomes.

Exercise 3.4.3 Verify that a measurement of the Pauli observable X is equivalent to a complete measurement with respect to the basis $\left\{\frac{1}{\sqrt{2}}(|0\rangle + |1\rangle), \frac{1}{\sqrt{2}}(|0\rangle - |1\rangle)\right\}$ basis.

Exercise 3.4.4

(a) Prove that performing a projective measurement with respect to P_0 and P_1 (defined above) on an n-qubit state is equivalent to measuring the observable $Z^{\otimes n}$.

(b) Explain why performing a complete Von Neumann measurement with respect to the computation basis, and then outputting the parity of the resulting string is not equivalent to performing a projective measurement of the parity.

Exercise 3.4.5 The observable formalism gives a convenient way to describe the expected value of a quantum measurement, where the eigenvalues m_i correspond to some relevant physical quantity. Such *expectation values* are particularly relevant for quantum experiments (particularly the early ones) where one does not measure individual quantum systems, but rather an ensemble of many independent and identically prepared systems, and where the measurement apparatus provides only cumulative results (e.g. the net magnetic field induced by an ensemble of nuclear spins). Consider a projective measurement described by projectors P_i, and suppose we measure the state $|\psi\rangle$. Show that the expected value of m_i is

$$E(m_i) = \text{Tr}(M|\psi\rangle\langle\psi|).$$

We have now seen how quantum measurements behave, starting with a postulate that describes a particular class of measurements, called (complete) Von Neumann measurements. The Measurement Postulate also described the behaviour of a measurement when we measure a subsystem of a larger composite quantum system. The Von Neumann measurement can be combined with other basic quantum operations to provide more general types of measurements, including general projective measurements, which canalso be phrased in terms of measuring an observable (which can be any Hermitean operator on the state space).

3.5   Mixed States and General Quantum Operations

In the preceding, we have always assumed that the state of a system has a definite state vector. Such a state is commonly referred to as a *pure* state. There are important situations, as we shall see, for which all we can say is that the qubit is described by one of a specific *set* of state vectors, with corresponding probabilities (the probabilities must add to 1). For example, suppose we know that a qubit is in the pure state $|\psi_1\rangle = \frac{1}{\sqrt{2}}|0\rangle + \frac{1}{\sqrt{2}}|1\rangle$ with probability $1/3$, and is in the pure state $|\psi_2\rangle = \frac{1}{\sqrt{2}}|0\rangle - \frac{1}{\sqrt{2}}|1\rangle$ with probability $2/3$. The state described by this probability distribution is called a *mixture* or *ensemble* of the states $|\psi_1\rangle$ and $|\psi_2\rangle$. We refer to the state of a system in such a situation as being a *mixed state*. In this section, we will define the standard mathematical tools used to describe mixed states and operations on mixed states. We will also discuss the partial trace operation, which will in general map a pure state to a mixed state, and a more general class of operations, which we call superoperators, that can be derived from the partial trace.

3.5.1   Mixed States

We can have mixed states on an ensemble of any number n of qubits. One way of representing a general mixed state on n qubits is as the ensemble

$$\left\{ (|\psi_1\rangle, p_1), (|\psi_2\rangle, p_2), \ldots, (|\psi_k\rangle, p_k) \right\} \qquad (3.5.1)$$

which means that the system is in the pure (n-qubit) state $|\psi_i\rangle$ with probability p_i, for $i = 1, 2, \ldots, k$. Note that a pure state can be seen as a special case of a mixed state, when all but one of the p_i equal zero.

To use a representation such as (3.5.1) in all our calculations would be quite cumbersome. There is an alternative, very useful, representation of mixed states in terms of operators on the Hilbert space $\mathcal{H}$. These are called *density operators*.[5] The matrix representation of a density operator is called a *density matrix*.

The density operator for a pure state $|\psi\rangle$ is defined as

$$\rho = |\psi\rangle\langle\psi|. \qquad (3.5.2)$$

If we apply the unitary operator U to state $|\psi\rangle$ we get the state $U|\psi\rangle$ which has density operator $U|\psi\rangle\langle\psi|U^\dagger$. Consider measuring the state with density operator

---

[5]It might seem unusual at first to use an 'operator' to describe a state. Nonetheless, it is useful to use such a mathematical object to describe the state of a system.

$\rho = |\psi\rangle\langle\psi|$ in the computational basis. Recalling Equation (3.4.2), the probability of getting 0 is given by

$$\langle 0|\psi\rangle\langle\psi|0\rangle = \langle 0|\rho|0\rangle. \tag{3.5.3}$$

Notice that $\langle 0|\psi\rangle\langle\psi|0\rangle$ evaluates to a real number. Since any number is the trace of a corresponding 1×1 matrix (whose only entry is that complex number), we can also write the probability of the measurement giving result 0 as

$$\begin{aligned}
\langle 0|\psi\rangle\langle\psi|0\rangle &= \mathrm{Tr}\big(\langle 0|\psi\rangle\langle\psi|0\rangle\big) \\
&= \mathrm{Tr}\big(|0\rangle\langle 0||\psi\rangle\langle\psi|\big)
\end{aligned} \tag{3.5.4}$$

where the last step follows from the cyclicity of trace (i.e. $\mathrm{Tr}(ABC) = \mathrm{Tr}(BCA) = \mathrm{Tr}(CAB)$).

Similarly, if we measure a qubit in a state with density operator $\rho = |\psi\rangle\langle\psi|$, the probability of obtaining the outcome $|1\rangle$ is $\mathrm{Tr}\big(|1\rangle\langle 1||\psi\rangle\langle\psi|\big)$. If only dealing with pure states, this notation is unnecessarily redundant; however, if we also consider mixed states it is a much more concise notation than used above in Equation (3.5.1).

The density operator for an ensemble of pure states such as (3.5.1) is

$$\rho = \sum_{i=1}^{k} p_i |\psi_i\rangle\langle\psi_i| \tag{3.5.5}$$

and captures all the relevant information about the state of the system.

For example, if we apply the unitary operator U to mixed state described in (3.5.1), we would get the mixed state

$$\Big\{ (U|\psi_1\rangle, p_1), (U|\psi_2\rangle, p_2), \dots, (U|\psi_k\rangle, p_k) \Big\} \tag{3.5.6}$$

which has density operator

$$\sum_{i=1}^{k} p_i U|\psi_i\rangle\langle\psi_i|U^{\dagger} = U\left(\sum_{i=1}^{k} p_i |\psi_i\rangle\langle\psi_i|\right) U^{\dagger} \tag{3.5.7}$$

$$= U\rho U^{\dagger}. \tag{3.5.8}$$

Note that the output density operator can be computed from the input density operator and the unitary U without knowing the precise decomposition of the input density operator.

Given the mixed state described by the density operator ρ of Equation (3.5.5), if we measure in the computational basis the probability of obtaining the outcome $|0\rangle$, for example, is

$$\sum_i p_i \mathrm{Tr}\left(|0\rangle\langle 0||\psi_i\rangle\langle\psi_i|\right) \tag{3.5.9}$$

$$= \mathrm{Tr}\sum_i p_i|0\rangle\langle 0||\psi_i\rangle\langle\psi_i| \tag{3.5.10}$$

$$= \mathrm{Tr}\left(|0\rangle\langle 0|\sum_i p_i|\psi_i\rangle\langle\psi_i|\right) \tag{3.5.11}$$

$$= \mathrm{Tr}\left(|0\rangle\langle 0|\rho\right). \tag{3.5.12}$$

For computing the statistics associated with measuring any observable property of a system, all that matters is the density operator itself, and not the precise decomposition of the density operator. In other words, two mixtures with the same density matrices are indistinguishable or equivalent (analogous to the way two pure states that differ only by a global phase are equivalent).

Exercise 3.5.1 Find the density matrices of the following states:

(a) $\left\{(|0\rangle, \frac{1}{2}), (|1\rangle, \frac{1}{2})\right\}$.

(b) $\frac{1}{\sqrt{2}}|0\rangle + \frac{1}{\sqrt{2}}|1\rangle$.

(c) $\left\{(\frac{1}{\sqrt{2}}|0\rangle + \frac{1}{\sqrt{2}}|1\rangle, \frac{1}{2}), (\frac{1}{\sqrt{2}}|0\rangle - \frac{1}{\sqrt{2}}|1\rangle, \frac{1}{2})\right\}$.

Exercise 3.5.2

(a) Prove that the density operator ρ for an ensemble of pure states satisfies the following conditions:

(i) $\mathrm{Tr}(\rho) = 1$.
(ii) ρ is a positive operator (i.e. for any $|v\rangle$, $\langle v|\rho|v\rangle$ is real and non-negative; equivalently, the eigenvalues of ρ are non-negative).

(b) Show that for any matrix ρ satisfying conditions 1 and 2, there exists a finite list of probabilities p_i and pure states $|\psi_i\rangle$ such that ρ is the density matrix of the mixed state

$$\left\{(|\psi_1\rangle, p_1), (|\psi_2\rangle, p_2), \ldots, (|\psi_k\rangle, p_k)\right\}. \tag{3.5.13}$$

Exercise 3.5.3 Consider any linear transformation T on a Hilbert space $\mathcal{H}$ of dimension N. This linear transformation T induces a transformation $\rho \mapsto T\rho T^\dagger$ on the set of linear operators on the Hilbert space $\mathcal{H}$. Prove that the above transformation is also linear.

Mixed States and the Bloch Sphere

Recall from Section 3.1 that pure states of a qubit can be represented by points on the surface of the Bloch sphere. Mixed states correspond to points in the interior of the Bloch sphere, which can be seen as follows. If $\rho = \sum_i p_i |\psi_i\rangle\langle\psi_i|$ and if the Bloch vector for $|\psi_i\rangle$ is $(\alpha_{x,i}, \alpha_{y,i}, \alpha_{z,i})$, then the Bloch vector for the mixed state ρ is

$$\rho = \sum_i p_i(\alpha_{x,i}, \alpha_{y,i}, \alpha_{z,i}) = \left(\sum_i p_i\alpha_{x,i}, \sum_i p_i\alpha_{y,i}, \sum_i p_i\alpha_{z,i}\right). \qquad (3.5.14)$$

There are of course many different convex combinations of points on the surface of the Bloch sphere that correspond to the same mixed state. One can compute the Bloch vector for a mixed state directly from its density matrix as follows. Recall in Section 3.2 we observed that any operator on a single qubit can be written as a linear combination of operators from $\{I, X, Y, Z\}$. The operators X, Y, Z all have trace 0. Since a density matrix must have trace 1 (Exercise 3.5.2), this means that any density operator for a single qubit can be written as

$$\rho = \tfrac{1}{2}I + \alpha_x X + \alpha_y Y + \alpha_z Z. \qquad (3.5.15)$$

The vector $(\alpha_x, \alpha_y, \alpha_z)$ gives the coordinates for the point in the Bloch sphere corresponding to the state ρ. For example, the totally mixed state (the ensemble $\{(|0\rangle\langle 0|, \tfrac{1}{2}), (|1\rangle\langle 1|, \tfrac{1}{2})\}$ corresponds to the point at the centre of the Bloch sphere.

3.5.2 Partial Trace

One of the most important uses for the density operator formulation is as a tool for describing the state of a *subsystem* of a composite system. Consider a pure state $|\psi\rangle_{AB} \in \mathcal{H}_A \otimes \mathcal{H}_B$ of two qubits. Recall that the general state of such a system may be entangled, and so it may not be possible to factor out the state vector $|\psi\rangle_A \in \mathcal{H}_A$ for the state of the first qubit. However, the state of the first qubit *can* in general be described as a *mixed state*. This means that it can be described by a density operator ρ^A on $\mathcal{H}_A$, sometimes called a *reduced density operator*. The mathematical operation for calculating the reduced density operator is the *partial trace*. The reduced density operator ρ_A is defined in terms of the density operator ρ^{AB} for the full 2-qubit system by

$$\rho^A \equiv \mathrm{Tr}_B\left(\rho^{AB}\right), \qquad (3.5.16)$$

where Tr_B is the *partial trace over system B*, defined as the linear extension of the operator defined on basis states by

$$\mathrm{Tr}_B\left(|a_1\rangle\langle a_2| \otimes |b_1\rangle\langle b_2|\right) \equiv |a_1\rangle\langle a_2|\mathrm{Tr}\left(|b_1\rangle\langle b_2|\right). \qquad (3.5.17)$$

Since

$$\mathrm{Tr}\big(|b_1\rangle\langle b_2|\big) = \mathrm{Tr}\big(\langle b_2|b_1\rangle\big) = \langle b_2|b_1\rangle, \qquad (3.5.18)$$

Equation (3.5.17) can be simplified to

$$\mathrm{Tr}_B\big(|a_1\rangle\langle a_2| \otimes |b_1\rangle\langle b_2|\big) = |a_1\rangle\langle a_2|\langle b_2|b_1\rangle. \qquad (3.5.19)$$

The operation of computing Tr_B is sometimes referred to as *tracing-out system B*. As an example, we illustrate the partial trace operation by tracing out the second qubit of the 2-qubit entangled state

$$\frac{1}{\sqrt{2}}\big(|00\rangle + |11\rangle\big). \qquad (3.5.20)$$

The density matrix for this state is

$$\rho = \tfrac{1}{2}\big(|00\rangle\langle 00| + |00\rangle\langle 11| + |11\rangle\langle 00| + |11\rangle\langle 11|\big). \qquad (3.5.21)$$

We compute the reduced density operator for the first qubit by tracing out qubit B.

$$\begin{aligned}
\rho^A &= \mathrm{Tr}_B(\rho) \\
&= \tfrac{1}{2}\mathrm{Tr}_2\big(|00\rangle\langle 00| + |00\rangle\langle 11| + |11\rangle\langle 00| + |11\rangle\langle 11|\big) \\
&= \tfrac{1}{2}\mathrm{Tr}_2\big(|0\rangle\langle 0| \otimes |0\rangle\langle 0| + |0\rangle\langle 1| \otimes |0\rangle\langle 1| + |1\rangle\langle 0| \otimes |1\rangle\langle 0| + |1\rangle\langle 1| \otimes |1\rangle\langle 1|\big) \\
&= \tfrac{1}{2}\Big(|0\rangle\langle 0|\mathrm{Tr}\big(|0\rangle\langle 0|\big) + |0\rangle\langle 1|\mathrm{Tr}\big(|0\rangle\langle 1|\big) + |1\rangle\langle 0|\mathrm{Tr}\big(|1\rangle\langle 0|\big) + |1\rangle\langle 1|\mathrm{Tr}\big(|1\rangle\langle 1|\big)\Big) \\
&= \tfrac{1}{2}\big(|0\rangle\langle 0|\langle 0|0\rangle + |0\rangle\langle 1|\langle 1|0\rangle + |1\rangle\langle 0|\langle 0|1\rangle + |1\rangle\langle 1|\langle 1|1\rangle\big) \\
&= \tfrac{1}{2}\big(|0\rangle\langle 0| + |1\rangle\langle 1|\big). \qquad (3.5.22)
\end{aligned}$$

Reduced density operators can be computed for composite systems consisting of more than two qubits in an analogous way.

In Section 3.5.3, we see that the partial trace can be combined with the other operations on quantum states that we have seen in order to induce a more general type of transformation on quantum states, which we call *superoperators*.

We conclude this section on partial trace by showing that the partial trace is very straightforward to compute when the joint state of the system being discarded and the system being kept is expressed in Schmidt form.

Exercise 3.5.4

(a) Given a bipartite state on $\mathcal{H}_A \otimes \mathcal{H}_B$, suppose we want to apply a unitary operation U on A, and then trace-out system B to give the resulting state for system A. Show that applying the unitary U on system A commutes with tracing-out system B. In other words, $Tr_B((U \otimes I)\rho(U^\dagger \otimes I)) = U(Tr_B\rho)U^\dagger$.

(b) Prove that one way to compute Tr_B is to assume that someone has measured system B in any orthonormal basis but does not tell you the measurement outcome.

Note: Part (b) shows that if some qubits in a computation will be discarded or ignored, one can assume for the sake of analysing the state of the remaining qubits that the discarded qubits have been measured. This is done, for example, in the analysis of the algorithms in Sections 6.5, 7.3.3, 7.4, and 7.5.

Exercise 3.5.5

(a) Find a pure state $\rho_{AB} \in \mathcal{H}_{AB}$ of a bipartite system AB, such that $\rho_{AB} \neq \text{Tr}_B (\rho_{AB}) \otimes \text{Tr}_A (\rho_{AB})$.

Note: The partial trace $\text{Tr}_B(\rho)$ contains all the relevant information about system A if system B is discarded. Similarly $\text{Tr}_A(\rho)$ contains all the relevant information about system B if system A is discarded. These local descriptions do not in general contain enough information to reconstruct the state of the whole system.

(b) Show that for any density operator ρ on a system A, there exists a pure state ψ on some larger system $A \otimes B$ such that $\rho = \text{Tr}_B |\psi\rangle\langle\psi|$ and $\dim(A) \geq \dim(B)$.

Partial Trace and the Schmidt Decomposition

When a bipartite vector is written in the Schmidt basis, it is very easy to compute the partial trace of either subsystem. For example, consider the following pure state on system AB, written in Schmidt form:

$$|\psi\rangle = \sum_i \sqrt{p_i}|\varphi_i^A\rangle|\varphi_i^B\rangle \qquad (3.5.23)$$

where we recall that $\{|\varphi_i^A\rangle\}$ is a basis for $\mathcal{H}_A$ and $\{|\varphi_i^B\rangle\}$ for $\mathcal{H}_B$. The density matrix for $|\psi\rangle$ is

$$
\begin{aligned}
|\psi\rangle\langle\psi| &= \left(\sum_i \sqrt{p_i}|\varphi_i^A\rangle|\varphi_i^B\rangle\right)\left(\sum_j \sqrt{p_j}\langle\varphi_j^A|\langle\varphi_j^B|\right) \\
&= \sum_{i,j} \sqrt{p_i}\sqrt{p_j}\,|\varphi_i^A\rangle|\varphi_i^B\rangle\langle\varphi_j^A|\langle\varphi_j^B| \\
&= \sum_{i,j} \sqrt{p_i}\sqrt{p_j}\,|\varphi_i^A\rangle\langle\varphi_j^A||\varphi_i^B\rangle\langle\varphi_j^B|.
\end{aligned}
$$

Now let us trace-out system B.

$$
\begin{aligned}
\text{Tr}_B|\psi\rangle\langle\psi| &= \sum_{i,j} \sqrt{p_i}\sqrt{p_j}\,\text{Tr}_B|\varphi_i^A\rangle\langle\varphi_j^A||\varphi_i^B\rangle\langle\varphi_j^B| \\
&= \sum_{i,j} \sqrt{p_i}\sqrt{p_j}\,|\varphi_i^A\rangle\langle\varphi_j^A|\langle\varphi_i^B|\varphi_j^B\rangle \\
&= \sum_{i,j} \sqrt{p_i}\sqrt{p_j}\,|\varphi_i^A\rangle\langle\varphi_j^A|\delta_{i,j} \\
&= \sum_i p_i|\varphi_i^A\rangle\langle\varphi_i^A|. \qquad (3.5.24)
\end{aligned}
$$

Similarly, $\text{Tr}_A|\psi\rangle\langle\psi| = \sum_i p_i|\varphi_i^B\rangle\langle\varphi_i^B|$.

Notice that in the Schmidt basis both reduced density operators are in diagonal form, and that their spectra (i.e. sets of eigenvalues) are the same. This suggest a method for computing the Schmidt decomposition, which is explained in Appendix A.7.

3.5.3 General Quantum Operations

We initially stated the postulates of quantum mechanics for closed systems, which involves pure states and unitary evolution. As we saw in the previous section, if we allow our system to interact with an external system, it is often appropriate to use mixed states to describe the state of our system. There is also a corresponding more general framework for describing quantum operations that involve external systems. Since we describe the behaviour of these more general operations on the density operators describing mixed states, we often call these operations superoperators. We will restrict attention to superoperators that do not require measurements.[6]

A superoperator or a 'general quantum operation' can take as input a system described by a density operator ρ_{in} corresponding to a Hilbert space of dimension N, add an ancilla of arbitrary size (in fact, it can be shown, using Caratheodory's Theorem, that the dimension of the ancilla never needs to be larger than N^2 and that we can assume without loss of generality that the ancilla is initialized to some fixed pure state), perform a unitary operation U on the joint system, and then discard some subsystem.[7]

More explicitly, this can be described as the map:

$$\rho_{in} \mapsto \rho_{out} = Tr_B(U(\rho_{in} \otimes |00\ldots0\rangle\langle00\ldots0|)U^\dagger) \qquad (3.5.25)$$

where the state $|00\ldots0\rangle$ is an ancilla state of arbitrary size (but without loss of generality has dimension at most N^2), U is a unitary operation acting on the joint system, and B is some subsystem of the joint system. We illustrate these operations using circuit diagrams in Figure 4.2 after we define quantum circuits in Section 4.1. If B is the original ancilla system, then the superoperator does not change the Hilbert space of the system. In general, we can describe states that change the dimension of the state space. In Exercise 10.4.2 it is shown that action of such a superoperator (restricting attention to operators that do not change the Hilbert space) can be described by a finite sum[8]

$$\rho_{in} \mapsto \sum_i A_i \rho_{in} A_i^\dagger \qquad (3.5.26)$$

---

[6]A more general notion of quantum operations also involving measurements are discussed briefly in Appendix A.8.

[7]It is important that the discarded system is never used again. Equivalently, it could be reset to some generic state. Otherwise, the partial trace does not capture all the relevant information about the state of system A.

[8]Since we are restricting to finite-dimensional ancillas, the number of terms one would derive would be finite. In general, one can consider an infinite number of A_i terms, but the resulting superoperator would have an equivalent formulation in terms of at most N^2 other Kraus terms.

where the A_i are called *Kraus operators*, which are linear operators[9] on the same Hilbert space as ρ_{in} and satisfy

$$\sum_i A_i^\dagger A_i = I. \qquad (3.5.27)$$

Conversely, every set of Kraus operators satisfying the completeness condition (Equation 3.5.26) can be realized by a map of the form in Equation 3.5.25 for some unitary U (which is unique up to a final unitary on the system that is traced out).

It it easy to verify that these superoperators are 'trace-preserving completely positive maps', because (see Exercise 3.5.7) they are maps that:

- map positive operators (in Exercise 3.5.2 we saw that density operators are positive) to positive operators (hence the term 'positive' map)
- when tensored with the identity operation, they still map positive operators to positive operators (e.g. the transpose map is positive but not completely positive; see Exercise 3.5.6)
- preserve the trace of the density operator (this equates to preserving the sum of the probabilities of the outcomes of a measurement).

Exercise 3.5.6 Prove that the transpose map, which maps $\rho \mapsto \rho^T$ is positive, but not completely positive.

Exercise 3.5.7 Prove that superoperators, as defined in Equation 3.5.25, are trace-preserving completely positive maps.

It can be proved, using the Stinespring dilation theorem, that any linear map from operators on one (finite-dimensional) Hilbert space to operators on another (finite-dimensional) Hilbert space that is trace-preserving and completely positive is equivalent to a superoperator of the form described above. Thus, linear trace-preserving completely positive maps exactly characterize the notion of 'general quantum operation' we have described.

---

[9]In general, the A_i could be linear transformations from $\mathcal{H}$ (of dimension N) to some other Hilbert space $\mathcal{H}'$ of dimension D.

4

A QUANTUM MODEL OF COMPUTATION

4.1 The Quantum Circuit Model

In Section 1.3, we introduced the circuit model of (classical) computation. We restricted attention to reversible circuits since they can simulate any non-reversible circuit with modest overhead. This model can be generalized to a model of *quantum circuits*. In the quantum circuit model, we have logical qubits carried along 'wires', and quantum gates that act on the qubits. A quantum gate acting on n qubits has the input qubits carried to it by n wires, and n other wires carry the output qubits away from the gate. A quantum circuit is often illustrated schematically by a *circuit diagram* as shown in Figure 4.1. The wires are shown as horizontal lines, and we imagine the qubits propagating along the wires from left to right in time. The gates are shown as rectangular blocks. For convenience, we will restrict attention to unitary quantum gates[1] (which are also reversible). Recall from Section 3.5.3 that non-unitary (non-reversible) quantum operations can be simulated by unitary (reversible) quantum gates if we allow the possibility of adding an ancilla and of discarding some output qubits. A circuit diagram describing a superoperator being implemented using a unitary operator is illustrated in Figure 4.2.

In the example of Figure 4.1, the 4-qubit state $|\psi_i\rangle = |0\rangle \otimes |0\rangle \otimes |0\rangle \otimes |0\rangle$ enters the circuit at the left (recall we often write this state as $|\psi_i\rangle = |0\rangle|0\rangle|0\rangle|0\rangle$ or $|\psi_i\rangle = |0000\rangle$.) These qubits are processed by the gates U_1, U_2, U_3, and U_4. At the output of the circuit we have the collective (possibly entangled) 4-qubit state $|\psi_f\rangle$. A measurement is then made of the resulting state. The measurement will often be a simple qubit-by-qubit measurement in the computational basis, but in some cases may be a more general measurement of the joint state. A measurement of a single qubit in the computational basis is denoted on a circuit diagram by a small triangle, as shown in Figure 4.1 (there are other

---

[1]We could consider measurements to be a special kind of gate that extracts or outputs some classical information about the quantum system. However, in this text we will restrict use of the word 'gate' to refer to operations that do not output such classical information. Thus the most general kind of operation implementable by a gate is a superoperator. Furthermore, for convenience, we will restrict attention to unitary gates.

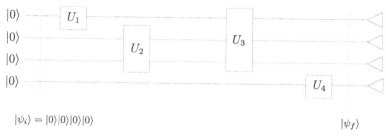

$$|\psi_i\rangle = |0\rangle|0\rangle|0\rangle|0\rangle \qquad\qquad\qquad |\psi_f\rangle$$

Fig. 4.1 A quantum circuit. The 4-qubit state $|0\rangle|0\rangle|0\rangle|0\rangle$ enters the circuit on the left. The boxes labelled U_1, U_2, U_3, U_4 represent *quantum gates* applied to the qubits (in the order indicated from left to right). The joint (possibly entangled) 4-qubit state after the gates are applied is $|\psi_f\rangle$. The small triangles at the right side of the circuit indicate that each of the four qubits of the final state are measured in the computational basis to provide the output of the circuit.

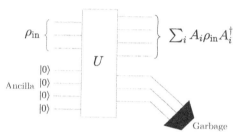

Fig. 4.2 A general (possibly irreversible) quantum operation or superoperator can be realized using a unitary operation by adding an ancilla and tracing out part of the output. Thus, we can restrict attention to unitary gates.

symbols used in the literature, but we adopt this one). The triangle symbol will be modified for cases in which there is a need to indicate different types of measurements. Recall that the measurement postulate stated that a measurement outputs a classical label 'i' indicating the outcome of the measurement and a quantum state $|\phi_i\rangle$. Thus, we could in general draw our measurement symbol with a 'quantum' wire carrying the quantum state resulting from the measurement, together with a classical wire carrying the classical label, as depicted in Figure 4.3.

Quite often, the quantum outcome is discarded or ignored, and we are only interested in the classical information telling us which outcome occurred. In such cases, we will not draw the quantum wire coming out of the measurement symbol. We will usually omit the classical wire from circuit diagrams as well.

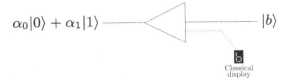

Fig. 4.3 The measurement of the quantum state $\alpha_0|0\rangle + \alpha_1|1\rangle$ results in a quantum output $|b\rangle$ with probability $|\alpha_b|^2$ ($b \in \{0, 1\}$) together with a classical label 'b' indicating which outcome was obtained. If the quantum output is discarded or ignored, we usually omit to draw the quantum wire on the right side of the measurement symbol. The classical wire carrying the output label is also usually omitted.

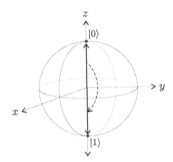

Fig. 4.4 The NOT gate rotating the state $|0\rangle$ to the state $|1\rangle$.

4.2 Quantum Gates

4.2.1 1-Qubit Gates

In Section 3.2, we said that any unitary operator acting on a 2-dimensional quantum system (a qubit) is called a '1-qubit quantum gate'. We gave the quantum NOT gate (sometimes called the Pauli X gate) as an example (and mentioned the other *Pauli gates*). Recall the Bloch sphere from Section 3.1. Every 1-qubit pure state is represented as a point on the surface of the Bloch sphere, or equivalently as a unit vector whose origin is fixed at the centre of the Bloch sphere. A 1-qubit quantum gate U transforms a quantum state $|\psi\rangle$ into another quantum state $U|\psi\rangle$. In terms of the Bloch sphere, the action of U on $|\psi\rangle$ can be thought of as a rotation of the Bloch vector for $|\psi\rangle$ to the Bloch vector for $U|\psi\rangle$. For example, the NOT gate takes the state $|0\rangle$ to the state $|1\rangle$ (and takes $|1\rangle$ to $|0\rangle$). In terms of the Bloch sphere, this action can be visualized as a rotation through an angle π about the x axis, as illustrated in Figure 4.4.

Recall in Section 2.5 we saw how to compute the exponential (and other functions) of operators. If we exponentiate the Pauli gates, we get unitary operators corresponding to very important classes of 1-qubit gates. These are the *rotation gates*, which correspond to rotations about the x-,y-, and z- axes of the Bloch sphere. They are defined in terms of the Pauli gates, and so for convenience, we remind you now of the definitions of the Pauli gates:

$$I \equiv \begin{bmatrix} 1 & 0 \\ 0 & 1 \end{bmatrix} \qquad X \equiv \begin{bmatrix} 0 & 1 \\ 1 & 0 \end{bmatrix}$$

$$Y \equiv \begin{bmatrix} 0 & -i \\ i & 0 \end{bmatrix} \qquad Z \equiv \begin{bmatrix} 1 & 0 \\ 0 & -1 \end{bmatrix}. \qquad (4.2.1)$$

The rotation gates are defined as follows:

$$R_x(\theta) \equiv e^{\frac{-i\theta X}{2}}$$

$$R_y(\theta) \equiv e^{\frac{-i\theta Y}{2}}$$

$$R_z(\theta) \equiv e^{\frac{-i\theta Z}{2}}. \qquad (4.2.2)$$

Exercise 4.2.1 Let x be a real number and A a matrix such that $A^2 = I$. Show that

$$e^{iAx} = \cos(x)I + i\sin(x)A.$$

It is easy to check that the Pauli operators X, Y, and Z satisfy the conditions $X^2 = I$, $Y^2 = I$, and $Z^2 = I$, and so using the result of Exercise 4.2.7 we can write the rotation gates as:

$$R_x(\theta) \equiv e^{\frac{-i\theta X}{2}} = \cos\left(\tfrac{\theta}{2}\right) I - i\sin\left(\tfrac{\theta}{2}\right) X$$

$$R_y(\theta) \equiv e^{\frac{-i\theta Y}{2}} = \cos\left(\tfrac{\theta}{2}\right) I - i\sin\left(\tfrac{\theta}{2}\right) Y$$

$$R_z(\theta) \equiv e^{\frac{-i\theta Z}{2}} = \cos\left(\tfrac{\theta}{2}\right) I - i\sin\left(\tfrac{\theta}{2}\right) Z. \qquad (4.2.3)$$

Knowing the matrices for I, X, Y, and Z in the computational basis, we can now write the rotation gates as matrices in the computational basis:

$$R_x(\theta) = \begin{bmatrix} \cos\left(\tfrac{\theta}{2}\right) & -i\sin\left(\tfrac{\theta}{2}\right) \\ -i\sin\left(\tfrac{\theta}{2}\right) & \cos\left(\tfrac{\theta}{2}\right) \end{bmatrix}$$

$$R_y(\theta) = \begin{bmatrix} \cos\left(\tfrac{\theta}{2}\right) & -\sin\left(\tfrac{\theta}{2}\right) \\ \sin\left(\tfrac{\theta}{2}\right) & \cos\left(\tfrac{\theta}{2}\right) \end{bmatrix}$$

$$R_z(\theta) = \begin{bmatrix} e^{-i\frac{\theta}{2}} & 0 \\ 0 & e^{i\frac{\theta}{2}} \end{bmatrix}. \qquad (4.2.4)$$

Consider an arbitrary 1-qubit state, written in terms of its Bloch vector angles σ and τ:

$$\cos\left(\frac{\sigma}{2}\right)|0\rangle + e^{i\tau}\sin\left(\frac{\sigma}{2}\right)|1\rangle. \tag{4.2.5}$$

In the computational basis, this can be written as the column vector

$$\begin{pmatrix} \cos\left(\frac{\sigma}{2}\right) \\ e^{i\tau}\sin\left(\frac{\sigma}{2}\right) \end{pmatrix}. \tag{4.2.6}$$

The effect of applying $R_z(\theta)$ on this state can be seen by performing a matrix multiplication:

$$\begin{bmatrix} e^{-i\frac{\theta}{2}} & 0 \\ 0 & e^{i\frac{\theta}{2}} \end{bmatrix} \begin{pmatrix} \cos\left(\frac{\sigma}{2}\right) \\ e^{i\tau}\sin\left(\frac{\sigma}{2}\right) \end{pmatrix} = \begin{pmatrix} e^{-i\frac{\theta}{2}}\cos\left(\frac{\sigma}{2}\right) \\ e^{i\frac{\theta}{2}}e^{i\tau}\sin\left(\frac{\sigma}{2}\right) \end{pmatrix}$$

$$= e^{-i\frac{\theta}{2}}\begin{pmatrix} \cos\left(\frac{\sigma}{2}\right) \\ e^{i\theta}e^{i\tau}\sin\left(\frac{\sigma}{2}\right) \end{pmatrix}$$

$$= e^{-i\frac{\theta}{2}}\left(\cos\left(\frac{\sigma}{2}\right)|0\rangle + e^{i(\tau+\theta)}\sin\left(\frac{\sigma}{2}\right)|1\rangle\right). \tag{4.2.7}$$

Since a global phase is insignificant, we have the state

$$\cos\left(\frac{\sigma}{2}\right)|0\rangle + e^{i(\tau+\theta)}\sin\left(\frac{\sigma}{2}\right)|1\rangle. \tag{4.2.8}$$

We see that effect of $R_z(\theta)$ has been to change the angle τ to $\tau + \theta$, which is a rotation of θ about the z-axis of the Bloch sphere. To see that $R_x(\theta)$ and $R_y(\theta)$ implement rotations about the x- and y-axes of the Bloch sphere is trickier, because such rotations involve changes to both angles σ and τ.

Exercise 4.2.2 Show that $R_x(\theta)$ and $R_y(\theta)$ implement rotations through an angle θ about the x- and y-axes of the Bloch sphere, respectively.

It will be useful to show how to decompose any given 1-qubit gate into a sequence of rotations about the main axes of the Bloch sphere. The following theorem tells us that we can decompose any 1-qubit gate into a sequence of two rotations about the z-axis and one rotation about the y-axis, along with a suitable phase factor.

Theorem 4.2.1 *Suppose U is a 1-qubit unitary gate. Then there exist real numbers $\alpha, \beta, \gamma,$ and δ such that*

$$U = e^{i\alpha}R_z(\beta)R_y(\gamma)R_z(\delta). \tag{4.2.9}$$

The proof of this follows from the fact that U is unitary, and the definition of the rotation matrices. There is nothing special about the y- and z-axes of the Bloch sphere. We can also give decompositions of 1-qubit gates in terms of rotations about any other two non-parallel axes of the Bloch sphere.

Theorem 4.2.2 *Suppose U is a 1-qubit unitary gate. Let l and m be any two non-parallel axes of the Bloch sphere. Then there exist real numbers $\alpha, \beta, \gamma,$ and δ such that*

$$U = e^{i\alpha} R_l(\beta) R_m(\gamma) R_l(\delta). \tag{4.2.10}$$

The following corollary of Theorem 4.2.1 will be used in the next section.

Corollary 4.2.1 *Any 1-qubit gate U can be written in the form*

$$U = e^{i\alpha} A X B X C, \tag{4.2.11}$$

where A, B, C are unitary operators satisfying $ABC = I$. (Recall that the Pauli gate X is the NOT *gate.)*

Exercise 4.2.3

(a) Prove $X R_y(\theta) X = R_y(-\theta)$ and $X R_z(\theta) X = R_z(-\theta)$.

(b) Prove Corollary 4.2.1.

Hint: Using Theorem 4.2.1 we can write

$$U = e^{i\alpha} R_z(\beta) R_y(\gamma) R_z(\delta). \tag{4.2.12}$$

Then take $A \equiv R_z(\beta) R_y(\gamma/2)$, $B \equiv R_y(-\gamma/2) R_z(-(\delta+\beta)/2)$, and $C \equiv R_z((\delta - \beta)/2)$.

4.2.2   Controlled-U Gates

Recall in Section 3.3 we introduced the *controlled*-NOT (CNOT) gate. This is a 2-qubit quantum gate that conditionally applies the NOT gate on the second (target) qubit when the first (control qubit) is in state $|1\rangle$. Remember that such a gate acts on quantum states in quantum superposition.

Exercise 4.2.4 Describe the effect of the CNOT gate with respect to the following bases.

(a) $B_1 = \left\{ |0\rangle \left(\frac{|0\rangle + |1\rangle}{\sqrt{2}} \right), |0\rangle \left(\frac{|0\rangle - |1\rangle}{\sqrt{2}} \right), |1\rangle \left(\frac{|0\rangle + |1\rangle}{\sqrt{2}} \right), |1\rangle \left(\frac{|0\rangle - |1\rangle}{\sqrt{2}} \right) \right\}$

(b) $B_2 = \left\{ \left(\frac{|0\rangle + |1\rangle}{\sqrt{2}} \right) \left(\frac{|0\rangle + |1\rangle}{\sqrt{2}} \right), \left(\frac{|0\rangle + |1\rangle}{\sqrt{2}} \right) \left(\frac{|0\rangle - |1\rangle}{\sqrt{2}} \right), \left(\frac{|0\rangle - |1\rangle}{\sqrt{2}} \right) \left(\frac{|0\rangle + |1\rangle}{\sqrt{2}} \right), \right.$

$\left. \left(\frac{|0\rangle - |1\rangle}{\sqrt{2}} \right) \left(\frac{|0\rangle - |1\rangle}{\sqrt{2}} \right) \right\}$

Express your answers both using Dirac notation, and also with matrix notation.

Given any 1-qubit gate U, we can similarly define a *controlled-U* gate, denoted c-U, which will be a 2-qubit gate corresponding to the following operation:

$$\text{c-}U|0\rangle|\psi\rangle = |0\rangle|\psi\rangle$$
$$\text{c-}U|1\rangle|\psi\rangle = |1\rangle U|\psi\rangle. \qquad (4.2.13)$$

Exercise 4.2.5 Prove that the c-U gate corresponds to the operator

$$|0\rangle\langle 0| \otimes I + |1\rangle\langle 1| \otimes U.$$

Exercise 4.2.6 We know that U and $e^{i\theta}U$ are equivalent since they only differ by a global phase. However, prove that c-$U \neq$ c-$(e^{i\theta}U)$ for θ not equal to an integer multiple of 2π.

The symbol commonly used for the c-U gate in a quantum circuit diagram is shown in Figure 4.5.

Exercise 4.2.7 For a given 1-qubit gate U, use the result of Corollary 4.2.1 to construct a circuit for implementing a c-U gate using only CNOT gates, and single-qubit gates.

Hint: Use the fact that the controlled application of $e^{i\alpha}I$ to the target qubit is equivalent to a 1-qubit phase rotation gate acting on the control qubit.

The construction of a controlled-U for any 1-qubit gate U is the subject of Exercise 4.2.7. This can be generalized to allow the implementation of a controlled version of any quantum circuit implementing a unitary operation U. Suppose we are given a circuit C_U implementing a unitary U, and we wish to implement a circuit for the controlled-U operation. The basic technique is to replace every gate G in C_U by a controlled gate c-G, as shown in Figure 4.6.

For 1-qubit gates G, the controlled gate c-G can be constructed using the method of Exercise 4.2.7. As we will see in Section 4.3, we can assume without loss of generality that C_U consists only of 1-qubit gates and CNOT gates. So the only thing that remains is to construct a controlled version of the CNOT gate. Recall

Fig. 4.5 The c-U gate.

Fig. 4.6 Given a circuit C_U implementing a unitary U, to implement a circuit for the controlled-U operation we replace every gate G in C_U by a controlled gate c-G.

Fig. 4.7 Suppose that at some point in a computation there is some qubit that will only be used as a control qubit in subsequent controlled-U_b operations before being discarded. The same result is obtained if one measures the qubit in the computational basis and then classically controls the U_b gates.

from Section 1.3 that a controlled-cnot gate is called a Toffoli gate. As we shall see in Section 4.3, the Toffoli gate can be implemented by a circuit containing CNOT gates and some 1-qubit gates. So we can use this replacement for each of the Toffoli gates generated in our construction of the controlled-U circuit. This completes the construction of a circuit for implementing the controlled-U operation.

Exercise 4.2.8 Suppose that at some point in a computation there is some qubit that will only be used as a control qubit in subsequent controlled-U_b operations before being discarded. By controlled-U_b we mean the transformation applies some unitary U_0 on some other qubit(s) in the computation if the control qubit is in state $|0\rangle$ (in the previous examples of controlled-gates, $U_0 = I$) and applies some unitary U_1 if the control qubit is in state $|1\rangle$. Prove that one obtains the same result if one measures the qubit in the computational basis and then classically controls whether to apply U_0 or U_1. (This is illustrated in Figure 4.7.)

4.3 Universal Sets of Quantum Gates

The gates we have seen so far have acted on either a single qubit, or on two qubits. An interesting quantum algorithm would, in general, be some complicated unitary operator acting non-trivially on n-qubits. In classical computing, we implement complicated operations as a sequence of much simpler operations. In practice, we want to be able to select these simple operations from some set of elementary gates. In quantum computing, we do the same thing. The goal is to choose some finite set of gates so that, by constructing a circuit using only gates from that set, we can implement non-trivial and interesting quantum computations.

When we use a circuit of quantum gates to implement some desired unitary operation, in practice, it suffices to have an implementation that *approximates* the desired unitary to some specified level of accuracy. We need to make precise the notion of the *quality of an approximation* of a unitary transformation. Suppose we approximate a desired unitary transformation U by some other unitary transformation V. The *error* in the approximation is defined to be

$$E(U, V) \equiv \max_{|\psi\rangle} \|(U - V)|\psi\rangle\| \qquad (4.3.1)$$

(recall Equation (2.2.11) for the definition of the norm). When we say that an operator U can be 'approximated to arbitrary accuracy', we mean that if we are given any error tolerance $\varepsilon > 0$, we can implement some unitary V such that $E(U, V) < \varepsilon$.

Exercise 4.3.1 Show that

$$E(U_2 U_1, V_2 V_1) \leq E(U_2, V_2) + E(U_1, V_1). \qquad (4.3.2)$$

From Exercise 4.3.1 it follows that

$$E(U_n U_{n-1} \ldots U_1, V_n V_{n-1} \ldots V_1) \leq E(U_n, V_n) + E(U_{n-1}, V_{n-1}) + \cdots + E(U_1, V_1). \qquad (4.3.3)$$

Definition 4.3.1 *A set of gates is said to be* universal *if for any integer $n \geq 1$, any n-qubit unitary operator can be approximated to arbitrary accuracy by a quantum circuit using only gates from that set.*

Finding convenient universal sets of gates is of great practical importance as well as of theoretical interest. Since a universal set of gates must be able to implement, for example, the CNOT, it will have to contain at least one non-trivial gate on two or more qubits.

Definition 4.3.2 *A 2-qubit gate is said to be an* entangling gate *if for some input product state $|\psi\rangle|\phi\rangle$ the output of the gate is not a product state (i.e. the output qubits are entangled).*

The following universality result is a useful starting point.

Theorem 4.3.3 *A set composed of any 2-qubit entangling gate, together with all 1-qubit gates, is universal.*

Theorem 4.3.3 implies, for example, that the CNOT gate together with all 1-qubit gates is universal.[2] The theorem gives sets that are universal in a stronger sense required by Definition 4.3.1. With an entangling 2-qubit gate and all 1-qubit gates, we can implement any n-qubit unitary *exactly*. A shortcoming of Theorem 4.3.3 is that the universal sets of gates it provides are infinite. It is useful to find a *finite* set of gates that is universal. A natural starting point in this direction is to look for a finite set of 1-qubit gates that can be used to approximate any 1-qubit gate to arbitrary accuracy.

Definition 4.3.4 *A set of gates is said to be* universal for 1-qubit gates *if any 1-qubit unitary gate can be approximated to arbitrary accuracy by a quantum circuit using only gates from that set.*

Theorem 4.2.2 states that for any two non-parallel axes l and m of the Bloch sphere, the set consisting of the rotation gates $R_l(\beta)$ and $R_m(\gamma)$ for all $\beta, \gamma \in [0, 2\pi)$ is universal for 1-qubit gates. This implies the following corollary (see Exercise 4.3.2).

Theorem 4.3.5 *If a set of two 1-qubit gates (rotations)* $\mathcal{G} = \{R_l(\beta), R_m(\gamma)\}$ *satisfies the conditions*

(i) l *and* m *are non-parallel axes of the Bloch sphere, and*
(ii) $\beta, \gamma \in [0, 2\pi)$ *are real numbers such that* $\frac{\beta}{\pi}$ *and* $\frac{\gamma}{\pi}$ *are not rational*

then $\mathcal{G}$ *is universal for 1-qubit gates.*

Exercise 4.3.2 Let $R_m(\theta_1), R_m(\theta_2)$ be 1-qubit rotations about the same axis.

(a) Show that distance between $R_m(\theta_1)$ and $R_m(\theta_2)$ satisfies $E(R_m(\theta_1), R_m(\theta_2)) \leq \left|e^{i\theta_1} - e^{i\theta_2}\right| \leq |\theta_1 - \theta_2|$.

(b) Let $\beta \in [0, 2\pi)$ is such that $\frac{\beta}{\pi}$ is not rational. Prove that for any $\varepsilon > 0$, and for any $\theta \in [0, 2\pi)$, there exists an integer n such that $E(R_m^n(\beta), R_m(\theta)) \leq \varepsilon$.

Hint: Use the pigeon-hole principle, which states the following. If $N > M$, then partitioning N elements into M disjoint sets, gives at least one set with more than 1 element.

As a concrete example, we give a simple set satisfying the conditions of Theorem 4.3.5. In this direction, we first take a short detour to introduce two important 1-qubit gates.

The *Hadamard* gate, H, is defined as that gate mapping the computational basis states as follows:

---

[2]Recall that for reversible classical computation, 1- and 2-bit reversible gates were not universal.

$$H|0\rangle = \tfrac{1}{\sqrt{2}}(|0\rangle + |1\rangle)$$
$$H|1\rangle = \tfrac{1}{\sqrt{2}}(|0\rangle - |1\rangle). \tag{4.3.4}$$

The Hadamard gate has the following matrix representation (with respect to the computational basis):

$$\frac{1}{\sqrt{2}}\begin{bmatrix} 1 & 1 \\ 1 & -1 \end{bmatrix}. \tag{4.3.5}$$

One useful property of the Hadamard gate is that it is self-inverse, meaning $H = H^{-1}$, and so

$$H\left(\tfrac{1}{\sqrt{2}}(|0\rangle + |1\rangle)\right) = |0\rangle$$
$$H\left(\tfrac{1}{\sqrt{2}}(|0\rangle - |1\rangle)\right) = |1\rangle. \tag{4.3.6}$$

Another 1-qubit gate that will be important for us is the $\frac{\pi}{8}$-phase gate, T, which acts on the computational basis states as follows:

$$T|0\rangle = |0\rangle$$
$$T|1\rangle = e^{i\frac{\pi}{4}}|1\rangle. \tag{4.3.7}$$

The $\frac{\pi}{8}$-phase gate has the following matrix representation:

$$T = \begin{bmatrix} 1 & 0 \\ 0 & e^{i\frac{\pi}{4}} \end{bmatrix}. \tag{4.3.8}$$

Note that T is equivalent to

$$\begin{bmatrix} e^{-i\frac{\pi}{8}} & 0 \\ 0 & e^{i\frac{\pi}{8}} \end{bmatrix} \tag{4.3.9}$$

(up to global phase), which is why we call it a $\frac{\pi}{8}$-gate.

The following result holds.

Lemma 4.3.6 *The set $G = \{HTHT, THTH\}$ satisfies the conditions of Theorem 4.3.5.*

This immediately gives the following corollary.

Corollary 4.3.1 *The set $\{H, T\}$ is universal for 1-qubit gates.*

Recalling Lemma 4.3.3, we now have the following universality result.

Theorem 4.3.7 *The set $\{\text{CNOT}, H, T\}$ is a universal set of gates.*

4.4 Efficiency of Approximating Unitary Transformations

In the previous section, we have stated that an arbitrary unitary transformation can be simulated using gates from a fixed universal set, such as $\{H, \text{CNOT}, T\}$

(Theorem 4.3.7). We have said nothing about how *efficiently* this can be done however. If we wish to implement a given unitary transformation U (corresponding to some computation), we would be interested in being able to do this using a *polynomial* number of gates from our universal set. Here, 'polynomial' is taken to mean 'polynomial in $\frac{1}{\epsilon}$ and in the number of qubits n', where ϵ is the desired quality of the estimate of U.

In fact, *most* unitary transformations *cannot* be *efficiently* approximated using gates from our universal set; this can be shown by counting arguments (since there are many more transformations than efficient circuits).

The difficulty in efficiently implementing some unitary transformations does not lie in the complexity of simulating arbitrary 1-qubit gates from a finite set of 1-qubit gates, since the decomposition described in Exercise 4.3.2 can be done in time polynomial in $\frac{1}{\epsilon}$ provided n-bit approximations[3] of all the coefficients of the gates can be computed in time polynomial in n. A result known as the *Solovay–Kitaev theorem* promises that we can do much better and find a set $\mathcal{G}$ of 1-qubit gates such that any arbitrary 1-qubit gate can be approximated to arbitrary accuracy using a sequence of a poly-logarithmic number of gates from $\mathcal{G}$. In other words, if we want to approximate a given unitary with error less than ε, we can do so using a number of gates that is polynomial in $\log(\frac{1}{\varepsilon})$.

It is worth discussing some of the consequences of the Solovay–Kitaev theorem. Suppose we are given a quantum circuit consisting of several CNOT gates, and m 1-qubit gates, and we wish to approximate this circuit using only gates from the universal set $\{\text{CNOT}\} \cup \mathcal{G}$. Suppose we approximate each 1-qubit gate in the circuit with error at most $\frac{\epsilon}{m}$. Then the overall error in the approximation of the circuit is bounded by ϵ (recall Equation 4.3.3). So, if we want to approximate the circuit using only gates from our universal set $\{\text{CNOT}\} \cup \mathcal{G}$, and if we want the total error in the approximation to be at most ϵ, we should aim to approximate each 1-qubit gate in the circuit with error at most $\frac{\epsilon}{m}$. We are now faced with the following question of efficiency: 'how many gates from $\mathcal{G}$ are required to approximate each 1-qubit gate with error at most $\frac{\epsilon}{m}$?' A special case of the Solovay–Kitaev theorem answers this question.

Theorem 4.4.1 *(Solovay–Kitaev) If $\mathcal{G}$ is a finite set of 1-qubit gates satisfying the conditions of Theorem 4.3.5 and also*

(iii) for any gate $g \in \mathcal{G}$, its inverse g^{-1} can be implemented exactly by a finite sequence of gates in $\mathcal{G}$,

then any 1-qubit gate can be approximated with error at most ϵ using $O\left(\log^c\left(\frac{1}{\epsilon}\right)\right)$ gates from $\mathcal{G}$, where c is a positive constant.

---

[3]By *n-bit approximation*, we mean a rational approximation of the form $\frac{x}{2^n}$ with error at most $\frac{1}{2^n}$.

Thus, according to the Solovay–Kitaev theorem, any 1-qubit gate can be approximated with error at most $\frac{\epsilon}{m}$ using $O\left(\log^c\left(\frac{m}{\epsilon}\right)\right)$ gates from a finite set $\mathcal{G}$ that is universal for 1-qubit gates, and that contains its own inverses (or whose inverses can be constructed exactly from a finite sequence of gates from $\mathcal{G}$). It is worth noting that if n-bit approximations of the coefficients of the gates in $\mathcal{G}$ can be computed in time polynomial in n, then the efficient decompositions can be found in time polynomial in $\log(\frac{1}{\epsilon})$.

Notice that the set $\{H, T\}$ satisfies these conditions. For a circuit having m 1-qubit gates, the approximation of these gates requires at most

$$O\left(m\log^c\left(\frac{m}{\epsilon}\right)\right) \tag{4.4.1}$$

gates from a universal set. This is a poly-logarithmic increase over the size of the original circuit.

4.5 Implementing Measurements with Quantum Circuits

In this section we examine how quantum circuits diagrams can be used to describe and implement the various types of quantum measurements described in Section 3.4, using only measurements of qubits with respect to the computational basis, and a universal set of unitary gates (for simplicity, in this section, we will assume that we can implement any unitary operation *exactly*).

After some examples of measuring simple two-state systems, we stated Postulate 4 in terms of a Von Neumann measurement with respect to some orthonormal basis $B = \{|\varphi_j\rangle\}$. Such 'complete' projective measurements are used commonly in quantum computing and quantum communication. In the next section, the superdense coding and quantum teleportation protocols will rely on the ability to perform certain Von Neumann measurements.

Given an orthonormal basis $|\varphi_j\rangle$, suppose we have a state $|\psi\rangle$, which we write in this basis:

$$|\psi\rangle = \sum_j \alpha_j |\varphi_j\rangle. \tag{4.5.1}$$

Recall that a Von Neumann measurement of $|\psi\rangle$ with respect to the basis $\{|\varphi_j\rangle\}$ is described by the orthogonal projectors $\{|\varphi_j\rangle\langle\varphi_j|\}$, and will output the result 'j' with probability

$$
\begin{aligned}
\mathrm{Tr}\left(|\psi\rangle\langle\psi||\varphi_j\rangle\langle\varphi_j|\right) &= \mathrm{Tr}\left(\langle\varphi_j|\psi\rangle\langle\psi|\varphi_j\rangle\right)\\
&= \langle\varphi_j|\psi\rangle\langle\psi|\varphi_j\rangle\\
&= |\langle\varphi_j|\psi\rangle|^2\\
&= |\alpha_j|^2. \tag{4.5.2}
\end{aligned}
$$

Given a device that will measure individual qubits in the computational basis, we can use a quantum circuit to implement Von Neumann measurements of

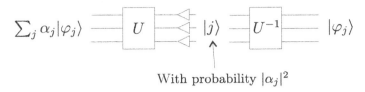

With probability $|\alpha_j|^2$

Fig. 4.8 Circuit implementing a Von Neumann measurement with respect to the basis $\{|\phi_j\rangle\}$. First U is applied to perform a basis change to the computational basis. Then a measurement is made in the computational basis, obtaining a specific (classical) outcome 'j' with probability $|\alpha_j|^2$. The state of the system after this measurement is $|j\rangle$. Finally U^{-1} is applied to change back to the $\{|\psi_j\rangle\}$-basis, leaving the post-measurement state $|\psi_j\rangle$.

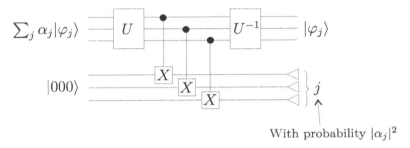

With probability $|\alpha_j|^2$

Fig. 4.9 Another circuit implementing the Von Neumann measurement. This time instead of directly measuring the state after the basis change effected by U, the measurement result is written to an ancillary register, creating the state $\sum_j \alpha_j |j\rangle|j\rangle$. The inverse basis change U^{-1} leaves the state $\sum_j |\phi_j\rangle|j\rangle$. A measurement of the ancillary register in the computational basis gives the result 'j' with probability $|\alpha_j|^2$ and leaves the main register in the state $|\phi_j\rangle$.

a multi-qubit register with respect to any orthonormal basis $\{|\varphi_j\rangle\}$. This can be done as follows. First, we construct a quantum circuit that implements the unitary transformation

$$U|\varphi_j\rangle = |j\rangle \tag{4.5.3}$$

(where the index j is assumed to be written in n-bit binary, $|j\rangle$ is the corresponding n-qubit computational basis state). The operator U performs a basis change from the $\{|\varphi_j\rangle\}$-basis to the computational basis. Given a general state $\sum_j \alpha_j |\varphi_j\rangle$, we use the circuit to perform the basis change U, and then make a measurement of the register in the computational basis. Finally, we perform the inverse basis change U^{-1} (by running the circuit for U backwards, replacing each gate by its inverse). This network is shown in Figure 4.8. An alternative approach is illustrated in Figure 4.9. In the alternative approach, we do not directly measure the state (with respect to the computational basis) after the basis

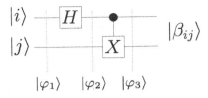

$|i\rangle$ — H — •
$|j\rangle$ — X — $|\beta_{ij}\rangle$

$|\varphi_1\rangle$ $|\varphi_2\rangle$ $|\varphi_3\rangle$

Fig. 4.10 A circuit implementing a basis change from the computational basis to the Bell basis.

change, but instead we 'copy'[4] the values onto an ancillary register, which we then measure in the computational basis.

As an example of how to implement the unitary basis change U, suppose we want to implement a Von Neumann measurement of a 2-qubit state, with respect to the orthonormal basis $\{|\beta_{00}\rangle, |\beta_{01}\rangle, |\beta_{10}\rangle, |\beta_{11}\rangle\}$ where

$$|\beta_{00}\rangle = \tfrac{1}{\sqrt{2}}|00\rangle + \tfrac{1}{\sqrt{2}}|11\rangle \qquad |\beta_{01}\rangle = \tfrac{1}{\sqrt{2}}|01\rangle + \tfrac{1}{\sqrt{2}}|10\rangle$$
$$|\beta_{10}\rangle = \tfrac{1}{\sqrt{2}}|00\rangle - \tfrac{1}{\sqrt{2}}|11\rangle \qquad |\beta_{11}\rangle = \tfrac{1}{\sqrt{2}}|01\rangle - \tfrac{1}{\sqrt{2}}|10\rangle. \qquad (4.5.4)$$

This basis is known as the *Bell* basis, and the four states $|\beta_{00}\rangle, |\beta_{01}\rangle, |\beta_{10}\rangle, |\beta_{11}\rangle$ are called the *Bell states* (also called *EPR pairs*). These states arise often in the study of quantum computation. A circuit that implements the basis change from the computational basis to the Bell basis is shown in Figure 4.10 (for the basis change from the Bell basis to the computational basis, we could run this circuit backwards). Suppose the input to the circuit in Figure 4.10 is the basis state $|\varphi_1\rangle = |00\rangle$. Consider the state as it passes through the circuit. After the Hadamard gate, the state is

$$|\varphi_2\rangle = \tfrac{1}{\sqrt{2}}\big(|0\rangle + |1\rangle\big)|0\rangle \qquad\qquad (4.5.5)$$
$$= \tfrac{1}{\sqrt{2}}\big(|00\rangle + |10\rangle\big). \qquad\qquad (4.5.6)$$

Note that the order of the qubits has been maintained in the above. Next, the controlled-NOT gate transforms this state into

$$|\varphi_3\rangle = \tfrac{1}{\sqrt{2}}\big(|00\rangle + |11\rangle\big). \qquad\qquad (4.5.7)$$

We have $|\varphi_3\rangle = |\beta_{00}\rangle$, and so we have verified that the circuit performs the basis change correctly on the input state $|00\rangle$. Similarly, the circuit performs the basis change correctly for the remaining three computational basis states $|01\rangle, |10\rangle$, and $|11\rangle$, transforming them to $|\beta_{01}\rangle, |\beta_{10}\rangle$, and $|\beta_{11}\rangle$, respectively.

In order to implement a 'Bell measurement' (i.e. a Von Neumann measurement with respect to the Bell basis), one could implement the circuit in Figure 4.9

---

[4]By 'copy' we mean that we perform the reversible (unitary) transformation that copies computational basis states. We are not cloning arbitrary superpositions.

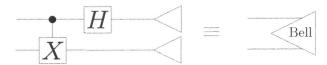

Fig. 4.11 A measurement with respect to the Bell basis can be implemented by the above circuit. Here we assume that we discard (or ignore) the resulting quantum state, and only output one of four labels $00, 01, 10,$ or 11 indicating the measurement outcome. Note that these two measurements are only equivalent in terms of their net result. In general, a Bell measurement does not *require* implementing a CNOT gate.

backwards, measure in the computational basis, and then apply the circuit in Figure 4.9 forwards again. If we only care about the classical measurement outcome, labelled by two bits $00, 01, 10,$ or 11, then we do not need to implement the Bell basis change again after the measurement. This equivalence is illustrated in Figure 4.11.

It will be very important for quantum computing, in particular for quantum error correction, to be able to implement general projective measurements, and not complete Von Neumann measurements. Consider a projective measurement with respect to the decomposition

$$I = \sum_i P_i, \qquad (4.5.8)$$

where P_i has rank r_i. In other words

$$P_i = \sum_{j=1}^{r_i} |\psi_{i,j}\rangle\langle\psi_{i,j}|$$

where the the states $\{|\psi_{i,j}\rangle\}$ are an orthonormal basis for the Hilbert space of dimension $N = \sum_i r_i$.

Let U_P be a circuit that maps $|\psi_{i,j}\rangle|0\rangle \mapsto |\psi_{i,j}\rangle|i\rangle$. One way (but not the only way) to implement U_P is to perform a basis change $U : |\psi_{i,j}\rangle \mapsto |i,j\rangle$, 'copy' j to the ancilla register, and then apply U^{-1}.

As an example, we consider a collection of projectors that are already diagonal in the computational basis, the parity projectors P_0 and P_1 (defined earlier in Section 3.4). Any input state $|\psi\rangle = \sum_x \beta_x |x\rangle$ can be rewritten as $|\psi\rangle = \alpha_0 |\psi_0\rangle + \alpha_1 |\psi_1\rangle$, where $\langle\psi_0|\psi_1\rangle = 0$, $\alpha_i = \sqrt{\langle\psi|P_i|\psi\rangle}$, and $|\psi_i\rangle = \frac{P_i|\psi\rangle}{\alpha_i}$ (as shown in Exercise 3.4.1). A parity measurement should output '0' and the state $|\psi_0\rangle$ with probability $|\alpha_0|^2$ and output '1' and the state $|\psi_1\rangle$ with probability $|\alpha_1|^2$.

One can implement U_P with a sequence of CNOT gates, as illustrated in Figure 4.12. Thus after the U_P circuit, we have the state

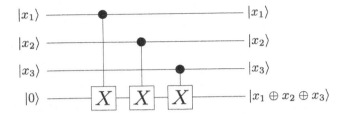

Fig. 4.12 A circuit computing the parity of three qubits.

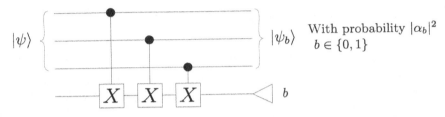

Fig. 4.13 A circuit implementing a parity measurement.

$$\sum_x \alpha_x |x\rangle |parity(x)\rangle = \sum_{parity(x)=0} \alpha_x |x\rangle |0\rangle + \sum_{parity(x)=1} \alpha_x |x\rangle |1\rangle$$

$$= \alpha_0 |\psi_0\rangle |0\rangle + \alpha_1 |\psi_1\rangle |1\rangle.$$

Thus measuring the ancilla qubit will leave the first register in the state $|\psi_0\rangle$ with probability $|\alpha_0|^2$ and in the state $|\psi_1\rangle$ with probability $|\alpha_1|^2$, as required. Therefore, this circuit will implement a parity measurement on an arbitrary 3-qubit state, as depicted in Figure 4.13.

It is worth emphasizing what differentiates this projective parity measurement from a Von Neumann measurement followed by classical post-processing to compute the parity. The projective measurement measures *only* the parity of the strings in the quantum state, and no other information, leaving one of the superposition states $|\psi_0\rangle$ or $|\psi_1\rangle$. A complete Von Neumann measurement would have extracted more information than needed, and we would have been left with a random basis state $|x\rangle$ of a specific parity instead of a superposition of all strings with the same parity.

We have introduced the basic building blocks of quantum circuits and presented circuit diagrams as a useful tool for describing quantum circuits and quantum operations in general. The remaining chapters will show how to construct quantum circuits to implement quantum protocols and algorithms. The quantum algorithms will be described in terms of uniform families of acyclic quantum circuits, where by *uniform* we mean that a classical computer can produce the quantum circuits in time polynomial in the size of the circuit.

5

SUPERDENSE CODING AND QUANTUM TELEPORTATION

We are now ready to look at our first protocols for quantum information. In this section, we examine two communication protocols which can be implemented using the tools we have developed in the preceding sections. These protocols are known as *superdense coding* and *quantum teleportation*. Both are inherently quantum: there are no classical protocols which behave in the same way. Both involve two parties who wish to perform some communication task between them. In descriptions of such communication protocols (especially in cryptography), it is very common to name the two parties 'Alice' and 'Bob', for convenience. We will follow this tradition. We will repeatedly refer to communication *channels*. A *quantum communication channel* refers to a communication line (e.g. a fiber-optic cable), which can carry qubits between two remote locations. A *classical communication channel* is one which can carry classical bits (but not qubits).[1] The protocols (like many in quantum communication) require that Alice and Bob initially share an entangled pair of qubits in the *Bell state*

$$|\beta_{00}\rangle = \tfrac{1}{\sqrt{2}}\big(|00\rangle + |11\rangle\big). \tag{5.0.1}$$

The above Bell state is sometimes referred to as an *EPR pair*. Such a state would have to be created ahead of time, when the qubits are in a lab together and can be made to interact in a way which will give rise to the entanglement between them. After the state is created, Alice and Bob each take one of the two qubits away with them. Alternatively, a third party could create the EPR pair and give one particle to Alice and the other to Bob. If they are careful not to let them interact with the environment, or any other quantum system, Alice and Bob's joint state will remain entangled. This entanglement becomes a *resource* which Alice and Bob can use to achieve protocols such as the following.

---

[1] Often the term 'channel' is used to refer to the mathematical transformation that occurs on bits or qubits when undergoing a general quantum operation. We will use this term in this sense in Chapter 10.

5.1 Superdense Coding

Suppose Alice wishes to send Bob two classical bits of information. Superdense coding is a way of achieving this task over a quantum channel, requiring only that Alice send one qubit to Bob. Alice and Bob must initially share the Bell state

$$|\beta_{00}\rangle = \tfrac{1}{\sqrt{2}}\big(|00\rangle + |11\rangle\big). \tag{5.1.1}$$

Suppose Alice is in possession of the first qubit and Bob the second qubit. Alice performs one of four 1-qubit gates, depending on the 2 classical bits she wishes to communicate to Bob. For convenience, we remind you again of the definitions of the Pauli gates:

$$I \equiv \begin{bmatrix} 1 & 0 \\ 0 & 1 \end{bmatrix} \qquad X \equiv \begin{bmatrix} 0 & 1 \\ 1 & 0 \end{bmatrix} \tag{5.1.2}$$

$$Y \equiv \begin{bmatrix} 0 & -i \\ i & 0 \end{bmatrix} \qquad Z \equiv \begin{bmatrix} 1 & 0 \\ 0 & -1 \end{bmatrix}. \tag{5.1.3}$$

If Alice wishes to send the bits 00 to Bob, she does nothing to her qubit (or equivalently, applies the identity gate I). If she wishes to send 01, she applies the X gate to her qubit. If she wishes to send 10, she applies the Z gate; and if she wishes to send 11, she applies $Z \cdot X$ (i.e. she applies the X gate followed by the Z gate). The following list summarizes the resulting joint 2-qubit state in each case:

To send	Transformation		
00	$I \otimes I:$	$\tfrac{1}{\sqrt{2}}\big(|00\rangle + |11\rangle\big) \mapsto \tfrac{1}{\sqrt{2}}\big(|00\rangle + |11\rangle\big) = |\beta_{00}\rangle$	
01	$X \otimes I:$	$\tfrac{1}{\sqrt{2}}\big(|00\rangle + |11\rangle\big) \mapsto \tfrac{1}{\sqrt{2}}\big(|01\rangle + |10\rangle\big) = |\beta_{01}\rangle$	
10	$Z \otimes I:$	$\tfrac{1}{\sqrt{2}}\big(|00\rangle + |11\rangle\big) \mapsto \tfrac{1}{\sqrt{2}}\big(|00\rangle - |11\rangle\big) = |\beta_{10}\rangle$	
11	$Z \cdot X \otimes I:$	$\tfrac{1}{\sqrt{2}}\big(|00\rangle + |11\rangle\big) \mapsto \tfrac{1}{\sqrt{2}}\big(|01\rangle - |10\rangle\big) = |\beta_{11}\rangle$	

You should verify the above states. After applying the appropriate gate, Alice sends her qubit to Bob. Then Bob is in possession of one of the four Bell states, depending on the classical bits Alice wished to send to him. Bob can now simply perform a measurement of the joint 2-qubit state *with respect to the Bell basis* (i.e. the basis $\{|\beta_{00}\rangle, |\beta_{01}\rangle, |\beta_{10}\rangle, |\beta_{11}\rangle\}$). Such a measurement can be implemented as described in Section 4.5 by first performing a change of basis to the Bell basis, and then performing a measurement in the computational basis (illustrated in Figure 4.11).

The outcome of the Bell measurement reveals to Bob which Bell state he possesses, and so allows him to determine with certainty the two classical bits Alice wanted to communicate to him. The superdense coding protocol is illustrated in Figure 5.1.

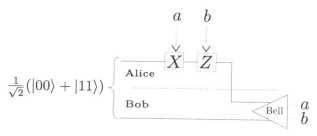

Fig. 5.1 The superdense coding protocol in which Alice sends two bits of classical information by sending one physical qubit to Bob. Alice and Bob initially share an EPR pair $\frac{1}{\sqrt{2}}(|00\rangle + |11\rangle)$. Alice applies the operation $U_{ab} = Z^b X^a$ depending on the classical bits a, b that she wishes to send. After sending her qubit to Bob, he measures his pair of qubits in the Bell basis. This measurement gives Bob the two values 'a' and 'b' corresponding to the Bell state $|\beta_{ab}\rangle$ in his possession.

5.2   Quantum Teleportation

For quantum teleportation, the scenario is that Alice wishes to communicate the state of a *qubit* to Bob. Suppose Alice only has a classical channel linking her to Bob. To send the state of a qubit *exactly*, it would seem that Alice would either have to send the physical qubit itself, or she would have to communicate the two complex amplitudes with *infinite precision*. However, if Alice and Bob possess an entangled state this intuition is wrong, and a quantum state can be sent exactly over a classical channel.

Teleportation is a protocol which allows Alice to communicate the state of a qubit exactly to Bob, sending only *two bits* of classical information to him. Like superdense coding, teleportation requires that Alice and Bob initially share the Bell state

$$|\beta_{00}\rangle = \tfrac{1}{\sqrt{2}}(|00\rangle + |11\rangle). \tag{5.2.1}$$

Suppose Alice wants to teleport the state $|\psi\rangle = \alpha_0|0\rangle + \alpha_1|1\rangle$ to Bob. Then, the circuit shown in Figure 5.2 implements the teleportation protocol, and transmits the state $|\psi\rangle$ from Alice to Bob.

The 3-qubit state possessed jointly by Alice and Bob is initially

$$|\psi\rangle|\beta_{00}\rangle. \tag{5.2.2}$$

Notice that by regrouping the qubits (but keeping them in the same order), this state can be written as

$$|\psi\rangle|\beta_{00}\rangle = \tfrac{1}{2}|\beta_{00}\rangle|\psi\rangle + \tfrac{1}{2}|\beta_{01}\rangle(X|\psi\rangle) + \tfrac{1}{2}|\beta_{10}\rangle(Z|\psi\rangle) + \tfrac{1}{2}|\beta_{11}\rangle(XZ|\psi\rangle). \tag{5.2.3}$$

Alice makes a measurement of the first two qubits in the Bell basis. The joint Alice–Bob state after this measurement is one of

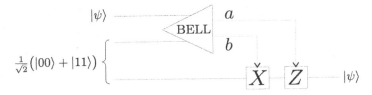

Fig. 5.2 A circuit implementing quantum teleportation. The top two lines represent Alice's qubits, and the bottom line represents Bob's qubit. Initially, Alice is in possession of the state $|\psi\rangle$, and she shares an EPR pair with Bob. Alice performs a joint measurement of $|\psi\rangle$ and her half of the EPR pair in the Bell basis. She sends the result of this measurement (classical bits, a and b) to Bob over a classical channel (shown in the figure as dashed arrows). The values of a and b are used to control the operations Bob performs on his qubit. After Bob performs his final operation, his qubit is left in the state $|\psi\rangle$.

$$|\beta_{00}\rangle|\psi\rangle, \tag{5.2.4}$$
$$|\beta_{01}\rangle(X|\psi\rangle), \tag{5.2.5}$$
$$|\beta_{10}\rangle(Z|\psi\rangle), \tag{5.2.6}$$
$$|\beta_{11}\rangle(XZ|\psi\rangle), \tag{5.2.7}$$

each with probability $\frac{1}{4}$. The classical bits a and b resulting from Alice's measurement indicate which of the four states is obtained. When Alice sends these two bits to Bob, he learns whether his qubit is left in the state $|\psi\rangle$, $X|\psi\rangle$, $Z|\psi\rangle$, or $XZ|\psi\rangle$. Depending on which state he has (i.e. depending on the values of the classical bits, a and b), Bob performs one of the following operations to transform his state into $|\psi\rangle$.

Exercise 5.2.1 Prove that

$$|\psi\rangle|\beta_{00}\rangle = \tfrac{1}{2}|\beta_{00}\rangle|\psi\rangle + \tfrac{1}{2}|\beta_{01}\rangle(X|\psi\rangle) + \tfrac{1}{2}|\beta_{10}\rangle(Z|\psi\rangle) + \tfrac{1}{2}|\beta_{11}\rangle(XZ|\psi\rangle). \tag{5.2.8}$$

M_1, M_2	**Bob performs**	
0,0	$I:$	$\alpha_0|0\rangle + \alpha_1|1\rangle \mapsto \alpha_0|0\rangle + \alpha_1|1\rangle = |\psi\rangle$
0,1	$X:$	$\alpha_0|1\rangle + \alpha_1|0\rangle \mapsto \alpha_0|0\rangle + \alpha_1|1\rangle = |\psi\rangle$
1,0	$Z:$	$\alpha_0|0\rangle - \alpha_1|1\rangle \mapsto \alpha_0|0\rangle + \alpha_1|1\rangle = |\psi\rangle$
1,1	$Z \cdot X:$	$\alpha_0|1\rangle - \alpha_1|0\rangle \mapsto \alpha_0|0\rangle + \alpha_1|1\rangle = |\psi\rangle$

So Bob conditionally applies Z and X to his qubit (classically) conditioned on the values a and b, respectively. After this transformation, Bob is guaranteed to have the state $|\psi\rangle$, and so the state has been successfully teleported from Alice to Bob. Note that it is somewhat remarkable that Alice could send a quantum state *exactly* to Bob without actually sending any quantum information; she only needs to send *2 bits of classical information*!

Teleportation provides a beautiful illustration of the power of *entanglement* as a resource for quantum computing and quantum communication. It allows us to replace the task of sending a qubit with the task of establishing one EPR pair of entanglement, sending two classical bits and performing a local Bell measurement. Establishing the EPR pair can be attempted repeatedly until successful, without damaging the state to be teleported. Sending classical bits does not require a quantum communication channel. Bob can also perform his Bell measurement without a quantum channel to Alice. So teleportation is a powerful tool for moving quantum information between locations that may be separated by a long distance.

5.3   An Application of Quantum Teleportation

Quantum teleportation turns out to have an interesting and remarkable application to quantum circuits. As we have seen, to implement quantum circuits in general, we need to have access to a universal set of quantum gates. Such a set always includes at least one gate that acts on two qubits. The CNOT gate is a common choice. It is often much more difficult technologically to implement gates that act on more than one qubit, since controlling coupled quantum systems is very challenging. It may be that a particular implementation of the CNOT gate is not perfect, but fails some of the time. If a CNOT gate fails in the middle of some long computation, the state of the qubits on which it was acting will be corrupted. Without some form of error correction, this will lead to an unreliable result for the computation.

One way around this problem might be to create a copy of the state we would like to apply the CNOT gate to, and keep the copy in a safe place. If the CNOT gate fails, then we can simply make another copy for safe keeping, and try the CNOT again. Unfortunately, this is impossible, by a result known as the *no-cloning* theorem, which says that it is impossible to implement a circuit that will perfectly copy an unknown quantum state. We will examine the no-cloning theorem in more detail in Section 10.4.2.

What we would like is a way of non-destructively applying the CNOT gate so that if it fails the quantum state of the relevant qubits is not corrupted, and we can simply try the CNOT gate again. Quantum teleportation gives us a way of doing this, provided we have the ability to prepare a Bell state, to do single bit rotations, and to measure Bell states directly. This scheme transforms the technological problem of implementing a CNOT gate into the technological problem of creating an entangled state. It is illustrated in the sequence of Figures 5.3–5.7. We wish to perform a CNOT gate between a control qubit in the state $\alpha_0|0\rangle + \alpha_1|1\rangle$ and a target qubit in the state $\gamma_0|0\rangle + \gamma_1|1\rangle$.

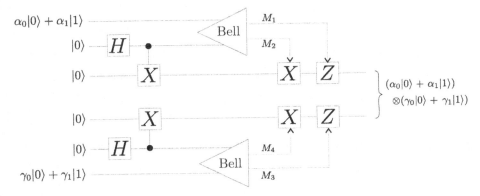

Fig. 5.3 Teleportation circuits to teleport the states $\alpha_0|0\rangle + \alpha_1|1\rangle$ and $\gamma_0|0\rangle + \gamma_1|1\rangle$. Note that the state of the two logical qubits is unaffected by this circuit, and so can be viewed as an implementation of the identity operation.

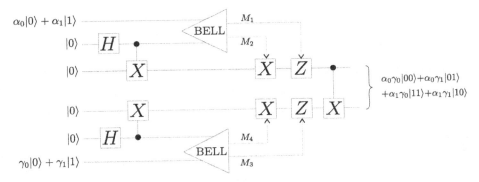

Fig. 5.4 A CNOT gate between the pair of teleported states. The overall effect on the state of the two logical qubits is the CNOT operation.

This could be done directly but at the risk of corrupting the quantum information when the gate fails. Instead, we can use two teleportation protocols: one for the control bit and the other for the target one, as shown in Figure 5.3.

In Figure 5.4, we apply the CNOT gate to the teleported states.

Figure 5.5 illustrates the 'trick'. We can add a pair of CNOT gates to the middle two qubits as shown. This does not change the overall behaviour of the circuit, since the combined effect of the two CNOT gates on those qubits is the identity. We can regroup the CNOT gates, as shown by the dashed boxes in Figure 5.5. It is easy to check that the effect of the portion ofthe circuit in the first (left)

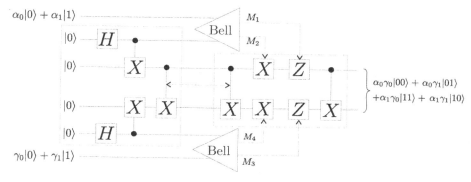

Fig. 5.5 A pair of CNOT gates added to the circuits. Notice that the pair of CNOT gates has no net effect.

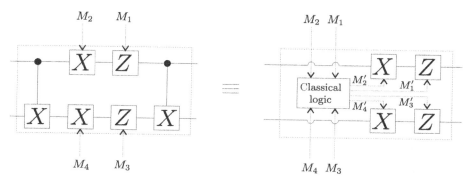

Fig. 5.6 The pair of CNOT gates can be removed if we modify the classical logic controlling the application of the X and Z gates.

dashed box is to create the 4-qubit entangled state

$$\frac{|0000\rangle + |0011\rangle + |1110\rangle + |1101\rangle}{2}.$$

Consider the portion of the circuit in the second (right) dashed box. The only impact of the CNOT gates is to alter the conditions on which the X and Z gates are applied separately to the two qubits. For example, if $M_1 = 0, M_2 = 0, M_3 = 1$, and $M_4 = 0$, the effect of the circuit in the dashed box is the same as applying Z separately to both qubits. For any combination of M_1, M_2, M_3, M_4, the desired effect can be achieved by applying some appropriate combination of X and Z gates individually to the two qubits in the dashed box. So this means we can remove the CNOT gates from this dashed box if we appropriately modify the classical logic controlling the X and Z gates. This is shown in Figure 5.6.

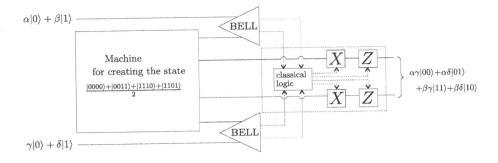

Fig. 5.7 A circuit for applying a CNOT gate between two qubits in a quantum computation, without risking destroying the state of the two qubits if the CNOT gate fails.

Exercise 5.3.1 Derive the 'classical logic' in Figure 5.6 (i.e. specify the mapping

$$M_1, M_2, M_3, M_4 \mapsto M_1', M_2', M_3', M_4'$$

for all values of M_1, M_2, M_3, M_4).

Note that we are only requiring a Bell measurement that provides the classical outcomes M_1, M_2. As we mentioned in the caption of Figure 4.11, a Bell measurement does not *require* implementing a CNOT gate. We also do not need the resulting Bell state $\beta M_1 M_2$ and thus the implementation of this measurement could for example destroy the Bell state in the process of measurement.

Notice that the first dashed box in Figure 5.6 makes use of CNOT gates. It is easy to verify that the effect of the circuit in this dashed box is only to create the state

$$\frac{|0000\rangle + |0011\rangle + |1110\rangle + |1101\rangle}{2}. \tag{5.3.1}$$

It suffices to have some machine that generates the above state, and some means of verifying that it has succeeded. Even though this machine uses CNOT gates, the point is that if it fails to create the state (5.3.1), our verification procedure will tell us this, and we can try the machine again with four freshly prepared qubits in the state $|0\rangle$. So in Figure 5.6, we replace the first dashed box with a generic machine for creating the state 5.3.1, which we assume will also contain a procedure for verifying that the state has been successfully created.

With the modifications described above, a circuit for implementing the CNOT gate on two qubits is shown in Figure 5.7.

6

INTRODUCTORY QUANTUM ALGORITHMS

In this chapter we will describe some of the early quantum algorithms. These algorithms are simple and illustrate the main ingredients behind the more useful and powerful quantum algorithms we describe in the subsequent chapters.

Since quantum algorithms share some features with classical probabilistic algorithms, we will start with a comparison of the two algorithmic paradigms.

6.1 Probabilistic Versus Quantum Algorithms

Classical probabilistic algorithms were introduced in Chapter 1. In this section we will see how quantum computation can be viewed as a generalization of probabilistic computation.

We begin by considering a simple probabilistic computation. Figure 6.1 illustrates the first two steps of such a computation on a register that can be in one of the four states, labelled by the integers $0, 1, 2$, and 3. Initially the register is in the state 0. After the first step of the computation, the register is in the state j with probability $p_{0,j}$. For example, the probability that the computation is in state 2 after the first step is $p_{0,2}$. In the second step of the computation, the register goes from state j to state k with probability $q_{j,k}$. For example, in the second step the computation proceeds from state 2 to state 3 with probability $q_{2,3}$.

Suppose we want to find the total probability that the computation ends up in state 3 after the second step. This is calculated by first determining the probability associated with each computation 'path' that could end up at the state 3, and then by adding the probabilities for all such paths. There are four computation paths that can leave the computation in state 3 after the first step. The computation can proceed from state 0 to state j and then from state j to state 3, for any of the four $j \in \{0, 1, 2, 3\}$. The probability associated with any one of these paths is obtained by multiplying the probability $p_{0,j}$ of the transition from state 0 to state j, with the probability $q_{j,3}$ of the transition from state j to state 3. The total probability of the computation ending up in state 3 is given

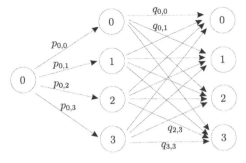

Fig. 6.1 A classical probabilistic computation acting on a register that can be in one of four states labelled $0, 1, 2, 3$. The $p_{0,j}$ are the probabilities for the computation proceeding from state 0 to state j in the first step. The $q_{j,k}$ represent the probabilities for the computation proceeding from state j to state k in the second step.

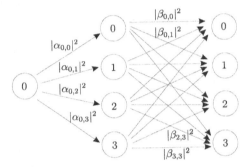

Fig. 6.2 The classical probabilistic computation viewed in a quantum setting. The transition probabilities as squared norms of quantum probability amplitudes. We have $p_{0,j} = |\alpha_{0,j}|^2$ and $q_{j,k} = |\beta_{j,k}|^2$. This can be viewed as a quantum computation in which the state is measured after each step.

by adding these four possibilities. So we have

$$\text{prob}(\text{final outcome is 3}) = \sum_j p_{0,j} q_{j,3}. \qquad (6.1.1)$$

Another way of looking at this computation is to suppose the register consists of two qubits, and let the labels $0, 1, 2, 3$ refer to the four basis states $|00\rangle, |01\rangle, |10\rangle, |11\rangle$, respectively. Then view each of the transition probabilities as a squared norm of a quantum probability amplitude, so that $p_{0,j} = |\alpha_{0,j}|^2$ and $q_{j,k} = |\beta_{j,k}|^2$. This approach is shown in Figure 6.2, which can be viewed as a quantum computation in which the state is measured after each step.

If we measured the state (in the computational basis) immediately after the first step of the computation, the probability associated with outcome 2 would be

$$\text{prob}(\text{measurement after first step gives 2}) = |\alpha_{0,2}|^2 = p_{0,2}. \qquad (6.1.2)$$

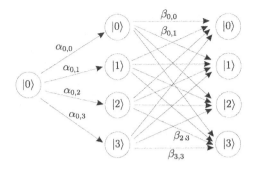

Fig. 6.3 A fully quantum computation. Here the state is not measured until after the second step.

As before, the total probability of measuring outcome 3 after the second step is

$$\text{prob(final outcome is 3)} = \sum_j |\alpha_{0,j}|^2 |\beta_{j,3}|^2 \qquad (6.1.3)$$

$$= \sum_j |\alpha_{0,j}\beta_{j,3}|^2 \qquad (6.1.4)$$

which is the same probability as in Equation 6.1.1.

In this example, since we assume that the state is measured after each step, we would know the intermediate state j, and thus we would know which computation path leading to the final state 3 was taken. The total probability of arriving at the final state 3 is determined by adding the squared norm of the probability amplitude $\alpha_{0,j}\beta_{j,3}$ associated with each path (i.e. we add the *probabilities* for the four paths, and not the probability amplitudes).

In a fully quantum algorithm, we would not measure the state immediately after the first step. This way the quantum probability amplitudes will have a chance to *interfere*. For example, some negative amplitudes could cancel with some positive amplitudes, significantly affecting the final probabilities associated with a given outcome. A quantum version of the algorithm above is illustrated in Figure 6.3.

This time the calculation of the total probability associated with outcome 3 in the measurement after the second step is different. Since there is no measurement after the first step of the computation, we do not learn the path taken by the computation to the final state 3. That is, when we obtain the output 3, we will have no information telling us which of the four paths was taken. In this case, instead of adding the probabilities associated with each of these four paths, we must add the probability *amplitudes*. The probability of a measurement after the second step giving the result 3 is obtained by taking the squared norm of the *total probability amplitude*.

$$\text{prob(final outcome is 3)} = \left| \sum_j \alpha_{0,j} \beta_{j,3} \right|^2 . \qquad (6.1.5)$$

Note the difference between Equations 6.1.4 and 6.1.5. In Exercise 6.1.2 you will examine sets of probability amplitudes for which the two equations give drastically different results.

Exercise 6.1.1 The transition probabilities $q_{i,j}$ of the classical probabilistic algorithm illustrated in Figure 1.1 form a 4×4 *stochastic* matrix for which $\sum_i q_{i,j} = 1$ for every j.

(a) Prove that for any unitary matrix $U = [u_{i,j}]$, the matrix $S = [|u_{i,j}|^2]$ is a stochastic matrix.

(b) Prove that not all stochastic matrices can be derived from a unitary U as described in the previous exercise.

Note that this means that not all classical probabilistic algorithms can be simulated by quantum algorithms in the way that is described in this section. However, the next exercise shows a simple way in which a quantum algorithm can simulate any classical probabilistic one.

(c) Show how a classical probabilistic transition on an M-state system can be simulated by a quantum algorithm by adding an additional M-state 'ancilla' system, applying a unitary operation to the joint system, and then measuring and discarding the ancilla system.

Exercise 6.1.2

(a) Describe complex numbers α_i, $i = 0, 1, \ldots, N - 1$ satisfying

$$\sum_i |\alpha_i|^2 = 1 \text{ and } \left| \sum_i \alpha_i \right|^2 = 0.$$

(b) Describe complex numbers α_i, $i = 0, 1, \ldots, N - 1$ satisfying

$$\sum_i |\alpha_i|^2 = \frac{1}{N} \text{ and } \left| \sum_i \alpha_i \right|^2 = 1.$$

Quantum interference has already been seen in Section 1.6 where we examined the photon and beam-splitter apparatus. We can revisit this example in the language of quantum circuits to provide a concrete example of interference in a quantum computation. Consider the quantum circuit in Figure 6.4. This circuit does not perform a purely quantum computation, because we make a measurement immediately after the first Hadamard gate (recall the definition of the Hadamard gate H, from Section 4.3).

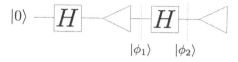

Fig. 6.4 A quantum circuit exhibiting no quantum interference.

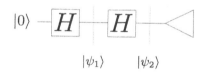

Fig. 6.5 A quantum circuit exhibiting interference.

The state $|\phi_1\rangle$ immediately after this measurement is

$$|\phi_1\rangle = \begin{cases} |0\rangle \text{ with probability } \frac{1}{2} \\ |1\rangle \text{ with probability } \frac{1}{2}. \end{cases} \qquad (6.1.6)$$

The state immediately after the second Hadamard gate is then

$$|\phi_2\rangle = \begin{cases} \frac{1}{\sqrt{2}}(|0\rangle + |1\rangle) \text{ with probability } \frac{1}{2} \\ \frac{1}{\sqrt{2}}(|0\rangle - |1\rangle) \text{ with probability } \frac{1}{2}. \end{cases} \qquad (6.1.7)$$

In either case, the final measurement will give the result 0 or 1 with equal probability.

Compare the above with the quantum circuit shown in Figure 6.5. This time there is no measurement after the first Hadamard gate, and the application of the second Hadamard gate will give rise to interference in the quantum amplitudes. The state immediately after the first Hadamard gate is

$$|\psi_1\rangle = \frac{1}{\sqrt{2}}|0\rangle + \frac{1}{\sqrt{2}}|1\rangle. \qquad (6.1.8)$$

This state is input directly to the second Hadamard gate, and the state after the second Hadamard gate is

$$|\psi_2\rangle = H\left(\frac{1}{\sqrt{2}}|0\rangle + \frac{1}{\sqrt{2}}|1\rangle\right) \qquad (6.1.9)$$

$$= \frac{1}{\sqrt{2}}H|0\rangle + \frac{1}{\sqrt{2}}H|1\rangle \qquad (6.1.10)$$

$$= \frac{1}{\sqrt{2}}\left(\frac{1}{\sqrt{2}}|0\rangle + \frac{1}{\sqrt{2}}|1\rangle\right) + \frac{1}{\sqrt{2}}\left(\frac{1}{\sqrt{2}}|0\rangle - \frac{1}{\sqrt{2}}|1\rangle\right) \qquad (6.1.11)$$

$$= \frac{1}{2}|0\rangle + \frac{1}{2}|1\rangle + \frac{1}{2}|0\rangle - \frac{1}{2}|1\rangle \qquad (6.1.12)$$

$$= |0\rangle. \qquad (6.1.13)$$

The total probability amplitude associated with $|1\rangle$ is 0, meaning that the probability for the second measurement giving result '1' is now 0. The second Hadamard gate acted on the basis states $|0\rangle$ and $|1\rangle$ in superposition, and the amplitudes of state $|1\rangle$ for the two paths in this superposition interfered, causing them to cancel out.

Note that if in Figure 6.5 we replace the Hadamard gate H with the 'square root of NOT' gate,

$$\begin{bmatrix} 1 & i \\ i & 1 \end{bmatrix}, \tag{6.1.14}$$

then we are describing the photon/beam-splitter experiment we saw in Section 1.6.

Classical probabilistic algorithms can be easily simulated by quantum algorithms (see Exercise 6.1.1 c). However, can classical probabilistic algorithms efficiently simulate quantum algorithms? We have seen how naively replacing each quantum gate with a probabilistic classical gate can give drastically different outcomes, and thus will not work in general. Simple attempts, like approximating the total amplitude of a given outcome by sampling a polynomial number of paths leading to that outcome, are also not efficient in general. However, in some restricted cases, such as quantum circuits using only the CNOT, H, X, Y, Z, and T gates (which generate what is known as the *Clifford group*), can be efficiently simulated on a classical computer (this is known as the Gottesman–Knill theorem). If there is no entanglement, or a sufficiently small amount of entanglement, then there are also efficient classical algorithms for simulating quantum systems. However, there is no known general purpose classical algorithm for simulating quantum systems (and, in particular, quantum computers). This leaves open the possibility that quantum algorithms might be able to solve some computational problems more efficiently than any classical probabilistic algorithm can.

6.2 Phase Kick-Back

In Exercise 4.2.4 we saw how, although when described in the classical basis, the CNOT gate appears to do nothing to the control qubit, it can in fact affect the control qubit just as much as it does the target qubit. For example, in the Hadamard basis, the role of control and target qubit is effectively switched, for example,

$$\text{CNOT:} \left(\frac{|0\rangle + |1\rangle}{\sqrt{2}} \right) \left(\frac{|0\rangle - |1\rangle}{\sqrt{2}} \right) \longmapsto \left(\frac{|0\rangle - |1\rangle}{\sqrt{2}} \right) \left(\frac{|0\rangle - |1\rangle}{\sqrt{2}} \right). \tag{6.2.1}$$

Notice that $\left(\frac{|0\rangle - |1\rangle}{\sqrt{2}}\right)$ is an eigenvector (or *eigenstate*) of the $X(\text{NOT})$ gate with eigenvalue -1, and an eigenvector of the identity gate with eigenvalue $+1$. Since the CNOT applies the NOT gate to the target qubit if the first qubit is in state $|1\rangle$, we get

$$\text{CNOT}: |1\rangle \left(\frac{|0\rangle - |1\rangle}{\sqrt{2}}\right) \longmapsto |1\rangle \left(\text{NOT}\left(\frac{|0\rangle - |1\rangle}{\sqrt{2}}\right)\right) \tag{6.2.2}$$

$$= |1\rangle \left((-1)\left(\frac{|0\rangle - |1\rangle}{\sqrt{2}}\right)\right) \tag{6.2.3}$$

$$= -|1\rangle \left(\frac{|0\rangle - |1\rangle}{\sqrt{2}}\right) \tag{6.2.4}$$

(where the second line follows from the first axiom of tensor products that we saw in Section 2.6). Since the CNOT applies the identity gate (i.e. does 'nothing') to the target qubit if the first qubit is in state $|0\rangle$, we get

$$\text{CNOT}: |0\rangle \left(\frac{|0\rangle - |1\rangle}{\sqrt{2}}\right) \longmapsto |0\rangle \left(\frac{|0\rangle - |1\rangle}{\sqrt{2}}\right). \tag{6.2.5}$$

Since the target qubit is in an eigenstate, it does not change, and we can effectively treat the eigenvalue as being 'kicked back' to the control register.

Note that this can be summarized as

$$\text{CNOT}: |b\rangle \left(\frac{|0\rangle - |1\rangle}{\sqrt{2}}\right) \longmapsto (-1)^{b}|b\rangle \left(\frac{|0\rangle - |1\rangle}{\sqrt{2}}\right), \tag{6.2.6}$$

where $b \in \{0, 1\}$. When the control qubit is in a superposition of $|0\rangle$ and $|1\rangle$, we have

$$\text{CNOT}: (\alpha_0|0\rangle + \alpha_1|1\rangle) \left(\frac{|0\rangle - |1\rangle}{\sqrt{2}}\right) \longmapsto (\alpha_0|0\rangle - \alpha_1|1\rangle) \left(\frac{|0\rangle - |1\rangle}{\sqrt{2}}\right) \tag{6.2.7}$$

(notice this corresponds to effecting the Z gate to the control qubit).

Let us consider the effect of a more general 2-qubit gate U_f implementing an arbitrary function $f\colon \{0, 1\} \to \{0, 1\}$ by mapping $U_f\colon |x\rangle|y\rangle \mapsto |x\rangle|y \oplus f(x)\rangle$ (as we saw in Section 1.5, this mapping is reversible even though the function f may not itself be invertible).

Let us fix the target register to the state $\frac{1}{\sqrt{2}}(|0\rangle - |1\rangle)$, and analyse the action of U_f on an arbitrary basis state in the control qubit:

$$U_f : |x\rangle \left(\frac{|0\rangle - |1\rangle}{\sqrt{2}} \right) \longmapsto \left(\frac{U_f|x\rangle|0\rangle - U_f|x\rangle|1\rangle}{\sqrt{2}} \right) \tag{6.2.8}$$

$$= \left(\frac{|x\rangle|0 \oplus f(x)\rangle - |x\rangle|1 \oplus f(x)\rangle}{\sqrt{2}} \right) \tag{6.2.9}$$

$$= |x\rangle \left(\frac{|0 \oplus f(x)\rangle - |1 \oplus f(x)\rangle}{\sqrt{2}} \right). \tag{6.2.10}$$

We know that the action of '$\oplus f(x)$' has no effect on a single bit if $f(x) = 0$ (i.e. $b \oplus 0 = b$), and '$\oplus f(x)$' flips the state of the bit if $f(x) = 1$.

Consider the expression $\frac{1}{\sqrt{2}}(|0 \oplus f(x)\rangle - |1 \oplus f(x)\rangle)$ in the two cases $f(x) = 0$ and $f(x) = 1$:

$$f(x) = 0 : \quad \frac{|0 \oplus f(x)\rangle - |1 \oplus f(x)\rangle}{\sqrt{2}} = \frac{|0\rangle - |1\rangle}{\sqrt{2}} \tag{6.2.11}$$

$$f(x) = 1 : \quad \frac{|0 \oplus f(x)\rangle - |1 \oplus f(x)\rangle}{\sqrt{2}} = \frac{|1\rangle - |0\rangle}{\sqrt{2}} = -\left(\frac{|0\rangle - |1\rangle}{\sqrt{2}} \right). \tag{6.2.12}$$

These two possibilities differ by a factor of (-1) which depends on the value of $f(x)$. We have

$$\frac{|0 \oplus f(x)\rangle - |1 \oplus f(x)\rangle}{\sqrt{2}} = (-1)^{f(x)} \left(\frac{|0\rangle - |1\rangle}{\sqrt{2}} \right). \tag{6.2.13}$$

So the above state can be rewritten as

$$|x\rangle(-1)^{f(x)} \left(\frac{|0\rangle - |1\rangle}{\sqrt{2}} \right). \tag{6.2.14}$$

Associating the $(-1)^{f(x)}$ factor with the first qubit, we have

$$U_f : |x\rangle \left(\frac{|0\rangle - |1\rangle}{\sqrt{2}} \right) \longmapsto (-1)^{f(x)}|x\rangle \left(\frac{|0\rangle - |1\rangle}{\sqrt{2}} \right). \tag{6.2.15}$$

When the control qubit is in a superposition of $|0\rangle$ and $|1\rangle$, we have

$$U_f : (\alpha_0|0\rangle + \alpha_1|1\rangle) \left(\frac{|0\rangle - |1\rangle}{\sqrt{2}} \right) \longmapsto \left((-1)^{f(0)}\alpha_0|0\rangle + (-1)^{f(1)}\alpha_1|1\rangle \right) \left(\frac{|0\rangle - |1\rangle}{\sqrt{2}} \right). \tag{6.2.16}$$

We can think of U_f as a 1-qubit operator $\widehat{U}_{f(x)}$ (which maps $|b\rangle \mapsto |b \oplus f(x)\rangle$) acting on the second qubit, *controlled* by the state $|x\rangle$ of the first register, as shown in Figure 6.6. We may sometimes write c-$\widehat{U}_{f(x)}$ instead of U_f.

Fig. 6.6 The 2-qubit gate $U_f : |x\rangle|y\rangle \mapsto |x\rangle|y \oplus f(x)\rangle$ can be thought of as a 1-qubit gate $\widehat{U}_{f(x)}$ acting on the second qubit, controlled by the first qubit.

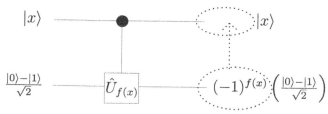

Fig. 6.7 The state $\frac{|0\rangle - |1\rangle}{\sqrt{2}}$ of the target register is an eigenstate of $\widehat{U}_{f(x)}$. The eigenvalue $(-1)^{f(x)}$ can be 'kicked back' in front of the target register.

Notice in Equation (6.2.15) that the state $\frac{|0\rangle - |1\rangle}{\sqrt{2}}$ of the second register is an eigenvector of $\widehat{U}_{f(x)}$.

This technique of inputting an eigenstate to the target qubit of an operator like the c-$\widehat{U}_{f(x)}$, and associating the eigenvalue with the state of the control register (as illustrated in Figure 6.7), will be used repeatedly in the remainder of this chapter and the next chapter.

6.3   The Deutsch Algorithm

We now look at our first quantum algorithm. The Deutsch algorithm is a very simple example of a quantum algorithm based on the Quantum Fouries Transform (to be defined in the next chapter). It is a good place to start, because while being very simple and easy to understand, the Deutsch algorithm illustrates the key ideas of *quantum parallelism* and *quantum interference* that are used in all useful quantum algorithms.

The problem solved by the Deutsch algorithm is the following. Suppose we are given a reversible circuit for computing an unknown 1-bit function $f : \{0,1\} \to \{0,1\}$ (see Section 1.5 for a discussion of reversible circuits). We treat this reversible circuit as a 'black box' or 'oracle'. This means that we can apply the circuit to obtain values of $f(x)$ for given inputs x, but we cannot gain any information about the inner workings of the circuit to learn about the function f. The problem is to determine the value of $f(0) \oplus f(1)$. If we determine that $f(0) \oplus f(1) = 0$, then we know that $f(0) = f(1)$ (although we do not know the value), and we say that f is 'constant'. If on the other hand we determine that $f(0) \oplus f(1) = 1$, then we know that $f(0) \neq f(1)$, and we say the function is 'balanced'. So determining $f(0) \oplus f(1)$ is equivalent to determining whether the function f is constant or balanced.

The Deutsch Problem

Input: A black box for computing an unknown function function $f : \{0,1\} \to \{0,1\}$.
Problem: Determine the value of $f(0) \oplus f(1)$ by making queries to f.

How many queries to the oracle for f must be made classically to determine $f(0) \oplus f(1)$? Clearly the answer is 2. Suppose we compute $f(0)$ using one (classical) query. Then the value of $f(1)$ could be 0, making $f(0) \oplus f(1) = 0$, or the value of $f(1)$ could be 1, making $f(0) \oplus f(1) = 1$. Without making a second query to the oracle to determine the value of $f(1)$, we can make no conclusion about the value of $f(0) \oplus f(1)$. The Deutsch algorithm is a quantum algorithm capable of determining the value of $f(0) \oplus f(1)$ by making only a *single query* to a quantum oracle for f.

The given reversible circuit for f can be made into a quantum circuit, by replacing every reversible classical gate in the given circuit with the analogous unitary quantum gate. This quantum circuit can be expressed as a unitary operator

$$U_f : |x\rangle|y\rangle \mapsto |x\rangle|y \oplus f(x)\rangle. \tag{6.3.1}$$

Having created a quantum version of the circuit for f, we can supply *quantum bits* as inputs. We define U_f so that if we set the second input qubit to be in the state $|y\rangle = |0\rangle$, then $|x\rangle = |0\rangle$ in the first input qubit will give $|0 \oplus f(0)\rangle = |f(0)\rangle$ in the second output bit, and $|x\rangle = |1\rangle$ in the first input qubit will give $|f(1)\rangle$. So we can think of $|x\rangle = |0\rangle$ as a quantum version of the (classical) input bit 0, and $|x\rangle = |1\rangle$ as a quantum version of the input bit 1. Of course, the state of the input qubit can be some *superposition* of $|0\rangle$ and $|1\rangle$. Suppose, still keeping the second input qubit $|y\rangle = |0\rangle$, we set the first input qubit to be in the superposition state

$$\frac{1}{\sqrt{2}}|0\rangle + \frac{1}{\sqrt{2}}|1\rangle. \tag{6.3.2}$$

Then the two qubit input to U_f is

$$\left(\frac{1}{\sqrt{2}}|0\rangle + \frac{1}{\sqrt{2}}|1\rangle\right)|0\rangle \tag{6.3.3}$$

$$= \frac{1}{\sqrt{2}}|0\rangle|0\rangle + \frac{1}{\sqrt{2}}|1\rangle|0\rangle. \tag{6.3.4}$$

The output of U_f will be the state

$$U_f \left(\frac{1}{\sqrt{2}}|0\rangle|0\rangle + \frac{1}{\sqrt{2}}|1\rangle|0\rangle \right) \tag{6.3.5}$$

$$= \frac{1}{\sqrt{2}}U_f|0\rangle|0\rangle + \frac{1}{\sqrt{2}}U_f|1\rangle|0\rangle \tag{6.3.6}$$

$$= \frac{1}{\sqrt{2}}|0\rangle|0 \oplus f(0)\rangle + \frac{1}{\sqrt{2}}|1\rangle|0 \oplus f(1)\rangle \tag{6.3.7}$$

$$= \frac{1}{\sqrt{2}}|0\rangle|f(0)\rangle + \frac{1}{\sqrt{2}}|1\rangle|0 \oplus f(1)\rangle. \tag{6.3.8}$$

In some sense, U_f has *simultaneously* computed the value of f on both possible inputs 0 and 1 in superposition. However, recalling how quantum measurement works from Section 3.4, if we now measure the output state in the computational basis, we will observe *either* $|0\rangle|f(0)\rangle$ (with probability $\frac{1}{2}$), or $|1\rangle|1 \oplus f(1)\rangle$ (with probability $\frac{1}{2}$). After the measurement, the output state will be either $|f(0)\rangle$ or $|f(1)\rangle$, respectively, and so any subsequent measurements of the output state will yield the same result. So this means that although we have successfully computed two values in superposition, only one of those values is accessible through a quantum measurement in the computational basis. Fortunately, this is not the end of the story.

Recall that for the Deutsch problem we are ultimately not interested in individual values of $f(x)$, but wish to determine the value of $f(0) \oplus f(1)$. The Deutsch algorithm illustrates how we can use *quantum interference* to obtain such *global information* about the function f, and how this can be done more efficiently than is possible classically. The Deutsch algorithm is implemented by the quantum circuit shown in Figure 6.8.

Note that the second input bit has been initialized to the state $\frac{|0\rangle - |1\rangle}{\sqrt{2}}$. This state can easily be created from the state $|1\rangle$ by applying a single Hadamard gate. We do not show this gate, however, to emphasize a certain symmetry that is characteristic of these algorithms. A convenient way to analyse the behaviour of a quantum algorithm is to work through the state at each stage of the circuit. First, the input state is

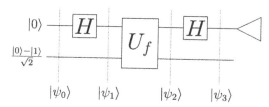

Fig. 6.8 A circuit implementing the Deutsch algorithm. The measured value equals $f(0) \oplus f(1)$.

$$|\psi_0\rangle = |0\rangle \left(\frac{|0\rangle - |1\rangle}{\sqrt{2}} \right). \tag{6.3.9}$$

After the first Hadamard gate is applied to the first qubit, the state becomes

$$|\psi_1\rangle = \left(\frac{1}{\sqrt{2}}|0\rangle + \frac{1}{\sqrt{2}}|1\rangle \right) \left(\frac{|0\rangle - |1\rangle}{\sqrt{2}} \right) \tag{6.3.10}$$

$$= \frac{1}{\sqrt{2}}|0\rangle \left(\frac{|0\rangle - |1\rangle}{\sqrt{2}} \right) + \frac{1}{\sqrt{2}}|1\rangle \left(\frac{|0\rangle - |1\rangle}{\sqrt{2}} \right). \tag{6.3.11}$$

Recalling Equation (6.2.15), after applying the U_f gate we have the state

$$|\psi_2\rangle = \frac{(-1)^{f(0)}}{\sqrt{2}}|0\rangle \left(\frac{|0\rangle - |1\rangle}{\sqrt{2}} \right) + \frac{(-1)^{f(1)}}{\sqrt{2}}|1\rangle \left(\frac{|0\rangle - |1\rangle}{\sqrt{2}} \right) \tag{6.3.12}$$

$$= \left(\frac{(-1)^{f(0)}|0\rangle + (-1)^{f(1)}|1\rangle}{\sqrt{2}} \right) \left(\frac{|0\rangle - |1\rangle}{\sqrt{2}} \right) \tag{6.3.13}$$

$$= (-1)^{f(0)} \left(\frac{|0\rangle + (-1)^{f(0) \oplus f(1)}|1\rangle}{\sqrt{2}} \right) \left(\frac{|0\rangle - |1\rangle}{\sqrt{2}} \right) \tag{6.3.14}$$

where the last equality uses the fact that $(-1)^{f(0)}(-1)^{f(1)} = (-1)^{f(0) \oplus f(1)}$.

If f is a constant function (i.e. $f(0) \oplus f(1) = 0$), then we have

$$|\psi_2\rangle = (-1)^{f(0)} \left(\frac{|0\rangle + |1\rangle}{\sqrt{2}} \right) \left(\frac{|0\rangle - |1\rangle}{\sqrt{2}} \right) \tag{6.3.15}$$

and so the final Hadamard gate on the first qubit transforms the state to

$$|\psi_3\rangle = (-1)^{f(0)}|0\rangle \left(\frac{|0\rangle - |1\rangle}{\sqrt{2}} \right). \tag{6.3.16}$$

The squared norm of the basis state $|0\rangle$ in the first qubit is 1. This means that for a constant function a measurement of the first qubit is certain to return the value $0 = f(0) \oplus f(1)$.

If f is a balanced function (i.e. $f(0) \oplus f(1) = 1$), then we have

$$|\psi_2\rangle = (-1)^{f(0)} \left(\frac{|0\rangle - |1\rangle}{\sqrt{2}} \right) \left(\frac{|0\rangle - |1\rangle}{\sqrt{2}} \right) \tag{6.3.17}$$

and so the final Hadamard gate on the first qubit transforms the state to

$$|\psi_3\rangle = (-1)^{f(0)}|1\rangle \left(\frac{|0\rangle - |1\rangle}{\sqrt{2}} \right). \tag{6.3.18}$$

In this case the squared norm of the basis state $|1\rangle$ in the first qubit is 1. This means that for a balanced function a measurement of the first qubit is certain to return the value $1 = f(0) \oplus f(1)$. So a measurement of the first qubit at the

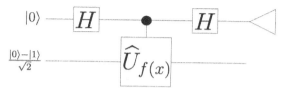

Fig. 6.9 The circuit for Deutsch's algorithm with the c-$\widehat{U}_{f(x)}$ drawn instead of U_f. When c-$\widehat{U}_{f(x)}$ is applied, the control qubit is in a superposition of $|0\rangle$ and $|1\rangle$, which pick up phase factors of $(-1)^{f(0)}$ and $(-1)^{f(1)}$, corresponding to the eigenvalues of $\widehat{U}_{f(x)}$ for $x = 0$ and 1, respectively. The Hadamard gate followed by a measurement in the computational basis determines the relative phase factor between $|0\rangle$ and $|1\rangle$.

end of the circuit for the Deutsch algorithm determines the value $f(0) \oplus f(1)$ and thus whether the function is constant or balanced.

To gain some insight into how the Deutsch algorithm can generalize, it is helpful to remember that the operator $U_f : |x\rangle|y\rangle \mapsto |x\rangle|y \oplus f(x)\rangle$ in the Deutsch algorithm can be viewed as a single-qubit operator $\widehat{U}_{f(x)}$, whose action on the second qubit is controlled by the state of the first qubit (see Figure 6.9). The state $(\frac{|0\rangle - |1\rangle}{\sqrt{2}})$ is an eigenstate of $\widehat{U}_{f(x)}$ with eigenvalue $(-1)^{f(x)}$. By encoding these eigenvalues in the phase factors of the control qubit, we are able to determine $f(0) \oplus f(1)$ by determining the relative phase factor between $|0\rangle$ and $|1\rangle$. Distinguishing $(\frac{|0\rangle + |1\rangle}{\sqrt{2}})$ and $(\frac{|0\rangle - |1\rangle}{\sqrt{2}})$ is done using the Hadamard gate.

We will see this technique of associating phase factors (corresponding to eigenvalues) with the control register, and then using quantum interference to determine the relative phase, applied throughout this chapter and the next chapter.

Exercise 6.3.1 In the Deutsch algorithm, when we consider U_f as a single-qubit operator $\widehat{U}_{f(x)}$, $\frac{|0\rangle - |1\rangle}{\sqrt{2}}$ is an eigenstate of $\widehat{U}_{f(x)}$, whose associated eigenvalue gives us the answer to the Deutsch problem. Suppose we were not able to prepare this eigenstate directly. Show that if we instead input $|0\rangle$ to the target qubit, and otherwise run the same algorithm, we get an algorithm that gives the correct answer with probability $\frac{3}{4}$ (note this also works if we input $|1\rangle$ to the second qubit). Furthermore, show that with probability $\frac{1}{2}$ we know for certainty that the algorithm has produced the correct answer.

Hint: write $|0\rangle$ in the basis of eigenvectors of U_f.

Note: Deutsch originally presented his algorithm in terms of the U_f operator with $|0\rangle$ input to the second qubit. Shor analysed his algorithm for finding orders (factoring) in an analogous manner. Later, it was found that analysing these algorithms in the eigenbasis of a suitable controlled operator is often convenient (Appendix A.6 discusses this issue; the operators are usually different from the $\widehat{U}_{f(x)}$ operators we describe in this exercise). Note that for many algorithms (including the algorithm for finding orders, which we will see in the next section), it is not possible to implement the 'trick' of inputting a desired eigenstate directly.

6.4   The Deutsch–Jozsa Algorithm

The Deutsch–Jozsa algorithm solves a problem that is a straight forward generalization of the problem solved by the Deutsch algorithm. The algorithm has exactly the same structure. As with the Deutsch algorithm, we are given a reversible circuit implementing an unknown function f, but this time f is a function from n-bit strings to a single bit. That is,

$$f \colon \{0,1\}^n \to \{0,1\}. \qquad (6.4.1)$$

We are also given the *promise* that f is either *constant* (meaning $f(x)$ is the same for all x), or f is *balanced* (meaning $f(x) = 0$ for exactly half of the input strings x, and $f(x) = 1$ for the other half of the inputs). The problem here is to determine whether f is constant, or balanced, by making queries to the circuit for f.

> **The Deutsch–Jozsa Problem**
>
> **Input:** A black-box for computing an unknown function $f \colon \{0,1\}^n \to \{0,1\}$.
> **Promise:** f is either a constant or a balanced function.
> **Problem:** Determine whether f is constant or balanced by making queries to f.

Consider solving this problem by a classical algorithm. Suppose we have used the oracle to determine $f(x)$ for exactly half of the possible inputs x (i.e. you have made 2^{n-1} queries to f), and that all queries have returned $f(x) = 0$. At this point, we would strongly suspect that f is constant. However, it is possible that if we queried f on the remaining 2^{n-1} inputs, we might get $f(x) = 1$ each time. So it is still possible that f is balanced. So in the worst case, using a classical algorithm we cannot decide with certainty whether f is constant or balanced using any less than $2^{n-1} + 1$ queries. The property of being constant or balanced is a global property of f. As for the Deutsch problem, a quantum algorithm can take advantage of quantum superposition and interference to determine this global property of f. The Deutsch–Jozsa algorithm will determine whether f is constant, or balanced, making only *one* query to a quantum version of the reversible circuit for f.

Analogous to what we did for the Deutsch algorithm, we will define the quantum operation

$$U_f \colon |\mathbf{x}\rangle |y\rangle \mapsto |\mathbf{x}\rangle |y \oplus f(\mathbf{x})\rangle. \qquad (6.4.2)$$

This time we write $\mathbf{x}$ in boldface, because it refers to an n-bit string. As before, we think of U_f as a 1-qubit operator $\widehat{U}_{f(\mathbf{x})}$, this time controlled by the *register*

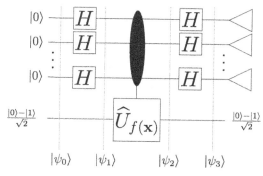

$$|\psi_0\rangle \qquad |\psi_1\rangle \qquad\qquad |\psi_2\rangle \qquad |\psi_3\rangle$$

Fig. 6.10 A circuit for the Deutsch–Jozsa algorithm. If the measured bit string is all 0s, then the function is constant. Otherwise, it is balanced.

of qubits in the state $|\mathbf{x}\rangle$. We can see that $\frac{|0\rangle-|1\rangle}{\sqrt{2}}$ is an eigenstate of $\widehat{U}_{f(\mathbf{x})}$ with eigenvalue $(-1)^{f(\mathbf{x})}$.

The circuit for the Deutsch–Jozsa algorithm is shown in Figure 6.10.

Notice the similarity between the circuit for the Deutsch algorithm, and the circuit for the Deutsch–Jozsa algorithm. In place of a simple 1-qubit Hadamard gate, we now have tensor products of n 1-qubit Hadamard gates (acting in parallel). This is denoted $H^{\otimes n}$. We use $|0\rangle^{\otimes n}$, or $|\mathbf{0}\rangle$ to denote the state that is the tensor product of n qubits, each in the state $|0\rangle$.

As we did for the Deutsch algorithm, we follow the state through the circuit. Initially the state is

$$|\psi_0\rangle = |0\rangle^{\otimes n}\left(\frac{|0\rangle - |1\rangle}{\sqrt{2}}\right). \tag{6.4.3}$$

Consider the action of an n-qubit Hadamard transformation on the state $|0\rangle^{\otimes n}$:

$$H^{\otimes n}|0\rangle^{\otimes n} = \left(\frac{1}{\sqrt{2}}\right)^n \underbrace{(|0\rangle + |1\rangle) \otimes (|0\rangle + |1\rangle) \otimes \cdots \otimes (|0\rangle + |1\rangle)}_{n}. \tag{6.4.4}$$

By expanding out the tensor product, this can be rewritten as

$$H^{\otimes n}|0\rangle^{\otimes n} = \frac{1}{\sqrt{2^n}} \sum_{\mathbf{x}\in\{0,1\}^n} |\mathbf{x}\rangle. \tag{6.4.5}$$

This is a very common and useful way of writing this state; the n-qubit Hadamard gate acting on the n-qubit state of all zeros gives a superposition of all n-qubit basis states, all with the same amplitude $\frac{1}{\sqrt{2^n}}$ (called an 'equally weighted superposition'). So the state immediately after the first $H^{\otimes n}$ in the Deutsch–Jozsa algorithm is

$$|\psi_1\rangle = \frac{1}{\sqrt{2^n}} \sum_{\mathbf{x}\in\{0,1\}^n} |\mathbf{x}\rangle \left(\frac{|0\rangle - |1\rangle}{\sqrt{2}}\right). \tag{6.4.6}$$

Notice that the query register is now in an equally weighted superposition of all the possible n-bit input strings. Now consider the state immediately after the U_f (equivalently the c-$\widehat{U}_{f(x)}$) gate. The state is

$$\begin{aligned}
|\psi_2\rangle &= \frac{1}{\sqrt{2^n}} U_f \left(\sum_{\mathbf{x}\in\{0,1\}^n} |\mathbf{x}\rangle \left(\frac{|0\rangle - |1\rangle}{\sqrt{2}}\right) \right) \\
&= \frac{1}{\sqrt{2^n}} \sum_{\mathbf{x}\in\{0,1\}^n} (-1)^{f(\mathbf{x})} |\mathbf{x}\rangle \left(\frac{|0\rangle - |1\rangle}{\sqrt{2}}\right)
\end{aligned} \tag{6.4.7}$$

where we have associated the phase shift of $(-1)^{f(\mathbf{x})}$ with the first qubit (recall Section 6.2).

To facilitate our analysis of the state after the interference is completed by the second Hadamard gate, consider the action of the n-qubit Hadamard gate on an n-qubit basis state $|\mathbf{x}\rangle$.

It is easy to verify that the effect of the 1-qubit Hadamard gate on a 1-qubit basis state $|x\rangle$ can be written as

$$H|x\rangle = \frac{1}{\sqrt{2}} \left(|0\rangle + (-1)^x |1\rangle\right) \tag{6.4.8}$$

$$= \frac{1}{\sqrt{2}} \sum_{z\in\{0,1\}} (-1)^{xz} |z\rangle. \tag{6.4.9}$$

Then we can see that the action of the Hadamard transformation on an n-qubit basis state $|\mathbf{x}\rangle = |x_1\rangle|x_2\rangle \ldots |x_n\rangle$ is given by

$$\begin{aligned}
H^{\otimes n}|\mathbf{x}\rangle &= H^{\otimes n}(|x_1\rangle|x_2\rangle \cdots |x_n\rangle) && \tag{6.4.10} \\
&= H|x_1\rangle H|x_2\rangle \cdots H|x_n\rangle && \tag{6.4.11} \\
&= \frac{1}{\sqrt{2}} \left(|0\rangle + (-1)^{x_1}|1\rangle\right) \frac{1}{\sqrt{2}} \left(|0\rangle + (-1)^{x_2}|1\rangle\right) \cdots \frac{1}{\sqrt{2}} \left(|0\rangle + (-1)^{x_n}|1\rangle\right) && \tag{6.4.12}
\end{aligned}$$

$$= \frac{1}{\sqrt{2^n}} \sum_{z_1 z_2 \ldots z_n \in\{0,1\}^n} (-1)^{x_1 z_1 + x_2 z_2 + \cdots + x_n z_n} |z_1\rangle|z_2\rangle \cdots |z_n\rangle. \tag{6.4.13}$$

Exercise 6.4.1 Prove that

$$\left(\frac{|0\rangle + (-1)^{x_1}|1\rangle}{\sqrt{2}}\right)\left(\frac{|0\rangle + (-1)^{x_2}|1\rangle}{\sqrt{2}}\right)\cdots\left(\frac{|0\rangle + (-1)^{x_n}|1\rangle}{\sqrt{2}}\right) \quad (6.4.14)$$

$$= \frac{1}{\sqrt{2^n}} \sum_{z_1 z_2 \ldots z_n \in \{0,1\}^n} (-1)^{x_1 z_1 + x_2 z_2 + \cdots + x_n z_n}|z_1\rangle|z_2\rangle\cdots|z_n\rangle. \quad (6.4.15)$$

The above equation above can be written more succinctly as

$$H^{\otimes n}|\mathbf{x}\rangle = \frac{1}{\sqrt{2^n}} \sum_{\mathbf{z}\in\{0,1\}^n} (-1)^{\mathbf{x}\cdot\mathbf{z}}|\mathbf{z}\rangle \quad (6.4.16)$$

where $\mathbf{x} \cdot \mathbf{z}$ denotes the bitwise inner product of $\mathbf{x}$ and $\mathbf{z}$, modulo 2 (we are able to reduce modulo 2 since $(-1)^2 = 1$). Note that addition modulo 2 is the same as the XOR operation. The state after the final n-qubit Hadamard gate in the Deutsch–Jozsa algorithm is

$$|\psi_3\rangle = \left(\frac{1}{\sqrt{2^n}} \sum_{\mathbf{x}\in\{0,1\}^n} (-1)^{f(\mathbf{x})} \frac{1}{\sqrt{2^n}} \sum_{\mathbf{z}\in\{0,1\}^n} (-1)^{\mathbf{x}\cdot\mathbf{z}}|\mathbf{z}\rangle\right)\left(\frac{|0\rangle - |1\rangle}{\sqrt{2}}\right)$$

$$= \frac{1}{2^n} \sum_{\mathbf{z}\in\{0,1\}^n} \left(\sum_{\mathbf{x}\in\{0,1\}^n} (-1)^{f(\mathbf{x})+\mathbf{x}\cdot\mathbf{z}}\right)|\mathbf{z}\rangle \left(\frac{|0\rangle - |1\rangle}{\sqrt{2}}\right). \quad (6.4.17)$$

At the end of the algorithm a measurement of the first register is made in the computational basis (just as was done for the Deutsch algorithm). To see what happens, consider the total amplitude (coefficient) of $|\mathbf{z}\rangle = |0\rangle^{\otimes n}$ in the first register of state $|\psi_3\rangle$. This amplitude is

$$\frac{1}{2^n} \sum_{\mathbf{x}\in\{0,1\}^n} (-1)^{f(\mathbf{x})}. \quad (6.4.18)$$

Consider this amplitude in the two cases: f constant and f balanced. If f is constant, the amplitude of $|0\rangle^{\otimes n}$ is either $+1$ or -1 (depending on what value $f(x)$ takes). So if f is constant, a measurement of the first register is *certain to return all 0s* (by 'all 0s' we mean the binary string $00\cdots0$). On the other hand, if f is balanced, then it is easy to see that the positive and negative contributions of the amplitudes cancel, and the overall amplitude of $|0\rangle^{\otimes n}$ is 0. So if f is balanced, a measurement of the first register *is certain not to return all 0s*. So to determine whether f is constant or balanced, the first register is measured. If the result of the measurement is all 0s, then the algorithm outputs 'constant', and otherwise it outputs 'balanced'.

Exercise 6.4.2

(a) Show that a probabilistic classical algorithm making 2 evaluations of f can with probability at least $\frac{2}{3}$ correctly determine whether f is constant or balanced.

Hint: Your guess does not need to be a deterministic function of the results of the two queries. Your result should not assume any particular a priori probabilities of having a constant or balanced function.

(b) Show that a probabilistic classical algorithm that makes $O(n)$ queries can with probability at least $1 - \frac{1}{2^n}$ correctly determine whether f is constant or balanced.

Hint: Use the Chernoff bound (Appendix A.1).

It is worth noting that although deterministic classical algorithms would require $2^{n-1} + 1$ queries in the worst case (compared to only 1 query for this quantum algorithm), as shown in Exercise 6.4.2, a probabilistic classical algorithm could solve the Deutsch–Jozsa problem with probability of error at most $\frac{1}{3}$ using 2 queries. The probability of error can be reduced to less than $\frac{1}{2^n}$ with only $n + 1$ queries. So although there is an exponential gap between deterministic classical and 'exact' quantum query complexity (see Definitions 9.4.1. and 9.4.2), the gap between classical probabilistic query complexity and the quantum computational query complexity is constant in the case of constant error, and can be amplified to a linear gap in the case of exponentially small error. The next section gives one of the first examples where a quantum algorithm can solve a problem with a polynomial number of queries, where any classical algorithm would require an exponential number of queries even to succeed with bounded error.

6.5   Simon's Algorithm

Consider a function $f \colon \{0,1\}^n \to X$, for some finite set X, where we have the promise that there is some 'hidden' string $\mathbf{s} = s_1 s_2 \ldots s_n$ so that $f(\mathbf{x}) = f(\mathbf{y})$ if and only if $\mathbf{x} = \mathbf{y}$ or $\mathbf{x} = \mathbf{y} \oplus \mathbf{s}$. In this section we will treat the domain $\{0,1\}^n$ of f as the vector space[1] Z_2^n over Z_2 (in general, one can treat it as additive group). For convenience, we will assume that $X \subseteq \{0,1\}^n$.

---

[1] To avoid potential confusion, it is worth pointing out that we are talking about two different types of vector spaces. On the one hand, we are referring to the vector space Z_2^n over Z_2, which consists of n-tuples of 0s and 1s. This vector space has dimension n since it can be generated by the n linearly independent vectors consisting of n-tuples with exactly one 1 in the kth position, for $k = 1, 2, \ldots n$. The quantum algorithm is executed in a complex vector (i.e. Hilbert) space whose basis elements are labelled by the elements of the vector space Z_2^n. This Hilbert space has dimension 2^n.

Simon's Problem

Input: A black-box for computing an unknown function $f : \{0,1\}^n \to X$, where X is some finite set.
Promise: There exists a string $\mathbf{s} = s_1 s_2 \ldots s_n$ so that $f(\mathbf{x}) = f(\mathbf{y})$ if and only if $\mathbf{x} = \mathbf{y}$ or $\mathbf{x} = \mathbf{y} \oplus \mathbf{s}$.
Problem: Determine the string $\mathbf{s}$ by making queries to f.

Simon's problem requires an exponential number of queries on a classical computer.

Theorem 6.5.1 *Any classical algorithm that solves this problem with probability at least $\frac{2}{3}$ for any such f must evaluate f a number of times in $\Omega(2^{n/3})$.*

Before we describe Simon's algorithm, let us make another observation about the n-qubit Hadamard transformation. We already saw that

$$H^{\otimes n}|\mathbf{x}\rangle = \frac{1}{\sqrt{2^n}} \sum_{\mathbf{z} \in \{0,1\}^n} (-1)^{\mathbf{x} \cdot \mathbf{z}} |\mathbf{z}\rangle. \tag{6.5.1}$$

What happens when we apply $H^{\otimes n}$ to a superposition of two basis states, say $|\mathbf{0}\rangle + |\mathbf{s}\rangle$?

$$H^{\otimes n}\left(\frac{1}{\sqrt{2}}|\mathbf{0}\rangle + \frac{1}{\sqrt{2}}|\mathbf{s}\rangle\right) = \frac{1}{\sqrt{2^{n+1}}} \sum_{\mathbf{z} \in \{0,1\}^n} |\mathbf{z}\rangle + \frac{1}{\sqrt{2^{n+1}}} \sum_{\mathbf{z} \in \{0,1\}^n} (-1)^{\mathbf{s} \cdot \mathbf{z}} |\mathbf{z}\rangle$$

$$\tag{6.5.2}$$

$$= \frac{1}{\sqrt{2^{n+1}}} \sum_{\mathbf{z} \in \{0,1\}^n} (1 + (-1)^{\mathbf{s} \cdot \mathbf{z}})|\mathbf{z}\rangle. \tag{6.5.3}$$

Note that if $\mathbf{s} \cdot \mathbf{z} = 1$ we have $1 + (-1)^{\mathbf{s} \cdot \mathbf{z}} = 0$ and the basis state $|\mathbf{z}\rangle$ vanishes in the above superposition, and otherwise, $|\mathbf{z}\rangle$ remains with amplitude $\frac{1}{\sqrt{2^{n-1}}}$. Let us define $\mathbf{s}^\perp = \{\mathbf{z} \in \{0,1\}^n | \mathbf{s} \cdot \mathbf{z} = 0\}$. Note that $\mathbf{s}^\perp$ is the vector subspace of Z_2^n that is orthogonal to the subspace $S = \{\mathbf{0}, \mathbf{s}\}$, also called the 'orthogonal complement of S' and denoted $S^\perp$. This implies that the $\dim(S) + \dim(S^\perp) = \dim(Z_2^n) = n$, and thus $\mathbf{s}^\perp$ has dimension $n - 1$.

$$H^{\otimes n}\left(\frac{1}{\sqrt{2}}|\mathbf{0}\rangle + \frac{1}{\sqrt{2}}|\mathbf{s}\rangle\right) = \frac{1}{\sqrt{2^{n-1}}} \sum_{\mathbf{z} \in \{\mathbf{s}\}^\perp} |\mathbf{z}\rangle. \tag{6.5.4}$$

Exercise 6.5.1 Let $\mathbf{x}, \mathbf{y} \in \{0,1\}^n$ and let $\mathbf{s} = \mathbf{x} \oplus \mathbf{y}$. Show that

$$H^{\otimes n}\left(\frac{1}{\sqrt{2}}|\mathbf{x}\rangle + \frac{1}{\sqrt{2}}|\mathbf{y}\rangle\right) = \frac{1}{\sqrt{2^{n-1}}} \sum_{\mathbf{z} \in \{\mathbf{s}\}^\perp} (-1)^{\mathbf{x} \cdot \mathbf{z}} |\mathbf{z}\rangle. \tag{6.5.5}$$

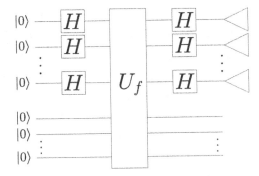

Fig. 6.11 A circuit for the quantum part of Simon's algorithm. The measured bit values correspond to a string $\mathbf{w}_i$ from $\mathbf{s}^{\perp}$.

In Exercise 6.5.1, we see how the Hadamard gate maps $\frac{1}{\sqrt{2}}|\mathbf{x}\rangle + \frac{1}{\sqrt{2}}|\mathbf{x} \oplus \mathbf{s}\rangle$ to a uniform superposition of states $\mathbf{z} \in \mathbf{s}^{\perp}$. This is the main ingredient to analysing the following algorithms for solving Simon's problem.

We assume that we have the following reversible black-box for implementing f:

$$U_f : |\mathbf{x}\rangle|\mathbf{b}\rangle \longmapsto |\mathbf{x}\rangle|\mathbf{b} \oplus f(\mathbf{x})\rangle.$$

Simon's algorithm is illustrated in Figure 6.11, and performs the following operations.

Algorithm for Simon's Problem

1. Set a counter $i = 1$.
2. Prepare $\frac{1}{\sqrt{2^n}} \sum_{\mathbf{x} \in \{0,1\}^n} |\mathbf{x}\rangle|\mathbf{0}\rangle$.
3. Apply U_f, to produce the state

$$\sum_{\mathbf{x} \in \{0,1\}^n} |\mathbf{x}\rangle|f(\mathbf{x})\rangle.$$

4. (optional[2]) Measure the second register.
5. Apply $H^{\otimes n}$ to the first register.
6. Measure the first register and record the value $\mathbf{w}_i$.
7. If the dimension of the span of $\{\mathbf{w}_i\}$ equals $n - 1$, then go to Step 8, otherwise increment i and go to Step 2.
8. Solve the linear equation $\mathbf{W}\mathbf{s}^T = \mathbf{0}^T$ and let $\mathbf{s}$ be the unique non-zero solution.
9. Output $\mathbf{s}$.

---

[2]This step is unnecessary, but can be helpful with the analysis.

Note that $\{0,1\}^n$ can be partitioned into 2^{n-1} pairs of strings of the form $\{\mathbf{x}, \mathbf{x} \oplus \mathbf{s}\}$ (in group theory language, these are the cosets of the subgroup $\{\mathbf{0}, \mathbf{s}\}$ in the additive group Z_2^n). Let I be a subset of $\{0,1\}^n$ consisting of one representative from each of these pairs (in group theory language, these are coset representatives of the cosets of $\{\mathbf{0}, \mathbf{s}\}$).

Note that the state in Step 3 can be rewritten as

$$\frac{1}{\sqrt{2^{n-1}}} \sum_{\mathbf{x} \in I} \frac{1}{\sqrt{2}} (|\mathbf{x}\rangle + |\mathbf{x} \oplus \mathbf{s}\rangle)|f(\mathbf{x})\rangle. \tag{6.5.6}$$

Thus, after we measure the 2nd register in Step 4 to obtain some value $f(\mathbf{x})$, the first register will be left in the superposition $\frac{1}{\sqrt{2}}(|\mathbf{x}\rangle + |\mathbf{x} \oplus \mathbf{s}\rangle)$. Exercise 6.5.1 shows that after the Hadamard transformation in Step 5, the first register will be in an equally weighted superposition of elements of $\mathbf{s}^\perp$. Thus the values $\mathbf{w}_i$ measured in Step 6 will be elements of $\mathbf{s}^\perp$ selected uniformly at random. This means that when in Step 7 the dimension of the span of the $\{\mathbf{w}_i\}$ equals $n-1$, then $\mathbf{span}\{\mathbf{w}_i\} = \mathbf{s}^\perp$. It follows that $\mathbf{0}$ and $\mathbf{s}$ are the only solutions to the linear equation in Step 8, which can be found by Gaussian elimination modulo 2 in time polynomial in n.

Exercise 6.5.2 We have defined $\mathbf{s}^\perp$, but more generally we can let S be a vector subspace of Z_2^n, and define $S^\perp = \{\mathbf{t} \in Z_2^n | \mathbf{t} \cdot \mathbf{s} = 0 \text{ for all } \mathbf{s} \in S\}$. So our previously defined $\mathbf{s}^\perp$ corresponds to $S^\perp$ where $S = \{\mathbf{0}, \mathbf{s}\}$ is the 2-dimensional vector space spanned by $\mathbf{s}$.

(a) Define $|S\rangle = \sum_{\mathbf{s} \in S} \frac{1}{\sqrt{2^m}} |\mathbf{s}\rangle$. Prove that $H^{\otimes n}|S\rangle = \sum_{\mathbf{w} \in S^\perp} \frac{1}{\sqrt{2^{n-m}}} |\mathbf{w}\rangle$.

(b) For any $\mathbf{y} \in \{0,1\}^n$ define $|\mathbf{y} + S\rangle = \sum_{\mathbf{s} \in S} \frac{1}{\sqrt{2^m}} |\mathbf{s}\rangle$. What is $H^{\otimes n}|\mathbf{y} + S\rangle$?

Exercise 6.5.3 Let W be a vector subspace of $\{0,1\}^n$ of dimension m.

Let $\mathbf{w}_1, \mathbf{w}_2, \ldots$ be a sequence of elements of W selected uniformly at random. Let V_i be the subspace spanned by $\mathbf{w}_1, \mathbf{w}_2, \ldots, \mathbf{w}_i$.

Define X_j to be the random variable denoting the lowest index i where V_i has dimension j. So X_m denotes the lowest index i where V_i has dimension m and therefore $V_i = W$.

Show that the expected value of X_m is less than $m+1$.

Hint: Define $Y_1 = X_1$, and $Y_j = X_j - X_{j-1}$ for $j > 1$, and note that $X_j = Y_1 + Y_2 + \ldots + Y_j$.

As shown in Exercise 6.5.3, the expected number of samples from $\mathbf{s}^\perp$ before the algorithm stops is less than $m + 1 = n$.

Theorem 6.5.2 *The above algorithm finds the hidden string* s *in Simon's Problem. The expected number of evaluations of f in the execution of the algorithm is less than n, and the expected number of other elementary gates is in $O(n^3)$.*

One might not be so satisfied with a polynomial *expected* running time; however, if one is willing to accept a small probability of not getting an answer, then we also have a polynomial worst-case running time. This is because one can generically convert an algorithm with expected running time T into one with a definite running time in $O(T)$ and with a bounded probability of successfully outputting an answer. We call this type of algorithm a 'zero-error' algorithm since when it does provide an answer, it is always correct.

It follows from Markov's inequality that any algorithm that terminates with an expected number of queries equal to T will terminate after at most $3T$ queries, with probability at least $\frac{2}{3}$ (see Appendix A.1). This means that if we simply abandon Simon's algorithm if it has not stopped after $3n$ queries, then with probability at least $\frac{2}{3}$ the algorithm will successfully solve Simon's problem. For any particular algorithm, it might be possible to do better than what Markov's inequality provides. For example, a more careful analysis shows that $n + 3$ uniformly random samples from $s^\perp$ will generate $s^\perp$ with probability at least $\frac{2}{3}$ (see A.3). We can thus alternatively describe the following zero-error version of Simon's algorithm that has a bounded running time.

Zero-Error Algorithm for Simon's Problem

1. Set a counter $i = 1$.
2. Prepare $\frac{1}{\sqrt{2^n}} \sum_{\mathbf{x} \in \{0,1\}^n} |\mathbf{x}\rangle |\mathbf{0}\rangle$.
3. Apply U_f, to produce the state

$$\sum_{\mathbf{x} \in \{0,1\}^n} |\mathbf{x}\rangle |f(\mathbf{x})\rangle.$$

4. (optional)[3] Measure the second register.
5. Apply $H^{\otimes n}$ to the first register.
6. Measure the first register and record the value $\mathbf{w}_i$.
7. If $i = n + 3$ then go to Step 8, otherwise increment i and go to Step 2.
8. Solve the linear system $\mathbf{W}\mathbf{s}^T = \mathbf{0}^T$, and let $\mathbf{s}_1, \mathbf{s}_2, \ldots$ be the generators of the solution space.
9. If the solution space has dimension 1, spanned by $\mathbf{s}_1$, output $\mathbf{s} = \mathbf{s}_1$. Otherwise, output 'FAILURE'.

Theorem 6.5.3 *The above algorithm solves Simon's problem with probability at least $\frac{2}{3}$ using $n + O(1)$ evaluations of f and $O(n^3)$ other elementary operations.*

---

[3]This step is unnecessary, but can be helpful with the analysis.

One can naturally generalize Simon's problem to the following.

Generalized Simon's Problem

Input: A black-box U_f, implementing some $f: \{0,1\}^n \to X$, where X is some finite set.
Promise: $f(\mathbf{x}) = f(\mathbf{y})$ if and only if $\mathbf{x} - \mathbf{y} \in S$ for some subspace $S \leq Z_2^n$.
Problem: Find a basis $\mathbf{s}_1, \mathbf{s}_2, \ldots, \mathbf{s}_m$ for S (where m is the dimension of the subspace S).

The algorithm for solving the generalized Simon's problem is essentially the same as the algorithm for Simon's problem. Note that if $S = \{\mathbf{0}, \mathbf{x}_1, \ldots, \mathbf{x}_{2^m-1}\}$ is an m-dimensional subspace of $Z_2^n = \{0,1\}^n$ over Z_2, then the set $\{0,1\}^n$ can be partitioned into 2^{n-m} subsets of the form $\{\mathbf{y}, \mathbf{y} \oplus \mathbf{x}_1, \mathbf{y} \oplus \mathbf{x}_2, \ldots, \mathbf{y} \oplus \mathbf{x}_{2^m-1}\}$ (which we often denote by $\mathbf{y} + S$). Let I be a subset of $\{0,1\}^n$ consisting of one representative from each of these 2^{n-m} disjoint subsets. Thus in Step 3, we can see that we have the state

$$\sum_{\mathbf{x}\in\{0,1\}^n} |\mathbf{x}\rangle|f(\mathbf{x})\rangle = \frac{1}{\sqrt{2^{n-m}}} \sum_{\mathbf{y}\in I} |\mathbf{y} + S\rangle|f(\mathbf{y})\rangle \tag{6.5.7}$$

where (as in Exercise 6.5.2) we define $|\mathbf{y} + S\rangle = \sum_{\mathbf{s}\in S} \frac{1}{\sqrt{2^m}}|\mathbf{s}\rangle$. Thus, after we measure the second register in Step 4, the first register is left in a state of the form $|\mathbf{y}+S\rangle$ for a random $\mathbf{y}$. In Exercise 6.5.2 we see that after applying the Hadamard transformation in Step 5, the first register contains a uniform superposition of elements of $S^\perp$. Thus the measurement of the first register in Step 6 results in a value $\mathbf{w}_i$ sampled uniformly at random from $S^\perp$. The only part of the algorithm that changes slightly is the last three steps.

If we know the dimension m of S, then we know that $S^\perp$ has dimension $n - m$, and we could substitute Steps 7, 8, and 9 in the first algorithm for Simon's problem with

7'. If the dimension of the span of $\{\mathbf{w}_i\}$ equals $n - m$, then go to Step 8, otherwise increment i and go to step 2.

8'. Solve the linear equation $\mathbf{W}\mathbf{s}^T = \mathbf{0}^T$ and let $\mathbf{s}_1, \mathbf{s}_2, \ldots, \mathbf{s}_m$ be generators of the solution space.

9'. Output $\mathbf{s}_1, \mathbf{s}_2, \ldots, \mathbf{s}_m$.

Theorem 6.5.4 *The modified algorithm described above solves the generalized Simon's problem when the dimension m of S is given. The expected number of evaluations of f in the execution of the algorithm is less than $n - m + 1$, and $O(n^3)$ other elementary operations are used.*

When we do not know m, we still know that whatever m is, that $m + 4$ samples suffice in order to generate $S^\perp$ with probability at least $\frac{2}{3}$, and thus $n + 4$ samples are certainly adequate. Thus for the generalized Simon's problem, we can run the zero-error algorithm for Simon's problem, with the following replacements:

7″. If $i = n + 4$ then go to Step 8, otherwise increment i and go to Step 2.

8″. Solve the linear equation $\mathbf{W}\mathbf{s}^T = \mathbf{0}^T$ and let $\mathbf{s}_1, \mathbf{s}_2, \ldots$ be generators of the solution space.

9″. Evaluate $f(\mathbf{0}), f(\mathbf{s}_1), f(\mathbf{s}_2), \ldots$. If the outputs all equal $f(\mathbf{0})$, then output $\mathbf{s}_1, \mathbf{s}_2, \ldots, \mathbf{s}_m$. Otherwise, output 'FAILURE'.

The following Theorem is proved in Appendix A.3.

Theorem 6.5.5 *The subspace $\langle \mathbf{w}_1, \mathbf{w}_2, \ldots, \mathbf{w}_{n+4} \rangle$ spanned by the $\mathbf{w}_i$ obtained in the modified zero-error algorithm for Simon's problem is a subspace of $S^{\perp}$. With probability at least $\frac{2}{3}$, we have $\langle \mathbf{w}_1, \mathbf{w}_2, \ldots, \mathbf{w}_{n+4} \rangle = S^{\perp}$.*

Corollary 6.5.6 *The hidden subspace S of f is contained in the span of $\mathbf{s}_1, \mathbf{s}_2, \ldots$. With probability at least $\frac{2}{3}$ we have $S = \langle \mathbf{s}_1, \mathbf{s}_2, \ldots \rangle$.*

Note that we can test if $f(\mathbf{s}_i) = 0$ for all i, and thus we can test if $S = \langle \mathbf{s}_1, \mathbf{s}_2, \ldots \rangle$ with $n + O(1)$ evaluations of f.

Theorem 6.5.7 *The modified algorithm described above is zero-error and solves the generalized Simon's problem with probability at least $\frac{2}{3}$ and uses $n - m + O(1)$ evaluations of f and $O(n^3)$ other elementary operations.*

It is worth noting that, since we never use the measurement outcome in Step 4, then that measurement step is not actually necessary (recall Exercise 3.5.4). It is included solely for the sake of helping analyse the algorithm.

If we view this problem in the language of group theory, the group S is usually called the 'hidden subgroup', as we describe in more detail in Section 7.5. We will see later in the next section how replacing Z_2^n with the group of integers Z gives us a problem that allows us to efficiently factor large integers.

7

ALGORITHMS WITH SUPERPOLYNOMIAL SPEED-UP

In this chapter we examine one of two main classes of algorithms: quantum algorithms that solve problems with a complexity that is superpolynomially less than the complexity of the best-known classical algorithm for the same problem. That is, the complexity of the best-known classical algorithm cannot be bounded above by any polynomial in the complexity of the quantum algorithm. The algorithms we will detail all make use of the quantum Fourier transform (QFT).

We start off the chapter by studying the problem of quantum phase estimation, which leads us naturally to the QFT. Section 7.1 also looks at using the QFT to find the period of periodic states, and introduces some elementary number theory that is needed in order to post-process the quantum algorithm. In Section 7.2, we apply phase estimation in order to estimate eigenvalues of unitary operators. Then in Section 7.3, we apply the eigenvalue estimation algorithm in order to derive the quantum factoring algorithm, and in Section 7.4 to solve the discrete logarithm problem. In Section 7.5, we introduce the hidden subgroup problem which encompasses both the order finding and discrete logarithm problem as well as many others. This chapter by no means exhaustively covers the quantum algorithms that are superpolynomially faster than any known classical algorithm, but it does cover the most well-known such algorithms. In Section 7.6, we briefly discuss other quantum algorithms that appear to provide a superpolynomial advantage.

7.1 Quantum Phase Estimation and the Quantum Fourier Transform

To introduce the idea of phase estimation, we begin by noting that the final Hadamard gate in the Deutsch algorithm, and the Deutsch–Jozsa algorithm, was used to get at information encoded in the relative phases of a state. The Hadamard gate is self-inverse and thus does the opposite as well, namely it can be used to encode information into the phases. To make this concrete, first consider H acting on the basis state $|x\rangle$ (where $x \in \{0,1\}$). It is easy to see that

$$H|x\rangle = \frac{1}{\sqrt{2}}|0\rangle + \frac{(-1)^x}{\sqrt{2}}|1\rangle \qquad (7.1.1)$$

$$= \frac{1}{\sqrt{2}} \sum_{y \in \{0,1\}} (-1)^{xy}|y\rangle. \qquad (7.1.2)$$

You can think about the Hadamard gate as having *encoded* information about the value of x into the relative phases between the basis states $|0\rangle$ and $|1\rangle$. The Hadamard gate is self-inverse, and so applying it to the state on the right side of Equation (7.1.2) we get $|x\rangle$ back again:

$$H\left(\frac{1}{\sqrt{2}}|0\rangle + \frac{(-1)^x}{\sqrt{2}}|1\rangle\right) = |x\rangle. \qquad (7.1.3)$$

Here the Hadamard gate can be thought of as *decoding* the information about the value of x that was encoded in the phases.

More generally, consider $H^{\otimes n}$ acting on the n-qubit basis state $|\mathbf{x}\rangle$, which we saw in Section 6.4 is:

$$H^{\otimes n}|\mathbf{x}\rangle = \frac{1}{\sqrt{2^n}} \sum_{\mathbf{y} \in \{0,1\}^n} (-1)^{\mathbf{x}\cdot\mathbf{y}}|\mathbf{y}\rangle. \qquad (7.1.4)$$

We can think about the n-qubit Hadamard transformation as having encoded information about the value of $\mathbf{x}$ into the phases $(-1)^{\mathbf{x}\cdot\mathbf{y}}$ of the basis states $|\mathbf{y}\rangle$. If we apply $H^{\otimes n}$ to this state we get $|\mathbf{x}\rangle$ back again:

$$H^{\otimes n}\frac{1}{\sqrt{2^n}} \sum_{\mathbf{y} \in \{0,1\}^n} (-1)^{\mathbf{x}\cdot\mathbf{y}}|\mathbf{y}\rangle = H^{\otimes n}\left(H^{\otimes n}|\mathbf{x}\rangle\right) \qquad (7.1.5)$$

$$= \left(H^{\otimes n}H^{\otimes n}\right)|\mathbf{x}\rangle \qquad (7.1.6)$$

$$= \mathbb{I}|\mathbf{x}\rangle \qquad (7.1.7)$$

$$= |\mathbf{x}\rangle. \qquad (7.1.8)$$

The n-qubit Hadamard gate here can be thought of as decoding the information about the value of $\mathbf{x}$ that was encoded in the phases.

Exercise 7.1.1 (Bernstein–Vazirani problem) Show how to find $\mathbf{a} \in Z_2^n$ given one application of a black box that maps $|\mathbf{x}\rangle|b\rangle \mapsto |\mathbf{x}\rangle|b \oplus \mathbf{x} \cdot \mathbf{a}\rangle$, for some $b \in \{0,1\}$.

Of course, $(-1)^{\mathbf{x}\cdot\mathbf{y}}$ are phases of a very particular form. In general, a phase is a complex number of the form $e^{2\pi i\omega}$, for any real number $\omega \in (0,1)$. The phase

-1 corresponds to $\omega = \frac{1}{2}$. The n-qubit Hadamard transformation is not able to fully access information that is encoded in more general ways. In this section we explore how to generalize the Hadamard gate to allow the determination of information encoded in phases in another special way.

Suppose we are given a state

$$\frac{1}{\sqrt{2^n}} \sum_{y=0}^{2^n-1} e^{2\pi i \omega y} |y\rangle, \qquad (7.1.9)$$

where $\omega \in (0,1)$. Previously we had considered the n-bit string $\mathbf{y}$ as an n-tuple of binary values, but now we consider the n-bit strings to be integers from 0 to $2^n - 1$. When we write $|y\rangle$, it is understood that we are referring to the basis state labelled by $|\mathbf{y}\rangle$, where $\mathbf{y}$ is the binary encoding of the integer y.

Given the state (7.1.9) above, we might be interested in determining ω. It may not be obvious now why this would be a useful thing to do, but the motivation will become clear later on. For reference, we state the problem below.

Phase Estimation Problem

Input: The state $\frac{1}{\sqrt{2^n}} \sum_{y=0}^{2^n-1} e^{2\pi i \omega y} |y\rangle$.
Problem: Obtain a good estimate of the phase parameter ω.

There is a quantum algorithm for solving the Phase Estimation Problem. It is described below.

We begin by showing you some standard notation for writing the kinds of expressions we will have. First note that ω can be written in binary as

$$\omega = 0.x_1 x_2 x_3 \cdots \qquad (7.1.10)$$

(this means $x_1 \cdot 2^{-1} + x_2 \cdot 2^{-2} + x_3 \cdot 2^{-3} + \cdots$).

Similarly, we can write power-of-2-multiples of ω as

$$2^k \omega = x_1 x_2 x_3 \cdots x_k . x_{k+1} x_{k+2} \cdots \qquad (7.1.11)$$

and since $e^{2\pi i k} = 1$ for any integer k, we have

$$e^{2\pi i (2^k \omega)} = e^{2\pi i (x_1 x_2 x_3 \cdots x_k . x_{k+1} x_{k+2} \cdots)}$$
$$= e^{2\pi i (x_1 x_2 x_3 \cdots x_k)} e^{2\pi i (0.x_{k+1} x_{k+2} \cdots)}$$
$$= e^{2\pi i (0.x_{k+1} x_{k+2} \cdots)}. \qquad (7.1.12)$$

Let us begin considering how to use a quantum circuit to determine ω, given the state $\sum_{y=0}^{2^n-1} e^{2\pi i \omega y} |y\rangle$ as input. If the input is a 1-qubit state(so $n = 1$), and if

$\omega = 0.x_1$, then the state can be written

$$\frac{1}{\sqrt{2}} \sum_{y=0}^{1} e^{2\pi i(0.x_1)y}|y\rangle = \frac{1}{\sqrt{2}} \sum_{y=0}^{1} e^{2\pi i\left(\frac{x_1}{2}\right)y}|y\rangle \qquad (7.1.13)$$

$$= \frac{1}{\sqrt{2}} \sum_{y=0}^{1} e^{\pi i(x_1 y)} \qquad (7.1.14)$$

$$= \frac{1}{\sqrt{2}} \sum_{y=0}^{1} (-1)^{x_1 y}|y\rangle \qquad (7.1.15)$$

$$= \frac{1}{\sqrt{2}} \left(|0\rangle + (-1)^{x_1}|1\rangle\right). \qquad (7.1.16)$$

Recalling Equation (7.1.3) we can use the single-qubit Hadamard gate to determine the value of x_1 (and thus of ω):

$$H\left(\frac{1}{\sqrt{2}}\left(|0\rangle + (-1)^{x_1}|1\rangle\right)\right) = |x_1\rangle. \qquad (7.1.17)$$

Before continuing to determining $\omega = 0.x_1 x_2 \cdots$ for more complicated states, make note of the following very useful identity.

$$\frac{1}{\sqrt{2^n}} \sum_{y=0}^{2^n-1} e^{2\pi i \omega y}|y\rangle = \left(\frac{|0\rangle + e^{2\pi i(2^{n-1}\omega)}|1\rangle}{\sqrt{2}}\right) \otimes \left(\frac{|0\rangle + e^{2\pi i(2^{n-2}\omega)}|1\rangle}{\sqrt{2}}\right) \otimes \cdots$$

$$\cdots \otimes \left(\frac{|0\rangle + e^{2\pi i(\omega)}|1\rangle}{\sqrt{2}}\right)$$

$$= \left(\frac{|0\rangle + e^{2\pi i(0.x_n x_{n+1}\cdots)}|1\rangle}{\sqrt{2}}\right) \otimes \left(\frac{|0\rangle + e^{2\pi i(0.x_{n-1}x_n x_{n+1}\cdots)}|1\rangle}{\sqrt{2}}\right) \otimes \cdots$$

$$\cdots \otimes \left(\frac{|0\rangle + e^{2\pi i(0.x_1 x_2\cdots)}|1\rangle}{\sqrt{2}}\right). \qquad (7.1.18)$$

Exercise 7.1.2 Prove the identity (7.1.18).

Suppose we have the 2-qubit state $\frac{1}{\sqrt{2^2}} \sum_{y=0}^{2^2-1} e^{2\pi i \omega y}|y\rangle$, and suppose that $\omega = 0.x_1 x_2$. Using the above identity, we can then write the state as

$$\frac{1}{\sqrt{2^2}} \sum_{y=0}^{2^2-1} e^{2\pi i(0.x_1 x_2)y}|y\rangle = \left(\frac{|0\rangle + e^{2\pi i(0.x_2)}|1\rangle}{\sqrt{2}}\right) \otimes \left(\frac{|0\rangle + e^{2\pi i(0.x_1 x_2)}|1\rangle}{\sqrt{2}}\right). \qquad (7.1.19)$$

Notice that x_2 can be determined from the first qubit, by applying a Hadamard gate (exactly the same as in the previous example). We still need to determine x_1, and this obviously has to come from the second qubit. If $x_2 = 0$, then the second qubit is in the state $\frac{1}{\sqrt{2}}|0\rangle + e^{2\pi i(0.x_1)}|1\rangle$, and we can determine x_1 using a Hadamard gate (just as we did for x_2). If $x_2 = 1$, however, this will not work, and we will need to do something else first. Define a 1-qubit *phase rotation operator* R_2 by the following matrix (with respect to the computational basis):

$$R_2 = \begin{bmatrix} 1 & 0 \\ 0 & e^{\frac{2\pi i}{2^2}} \end{bmatrix} = \begin{bmatrix} 1 & 0 \\ 0 & e^{2\pi i(0.01)} \end{bmatrix}, \tag{7.1.20}$$

where 0.01 in the exponent is written in base 2 (so $0.01 = 2^{-2}$). The *inverse* of R_2 is

$$R_2^{-1} = \begin{bmatrix} 1 & 0 \\ 0 & e^{-2\pi i(0.01)} \end{bmatrix}. \tag{7.1.21}$$

If $x_2 = 1$, consider the effect of applying R_2^{-1} to the second qubit:

$$R_2^{-1}\left(\frac{|0\rangle + e^{2\pi i(0.x_1 1)}|1\rangle}{\sqrt{2}}\right) = \frac{|0\rangle + e^{2\pi i(0.x_1 1 - 0.01)}|1\rangle}{\sqrt{2}}$$
$$= \frac{|0\rangle + e^{2\pi i(0.x_1)}|1\rangle}{\sqrt{2}}. \tag{7.1.22}$$

After R_2^{-1} is applied, the Hadamard gate can be used to determine x_1. Whether to apply R_2^{-1} to the second qubit before applying the Hadamard gate is determined by whether $x_2 = 1$ or $x_2 = 0$. Recall that after we applied the Hadamard gate to the first qubit, the state of the first qubit became $|x_2\rangle$. So we can use a *controlled*-R_2^{-1} gate on the second qubit, controlled by the state of the first qubit. In summary, for the case of a 2-qubit state with $\omega = 0.x_1 x_2$, the circuit shown in Figure 7.1 solves the Phase Estimation Problem (note that here the 'estimation' is exact).

It is worth noting that the controlled-R gate, for any phase rotation gate R is symmetric with respect to swapping the control and target bits, as illustrated in Figure 7.2. However, it is convenient when doing phase estimation to think of it as being a controlled phase shift.

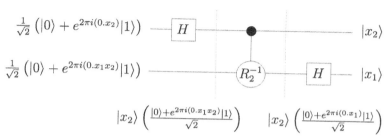

Fig. 7.1 A circuit for the 2-qubit phase estimation algorithm.

Fig. 7.2 A controlled phase shift of $e^{i\phi}$ is symmetric with respect to swapping the control and target bits.

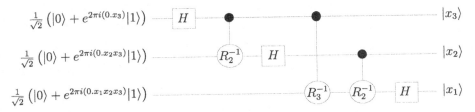

Fig. 7.3 A circuit for the 3-qubit phase estimation algorithm.

The above approach to phase estimation can be generalized. To illustrate this, we give one more example. Suppose we wish to determine $\omega = 0.x_1x_2x_3$ for a 3-qubit state $\frac{1}{\sqrt{2^3}}\sum_{y=0}^{2^3-1} e^{2\pi i(0.x_1x_2x_3)y}|y\rangle$. This state can be written

$$\sum_{y=0}^{2^3-1} e^{2\pi i(0.x_1x_2x_3)y}|y\rangle \tag{7.1.23}$$

$$= \left(\frac{|0\rangle + e^{2\pi i(0.x_3)}|1\rangle}{\sqrt{2}}\right) \otimes \left(\frac{|0\rangle + e^{2\pi i(0.x_2x_3)}|1\rangle}{\sqrt{2}}\right) \otimes \left(\frac{|0\rangle + e^{2\pi i(0.x_1x_2x_3)}|1\rangle}{\sqrt{2}}\right).$$

We define a general 1-qubit phase rotation gate R_k by

$$R_k = \begin{bmatrix} 1 & 0 \\ 0 & e^{\frac{2\pi i}{2^k}} \end{bmatrix}. \tag{7.1.24}$$

The inverse R_k^{-1} has the following effect on the basis states

$$R_k^{-1} : |0\rangle \mapsto |0\rangle$$
$$R_k^{-1} : |1\rangle \mapsto e^{-2\pi i(0.0...01)}|1\rangle, \tag{7.1.25}$$

where the 1 in the exponent is in the kth position.

We argue just as we did for the 2-qubit case above. This time, for the third qubit we have to conditionally 'rotate off' both x_2 and x_3. The circuit in Figure 7.3 implements the phase estimation algorithm for the 3-qubit state (7.1.23). A measurement of the state at the output of the circuit tells us $\omega = 0.x_1x_2x_3$.

It should be clear now how this phase estimation circuit generalizes.

We have only argued that the above phase estimation algorithm works for the n-qubit state $\frac{1}{\sqrt{2^n}}\sum_{y=0}^{2^n-1}e^{2\pi i\omega y}|y\rangle$ when the phase is of the form $\omega = 0.x_1 x_2 \cdots x_n$. That is, we have only seen that the phase estimation algorithm returns x when ω is of the form $\frac{x}{2^n}$, for some integer x. As we shall see in the next section, for *arbitrary* ω, the phase estimation circuit will return x such that $\frac{x}{2^n}$ is closest to ω with high probability (this is why we use the word 'estimation' for this algorithm). So we just have to choose n (i.e. the number of qubits to use for our approximation) so that this estimate is close enough.

Notice that the output of Figure 7.3 is the state $|x\rangle = |x_3 x_2 x_1\rangle$. For the analogous circuit on n qubits estimating a phase of the form $x = 0.x_1 x_2 \ldots x_n$, the output of the circuit would be the state $|x_n \ldots x_2 x_1\rangle$. If we add some gates to reverse the order of the qubits at the end, we have an efficient circuit (with $O(n^2)$ gates) that implements

$$\frac{1}{\sqrt{2^n}}\sum_{y=0}^{2^n-1}e^{2\pi i\frac{x}{2^n}y}|y\rangle \longmapsto |x\rangle. \qquad (7.1.26)$$

Note that in practice we do not actually have to implement the reversal of the order of the qubits; it suffices simply to logically relabel the qubits (in reverse order).

Consider the inverse of (7.1.26):

$$|x\rangle \longmapsto \frac{1}{\sqrt{2^n}}\sum_{y=0}^{2^n-1}e^{2\pi i\frac{x}{2^n}y}|y\rangle. \qquad (7.1.27)$$

Note that this is simply the unitary transformation realized by applying the phase estimation circuit backwards.[1] Equation (7.1.27) bares a strong resemblance to the *discrete Fourier transform*, which appears often in science and engineering. We call Equation (7.1.27) the *Quantum Fourier Transform* (QFT) on n qubits, written QFT_{2^n}. We often just write QFT instead of QFT_{2^n} when the intended meaning is clear. The QFT extends linearly to arbitrary superpositions of basis states.

Since the QFT is the inverse of the phase estimation operation, we have an efficient circuit for performing the QFT (just the phase estimation circuit backwards). For reference, a quantum circuit for the QFT is shown in Figure 7.4.

In general, QFT_m is used to denote the QFT defined on basis states $|0\rangle, |1\rangle, \ldots, |m-1\rangle$ according to

$$\text{QFT}_m : |x\rangle \mapsto \frac{1}{\sqrt{m}}\sum_{y=0}^{m-1}e^{2\pi i\frac{x}{m}y}|y\rangle. \qquad (7.1.28)$$

---

[1] Recall that running or applying a circuit 'backwards' means to replace each gate with its inverse, and run the circuit in reverse order.

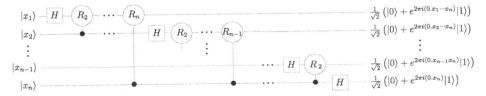

Fig. 7.4 A circuit for the QFT, up to a permutation of the output qubits to reverse their order. Note that in practice, we do not need to physically implement this permutation, but can achieve the desired result by simply logically relabelling the qubits.

Note however that a circuit like that in Figure 7.4 will only implement QFT QFT_m where $m = 2^n$ is a power of 2.

Theorem 7.1.1 *There is a uniform family of circuits $C_{m,T}$ with size polynomial in $\log m$ and $\log T$ that implements QFT_m with error[2] less than $\frac{1}{T}$.*

Also for reference, we state the action of the inverse QFT (denoted QFT_m^{-1}) on the basis states $|0\rangle, |1\rangle, \ldots, |m-1\rangle$:

$$\mathrm{QFT}_m^{-1} : |x\rangle \mapsto \frac{1}{\sqrt{m}} \sum_{y=0}^{m-1} e^{-2\pi i \frac{x}{m} y} |y\rangle. \tag{7.1.29}$$

7.1.1   Error Analysis for Estimating Arbitrary Phases

In our discussion of phase estimation we assumed that ω was of the form $\omega = \frac{x}{2^n}$. The QFT^{-1} then returns the integer x, encoded in binary by an n-qubit state. In this section we examine the error that occurs when ω is not an integer multiple of $\frac{1}{2^n}$.

In general, the QFT^{-1} will output some superposition $|\tilde{\omega}\rangle = \sum_x \alpha_x(\omega)|x\rangle$ which, after the measurement, outputs x with probability $|\alpha_x(\omega)|^2$. The output x corresponds to the estimate $\tilde{\omega} = \frac{x}{2^n}$. We show in this section that with high probability the estimate $\tilde{\omega}$ will be a good estimate of ω. Note that although $\tilde{\omega}$ is a particular value that is output according to a probability distribution, we use $|\tilde{\omega}\rangle$ as shorthand for the superposition of the values x which, when measured, gives a good estimate of ω with high probability. (i.e. $|\tilde{\omega}\rangle$ does not refer to a computational basis state with value '$\tilde{\omega}$'.)

We begin by showing that if we use n qubits, then the phase estimation algorithm returns the integer $\hat{x}$ such that $\frac{\hat{x}}{2^n}$ is the closest integer multiple of $\frac{1}{2^n}$ to ω, with probability at least $\frac{4}{\pi^2}$. (If ω is exactly halfway between two integer multiples of $\frac{1}{2^n}$, the phase estimation algorithm returns each of these with probability at least $\frac{4}{\pi^2}$.) Then we will investigate how many qubits we need to use to ensure

---

[2]Recall the definition of this error in Equation 4.3.1.

that we get ω accurate to n bits, with a probability of error below a prespecified level. To illustrate our discussion, it is convenient to represent phase values on a circle having circumference 1. The value ω (corresponding to the phase parameter $2\pi\omega$) is a real number in the interval $[0, 1)$. We can choose a reference point on the circle to represent the value 0, and count points around the circle counterclockwise, up to the value 1 where we return to the starting point. To represent phase values that can be encoded on an n-qubit quantum computer, we place a dot on the circle at each integer multiple of $\frac{1}{2^n}$. There will be 2^n such dots on the circle. Of course, a real phase parameter ω may not be an integer multiple of $\frac{1}{2^n}$, and so may lie between the dots on the circle. This representation for the phase is illustrated in Figure 7.5.

Suppose the phase being estimated is ω, and let $\hat{\omega}$ be the nearest integer multiple of $\frac{1}{2^n}$ to ω, as shown in Figure 7.6. That is, $\hat{x}$ is chosen as the integer between 0 and $2^n - 1$ such that $\hat{\omega} = \frac{\hat{x}}{2^n}$ is the closest number of this form to ω. If ω is exactly halfway between two numbers of this form, choose $\hat{w} = \frac{\hat{x}}{2^n}$ to be one of the two. For ease of notation, in this section, we will abuse the usual absolute value notation and, for any real numbers $\omega, \tilde{\omega} \in [0, 1)$, we let $|\omega - \tilde{\omega}|$ be such that $2\pi|\omega - \tilde{\omega}|$ is the shortest arclength between $e^{2\pi i \omega}$ and $e^{2\pi i \tilde{\omega}}$ along the unit circle. That is, we will use $|\omega - \tilde{\omega}|$ to denote $\min\{|\omega - \tilde{\omega}|, |\omega - \tilde{\omega} + 1|, |\omega - \tilde{\omega} - 1|\}$.

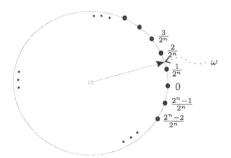

Fig. 7.5 Representation of a phase ω as a point on a circle.

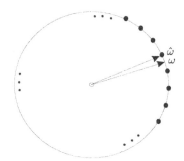

Fig. 7.6 $\hat{\omega} = \frac{\hat{x}}{2^n}$ is the nearest integer multiple of $\frac{1}{2^n}$ to ω.

Our first goal is to show that the phase estimation algorithm returns the integer $\hat{x}$ with probability at least $\frac{4}{\pi^2}$. We begin with a lemma which follows easily by computing a simple geometric sum and recalling that $|1 - e^{i2\theta}| = |e^{-i\theta} - e^{i\theta}| = 2|\sin(\theta)|$.

Lemma 7.1.2 *Let* $\omega = \frac{x}{2^n} = 0.x_1x_2\ldots x_n$ *be some fixed number. The phase estimation algorithm applied to the input state* $|\psi\rangle = \frac{1}{\sqrt{2^n}}\sum_{y=0}^{2^n-1} e^{2\pi i \omega y}|y\rangle$ *outputs the integer* x *with probability:*

$$p(x) = \frac{1}{2^{2n}} \frac{\sin^2\left(\pi(2^n\omega - x)\right)}{\sin^2\left(\pi(\omega - x/2^n)\right)}. \tag{7.1.30}$$

The following lemma will be useful.

Lemma 7.1.3 *If* $|\theta| \le \frac{\pi}{2}$ *then* $\frac{1}{M^2}\frac{\sin^2(M\theta)}{\sin^2(\theta)} \ge \frac{4}{\pi^2}$, *for any* $M \ge 1$.

Together with Lemma 7.1.3, Lemma 7.1.2 implies the following theorem.

Theorem 7.1.4 *Let* $\hat{\omega} = \frac{\hat{x}}{2^n}$ *be an integer multiple of* $\frac{1}{2^n}$ *closest to* ω. *The phase estimation algorithm returns* $\hat{x}$ *with probability at least* $\frac{4}{\pi^2}$.

In other words, with probability at least $\frac{4}{\pi^2}$ the phase estimation algorithm outputs an estimate $\tilde{x}$ such that $|\frac{\tilde{x}}{2^n} - \omega| \le \frac{1}{2^{n+1}}$.

Note that if ω lies exactly in between $\frac{x}{2^n}$ and $\frac{x+1}{2^n}$ (i.e. $\omega = \frac{k}{2^n} + \frac{1}{2^{n+1}}$), then we will measure one of the two closest estimates of ω with probability at least $\frac{8}{\pi^2}$. In fact, this is true for any ω as we summarize in the following theorem.

Theorem 7.1.5 *If* $\frac{x}{2^n} \le \omega \le \frac{x+1}{2^n}$, *then the phase estimation algorithm returns one of* x *or* $x+1$ *with probability at least* $\frac{8}{\pi^2}$.

In other words, with probability at least $\frac{8}{\pi^2}$ the phase estimation algorithm outputs an estimate $\hat{x}$ such that $|\frac{\hat{x}}{2^n} - \omega| \le \frac{1}{2^n}$.

It is easy to verify that with probability at least $1 - \frac{1}{2(k-1)}$, the phase estimation algorithm will output one of the $2k$ closest integer multiples of $\frac{1}{2^n}$ (see Figure 7.7). This implies that with probability at least $1 - \frac{1}{2(k-1)}$, the output $\tilde{\omega}$ of the phase estimation algorithm will satisfy $|\omega - \tilde{\omega}| \le \frac{k}{2^n}$. In other words, in order to obtain an estimate $\tilde{\omega}$ such that with probability at least $1 - \frac{1}{2^m}$ we have $|\tilde{\omega} - \omega| \le \frac{1}{2^r}$, it suffices to do a phase estimation with $n = m + r + 1$. It is worth noting that this algorithm is quite likely to get an estimate that has error much smaller than $\frac{1}{2^r}$. For example, with probability at least $\frac{8}{\pi^2}$ the error will be at most $\frac{1}{2^{r+m}}$. If we only care about having an estimate with error at most $\frac{1}{2^r}$, in Exercise 7.1.3 you will show how to do so using $O(\log r)$ repetitions of the phase estimation

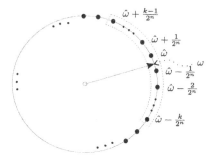

Fig. 7.7 The phase estimation algorithm will output one of the $2k$ closest integer multiples of $\frac{1}{2^n}$ to ω with probability at least $1 - \frac{1}{2(k-1)}$.

algorithm with parameter $n = m$. Depending on the intrinsic cost of computing higher-order phase shifts, this could be a much more efficient algorithm.

Exercise 7.1.3 Prove that $O(\log_2(r))$ phase estimations with $n = m$ and taking the outcome that occurs most often provides an estimate $\tilde{\omega}$ of the phase ω which will with probability at least $1 - \frac{1}{2^r}$ have error $|\omega - \tilde{\omega}| \le \frac{1}{2^m}$.

Hint: Find an upper bound on the probability of obtaining anything other than one of the two closest estimates, and then guarantee that with high probability the outcome is one of the two closest estimates.

Exercise 7.1.4

(a) Give a concise description of the operation performed by the square of the QFT.

(a) What are the eigenvalues of the QFT?

7.1.2   Periodic States

We have studied in detail the behaviour of the QFT (or its inverse) on computational basis states, and on states of the form

$$\sum_x e^{2\pi i \omega x} |x\rangle. \tag{7.1.31}$$

It is also interesting and useful to study behaviour of the QFT on what we often call *periodic* states.

A periodic superposition of states is one of the form

$$|\phi_{r,b}\rangle = \frac{1}{\sqrt{m}} \sum_{z=0}^{m-1} |zr + b\rangle. \tag{7.1.32}$$

We say this state is periodic with *period r*, *shift b*, and m repetitions of the period. Consider the following problem:

Finding the Period a of a Periodic State, Given mr

Input:

- Integer mr
- A black-box generating quantum states

$$|\phi_{r,b}\rangle = \frac{1}{\sqrt{m}} \sum_{z=0}^{m-1} |zr + b\rangle \qquad (7.1.33)$$

where b is chosen uniformly at random from $\{0, 1, \ldots, r-1\}$.
Problem: Find r.

If we measure $|\phi_{r,b}\rangle$ in the computational basis, we get $zr + b$ for some value $z \in \{0, 1, \ldots, m-1\}$ chosen uniformly at random. Since $b \in \{0, 1, \ldots, r-1\}$ is also chosen uniformly at random, the probability of the measurement producing any particular integer $x \in \{0, 1, \ldots, mr-1\}$ is uniformly $\frac{1}{mr}$ and thus this outcome gives us no useful information about the value of r.

Exercise 7.1.5 Prove

$$\mathrm{QFT}_{mr}^{-1}|\phi_{r,b}\rangle = \frac{1}{\sqrt{r}} \sum_{k=0}^{r-1} e^{-2\pi i \frac{b}{r} k} |mk\rangle. \qquad (7.1.34)$$

However, if we apply[3] QFT_{mr}^{-1} to $|\phi_{r,b}\rangle$ then the resulting state is the superposition $\mathrm{QFT}_{mr}^{-1}|\phi_{r,b}\rangle = \frac{1}{\sqrt{r}} \sum_{k=0}^{r-1} e^{-2\pi i \frac{b}{r} k} |mk\rangle$. If we measure this state we will obtain a value $x = mk$ for some random integer k between 0 and $r-1$. Since we know mr, we can compute $\frac{x}{mr} = \frac{k}{r}$ and express it in lowest terms. Note however that if k and r share a non-trivial common factor, the denominator of the reduced fraction for $\frac{x}{mr} = \frac{k}{r}$ will not be r, but rather some divisor of r. For example, suppose $m = 3$, $r = 20$, $x = 24$; in other words, we initially know $mr = 60$, and measuring $\mathrm{QFT}_{60}^{-1}|\phi_{r,b}\rangle$ gave us the number $x = 24$. So in this case $\frac{24}{60} = \frac{8}{20}$ and $k = 8$. However, since we only know $mr = 60$ and $x = 24$, we would reduce to lowest terms and obtain $\frac{24}{60} = \frac{2}{5}$. The denominator 5 is a divisor of $r = 20$, but we 'lost' the factor of 4 because 4 was also a factor of $k = 24$.

---

[3]Note that QFT_{mr} would also work. We choose to use QFT_{mr}^{-1} for consistency with the phase estimation algorithm.

One answer to this potential problem is to simply note that with probability in $\Omega(\frac{1}{\log r \log r})$, the integer k will not have a non-trivial common factor with r. Thus we only need to repeat this entire procedure an expected number of times in $O(\log \log r)$ before we find r.

In the next section, we introduce some mathematical notation and elementary techniques that give us a better method for finding r, and will also be useful elsewhere in this chapter.

One important technical question is how to know we have the correct r. In the applications of this period-finding tool we use later, there will be an easy classical means for verifying the correct r. In the example of this section, since each denominator of the reduced fractions will be a divisor of r, then when r should eventually appear in the list, it will be the largest element in the list. Thus our algorithm should output the largest value in the list as the guess for r. In Exercise 7.1.6, we introduce an interesting tool that gives us another way to test if we have the correct value of r (note that we know our guess will be a divisor of r, so to prove it equals r, it suffices to verify that it is also a multiple of r).

Exercise 7.1.6 Suppose you are given the state $|\phi_{r,b}\rangle$ and a candidate r'. Devise a '1-sided' test, which always outputs 0 if r' is a multiple of r, and outputs 1 with probability at least 50% otherwise.

Hint: What happens if we add $r' \mod mr$ to the basis states of $|\phi_{r,b}\rangle$?

For now, let us move on to the case that we do not actually know the product mr, and instead we have the following problem.

Finding the Period of a Periodic State

Input:

- Integer n
- A black-box generating quantum states

$$|\phi_{r,b}\rangle = \sqrt{\frac{1}{m_b}} \sum_{z:0 \le zr+b<2^n} |zr + b\rangle \qquad (7.1.35)$$

where b is chosen from $\{0, 1, \ldots, r-1\}$, and $m_b \approx \frac{2^n}{r}$ is the value that makes the state have norm equal to 1.[4]

Problem: Find r.

---

[4]In order for the state to be normalized, we must have $m_b \equiv |\{z : 0 \le zr + b < 2^n\}| = \lfloor \frac{2^n - b - 1}{r} \rfloor + 1$. This can also be written as $m_b = \frac{2^n - (2^n \mod r)}{r} + 1$ if $0 \le b < (2^n \mod r)$, and $m_b = \frac{2^n - (2^n \mod r)}{r}$ if $(2^n \mod r) \le b < r$.

If we apply $QFT_{2^n}^{-1}$ then with high probability a measurement will give a value x such that $\frac{x}{2^n}$ is close to $\frac{k}{r}$ for a random integer $k \in \{0, 1, 2, \ldots, r\}$. More specifically, we have the following theorem.

Theorem 7.1.6 *Let x be the outcome of measuring $QFT_{2^n}^{-1}|\phi_{r,b}\rangle$. For each value x satisfying*

$$\left| \frac{x}{2^n} - \frac{k}{r} \right| \le \frac{1}{2m_b r} \tag{7.1.36}$$

for some integer k, the probability of obtaining x is at least $\frac{m_b}{2^n} \frac{4}{\pi^2}$.

This theorem can be obtained by computing a simple geometric sum and using Lemma 7.1.3.

The important part about this bound on the error is that as long as $m \ge r$ (it suffices to have $2^n \ge 2r^2$), then $\frac{1}{2m_b r} \le \frac{1}{2r^2}$. This allows us to find the fraction $\frac{k}{r}$ using the continued fractions algorithm.

The continued fractions algorithm is an algorithm that approximates any real number with a sequence of rational approximations. We will summarize the facts about continued fractions that are relevant for this textbook.

Theorem 7.1.7 *Each rational number $\frac{x}{2^n}$ has a sequence of $O(n)$ rational approximations, called convergents, $\frac{a_1}{b_1}, \frac{a_2}{b_2}, \ldots, \frac{a_m}{b_m}$, where $\frac{a_m}{b_m} = \frac{x}{2^n}$, with the following properties:*

- $a_1 < a_2 < \cdots < a_m$, $b_1 < b_2 < \cdots < b_m$.
- *The list of convergents of $\frac{x}{2^n}$ can be computed in time polynomial in n.*
- *If some fraction $\frac{k}{r}$ satisfies*

$$\left| \frac{x}{2^n} - \frac{k}{r} \right| \le \frac{1}{2r^2},$$

then $\frac{k}{r}$ appears in the list of convergents of $\frac{x}{2^n}$.

Note that Theorem 7.1.7 implies that if $2^n \ge 2r^2$ and if we measure one of the two closest estimates of $\frac{k}{r}$, we will be able to recognize which convergent equals $\frac{k}{r}$ (see Exercise 7.1.7).

Exercise 7.1.7 (a) Prove that there can be at most one convergent $\frac{a_i}{b_i} \ne \frac{x}{2^n}$ satisfying $|\frac{x}{2^n} - \frac{a_i}{b_i}| \le \frac{1}{2r^2}$ and $b_i \le r$.

(b) Prove that if $2^n \ge 2r^2$ and $|\frac{x}{2^n} - \frac{k}{r}| \le \frac{1}{2^n}$, then $\frac{a_i}{b_i} = \frac{k}{r}$ will be the only convergent of $\frac{x}{2^n}$ with $b_i \le 2^{\frac{(n-1)}{2}}$.

7.1.3   GCD, LCM, the Extended Euclidean Algorithm

We begin by reviewing some basic definitions from number theory, and then state an algorithm which will be useful for some of the classical reductions we will see in this chapter, in particular for finding r given a close estimate of $\frac{k}{r}$ for random integers k.

Definition 7.1.8 *An integer x is said to divide an integer y, written $x|y$, if there exists another integer z such that $y = xz$.*

Definition 7.1.9 *The greatest common divisor (GCD) of two integers x and y, denoted $GCD(x, y)$, is the largest positive integer z that divides both x and y. In the case that $x = y = 0$, we define $GCD(x, y) = 0$.*

Two numbers x and y are said to be *coprime* or *relatively prime* if the GCD of x and y, denoted $GCD(x, y)$, equals 1.

Definition 7.1.10 *The lowest common multiple (LCM) of two integers x and y, denoted $LCM(x, y)$, is the smallest integer z that is divisible by both x and y.*

A well-known algorithm called the *extended Euclidean algorithm* (EEA) provides an efficient way to compute LCMs and GCDs.

The Extended Euclidean Algorithm

The EEA takes two positive integers $x, y < 2^n$ and outputs three integers $a, b, d < 2^n$ with the following properties:

$$d = GCD(x, y) \tag{7.1.37}$$
$$ax + by = d. \tag{7.1.38}$$

The total running time is in $O(n^2)$.

Corollary 7.1.11 *(EEA): Given non-zero integers x and y, the EEA can be used to efficiently find:*

1. $GCD(x, y)$
2. $LCM(x, y) = \frac{xy}{GCD(x,y)}$
3. *The fraction x/y reduced to lowest terms (i.e. find x_1, y_1 such that $x/y = x_1/y_1$ and $GCD(x_1, y_1) = 1$; note that $x_1 = \frac{x}{GCD(x,y)}$, $y_1 = \frac{y}{GCD(x,y)}$)*
4. *The inverse of x modulo y (assuming $GCD\ (x, y) = 1$).*

Let us return to the problem of finding r given the fraction $\frac{k}{r}$ expressed in lowest terms for an integer $k \in \{0, 1, 2, \ldots, r-1\}$ selected uniformly at random.

Suppose we repeat the procedure to obtain two measurement results x_1 and x_2, such that $\frac{x_1}{mr} = \frac{k_1}{r}$ and $\frac{x_2}{mr} = \frac{k_2}{r}$, for integers k_1, k_2 between 0 and $r-1$ selected uniformly at random.

We can efficiently find integers c_1, r_1, c_2, r_2 with $GCD(c_1, r_1) = GCD(c_2, r_2) = 1$ so that $\frac{k_1}{r} = \frac{c_1}{r_1}$ and $\frac{k_2}{r} = \frac{c_2}{r_2}$. Note that this means that r_1 and r_2 both divide r (i.e. r is a common multiple of r_1 and r_2).

Theorem 7.1.12 *Let r be a positive integer. Suppose the integers k_1 and k_2 are selected independently and uniformly at random from $\{0, 1, \ldots, r-1\}$. Let c_1, r_1, c_2, r_2 be integers so that $GCD(r_1, c_1) = GCD(r_2, c_2) = 1$ and $\frac{k_1}{r} = \frac{c_1}{r_1}$ and $\frac{k_2}{r} = \frac{c_2}{r_2}$.*

Then with probability at least $\frac{6}{\pi^2}$ we have $r = LCM(r_1, r_2)$. Furthermore, the numbers c_1, r_1, c_2, r_2, and r can be computed in time in $O(\log^2 r)$.

7.2 Eigenvalue Estimation

When we looked at the Deutsch algorithm (and similarly the Deutsch–Jozsa and Simon algorithms), we mentioned that we could think of the operator U_f as a controlled operator c-$\widehat{U}_{f(x)}$. We saw that the state $\frac{|0\rangle - |1\rangle}{\sqrt{2}}$ of the target qubit was an eigenvector of $\widehat{U}_f(x)$, with corresponding eigenvalue $(-1)^{f(x)}$, and we showed that we can associate this eigenvalue with the control qubit. We generalize this idea here, and show how we can construct a quantum circuit for estimating eigenvalues of a given multi-qubit unitary operator U.

Consider an n-qubit unitary operator U with eigenvector $|\psi\rangle$ and corresponding eigenvalue $e^{2\pi i \omega}$. Suppose that we have an efficient quantum network for implementing U. Now consider a controlled-U gate (i.e. a circuit for performing the controlled-U operation, which we bundle-up and represent as single 'gate'. Recall Exercise 4.2.7 on how to implement this). Suppose the second (target) register is prepared in the eigenstate $|\psi\rangle$. If the control qubit is in state $|0\rangle$, U is not applied to the qubits of the second register. If the control bit is in the state $|1\rangle$, U is applied. In this case, denoting the controlled-U gate by c-U, we have

$$\text{c-}U|1\rangle|\psi\rangle = |1\rangle U|\psi\rangle$$
$$= |1\rangle e^{2\pi i \omega}|\psi\rangle$$
$$= e^{2\pi i \omega}|1\rangle|\psi\rangle. \tag{7.2.1}$$

This is shown in Figure 7.8.

Suppose the control qubit is prepared in a superposition $\alpha|0\rangle + \beta|1\rangle$. Then the effect of applying the controlled-U is to encode the eigenvalue of U into the relative phase factor between the basis states $|0\rangle$ and $|1\rangle$ in the control qubit's state. As a relative phase, it becomes a measurable quantity (through quantum interference). This effect of encoding the eigenvalue of U into the phase of the control register of a controlled-U operation is illustrated in Figure 7.9.

In this section we are going to apply this idea of encoding eigenvalues in the phases of a control qubit together with the phase estimation algorithm to solve the following problem.

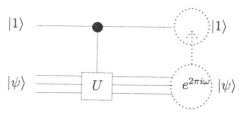

Fig. 7.8 When we analyse the action of the controlled-U on the state $|1\rangle|\psi\rangle$ for an eigenstate $|\psi\rangle$ with eigenvalue $e^{2\pi i\omega}$, the phase shift corresponding to the eigenvalue of U can be associated with the control qubit, since $|1\rangle\left(e^{2\pi i\omega}|\psi\rangle\right) = \left(e^{2\pi i\omega}|1\rangle\right)|\psi\rangle$. That is, the eigenvalue of U on $|\psi\rangle$ can be considered to have been 'kicked back' to the control qubit.

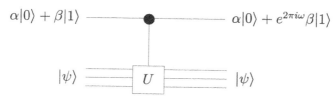

Fig. 7.9 When the control bit is in a superposition of $|0\rangle$ and $|1\rangle$, the $|0\rangle$ component does not pick up a phase of $e^{2\pi i\omega}$, and the $|1\rangle$ component does. Thus the eigenvalue turns up as a relative phase between the $|0\rangle$ and $|1\rangle$ components of the control bit superposition.

Eigenvalue Estimation Problem

Input: A quantum circuit implementing an operator U, and an eigenstate $|\psi\rangle$ with corresponding eigenvalue $e^{2\pi i\omega}$.
Problem: Obtain a good estimate for ω.

Recall that the inverse QFT (which we showed was a good algorithm for phase estimation) allows us to estimate ω given the state

$$\frac{1}{\sqrt{2^n}} \sum_{y=0}^{2^n-1} e^{2\pi i \omega y} |y\rangle \tag{7.2.2}$$

$$= \left(\frac{|0\rangle + e^{2\pi i(2^{n-1}\omega)}|1\rangle}{\sqrt{2}}\right)\left(\frac{|0\rangle + e^{2\pi i(2^{n-2}\omega)}|1\rangle}{\sqrt{2}}\right)\cdots\left(\frac{|0\rangle + e^{2\pi i(\omega)}|1\rangle}{\sqrt{2}}\right). \tag{7.2.3}$$

So if we can devise a quantum circuit that creates this state, we can then use QFT^{-1} to estimate the eigenvalue. To see how this can be done, notice that $|\psi\rangle$

is also an eigenvector of U^2, with corresponding eigenvalue $\left(e^{2\pi i\omega}\right)^2 = e^{2\cdot 2\pi i\omega}$. Similarly, for any integer x, we know that $|\psi\rangle$ is an eigenvector of U^x with corresponding eigenvalue $e^{x\cdot 2\pi i\omega}$. So if we implement a controlled-U^{2^j}, and set the control qubit to $\frac{|0\rangle+|1\rangle}{\sqrt{2}}$, and the target qubit to the eigenstate $|\psi\rangle$, then the result is

$$\text{c-}U^{2^j}\left(\left(\frac{|0\rangle+|1\rangle}{\sqrt{2}}\right)|\psi\rangle\right) = \left(\frac{|0\rangle + e^{2\pi i(2^j\omega)}|1\rangle}{\sqrt{2}}\right)|\psi\rangle. \qquad (7.2.4)$$

With these observations, it is easy to see that the circuit in Figure 7.10 creates the state (7.2.2).

As we have seen, if we now apply the QFT^{-1} to the output of the circuit shown in Figure 7.10, we will obtain a state $|\tilde{\omega}\rangle$, which provides (with high probability) a good estimate of the eigenvalue parameter ω. Therefore, the circuit shown in Figure 7.11 solves the eigenvalue estimation problem.

We have a sequence of controlled-U^{2^k} operations controlled on the kth significant bit x_k of $x = 2^{n-1}x_{n-1} + \ldots + 2x_1 + x_0$, for each of $k = 1, 2, \ldots, n$. It is easy to see that this has the overall effect of applying U a total of x times (exponentiating U). We can write this as a single U^x operator. We therefore define a c-U^x operator that maps

$$\text{c-}U^x : |x\rangle|\phi\rangle \mapsto |x\rangle U^x|\phi\rangle. \qquad (7.2.5)$$

Exercise 7.2.1 Let $N \leq 2^n$. Given $a \in \{2, \ldots, N-2\}$, explain how $a^{2^m} \bmod N$ can be computed in time polynomial in $m + n$, and with space in $O(n)$.

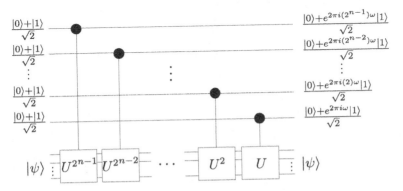

Fig. 7.10 First stage of eigenvalue estimation.

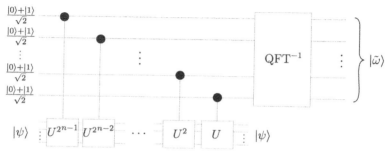

Fig. 7.11 A circuit for eigenvalue estimation. We measure the state $|\tilde{\omega}\rangle$ and obtain a string x corresponding to the binary representation of an integer. Our estimate for ω is $2\pi\frac{x}{2^n}$.

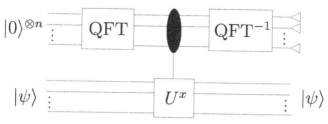

Fig. 7.12 A circuit for estimating the eigenvalue $e^{2\pi i\omega}$ of the operator U on eigenvalue $|\psi\rangle$.

The qubits in the first (control) register can be prepared in the state

$$\left(\frac{|0\rangle + |1\rangle}{\sqrt{2}}\right)\left(\frac{|0\rangle + |1\rangle}{\sqrt{2}}\right)\cdots\left(\frac{|0\rangle + |1\rangle}{\sqrt{2}}\right) \qquad (7.2.6)$$

by starting with the state $|0\rangle^{\otimes n}$, and applying the n-qubit Hadamard transformation $H^{\otimes n}$. We have seen before that the tensor product factors can be expanded out, and the result can be written more concisely as

$$H^{\otimes n}|0\rangle^{\otimes n} = \frac{1}{\sqrt{2^n}}\sum_{x=0}^{2^n-1}|x\rangle. \qquad (7.2.7)$$

It is easy to check from the definition of the QFT that

$$\text{QFT}|0\rangle^{\otimes n} = H^{\otimes n}|0\rangle^{\otimes n} \qquad (7.2.8)$$

and so we can use a QFT in place of a Hadamard gate.

With the above observations, the circuit for eigenvalue estimation can be drawn more concisely as shown in Figure 7.12.

The eigenvalue estimation algorithm implemented by the circuit in Figure 7.12 is summarized below.

Eigenvalue Estimation Algorithm

1. Initialize an n-qubit register to $|0\rangle^{\otimes n}$. Call this the *control register*.
2. Apply the QFT to the control register.
3. Apply c-U^x to the given eigenstate $|\psi\rangle$, controlled on the state of the control register.
4. Apply the QFT^{-1} to the control register.
5. Measure the control register to obtain a string of bits encoding the integer x. Output the value $\frac{x}{2^n}$ as the estimate for ω.

Suppose we apply the eigenvalue estimation circuit with the second register initially in an arbitrary state $|\psi\rangle$ which is not necessarily an eigenvector of the n-qubit operator U. By the spectral theorem (see Section 2.4), the eigenvectors of U form a basis for the 2^n-dimensional vector space on which U acts. This means that any state in this space can be written as a linear combination of the eigenvectors of U. So we have

$$|\psi\rangle = \sum_{j=0}^{2^n-1} \alpha_j |\psi_j\rangle \tag{7.2.9}$$

where $|\psi_j\rangle$ are the eigenvectors of U with corresponding eigenvalues $e^{2\pi i \omega_j}$, for $i = 0, 1, \ldots, 2^n - 1$. We know the eigenvalue estimation algorithm maps $|0\rangle^{\otimes n}|\psi_j\rangle \mapsto |\tilde{\omega}_j\rangle|\psi_j\rangle$. Thus, by linearity, if we apply the eigenvalue estimation circuit with the second register in the state $|\psi\rangle = \sum_{j=0}^{2^n-1} \alpha_j |\psi_j\rangle$, we obtain the superposition

$$\sum_{j=0}^{2^n-1} \alpha_j |\tilde{\omega}_j\rangle|\psi_j\rangle. \tag{7.2.10}$$

This is illustrated in Figure 7.13. We will see this idea applied in the next section.

Note that measuring the first register is equivalent to being given $|\tilde{\omega}_j\rangle|\psi_j\rangle$ with probability $|\alpha_j|^2$ and then measuring the first register.

Recall from Exercise 3.5.4 (a) that measuring the first register and then tracing out (i.e. discarding or ignoring) the second register is equivalent to tracing out

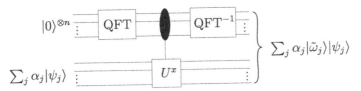

Fig. 7.13 The eigenvalue estimation circuit applied with the second register in the state $|\psi\rangle$, which is a superposition of the eigenstates of U.

the second register before measuring the first register. In Exercise 3.5.4 (b), we verify that tracing out the second system is equivalent to measuring it and then discarding it without revealing the measurement outcome. For convenience, we can therefore assume that the second register was measured in the basis of eigenstates and then traced out. Thus, in the case of the state in Equation 7.2.10, tracing out the second register leaves the first register in the mixture consisting of the state $|\tilde{\omega}_j\rangle$ with probability $|\alpha_j|^2$. This way of describing the state of the first register will be a useful way of analysing many of the algorithms in this chapter.

Exercise 7.2.2

(a) Recall in Section 4.5 it was shown how to implement a parity measurement using a quantum circuit. In Exercise 3.4.4, it was shown how the parity measurement is equivalent to measuring the observable $Z^{\otimes n}$. Describe an alternative algorithm (and draw the corresponding circuit diagram) for measuring the observable $Z \otimes Z \otimes Z$ using one application of a c-$(Z \otimes Z \otimes Z)$ gate.

(b) Consider the observable $M = \sum_i m_i P_i$, where we assume for convenience that $m_i \in \{0, 1, 2, \ldots, N-1\}$. Let $U = e^{\frac{2\pi i}{N} M}$. Describe an algorithm (and draw the corresponding circuit diagram) for measuring the observable M given one application of a c-U^x which maps $|x\rangle|\psi\rangle \mapsto |x\rangle U^x|\psi\rangle$, for $x \in \{0, 1, \ldots, N-1\}$.

7.3   Finding-Orders

7.3.1   The Order-Finding Problem

In the preceding sections we have developed tools that now allow us to describe an algorithm that has been one of the most important developments in the history of quantum computation. This is the quantum factoring algorithm, discovered by Peter Shor in 1994. The *RSA cryptosystem* is a public key protocol widely used in industry and government to encrypt sensitive information. The security of RSA rests on the assumption that it is difficult for computers to factor large numbers. That is, there is no known (classical) computer algorithm for finding the factors of an n-bit number in time that is polynomial in n. If such an algorithm were found, it would undermine the security of RSA. So when Peter Shor discovered that a *quantum* computer *is* capable of factoring large numbers efficiently, this generated much excitement and catalysed industry and government's interest in the potential of quantum computation.

Before we continue to describe this and other similar algorithms in more detail, we include a short section describing some of the relevant mathematics we will be discussing.

7.3.2 Some Mathematical Preliminaries

The *integers mod N* is the set of integers $\{0, 1, \ldots, N-1\}$, which we will denote as $\mathbb{Z}_N$. Two integers s and t are said to be *equivalent mod N* if N divides $s - t$ with zero remainder. In this case we write

$$s \equiv t \pmod{N}. \qquad (7.3.1)$$

Any integer k can be *reduced mod N* by taking the remainder r after division of k by N. In this case we write

$$r = k \bmod N. \qquad (7.3.2)$$

One important property is that if $GCD(a, N) = 1$, then the number 1 will eventually appear in the sequence $a \bmod N$, $a^2 \bmod N$, $a^3 \bmod N, \ldots$ and then the sequence continues to repeat itself in a periodic fashion. This motivates the following definition.

Definition 7.3.1 *Given integers a and N, such that $GCD(a, N) = 1$, the order of a (mod N) is the smallest positive integer r so that $a^r \equiv 1 \pmod{N}$.*

Exercises 7.3.1 and 7.3.2 provide some practice working with modular arithmetic, and prove some basic results.

Exercise 7.3.1

(a) Compute $118 \bmod 5$.

(b) Prove that $xy \bmod N = (x \bmod N)(y \bmod N) \bmod N$.

Exercise 7.3.2

(a) What is the order of 2 mod 5?

(b) What is $2^{2005} \bmod 5$?

(c) What is the order of 2 mod 11?

(d) Let r be the order of 2 mod 55.

   (i) Find r.
   (ii) Find $GCD(55, 2^{\frac{r}{2}} - 1)$ and $GCD(55, 2^{\frac{r}{2}} + 1)$.

If p is prime, then $\mathbb{Z}_p$, with the operations of addition modulo p and multiplication modulo p is a *finite field* or *Galois field* often denoted $\mathbb{F}_p$ or $GF(p)$. If N is not prime, then $\mathbb{Z}_N$ is not a finite field. For any integer N, we let $\mathbb{Z}_N^*$ denote the set of numbers x in $\mathbb{Z}_N$ where x and N are coprime. These are precisely the integers $x \in \{0, 1, 2, \ldots, N-1\}$ for which there exists an integer y with $xy \equiv yx \equiv 1 \pmod{N}$; for each such x, y is unique and is called the *inverse* of x modulo N. We call $\mathbb{Z}_N^*$ (with the operation of multiplication mod N) the *multiplicative group* of the *ring* $\mathbb{Z}_N$.

For every prime power p^m, $m > 1$ there also exists a finite field $\mathbb{F}_{p^m}$ of that order, but it is not equivalent to $\mathbb{Z}_{p^m}$. For most of this introductory textbook, we do not need to work with the more general notions of groups, rings, and fields, and will usually just work with very simple concrete examples of such objects like $\mathbb{Z}_N$. We will just point out that the problems of finding orders and discrete logarithms (to be described in the following sections) can be defined in more general families of *groups* including $\mathbb{F}_{p^m}^*$ (the multiplicative group of the finite field $\mathbb{F}_{p^m}$), $\mathbb{Z}_N^*$, and even very different looking groups like the additive group of points on an elliptic curve (of much use today in public key cryptography). No knowledge of group theory (beyond the most basic properties of groups like $\mathbb{Z}_N^*$) is required to understand the algorithms in this chapter. We will illustrate the mechanics of these algorithms using the simple concrete groups of the form $\mathbb{Z}_N^*$.

Integer Factorization Problem

Input: An integer N.
Problem: Output positive integers $p_1, p_2, \ldots, p_l, r_1, r_2, \ldots, r_l$ where the p_i are distinct primes and $N = p_1^{r_1} p_2^{r_2} \cdots p_l^{r_l}$.

Suppose we wish to factor the integer N. Since it is easy to remove factors of 2, we will assume N is odd. Furthermore, one can easily factor any integer N that is a prime power (see Exercise 7.3.3). Thus, we will further assume that the factorization of N contains at least two distinct odd prime factors. If we could split any odd non-prime-power integer into two non-trivial factors, then we can completely factor N into its prime factors using at most $\log N$ splittings. There are efficient classical probabilistic algorithms for testing primality, and also polynomial time classical deterministic algorithms (though at present the polynomials have a fairly high degree), so we know when we can stop trying to split the factors. Thus, the problem of factoring N can be reduced to $O(\log N)$ instances of the problem of splitting an odd non-prime-power integer.

Splitting an Odd Non-Prime-Power Integer

Input: An odd integer N that has at least two distinct prime factors.
Problem: Output two integers N_1, N_2, $1 < N_1 < N$, $1 < N_2 < N$, such that $N = N_1 \times N_2$.

Exercise 7.3.3 Suppose $N = m^n$ for some integers $m > 1$ and $n > 1$. Show how to find a non-trivial splitting of N in time polynomial in $\log(N)$.

Miller showed in 1975 how the problem of splitting integers *reduces* probabilistically to the problem of *order finding*. This means that if we have an efficient algorithm for order finding, it is possible to give an efficient probabilistic algorithm for splitting integers (the splitting algorithm will use the order finding algorithm as a subroutine). We will sketch this reduction.

Order-Finding Problem

Input: Integers a and N such that $GCD(a, N) = 1$ (i.e. a is relatively prime to N).
Problem: Find the order of a modulo N.

To split N, we would start by finding the order of a random integer a that is coprime with N. To do this, we first need to have some means of finding such an integer a. If a is not coprime with N, then the GCD of a and N, denoted $GCD(a, N)$, is a non-trivial factor of N. As we saw in Section 7.1.3, the GCD of two numbers can be found efficiently using the EEA. So one can uniformly sample elements a coprime to N by uniformly sampling $\{2, 3, \ldots, N-2\}$ and then applying the EEA to test if the sampled integer is coprime with N. (If $GCD(a, N) > 1$, then we have hit the jackpot as we have already found a non-trivial factor of N.) If a is randomly selected with $GCD(a, N) = 1$, then the order r of a will be even with probability at least $\frac{1}{2}$. If r is even, then $b = a^{r/2} \bmod N$ satisfies $b^2 - 1 = 0 \bmod N$, and thus N divides $(b-1)(b+1)$. The hope is that $GCD(b - 1, N)$ will be a non-trivial factor of N. If N has at least two distinct prime factors, then for an integer a selected uniformly at random with even order r, the probability that $GCD(a^{r/2} - 1 \bmod N, N)$ is a non-trivial factor of N is at least $\frac{1}{2}$. Thus, only a constant number of values a need to be tried in order to successfully split N with high probability.

Recalling Theorem 7.1.12, we can reduce the order-finding problem to the task of sampling fractions $\frac{k}{r}$ for integers k chosen uniformly at random between 1 and $r - 1$. Using a beautiful piece of number theory, the theory of continued fractions (recall Theorem 7.1.7), we can reduce the task of exactly determining a fraction $\frac{k}{r}$ to the task of finding an estimate $\frac{x}{2^n}$ with $\left| \frac{k}{r} - \frac{x}{2^n} \right| \leq \frac{1}{2r^2}$.

It is important to note that all of the above reductions are classical. To summarize, therefore, finding the order r of a modulo N with bounded error can be reduced to the following sampling problem.

Sampling Estimates
to an Almost Uniformly Random Integer Multiple of $\frac{1}{r}$

Input: Integers a and N such that $GCD(a, N) = 1$. Let r denote the (unknown) order of a.

Problem: Output a number $x \in \{0, 1, 2, \ldots, 2^{n-1}\}$ such that for each $k \in \{0, 1, \ldots, r-1\}$ we have

$$\Pr\left(\left| \frac{x}{2^n} - \frac{k}{r} \right| \leq \frac{1}{2r^2} \right) \geq c\frac{1}{r}$$

for some constant $c > 0$.

Fact: Write $a \implies b$ to mean that problem a reduces to a problem b. We have

Factoring any integer

$\Downarrow$ deterministic classical polytime reduction

Splitting odd non-prime-power N

$\Downarrow$ probabilistic classical polytime reduction

Finding the orders of integers modulo N

$\Downarrow$ probabilistic classical polytime reduction

Sampling estimates to a random integer multiple of $\dfrac{1}{r}$

(where r is the order of some integer a mod N).

This sampling problem is where a quantum algorithm is used. In the following section we show how eigenvalue estimation can solve the above sampling problem (and thus the integer factorization problem).

7.3.3   The Eigenvalue Estimation Approach to Order Finding

As we show later, Shor's order-finding algorithm can be viewed as an application of the eigenvalue estimation algorithm we saw in Section 7.2.

Let U_a be the operator that maps

$$U_a : |s\rangle \mapsto |sa \bmod N\rangle, \qquad 0 \leq s < N. \tag{7.3.3}$$

Since a is coprime with N, then a has an inverse modulo N, and so the transformation performed by U_a is reversible and thus unitary. Also, U_a can be implemented efficiently. When implementing this operation say using m qubits where $2^m > N$, we can simply extend the action of U_a in any reversible way, for example

$$U_a : |s\rangle \mapsto |sa \bmod N\rangle, \qquad s < N$$
$$|s\rangle \mapsto |s\rangle, \qquad 0 \leq s \geq N. \tag{7.3.4}$$

We will restrict attention to the action of U_a restricted to the state space spanned by $\{|0\rangle, |1\rangle, \ldots, |N-1\rangle\}$.

Note that since $a^r \equiv 1 \pmod{N}$, we have

$$U_a^r : |s\rangle \mapsto |sa^r \bmod N\rangle = |s\rangle. \tag{7.3.5}$$

That is, U_a is an rth root of the identity operation.

In other words, since we know how to multiply by a modulo N, we therefore know how to implement a unitary transformation that is an rth root of the identity operation. In Exercise 7.3.4 you will verify that the eigenvalues of a unitary operation that is an rth root of the identity operation must be rth roots of 1, that is, of the form $e^{2\pi i \frac{k}{r}}$ for some integer k.

Exercise 7.3.4 Prove that if a operator U satisfies $U^r = I$, then the eigenvalues of U must be rth roots of 1.

Consider the state

$$|u_k\rangle = \frac{1}{\sqrt{r}} \sum_{s=0}^{r-1} e^{-2\pi i \frac{k}{r} s} |a^s \bmod N\rangle. \tag{7.3.6}$$

We have

$$U_a |u_k\rangle = \frac{1}{\sqrt{r}} \sum_{s=0}^{r-1} e^{-2\pi i \frac{k}{r} s} U_a |a^s \bmod N\rangle$$

$$= \frac{1}{\sqrt{r}} \sum_{s=0}^{r-1} e^{-2\pi i \frac{k}{r} s} |a^{s+1} \bmod N\rangle$$

$$= e^{2\pi i \frac{k}{r}} \frac{1}{\sqrt{r}} \sum_{s=0}^{r-1} e^{-2\pi i \frac{k}{r}(s+1)} |a^{s+1} \bmod N\rangle$$

$$= e^{2\pi i \frac{k}{r}} |u_k\rangle \tag{7.3.7}$$

and so $|u_k\rangle$ is an eigenstate for U_a with eigenvalue $e^{2\pi i \frac{k}{r}}$. The last equality in the above equations follows from the fact that $e^{2\pi i \frac{k}{r} r} |a^r \bmod N\rangle = e^{2\pi i \frac{k}{r} 0} |a^0 \bmod N\rangle$.

Exercise 7.3.5 Let b be an integer coprime with N. Give a set of eigenvectors $|\psi_j^b\rangle$ of U_a so that $|b\rangle = \sum_{j=0}^{r-1} \frac{1}{\sqrt{r}} |\psi_j^b\rangle$.

For any value of k between 0 and $r-1$, if we were given the state $|u_k\rangle$, we could apply the eigenvalue estimation algorithm and perform

$$|0\rangle|u_k\rangle \longmapsto |\widetilde{k/r}\rangle|u_k\rangle. \tag{7.3.8}$$

Referring to Theorem 7.1.5, we see that measuring the first register of this state would solve the sampling problem, and therefore solve the order finding problem.

Without knowing r, we do not know how to prepare such states $|u_k\rangle$. Fortunately, we do not have to. The key insight is the following. Instead of preparing an eigenstate having eigenvalue $e^{2\pi i \frac{k}{r}}$ for a randomly selected $k \in \{0, \dots, r-1\}$, it would suffice to prepare any superposition or mixture that contains each eigenvalue with sufficient weight. For example, a uniform superposition of the eigenstates would suffice. Then the eigenvalue estimation algorithm will produce a superposition of these eigenstates entangled with estimates of their eigenvalues, and when a measurement is performed, the result is an estimate of a random eigenvalue. We shall see that such a superposition of eigenstates *is* possible to prepare, without knowing r. Consider

$$\frac{1}{\sqrt{r}} \sum_{k=0}^{r-1} |u_k\rangle = \frac{1}{\sqrt{r}} \sum_{k=0}^{r-1} \frac{1}{\sqrt{r}} \sum_{s=0}^{r-1} e^{-2\pi i \frac{k}{r} s} |a^s \bmod N\rangle. \tag{7.3.9}$$

Notice that $|a^s \bmod N\rangle = |1\rangle$ iff $s \equiv 0 \pmod r$. The amplitude of $|1\rangle$ in the above state is then the sum over the terms for which $s = 0$. This is

$$\frac{1}{\sqrt{r}} \frac{1}{\sqrt{r}} \sum_{k=0}^{r-1} e^{-2\pi i \frac{k}{r} 0} = \frac{1}{r} \sum_{k=0}^{r-1} (1)$$

$$= 1. \tag{7.3.10}$$

So the amplitude of state $|1\rangle$ is 1, and thus the amplitude of all other basis states must be 0. So we have

$$\frac{1}{\sqrt{r}} \sum_{k=0}^{r-1} |u_k\rangle = |1\rangle. \tag{7.3.11}$$

This means that the eigenvalue estimation algorithm maps the input state

$$|0\rangle|1\rangle = |0\rangle \left(\frac{1}{\sqrt{r}} \sum_{k=0}^{r-1} |u_k\rangle \right) \tag{7.3.12}$$

$$= \frac{1}{\sqrt{r}} \sum_{k=0}^{r-1} |0\rangle|u_k\rangle \tag{7.3.13}$$

to the output state

$$\frac{1}{\sqrt{r}} \sum_{k=0}^{r-1} |\widetilde{k/r}\rangle |u_k\rangle. \qquad (7.3.14)$$

If we trace out or ignore the second register, we see that the first register is in an equally weighted mixture of the states $|\widetilde{k/r}\rangle$, for $k \in \{0, 1, \dots, r-1\}$. Therefore, a measurement of the first register at the end of the eigenvalue estimation algorithm yields an integer x such that $\frac{x}{2^n}$ is an estimate of $\frac{k}{r}$ for some $k \in \{0, 1, \dots, r-1\}$ selected uniformly at random. As mentioned above, with high probability this estimate will allow us to exactly determine the fraction $\frac{k}{r}$, using the continued fractions algorithm.

A quantum circuit implementing the quantum part of the order-finding algorithm is shown in Figure 7.14.

The order-finding algorithm is summarized below.

Order-Finding Algorithm

1. Choose an integer n so that $2^n \geq 2r^2$. The value $n = \lceil 2 \log N \rceil$ will suffice.
2. Initialize an n-qubit register to $|0\rangle^{\otimes n}$. Call this the *control register*.
3. Initialize an n-qubit register to $|1\rangle = |00\dots01\rangle$. Call this the *target register*.
4. Apply the QFT to the control register.
5. Apply c-U_a^x control and target registers.
6. Apply the QFT^{-1} to the control register.
7. Measure the control register to obtain an estimate $\frac{x_1}{2^n}$ of a random integer multiple of $\frac{1}{r}$.
8. Use the continued fractions algorithm to obtain integers c_1 and r_1 such that $|\frac{x_1}{2^n} - \frac{c_1}{r_1}| \leq \frac{1}{2^{\frac{n-1}{2}}}$. If no such pair of integers is found, output 'FAIL'.
9. Repeat Steps 1–7 to obtain another integer x_2 and a pair of integers c_2 and r_2 such that $|\frac{x_2}{2^n} - \frac{c_2}{r_2}| \leq \frac{1}{2^{\frac{n-1}{2}}}$. If no such pair of integers is found, output 'FAIL'.
10. Compute $r = \text{LCM}(r_1, r_2)$. Compute $a^r \bmod N$.
11. If $a^r \bmod N = 1$, then output r. Otherwise, output 'FAIL'.

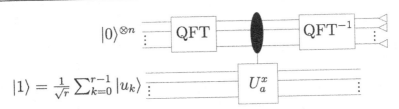

Fig. 7.14 A circuit for sampling estimates to a random integer multiple of $\frac{1}{r}$, which can be used to solve the order-finding problem. The measured bits are a binary representation of an integer x such that $\frac{x}{2^n}$ is an estimate of $\frac{k}{r}$ for a random integer k.

To see why this algorithm works, note that Step 6 is effectively measuring $|\widetilde{\frac{k}{r}}\rangle$ for an integer k selected uniformly at random from $\{0, 1, \ldots, r-1\}$. The following theorem thus follows by the reductions given in Section 7.3.2.

Theorem 7.3.2 *The order-finding algorithm will output the correct order r of a with probability at least $\frac{384}{\pi^6} > 0.399$, and otherwise outputs a multiple of r or 'FAIL'.*

The computational bottleneck of this algorithm is the controlled exponentiations of the operator U_a, that is, the c-$U_a^{2^j}$ operations for $j = 0, 1, 2, \ldots, 2^{n-1}$ that constitute the c-U_a^x, as we saw for eigenvalue estimation in Section 7.2. The obvious way to compute c-$U_a^{2^j}$ requires 2^j applications of the c-U_a operation. A critical observation is that c-$U_a^{2^j} = $ c-$U_{a^{2^j}}$; in other words, multiplying by a modulo N a total of 2^j times is equivalent to multiplying by $a^{2^j} \bmod N$ only once. We can (classically) precompute $a^{2^j} \bmod N$ with only j multiplications modulo N (by repeated squaring modulo N, starting with a), which provides an exponential improvement over multiplying by a modulo N a total of 2^j times. The quantum circuit we would implement would simply be a circuit for multiplying by the number $a^j \bmod N$ (which is a number between 1 and $N-1$). Standard arithmetic techniques can implement this multiplication with only $O((\log N) \log \log(N) \log \log \log(N))$ elementary gates. Thus, the required exponentiation can be done with only $O((\log N)^2 \log \log(N) \log \log \log(N))$ elementary gates. The QFT require $O((\log N)^2)$ gates. Thus this quantum circuit requires only $O((\log N)^2 \log \log(N) \log \log \log(N))$ elementary quantum gates. Note that it only needs to be repeated a constant number of times to successfully factor N into two non-trivial factors with a high probability of success.

In contrast, the best-known 'heuristic' classical algorithm uses $e^{O((\log N)^{\frac{1}{3}} (\log \log N)^{\frac{2}{3}})}$ elementary classical gates. The best-known rigorous classical algorithm uses $e^{O((\log N)^{\frac{1}{2}} (\log \log N)^{\frac{1}{2}})}$.

It is important to note that the order-finding algorithm will work for any group for which we can represent group elements uniquely and perform the group operation. In other words, the order-finding algorithm works for 'black-box groups' (with unique encodings[5]). In the black-box group model, each element is encoded by a string of some length n, and one can perform group operations (multiplication, inverse, and recognizing the group identity element) on these encodings via a black-box. An algorithm in this model cannot access any information about the structure of the group except through the black-box. The complexity of

---

[5]In order for quantum interference to occur, each group element must be represented by some unique quantum encoding. Thus, it is sufficient if each group element has a unique classical encoding. However, more sophisticated unique quantum encodings might also possible, such as letting each group element be represented by a uniform superposition of all its valid classical encodings.

algorithms in the black-box model can be measured in terms of the number of applications of the black box (as well as the number of other operations). Appendix A.6 discusses the black-box group model in more detail.

The classical and quantum complexities for order finding are summarized below.

Complexities for Order Finding

- Finding the order of a random element in Z_N^*
    - Quantum complexity is in $O((\log N)^2 \log \log(N) \log \log \log(N))$.
    - Best-known rigorous probabilistic classical algorithm has complexity in $e^{O(\sqrt{\log N \log \log N})}$.
    - Best-known heuristic[6] probabilistic classical algorithm has complexity in $e^{O((\log N)^{\frac{1}{3}}(\log \log N)^{\frac{2}{3}})}$.
- Order finding in a black-box group
    - Quantum black-box complexity (for groups with unique encodings of group elements) is $O(\log r)$ black-box multiplications and $O(n + \log^2 r)$ other elementary operations.
    - Classical black-box complexity is in $\Theta(\sqrt{r})$ black-box multiplications.

7.3.4 Shor's Approach to Order Finding

The above is not the analysis outlined by Shor in his landmark 1994 paper on integer factorization. It is equivalent, however, as we will show in this section. Understanding both approaches is useful when trying to generalize the algorithms to solve other problems.

The original approach to order finding (in particular, to estimating a random integer multiple of $\frac{1}{r}$) was the following:

Original Approach to Estimating a Random Integer Multiple of $\frac{1}{r}$

1. Create the state

$$|\psi_0\rangle = \sum_{x=0}^{2^n-1} \frac{1}{\sqrt{2^n}} |x\rangle |a^x \bmod N\rangle. \tag{7.3.15}$$

We can rewrite the above state as (see Exercise 7.3.6)

$$|\psi_0\rangle = \sum_{b=0}^{r-1} \left(\frac{1}{\sqrt{2^n}} \sum_{z=0}^{m_b-1} |zr+b\rangle \right) |a^b \bmod N\rangle. \tag{7.3.16}$$

where m_b is the largest integer so that $(m_b - 1)r + b \leq 2^n - 1$ (see Equation (7.1.35)).

---

[6]By 'heuristic' algorithm, we mean the proof of its running time makes some plausible but unproven assumptions.

2. Measure the second register. We will get a value $a^b \bmod N$ for b chosen almost[7] uniformly at random from $\{0, 1, \ldots, r-1\}$. The first register will be left in a superposition of the form

$$\frac{1}{\sqrt{m_b}} \sum_{z=0}^{m_b-1} |zr+b\rangle. \qquad (7.3.17)$$

If we were able to implement the $\mathrm{QFT}_{m_b r}^{-1}$ and apply it to the above state (recall Section 7.1.2), then we would produce the superposition

$$\sum_{j=0}^{r-1} e^{-2\pi i \frac{b}{r} j} |m_b j\rangle. \qquad (7.3.18)$$

In other words, we will only measure values x such that $\frac{x}{rm_b} = \frac{j}{r}$ for some integer j. However, since we do not know what r and m_b are, we use $\mathrm{QFT}_{2^n}^{-1}$.

3. Apply $\mathrm{QFT}_{2^n}^{-1}$ to the first register, and then measure. Let x denote the measured value.

4. Output $\frac{x}{2^n}$.

The rest of the algorithm can proceed identically to the algorithm in Section 7.3.3.

Theorem 7.3.3 *The above algorithm outputs an integer $x \in \{0, 1, 2, \ldots, 2^n-1\}$ such that for each $j \in \{0, 1, 2, \ldots, r-1\}$ with probability at least $\frac{4}{r\pi^2}$ we have $\left|\frac{x}{2^n} - \frac{j}{r}\right| \le \frac{1}{2^{n+1}}$.*

Therefore, this algorithm solves the problem of estimating an almost uniformly random integer multiple of $\frac{1}{r}$.

Exercise 7.3.6

(a) For every integer $x \in \{0, 1, 2, \ldots, 2^n - 1\}$ show that there are unique integers z_x and b_x where $x = z_x r + b_x$ and $0 \le b_x < r$.

(b) Using the result of part (a) above, show that Equation (7.3.15) can be rewritten as Equation (7.3.16).

---

[7] Note that for the values b satisfying $0 \le b < (2^n \bmod r)$ the probability of measuring a^b is $\frac{1}{r} + \frac{r-(2^n \bmod r)}{r2^n}$, and for b satisfying $(2^n \bmod r) \le b < r$, the probability of measuring a^b is $\frac{1}{r} - \frac{(2^n \bmod r)}{r2^n}$. In other words, the probability lies in the interval $(\frac{1}{r} - \frac{1}{2^n}, \frac{1}{r} + \frac{1}{2^n})$.

Note that, as was the case in Simon's algorithm, since we never use the measured value in Step 2, we can ignore that step. Furthermore, a very natural way to create the state in Step 1 is to first prepare the state

$$|\psi_0\rangle = \sum_{x=0}^{2^n-1} \frac{1}{\sqrt{2^n}} |x\rangle|1\rangle \qquad (7.3.19)$$

and then perform the operation that maps $|x\rangle|y\rangle \mapsto |x\rangle|ya^x \bmod N\rangle$.

Thus Shor's algorithm is implemented by the circuit in Figure 7.15. Note that this is exactly the same circuit we described in the previous section. The only difference between the two approaches is the basis in which the state of the system is analysed. In the previous section we expressed the state of the second register in the eigenvector basis. In this section we expressed the state of the second register in the computational basis. This equivalence is illustrated in Figure 7.16.

Note that constructing a circuit that implements c-$U_a^x : |x\rangle|y\rangle \mapsto |x\rangle|ya^x \bmod N\rangle$ is not actually necessary. It suffices to create the state $\sum_x |x\rangle|a^x\rangle$ which can instead be constructed easily using a circuit that implements $V_a : |x\rangle|y\rangle \mapsto |x\rangle|y \oplus a^x\rangle$. Appendix A.6 discusses the relationship between these different types of black-boxes.

Exercise 7.3.7 Show how the order-finding algorithm can be generalized to solve a special case of the period finding problem. More specifically, let $f : Z \to X$, for some finite set X, be a periodic function with period r. That is, for any x we have $f(x) = f(x+r) = f(x+2r) = \ldots$. In other words, $f(x) = f(y)$ if $r|x-y$ (where $r|x-y$ denotes the condition that r divides $x - y$). Furthermore, assume that $f(x) \neq f(y)$ unless $r|x - y$, so that $f(x) = f(y)$ if and only if $r|x - y$. Given a black-box U_f that maps $|x\rangle|0\rangle \mapsto |x\rangle|f(x)\rangle$, describe an algorithm for finding the period of f, and prove that it works.

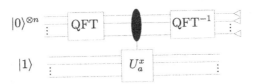

Fig. 7.15 A circuit for implementing the quantum part of Shor's algorithm. The measured string x gives an estimate $\frac{x}{2^n}$ of a random integer multiple of $\frac{1}{r}$.

Equivalence of the two approaches to analyzing the order finding algorithm

	Shor's Analysis	Eigenvalue Estimation Analysis
Initial state	$\lvert 0\rangle\lvert 1\rangle$	$\sum_k \lvert 0\rangle\lvert u_k\rangle$
$\xrightarrow{\text{QFT}}$	$\sum_x \lvert x\rangle\lvert 1\rangle$	$\sum_k \sum_x \lvert x\rangle\lvert u_k\rangle$
$\xrightarrow{\text{c-}U_a^x}$	$\sum_b\left(\sum_z \lvert zr+b\rangle\right)\lvert a^b\rangle$	$\sum_k\left(\sum_x e^{2\pi i\frac{kx}{r}}\lvert x\rangle\right)\lvert u_k\rangle$
$\xrightarrow{\text{QFT}^{-1}}$	$\sum_b\lvert\text{⩘}\rangle\lvert a^b\rangle$	$\sum_s\lvert\text{⩘}\rangle\lvert u_k\rangle$
$\xrightarrow{\text{Tr}_2}$	$\sum_b\lvert\text{⩘}\rangle\langle\text{⩘}\rvert$	$\sum_k\lvert\text{⩘}\rangle\langle\text{⩘}\rvert$

Fig. 7.16 Equivalence of Shor's analysis and the eigenvalue estimation analysis of the order-finding algorithm. Each column represents the same state as viewed in each of the two analyses at each step of the algorithm. The last line illustrates the state after tracing out the second register. In the last two lines of the table, we illustrate the amplitudes of the states graphically, by drawing peak where the probability amplitude will be concentrated.

7.4   Finding Discrete Logarithms

Not all public key cryptosystems in use today rely on the difficulty of factoring. Breaking many cryptosystems in use today can be reduced to finding *discrete logarithms* in groups such as the multiplicative group of finite fields or the additive group of points on elliptic curves. Shor also showed how to find discrete logarithms in $\mathbb{Z}_p^*$ and the algorithm easily extends to other groups, including the widely used elliptic curve groups.

The discrete logarithm problem in $\mathbb{Z}_p^*$ is the following.

The Discrete Logarithm Problem

Input: Elements b and $a = b^t$ in $\mathbb{Z}_p^*$, where t is an integer from $\{0, 1, 2, \ldots, r-1\}$ and r is the order of a.
Problem: Find t. (The number t is called the discrete logarithm of b with respect to the base a.)

As in Section 7.3.3, let U_a be the operator that maps

$$U_a : |s\rangle \mapsto |sa \bmod N\rangle, \qquad s < N, \tag{7.4.1}$$

and let U_b be the operator that maps

$$U_b : |s\rangle \mapsto |sb \bmod N\rangle, \qquad s < N. \tag{7.4.2}$$

We assume that we know r, the order of b.

Because of the quantum factoring algorithm, we assume that we can factor r into its prime factors, and we can therefore reduce the discrete logarithm problem to the base a to less than $\log r$ instances of the discrete logarithms problem for elements a' of prime order (see Appendix A.2). We will therefore assume for convenience that r is prime, but the algorithm would also work for composite r with a slightly more complicated analysis.

The operators U_a and U_b share the eigenvectors $|u_k\rangle$ defined in Section 7.3.3, with respective eigenvalues $e^{2\pi i \frac{k}{r}}$ and $e^{2\pi i \frac{kt}{r}}$. The idea is to apply the eigenvalue estimation algorithm to estimate[8] these two eigenvalues accurately enough to determine both $\frac{k}{r}$ and $\frac{kt \bmod r}{r}$. Since (unlike with the order-finding problem) we know r, we only need to estimate these eigenvalues with an error of at most $\frac{1}{2r}$ in order to find the correct numerator (which only requires $n \geq \log_2 r + 1$). In particular, since we know r we do *not* need to apply the continued fractions algorithm (which used $n \geq \log_2^2 r + 1$). If $k \neq 0$ (which occurs with probability $1 - \frac{1}{r}$) we can simply compute

$$t \equiv k^{-1} kt \bmod r \equiv (k \bmod r)^{-1} (kt \bmod r) \bmod r. \tag{7.4.3}$$

Thus, we can apply the eigenvalue estimation algorithm twice, as shown in Figure 7.17 in order to find discrete logarithms.

The circuit in Figure 7.17 maps $|0\rangle^{\otimes n} |0\rangle^{\otimes n} |u_k\rangle$ to $|\frac{\tilde{k}}{r}\rangle |\widetilde{\frac{kt \bmod r}{r}}\rangle |u_k\rangle$. Therefore starting with $|0\rangle^{\otimes n} |0\rangle^{\otimes n} |1\rangle = |0\rangle^{\otimes n} |0\rangle^{\otimes n} \sum_{k=0}^{r-1} |u_k\rangle$ yields the state

$$\sum_{k=0}^{r-1} |\frac{\tilde{k}}{r}\rangle |\widetilde{\frac{kt \bmod r}{r}}\rangle |u_k\rangle. \tag{7.4.4}$$

Tracing out the last register, the first two registers are in an equally weighted mixture of the states $|\frac{\tilde{k}}{r}\rangle |\widetilde{\frac{kt \bmod r}{r}}\rangle$ for $k \in \{0, 1, \ldots, r-1\}$.

---

[8]In fact, by Theorem 7.1.1, since we know r, we efficiently approximate the QFT_r with arbitrary precision. Thus we could assume for convenience that we can implement the QFT_r and QFT_r^{-1} exactly, which allows us to obtain k and $kt \bmod r$ exactly. We will make this assumption for the hidden subgroup algorithm later, but for this section we will stick with QFT_{2^n} which we have shown how to implement in detail.

Note that with probability at least $\left(\frac{8}{\pi^2}\right)^2$, the two values x and y that are measured will simultaneously satisfy

$$\left|\frac{x}{2^n} - \frac{k}{r}\right| \leq \frac{1}{2^n} \tag{7.4.5}$$

and

$$\left|\frac{y}{2^n} - \frac{kt \bmod r}{r}\right| \leq \frac{1}{2^n}. \tag{7.4.6}$$

In other words,

$$\left|\frac{xr}{2^n} - k\right| \leq \frac{r}{2^n} \tag{7.4.7}$$

and

$$\left|\frac{yr}{2^n} - kt \bmod r\right| \leq \frac{r}{2^n}. \tag{7.4.8}$$

Thus if we choose n so that $2r \leq 2^n$, we can determine the integers k and $kt \bmod r$ by simply rounding off $\frac{x}{2^n}$ and $\frac{y}{2^n}$ to the nearest integers.

In summary, the quantum circuit shown in Figure 7.17, followed by the above post-processing will find the correct value of t with probability at least $\frac{r-1}{r}\left(\frac{8}{\pi^2}\right)^2 > 0.657\frac{r-1}{r}$. As with the order-finding circuit, this quantum circuit requires only $O((\log N)^2 \log\log(N) \log\log\log(N))$ elementary quantum gates.

The discrete logarithm algorithm is summarized below.

Discrete Logarithm Algorithm

1. Initialize two n-qubit register to $|0\rangle^{\otimes n}$. Call this these the *first* and *second* control registers respectively.
2. Initialize an n-qubit register to $|1\rangle = |00\dots01\rangle$. Call this the *target register*.
3. Apply the QFT to each of the first and second registers.
4. Apply c-U_a^x to the target register and first control register.
5. Apply c-U_b^x to the target register and second control register.
6. Apply the QFT^{-1} to each of the first and second registers.
7. Measure the first register to obtain an estimate $\frac{x}{2^n}$ of $\frac{k}{r}$ for a randomly selected $k \in \{0, 1, \dots, r-1\}$.
8. Measure the second register to obtain the estimate $\frac{y}{2^n}$ of $\frac{kt \bmod r}{r}$ (for the same k as obtained in the previous step).
9. Round off $\frac{ry}{2^n}$ to the nearest integer $\tilde{y}$. Round off $\frac{xr}{2^n}$ to the nearest integer $\tilde{x}$. If $\tilde{x} = 0$, output 'FAIL'. If $\tilde{x} \neq 0$, compute $\tilde{t} = \tilde{y}\tilde{x}^{-1} \bmod r$. If $b = a^{\tilde{t}} \bmod p$, then output $\tilde{t}$. Otherwise, output 'FAIL'.

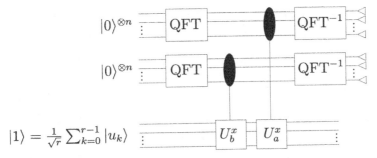

Fig. 7.17 A circuit for finding the discrete logarithm of a to the base b. The value x measured at the first register provides the estimate $\frac{x}{2^n}$ of $\frac{k}{r}$ for a random $k \in \{0, 1, \dots, r-1\}$, and the outcome measured at the second register provides an estimate of $\frac{(kt \bmod r)}{r}$ for the same random k.

As was the case with the order-finding algorithm, the discrete logarithm algorithm will work for any group for which we can represent group elements uniquely and perform the group operation. That is, the discrete logarithm algorithm works in 'black-box groups' (with unique encodings). Thus, this algorithm also applies to the additive group of points on an elliptic curve, which is commonly used in public-key cryptography.

Furthermore, it suffices to have any circuit that produces the state $\sum_{x,y} |x\rangle |y\rangle \, |b^x a^y\rangle$ (which equals the state in Equation 7.4.4), for example, using the mapping $V_{a,b} : |x\rangle |y\rangle |z\rangle \mapsto |x\rangle |y\rangle |z \oplus a^x b^y\rangle$ would also suffice (as discussed in Appendix A.6).

The classical and quantum complexities for the discrete logarithm problem are summarized below.

Complexities of the Discrete Logarithm Problem

- Finding discrete logarithms in F_q^*
  - Quantum complexity is in $O((\log q)^2 \log \log(q) \log \log \log(q))$.
  - Best-known rigorous probabilistic classical algorithm has complexity in $e^{O(\sqrt{\log q \log \log q})}$.
  - Best-known heuristic probabilistic classical algorithm has complexity in $e^{O((\log q)^{\frac{1}{3}} (\log \log q)^{\frac{2}{3}})}$.
- Discrete logarithms in a black-box group represented with strings of length n
  - Quantum black-box complexity (for groups with unique encodings of group elements) is $O(\log r)$ black-box multiplications and $O(n + \log^2 r)$ other elementary operations.
  - Classical black-box complexity is in $\Theta(\sqrt{r})$.

The discrete logarithm algorithm was originally discovered by Shor in a manner analogous to the order-finding algorithm description in Section 7.3.4. In the next section, we show a generalization of the order-finding and discrete logarithm algorithms, and analyse it in this way.

7.5   Hidden Subgroups

In Section 6.5 we stated a generalized version of Simon's problem, which is a special case of the 'Hidden Subgroup Problem'.

The problem can be stated for any group G.

The Hidden Subgroup Problem

Let $f : G \to X$ map a group G to some finite set X with the property that there exists some subgroup $S \leq G$ such that for any $x, y \in G$, $f(x) = f(y)$ if and only if $x + S = y + S$. In other words, f is constant on cosets of S and distinct on different cosets.

Notice how we can rephrase most of the problems we have already discussed, along with some other ones, in this framework.

Hidden Subgroup Problems

Deutsch's Problem:
$G = \mathbb{Z}_2$, $X = \{0, 1\}$, and $S = \{0\}$ if f is balanced, and $S = \mathbb{Z}_2$ if f is constant.

Generalized Simon's problem:
$G = \mathbb{Z}_2^n$, $X = \{0, 1\}^n$, and S is any subgroup of $\mathbb{Z}_2^n$.

Finding orders:
$G = \mathbb{Z}$, $X =$ any finite group H, r is the order of $a \in H$. The subgroup $S = r\mathbb{Z}$ is the hidden subgroup of G, and a generator for S reveals r.

Finding the period of a function:
$G = \mathbb{Z}$, $X =$ any set, r is the period of f (see Exercise 7.3.7). The subgroup $S = r\mathbb{Z}$ is the hidden subgroup of G, and a generator for S reveals the period r.

Discrete logarithms in any group: $G = \mathbb{Z}_r \times \mathbb{Z}_r$, $X =$ any group H. Let a be an element of H with $a^r = 1$ and suppose $b = a^k$. Consider the function $f(x_1, x_2) = a^{x_1} b^{x_2}$. We have $f(x_1, x_2) = f(y_1, y_2)$ if and only if $(x_1, x_2) - (y_1, y_2) \in \{(t, -tk), t = 0, 1, \ldots, r - 1\}$. The hidden subgroup S is the subgroup generated by $(1, -k)$ (k is the discrete logarithm).

Hidden linear functions: $G = \mathbb{Z} \times \mathbb{Z}$. Let g be some permutation of $\mathbb{Z}_N$ for some integer N. Let h be a function from $\mathbb{Z} \times \mathbb{Z}$ to $\mathbb{Z}_N$ defined by $h(x, y) = x + ay \bmod N$. Let $f = g \circ h$. The subgroup S is the hidden subgroup generated by $(-a, 1)$, and the generator reveals the hidden linear function h.

Self-shift-equivalent polynomials: Given a polynomial P in l variables $X_1, X_2, \ldots, X_l$ over $\mathbb{F}_q$ (the finite field with q elements), the function f which maps $(a_1, a_2, \ldots, a_l) \in \mathbb{F}_q^l$ to $P(X_1 - a_1, X_2 - a_2, \ldots, X_l - a_l)$ is constant on cosets of a subgroup S of $\mathbb{F}_q^l$. This subgroup S is the set of self-shift equivalences of the polynomial P.

Abelian stabilizer problem: Let G be any group acting on a finite set X. That is, each element of G acts as a map from X to X in such a way that for any two elements $a, b \in G$, $a(b(x)) = (ab)(x)$ for all $x \in X$. For a particular element $x \in X$, the set of elements which fix x (i.e. the elements $a \in G$ such that $a(x) = x$) form a subgroup. This subgroup is called the stabilizer of x in G, denoted $\mathrm{St}_G(x)$. Let f_x denote the function from G to X which maps $g \in G$ to $g(x)$. The hidden subgroup of f_x is $\mathrm{St}_G(x)$.

Graph automorphism problem: Consider $G = S_n$, the symmetric group on n elements, which corresponds to the permutations of $\{1, 2, \ldots, n\}$. Let $\mathbf{G}$ be a graph on n vertices labelled $\{1, 2, \ldots, n\}$. For any permutation $\sigma \in S_n$, let $f_{\mathbf{G}}$ map S_n to the set of n-vertex graphs by mapping $f_{\mathbf{G}}(\sigma) = \sigma(\mathbf{G})$, where $\sigma(\mathbf{G})$ is the graph obtained by permuting the vertex labels of $\mathbf{G}$ according to σ. For the function $f_{\mathbf{G}}$, the hidden subgroup of G is the automorphism group of G.

Note that for the graph automorphism problem above, the group G is non-Abelian.[9] If we restrict attention to finite Abelian groups, or more generally, finitely generated Abelian groups, then we can efficiently solve the hidden subgroup problem. Below we outline how the algorithm works for finite Abelian groups.

7.5.1 More on Quantum Fourier Transforms

We have seen two generalizations of the Hadamard transformation. The first was formed by taking the tensor product $H^{\otimes n} = H \otimes H \otimes \cdots \otimes H$ of several Hadamard transformations. The second generalization was formed by increasing the dimension of the single system, giving the QFT_N, for arbitrarily large N, where $\mathrm{QFT}_2 = H$.

We can perform both type of generalizations at the same time, giving us $\mathrm{QFT}_N^{\otimes n} = \mathrm{QFT}_N \otimes \mathrm{QFT}_N \otimes \cdots \otimes \mathrm{QFT}_N$ or even more generally $\mathrm{QFT}_{N_1} \otimes \mathrm{QFT}_{N_2} \otimes \cdots \otimes \mathrm{QFT}_{N_k}$, for possibly different N_i.

Note that
$$\mathrm{QFT}_{N_1} \otimes \mathrm{QFT}_{N_2} \otimes \cdots \otimes \mathrm{QFT}_{N_k} \qquad (7.5.1)$$

operates on the vector space $H_{N_1} \otimes H_{N_2} \otimes \cdots \otimes H_{N_k}$, and we also denote it as $\mathrm{QFT}_{N_1, N_2, \ldots, N_k}$.

---

[9]A group is said to be *Abelian* if for any two group elements x, y, we have $xy = yx$ (i.e. if the group operation is commutative).

We can verify that

$$\text{QFT}_{N_1,N_2,\dots,N_k}|x_1\rangle|x_2\rangle\cdots|x_k\rangle = \sum_{\substack{(y_1,y_2,\dots,y_k) \\ \in Z_{N_1}\times Z_{N_2}\times\cdots\times Z_{N_k}}} e^{2\pi i\left(\frac{y_1 x_1}{N_1}+\frac{y_2 x_2}{N_2}+\cdots+\frac{x_k y_k}{N_k}\right)}|y_1\rangle|y_2\rangle\cdots|y_k\rangle.$$

(7.5.2)

If $N_1 = N_2 = \cdots = N_k$ we can more compactly write

$$\text{QFT}_N^{\otimes k}|\mathbf{x}\rangle = \frac{1}{\sqrt{N^k}} \sum_{\mathbf{y}\in Z_N^k} e^{\frac{2\pi i}{N}\mathbf{x}\cdot\mathbf{y}}|\mathbf{y}\rangle$$

(7.5.3)

where $\mathbf{x}\cdot\mathbf{y} = x_1 y_1 + x_2 y_2 + \cdots + x_k y_k \bmod N$.

Let S be any subgroup of Z_N^k, and define

$$|S\rangle = \frac{1}{\sqrt{|S|}} \sum_{\mathbf{s}\in S}|\mathbf{s}\rangle.$$

(7.5.4)

We let $S^\perp$ denote $\{\mathbf{t} : \mathbf{t}\cdot\mathbf{s} = 0 \text{ for all } \mathbf{s}\in S\}$. We can verify that $\text{QFT}_N^{\otimes k}|S\rangle = \sum_{\mathbf{t}\in S^\perp}|\mathbf{t}\rangle$. For any $\mathbf{b}\in Z_N^k$ we define $\mathbf{b}+S = \{\mathbf{b}+\mathbf{s} : \mathbf{s}\in S\}$, and

$$|\mathbf{b}+S\rangle = \frac{1}{\sqrt{|S|}} \sum_{\mathbf{s}\in S}|\mathbf{b}+\mathbf{s}\rangle.$$

(7.5.5)

We can verify that $\text{QFT}_N^{\otimes k}|\mathbf{b}+S\rangle = \frac{1}{\sqrt{|S^\perp|}}\sum_{\mathbf{t}\in S^\perp}e^{\frac{2\pi i}{N}\mathbf{t}\cdot\mathbf{b}}|\mathbf{t}\rangle$.

More generally, we can consider any Abelian group $G = Z_{N_1}\times Z_{N_2}\times\cdots\times Z_{N_k}$, and for any subgroup $S\leq G$, we similarly define

$$|S\rangle = \frac{1}{\sqrt{|S|}} \sum_{\mathbf{s}\in S}|\mathbf{s}\rangle$$

(7.5.6)

and for any coset $\mathbf{b}+S$ of S we define

$$|\mathbf{b}+S\rangle = \sum_{\mathbf{s}\in S}|\mathbf{b}+\mathbf{s}\rangle.$$

(7.5.7)

We can define $S^\perp$ to be the set $\{\mathbf{t} : \frac{t_1 s_1}{N_1}+\frac{t_2 s_2}{N_2}+\cdots+\frac{t_k s_k}{N_k} = 0 \bmod 1 \text{ for all } \mathbf{s}\in S\}$, where $x = 0 \bmod 1$ if $x\in Z$. Another way of expressing the condition that

$$\frac{t_1 s_1}{N_1} + \frac{t_2 s_2}{N_2} + \cdots + \frac{t_k s_k}{N_k} = 0 \bmod 1$$

(7.5.8)

is to say that

$$e^{2\pi i\left(\frac{t_1 s_1}{N_1}+\frac{t_2 s_2}{N_2}+\cdots+\frac{t_k s_k}{N_k}\right)} = 1.$$

(7.5.9)

For convenience, let us denote

$$\chi_{\mathbf{t}}(\mathbf{s}) = e^{2\pi i\left(\frac{t_1 s_1}{N_1}+\frac{t_2 s_2}{N_2}+\cdots+\frac{t_k s_k}{N_k}\right)}.$$

(7.5.10)

For the reader familiar with group representation theory, the function $\chi_{\mathbf{t}}$ is a character of the Abelian group G, and for Abelian groups there is a one-to-one correspondence between G and the characters of G by the obvious correspondence $\mathbf{t} \leftrightarrow \chi_{\mathbf{t}}$. The QFT_G maps $|\mathbf{x}\rangle \mapsto \sum_{\mathbf{y} \in G} \chi_{\mathbf{y}}(\mathbf{x}) |\mathbf{y}\rangle$.

One important observation is that

$$\mathrm{QFT}_G^{-1}|\mathbf{b} + S\rangle = \sum_{\mathbf{t} \in S^\perp} \chi_{\mathbf{t}}(\mathbf{b})|\mathbf{t}\rangle. \qquad (7.5.11)$$

Exercise 7.5.1 Prove Equation (7.5.11).

7.5.2 Algorithm for the Finite Abelian Hidden Subgroup Problem

For convenience, we will assume that we can efficiently perform the QFT_N exactly for any N. In practice, we can perform it with arbitrary precision, as we described in Theorem 7.1.1

Let $N = \prod_i N_i$. Let $N = p_1^{n_1} p_2^{n_2} \ldots p_l^{n_l}$ be the prime factorization of N, and let $n = \sum_j n_j$. We have the following algorithm for the finite Abelian hidden subgroup problem. We let $\mathcal{H}_X$ denote the Hilbert space of the output register of U_f.

Algorithm for the Finite Abelian HSP

1. Set $i = 1$.
2. Start with

$$|0\rangle|0\rangle \cdots |0\rangle|0\rangle \in \mathcal{H}_{N_1} \otimes \mathcal{H}_{N_2} \otimes \ldots \otimes \mathcal{H}_{N_k} \otimes \mathcal{H}_X. \qquad (7.5.12)$$

3. Apply $\mathrm{QFT}_{N_1, N_2, \ldots, N_k}$ to the input registers.
4. Apply U_f to create the state

$$\sum_{\mathbf{x}} |\mathbf{x}\rangle|f(\mathbf{x})\rangle. \qquad (7.5.13)$$

5. (optional) Measure the second register.
6. Apply $\mathrm{QFT}_{N_1, N_2, \ldots, N_k}^{-1}$ to the input registers.
7. Measure the first register to obtain a value $\mathbf{t}_i$.
8. If $i < n + 4$, increment i and go to Step 1; otherwise proceed to Step 7.
9. Find generators $\mathbf{k}_1, \mathbf{k}_2, \ldots$ for the solution space of the equation

$$\mathbb{T}\mathbf{x}^T = \mathbf{0} \bmod 1 \qquad (7.5.14)$$

where $\mathbb{T}$ is the matrix whose ith row is $(\frac{t_{i,1}}{N_i}, \frac{t_{i,2}}{N_i}, \ldots, \frac{t_{i,k}}{N_i})$.
10. Output $\mathbf{k}_1, \mathbf{k}_2, \ldots \ldots$

Note that the group $G = Z_{N_1} \times Z_{N_2} \times \cdots \times Z_{N_k}$ can be partitioned into the cosets $\mathbf{y} + S$ of the subgroup S, and we can rewrite the state in Step 3 as

$$\sum_{\mathbf{y}} |\mathbf{y} + S\rangle |f(\mathbf{y})\rangle \qquad (7.5.15)$$

where the summation is over a set of coset representatives. Thus the (optional) measurement in Step 4 will leave the first register in a random coset state $|\mathbf{y}+S\rangle$. As we saw in Equation 7.5.11, the final QFT_G^{-1} produces a uniform superposition of elements of $S^\perp$ (where the value of the coset representative $\mathbf{y}$ is encoded in the phase factors). Thus the values $\mathbf{t_i}$ we measure in Step 7 will be elements of $S^\perp$ and thus satisfy the linear equation in Equation 7.5.8. With high probability (see Theorem 7.5.1), the values $\mathbf{t}_1, \mathbf{t}_2, \ldots, \mathbf{t}_{n+4}$ will generate $S^\perp$, in which case the elements of S will be the only solutions to the linear system in Equation 7.5.14. The linear system can be solved in time polynomial in n.

Theorem 7.5.1 *The group $\langle \mathbf{t}_1, \mathbf{t}_2, \ldots, \mathbf{t}_{n+4}\rangle$ generated by the $\mathbf{t}_i$ is a subgroup of $K^\perp$. With probability at least $\frac{2}{3}$ we have $\langle \mathbf{t}_1, \mathbf{t}_1, \ldots, \mathbf{t}_{n+4}\rangle = K^\perp$.*

The proof of this theorem follows by a similar argument to that used in the proof of Theorem A.3.1 in Appendix A.3 (which was used in analysing the zero-error version of Simon's algorithm).

Corollary 7.5.2 *The hidden subgroup K of f is contained in the span of $\mathbf{k}_1, \mathbf{k}_2, \ldots$ With probability at least $\frac{2}{3}$ we have $K = \langle \mathbf{k}_1, \mathbf{k}_2, \ldots \rangle$.*

Note that we can test if $f(\mathbf{k}_i) = 0$ for all i, and thus we can test if $K = \langle \mathbf{k}_1, \mathbf{k}_2, \ldots \rangle$ with $n + O(1)$ evaluations of f.

Corollary 7.5.3 *There exists a bounded-error quantum algorithm for finding generators for the hidden subgroup $K \leq G = Z_{N_1} \times Z_{N_2} \times \cdots \times Z_{N_l}$ of f using $O(\log N)$ evaluations of f and $O(\log^3 N)$ other elementary operations.*

Exercise 7.5.2 Assume that N is prime.

(a) Find a basis for the Hilbert space spanned by $\{|f(\mathbf{x})\rangle : \mathbf{x} \in Z_N^{\otimes k}\}$ that consists of eigenvectors of the maps $|f(\mathbf{x})\rangle \mapsto |f(\mathbf{x}+\mathbf{y})\rangle$.

Hint: There is a one-to-one correspondence between these eigenvectors and the elements of $S^\perp$.

(b) Rewrite Equation 7.5.13 by expressing the state of the second register in this new basis.

(c) What is the result of applying the inverse of $\text{QFT}_N^{\otimes k}$ to the first register, with the second register expressed in this new basis?

Exercise 7.5.3 Show that the hidden subgroup problem can be efficiently reduced to the finite Abelian hidden subgroup problem if G is finitely generated, generators $g_1, g_2, \ldots, g_n$ are given, and X is finite.

7.6   Related Algorithms and Techniques

The great success of quantum algorithms for solving the Abelian hidden subgroup problem leads to the natural question of whether it can solve the hidden subgroup problem for non-Abelian groups. This question has been studied by many researchers, and quantum algorithms can be found for some non-Abelian groups. However, at present, there is no algorithm for most non-Abelian groups, like the symmetric group (which would directly solve the graph automorphism problem). One can generalize the QFT to non-Abelian groups, and it can be implemented efficiently in some cases. However, it is not yet clear if an efficient QFT for a group suffices in order to efficiently solve the hidden subgroup problem for that group.

There are also a handful of problems, such as 'hidden shift' problems, and approximating the Jones polynomial, for which quantum algorithms offer a superpolynomial advantage over the best-known classical algorithms. These algorithms do not seem to be a special case of the hidden subgroup problem.

One very important class of problems, which in fact motivated Feynman to invent the notion of a quantum computer, is that of simulating quantum mechanical systems. There are quantum algorithms that can simulate quantum mechanical systems exponentially more efficiently than any known classical algorithm.

Last, we have focussed attention on quantum algorithms for solving classical problems. But there are many information-processing tasks like entanglement concentration and quantum data compression (which we do not deal with in this textbook), where both the input and output are quantum, so they cannot be done at all using classical computation.

8

ALGORITHMS BASED ON AMPLITUDE AMPLIFICATION

8.1 Grover's Quantum Search Algorithm

In this section, we discuss a broadly applicable quantum algorithm that provides a polynomial speed-up over the best-known classical algorithms for a wide class of important problems.

The quantum search algorithm performs a generic search for a solution to a very wide range of problems. Consider any problem where one can efficiently recognize a good solution and wishes to search through a list of potential solutions in order to find a good one. For example, given a large integer N, one can efficiently recognize whether an integer p is a non-trivial factor of N, and thus one naive strategy for finding non-trivial factors of N is to simply search through the set $\{2, 3, 4, \ldots, \lfloor \sqrt{N} \rfloor\}$ until a factor is found. The factoring algorithm we described in Chapter 7 is not such a naive algorithm, as it makes profound use of the structure of the problem. However, for many interesting problems, there are no known techniques that make much use of the structure of the problem, and the best-known algorithm for solving these problems is to naively search through the potential solutions until one is found. Typically the number of potential solutions is exponential in the size of the problem instance, and so the naive algorithm is not efficient. Often the best-known classical search makes some very limited use of the structure of the problem, perhaps to rule out some obviously impossible candidates, or to prioritize some more likely candidates, but the overall complexity of the search is still exponential.

Quantum searching is a tool for speeding up these sorts of generic searches through a space of potential solutions.

It is worth noting that having a means of recognizing a solution to a problem, and knowing the set of possible solutions, means that in some sense one 'knows' the solution. However, one cannot necessarily efficiently produce the solution.

For example, it is easy to recognize the factors of a number, but finding those factors can take a long time.

We give this problem a more general mathematical structure as follows. We assume that the solutions are expressible as binary strings of length n. Define a function $f : \{0,1\}^n \to \{0,1\}$ so that $f(x) = 1$ if x is the binary encoding of a 'good' string (i.e. a solution to the search problem), and $f(x) = 0$ otherwise.

The Search Problem

Input: A   black   box U_f for   computing   an   unknown   function $f : \{0,1\}^n \to \{0,1\}$.
Problem: Find an input $x \in \{0,1\}^n$ such that $f(x) = 1$.

If the function f is only provided as such a black box, then $\Omega(\sqrt{2^n})$ applications of the black box are necessary in order to solve the search problem with high probability for any input (see Section 9.2). Thus quantum algorithms can provide at most a quadratic speed-up over classical exhaustive search.

For convenience, let us initially restrict attention to functions with exactly one solution $x = w$. Let us assume that we wish our procedure to find the solution with probability at least $\frac{2}{3}$ for every such function f.[1]

If we are only allowed to make one query, the best our algorithm can do is to guess a solution x_1 uniformly at random, and then use the query to check if $f(x_1) = 1$. If x_1 is the correct answer, output x_1. Otherwise, guess a string x_2 uniformly at random from the set $\{0,1\}^n - \{x_1\}$ and output x_2. Note that this procedure outputs the correct value $x = w$ with probability $\frac{2}{2^n}$.

If we have two queries, the best we can do is to continue with the above procedure, and use the second query to test if $f(x_2) = 1$. If $f(x_2) = 1$, we output x_2, and otherwise, we guess a string x_3 uniformly at random from $\{0,1\}^n - \{x_1, x_2\}$, and output the guess x_3. This procedure outputs $x = w$ with probability $\frac{3}{2^n}$.

If we continue the above procedure, with k queries, for $k < 2^n$, the procedure will output the correct value $x = w$ with probability $\frac{k+1}{2^n}$. Note that we can guess the correct answer with probability $\frac{1}{2^n}$ without any queries, and that each additional query boosts the probability of outputting the correct answer by $\frac{1}{2^n}$.

Consider a quantum version of the naive algorithm that makes a guess without making any queries. This procedure guesses the correct answer with probability $\frac{1}{2^n}$, and so the quantum version does this with a probability amplitude of $\frac{1}{\sqrt{2^n}}$. If there were some quantum way to boost the amplitude by $\frac{1}{\sqrt{2^n}}$ after each query, then we could solve the search problem with only $O\left(\sqrt{2^n}\right)$ queries. Finding such

---

[1] As pointed out in Appendix A.1, the choice of the value $\frac{2}{3}$ for the success probability is arbitrary. Any constant strictly between $\frac{1}{2}$ and 1 would suffice.

a quantum-boosting algorithm is not straightforward since we are constrained by laws of quantum mechanics; therefore, we are not able to use handy tools like cloning. Grover devised a quantum algorithm that achieves this amplitude boosting.

Grover's algorithm performs the search *quadratically* faster than can be done classically. If there is exactly one solution, a classical deterministic brute-force search takes $2^n - 1$ queries in the worst case. In fact, any classical algorithm, that for any function f finds a solution with probability at least $\frac{2}{3}$, must make $\Omega(2^n)$ queries in the worst case. Grover's quantum search algorithm takes only $O\left(\sqrt{2^n}\right) = O\left(2^{\frac{n}{2}}\right)$ queries.

Although this is not as dramatic as the exponential quantum advantage achieved by Shor's algorithm for factoring, the extremely wide applicability of searching problems makes Grover's algorithm interesting and important. In particular, Grover's algorithm gives a quadratic speed-up in the solution of NP-complete problems (see Section 9.1.1), which account for many of the important hard problems in computer science. We describe Grover's algorithm in the remainder of this section.

We assume we have a means for recognizing a solution, and therefore, we can without loss of generality assume we have a quantum black box U_f for f as follows.

$$U_f : |x\rangle|b\rangle \mapsto |x\rangle|b \oplus f(x)\rangle. \tag{8.1.1}$$

Suppose we set the target register $|b\rangle$ (which consists of a single qubit) to $|0\rangle$. Then, given a query value x encoded in the query register as $|x\rangle$, suppose we query U_f. The result is

$$|x\rangle|0\rangle \xrightarrow{U_f} |x\rangle|f(x)\rangle \tag{8.1.2}$$

and by measuring the target qubit, we get the answer to the oracle query to f. But this is no better than just applying the oracle for f classically. As was the case for the QFT algorithms, to gain a 'quantum advantage', we need to use quantum superpositions.

We can easily prepare the first register in a superposition of all possible query values, $\frac{1}{\sqrt{N}} \sum_{x=0}^{N-1} |x\rangle$ (where $N = 2^n$).

We can split the sum $\frac{1}{\sqrt{N}} \sum_{x=0}^{N-1} |x\rangle$ into two parts. The first part is a sum over all the x for which $f(x) = 0$; that is, the 'bad' x that are *not* solutions to the search problem. Let X_{bad} be the set of such bad x. The second part is a sum over all the x for which $f(x) = 1$; that is, the 'good' solutions to the search problem. Let X_{good} be the set of such good x. For convenience, let us assume for now that there is only one solution, w, so $X_{good} = \{w\}$.

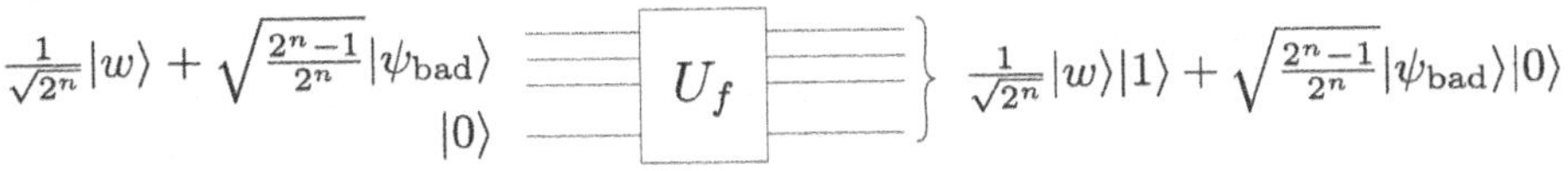

$$\frac{1}{\sqrt{2^n}}|w\rangle + \sqrt{\frac{2^n-1}{2^n}}|\psi_{\text{bad}}\rangle$$
$$|0\rangle$$

$$\left.\begin{array}{c}\end{array}\right\} \quad \frac{1}{\sqrt{2^n}}|w\rangle|1\rangle + \sqrt{\frac{2^n-1}{2^n}}|\psi_{\text{bad}}\rangle|0\rangle$$

Fig. 8.1 The oracle U_f for quantum searching.

Define the states

$$|\psi_{\text{good}}\rangle = |w\rangle$$
$$|\psi_{\text{bad}}\rangle = \frac{1}{\sqrt{N-1}} \sum_{x \in X_{\text{bad}}} |x\rangle. \tag{8.1.3}$$

Suppose we prepare the target qubit of U_f in the state $|0\rangle$, and the query register in a superposition of the form

$$\frac{1}{\sqrt{N}} \sum_{x=0}^{N-1} |x\rangle = \frac{1}{\sqrt{N}}|w\rangle + \sqrt{\frac{N-1}{N}}|\psi_{\text{bad}}\rangle, \tag{8.1.4}$$

as shown in Figure 8.1.

Now with probability $\frac{1}{N}$ a measurement of the target qubit will give $|1\rangle$, and the query qubits will be left in the good state $|w\rangle$. Although this procedure uses the quantum superposition principle, it does not make any use of quantum interference and can easily be simulated using classical randomness. This procedure is equivalent to simply sampling an input x uniformly at random and computing $f(x)$.

The quantum search algorithm is an iterative procedure that uses quantum interference to nudge up the amplitude of the good state $|w\rangle$ before measuring the query register.

We saw in Chapter 6 that if we set the query register to some query index $|x\rangle$, and we set the target qubit to $\frac{1}{\sqrt{2}}(|0\rangle - |1\rangle)$ the effect of the oracle is:

$$|x\rangle \left(\frac{|0\rangle - |1\rangle}{\sqrt{2}}\right) \overset{U_f}{\longmapsto} (-1)^{f(x)}|x\rangle \left(\frac{|0\rangle - |1\rangle}{\sqrt{2}}\right). \tag{8.1.5}$$

Since the second register is in an eigenstate, we can ignore it, considering only the effect on the first register.

$$U_f : |x\rangle \longmapsto (-1)^{f(x)}|x\rangle. \tag{8.1.6}$$

So the effect is to encode the answer to the oracle query in a phase shift (recall this idea of encoding an answer in a quantum phase was key to the operation of the QFT algorithms as well). It is convenient, for the rest of this chapter, to redefine U_f to be the n-qubit operator that performs the transformation of (8.1.6).

Exercise 8.1.1 Suppose $f : \{0, 1, \ldots N\} \to \{0, 1\}$, with the promise that $f(0) = 0$. Show how one application of an oracle that maps $|x\rangle \mapsto (-1)^{f(x)}|x\rangle$ can be used to implement the oracle that maps $|x\rangle|b\rangle \mapsto |x\rangle|b \oplus f(x)\rangle$.

We will also define an n-qubit phase shift operator $U_{0^\perp}$ that acts as follows:

$$U_{0^\perp} : \begin{cases} |x\rangle \mapsto -|x\rangle, & x \neq 0 \\ |0\rangle \mapsto |0\rangle \end{cases} . \tag{8.1.7}$$

This operator applies a phase shift of -1 to all n-qubit states orthogonal to the state $|00\ldots0\rangle$. If we denote the vector space spanned by the basis state $|0\rangle$ by V_0, then the vector space orthogonal to V_0 is the space spanned by all the basis states $|x\rangle \neq |00\ldots0\rangle$, and can be denoted by $V_0^\perp$. The operator $U_{0^\perp}$ applies a phase shift of -1 to vectors in $V_0^\perp$.

Now we can define the operator that does the job of increasing the amplitude of $|\psi_{\text{good}}\rangle = |w\rangle$. This operator $G = HU_{0^\perp}HU_f$ is called the *Grover iterate* or the *quantum search iterate*. It is defined by the following sequence of transformations.

The Grover Iterate G

1. Apply the oracle U_f.
2. Apply the n-qubit Hadamard gate H.
3. Apply $U_{0^\perp}$.
4. Apply the n-qubit Hadamard gate H.

A circuit implementing the Grover iterate is shown in Figure 8.2. Note that the target qubit for the oracle operator U_f (which we prepared in the eigenstate $\frac{1}{\sqrt{2}}(|0\rangle - |1\rangle)$) is omitted in Figure 8.2, since we are working with the simplified definition of U_f as described by Equation (8.1.6) above.

Now that we have defined the Grover iterate, Grover's quantum searching algorithm can be written succinctly as follows.

$$G$$

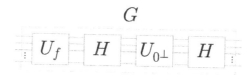

Fig. 8.2 The Grover iterate.

Grover's Quantum Search Algorithm

1. Start with the n-qubit state $|00\ldots0\rangle$.
2. Apply the n-qubit Hadamard gate H to prepare the state $\frac{1}{\sqrt{N}}|\psi\rangle = \sum_{x=0}^{N-1}|x\rangle$ (where $N = 2^n$).
3. Apply the Grover iterate G a total of $\left\lfloor \frac{\pi}{4}\frac{1}{\sqrt{N}} \right\rfloor$ times.
4. Measure the resulting state.

Grover's algorithm is shown schematically in Figure 8.3.

We next show that the Grover iterate G actually does the job of increasing the probability amplitude of $|w\rangle$.

Let

$$|\psi\rangle = H|00\ldots0\rangle, \tag{8.1.8}$$

consider the action of the operator $HU_{0\perp}H$. We have that

$$HU_{0\perp}H \;:\; |\psi\rangle \mapsto |\psi\rangle. \tag{8.1.9}$$

Let $V_\psi^\perp$ denote the vector space orthogonal to $|\psi\rangle$. This space is spanned by the states $H|x\rangle$ for $x \neq 00\ldots0$, and for all such states we have

$$HU_{0\perp}H \;:\; H|x\rangle \mapsto -H|x\rangle. \tag{8.1.10}$$

So the operator $HU_{0\perp}H$ applies a phase shift of -1 to vectors in $V_\psi^\perp$. We can therefore denote

$$U_{\psi^\perp} = HU_{0\perp}H \tag{8.1.11}$$

and write the Grover iterate more succinctly as

$$G = U_{\psi^\perp}U_f. \tag{8.1.12}$$

Exercise 8.1.2 Let $|\psi\rangle = \frac{1}{\sqrt{N}}\sum_{x=0}^{N-1}|x\rangle$. Show that the operator $HU_{0\perp}H$ can be written as $(2|\psi\rangle\langle\psi| - \mathbb{I})$.

Exercise 8.1.3 Prove that any n-qubit state $|\phi\rangle$ that is orthogonal to $H|00\ldots0\rangle$ has the sum of its amplitudes equal to 0.

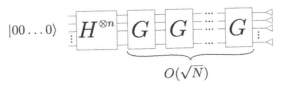

Fig. 8.3 Grover's quantum searching algorithm.

Exercise 8.1.4 Prove that $U_{\psi\perp}$ 'inverts about the mean'. More precisely, consider any superposition

$$|\phi\rangle = \sum_x \alpha_x |x\rangle$$

where

$$\mu = \frac{1}{N} \sum_x \alpha_x$$

is the mean of the amplitudes. Show that $U_{\psi\perp}|\phi\rangle = \sum_x (\mu - \alpha_x)|x\rangle$.

Hint: Decompose $|\phi\rangle$ as $|\phi\rangle = \alpha|\psi\rangle + \beta|\overline{\psi}\rangle$ where $|\overline{\psi}\rangle$ is orthogonal to $|\psi\rangle$.

Since $H|00\ldots0\rangle$ has only real amplitudes, and the Grover iterate does not introduce any complex phases, then the amplitudes always remain real. This allows us to represent the amplitudes as lines above (for positive amplitudes) or below (for negative amplitudes), an axis labelled by the N possible inputs, as done in Figure 8.4. Initially, the state is $|\psi\rangle = H|00\ldots0\rangle$, so the mean value of the amplitudes is simply $\frac{1}{\sqrt{N}}$.

After the application of U_f, the amplitude of $|w\rangle$ picks up a -1 phase shift, and thus the mean value of the amplitudes shifts down slightly, as illustrated in Figure 8.5.

The operator $U_{\psi\perp}$ can be viewed as an 'inversion about the mean', which nearly triples the size of the amplitude of $|w\rangle$, and slightly nudges down the amplitudes of all the other basis states, as illustrated in Figure 8.6.

Another application of U_f makes the amplitude of $|w\rangle$ negative again, slightly pushing down the mean value of the amplitudes, and the inversion about the mean operation adds roughly another $\frac{2}{\sqrt{N}}$ to the size of the amplitude of $|w\rangle$ and slightly nudges down the amplitudes of all the other basis states.

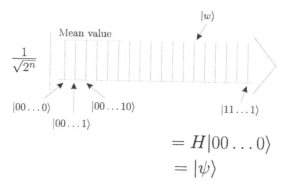

Fig. 8.4 Real valued amplitudes represented as lines above and below a horizontal axis labelled by the N possible inputs to the search problem. The state $|\psi\rangle$ depicted above is a uniform superposition over all possible inputs.

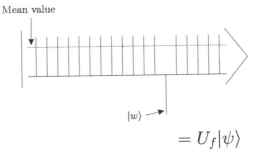

Fig. 8.5 State after a single application of U_f (omitting the normalization factor).

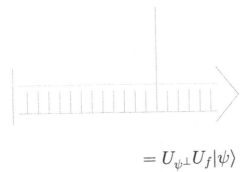

Fig. 8.6 Inversion about the mean.

We can see that roughly $\frac{\sqrt{N}}{2}$ iterations of the Grover iterate should boost the amplitude of $|w\rangle$ to be close to 1. The following is a precise analysis.

First note that we can write $|\psi\rangle = H|00\ldots0\rangle$ in terms of $|w\rangle$ and $|\psi_{\text{bad}}\rangle$ as

$$|\psi\rangle = \tfrac{1}{\sqrt{N}}|w\rangle + \sqrt{\tfrac{N-1}{N}}|\psi_{\text{bad}}\rangle. \qquad (8.1.13)$$

It is important to observe that starting in the state $|\psi\rangle$ and repeatedly applying U_f and $U_{\psi^\perp}$ leaves the state of the system in the subspace spanned by $|w\rangle$ and $|\psi_{\text{bad}}\rangle$, that is, a 2-dimensional subspace of the $N = 2^n$-dimensional state space.

In order to analyse Grover's algorithm, it helps to define two bases for this 2-dimensional subspace:

$$\{|w\rangle, |\psi_{\text{bad}}\rangle\} \qquad (8.1.14)$$

and

$$\{|\psi\rangle, |\overline{\psi}\rangle\} \qquad (8.1.15)$$

where we define the state $|\overline{\psi}\rangle$ orthogonal to $|\psi\rangle$:

$$|\overline{\psi}\rangle = \sqrt{\tfrac{N-1}{N}}|w\rangle - \tfrac{1}{\sqrt{N}}|\psi_{\text{bad}}\rangle. \qquad (8.1.16)$$

Note that the mean value of the amplitudes of $|\overline{\psi}\rangle$ is 0 (see Exercise 8.1.3).

Define θ so that

$$\sin(\theta) = \frac{1}{\sqrt{N}}. \tag{8.1.17}$$

Then we have $\cos(\theta) = \sqrt{\frac{N-1}{N}}$.

Note that

$$|\psi\rangle = \sin(\theta)|w\rangle + \cos(\theta)|\psi_{\text{bad}}\rangle, \tag{8.1.18}$$
$$|\overline{\psi}\rangle = \cos(\theta)|w\rangle - \sin(\theta)|\psi_{\text{bad}}\rangle \tag{8.1.19}$$

and also

$$|w\rangle = \sin(\theta)|\psi\rangle + \cos(\theta)|\overline{\psi}\rangle, \tag{8.1.20}$$
$$|\psi_{\text{bad}}\rangle = \cos(\theta)|\psi\rangle - \sin(\theta)|\overline{\psi}\rangle \tag{8.1.21}$$

so we can easily convert between the two bases.

Figures 8.7 and 8.8 illustrate the states $|\psi\rangle$ and $|\overline{\psi}\rangle$ in terms of $|w\rangle$ and $|\psi_{\text{bad}}\rangle$. The quantum searching algorithm starts off in the state

$$|\psi\rangle = \sin(\theta)|w\rangle + \cos(\theta)|\psi_{\text{bad}}\rangle.$$

The operator U_f gives the state

$$U_f|\psi\rangle = -\sin(\theta)|w\rangle + \cos(\theta)|\psi_{\text{bad}}\rangle = \cos(2\theta)|\psi\rangle - \sin(2\theta)|\overline{\psi}\rangle$$

illustrated in Figures 8.9 and 8.10.

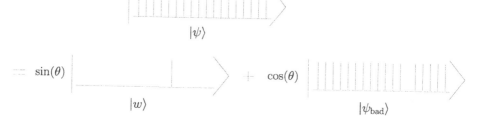

Fig. 8.7 The state $|\psi\rangle$ in terms of $|w\rangle$ and $|\psi_{\text{bad}}\rangle$. Note that θ satisfies $\sin(\theta) = \frac{1}{\sqrt{2^n}}$.

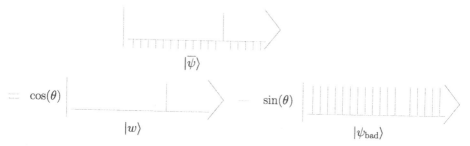

Fig. 8.8 The state $|\overline{\psi}\rangle$ in terms of $|w\rangle$ and $|\psi_{\text{bad}}\rangle$.

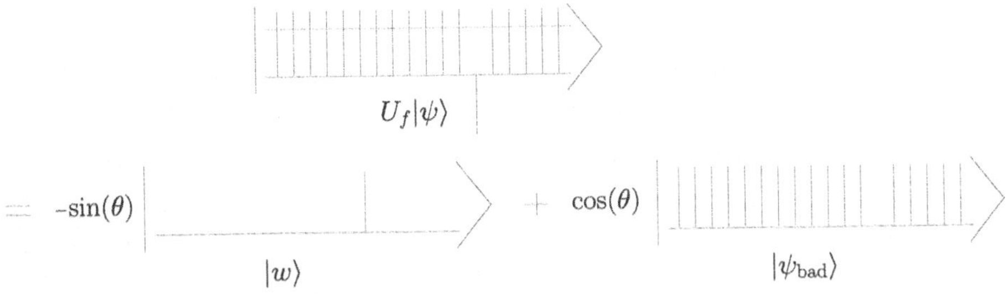

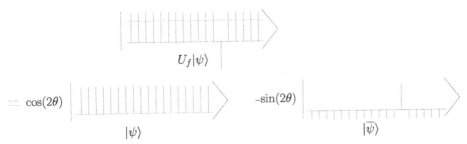

Fig. 8.9 The state after one application of U_f. Compare with Figure 8.7.

$U_f|\psi\rangle$

$\cos(2\theta)$ |$\psi\rangle$ $-\sin(2\theta)$ $|\overline{\psi}\rangle$

Fig. 8.10 The state in Figure 8.9 can be expressed in terms of the $\{|\psi\rangle, |\overline{\psi}\rangle\}$ basis.

Then the inversion about the mean, $U_\psi^\perp$, gives the state

$$U_\psi^\perp U_f|\psi\rangle = \cos(2\theta)|\psi\rangle + \sin(2\theta)|\overline{\psi}\rangle = \sin(3\theta)|w\rangle + \cos(3\theta)|\psi_{\text{bad}}\rangle,$$

illustrated in Figures 8.11 and 8.12.

It is easy to verify by induction that after k iterations of the Grover iterate starting with state $|\psi\rangle = H|00\ldots0\rangle$, we are left with the state

$$(U_\psi^\perp U_f)^k|\psi\rangle = \cos(2k\theta)|\psi\rangle + \sin(2k\theta)|\overline{\psi}\rangle$$
$$= \sin\big((2k+1)\theta\big)|w\rangle + \cos\big((2k+1)\theta\big)|\psi_{\text{bad}}\rangle, \qquad (8.1.22)$$

illustrated in Figure 8.13.

Exercise 8.1.5 Verify that for any real number j

$$\sin((2j+1)\theta)|w\rangle + \cos((2j+1)\theta)|\psi_{\text{bad}}\rangle = \cos(2j\theta)|\psi\rangle + \sin(2j\theta)|\overline{\psi}\rangle.$$

In order to have a high probability of obtaining $|w\rangle$, we wish to select k so that $\sin((2k+1)\theta) \approx 1$, which means that we would like $(2k+1)\theta \approx \frac{\pi}{2}$, and thus $k \approx \frac{\pi}{4\theta} - \frac{1}{2} \approx \frac{\pi}{4}\sqrt{N}$.

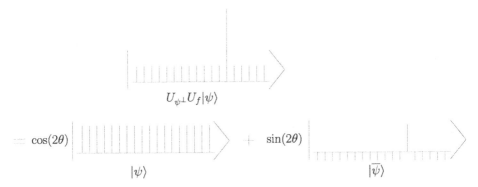

Fig. 8.11 The state after the inversion about the mean.

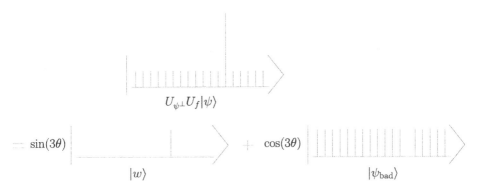

Fig. 8.12 The state in Figure 8.11 expressed in terms of the $\{|w\rangle, |\psi_{\text{bad}}\rangle\}$ basis.

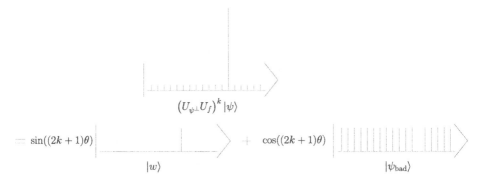

Fig. 8.13 The state after k iterations of the Grover iterate.

Let $\tilde{k}$ satisfy $(2\tilde{k}+1)\theta = \frac{\pi}{2}$. Let $k = \lfloor \tilde{k} \rfloor$.

Note that $(2k+1)\theta = \frac{\pi}{2} + \varepsilon$ where $|\varepsilon| \in O\left(\frac{1}{\sqrt{N}}\right)$. Thus, $\sin\left(\frac{\pi}{2} + \varepsilon\right) = \cos(\varepsilon) \geq 1 - \frac{\varepsilon^2}{2} \in 1 - O\left(\frac{1}{N}\right)$.

Rounding off

For any real number x we are using the standard notation $\lceil x \rceil$ and $\lfloor x \rfloor$ to denote the nearest integer greater than x (rounding x 'up') and the nearest integer less than x (rounding x 'down'), respectively.

We also use the notation $[x]$ to denote the nearest integer to x (in the case that x is exactly in between two integers, rounding off to either one will do for the purposes of this textbook).

Since in some cases the algorithms we describe require us to round off a real number x, given as an expression like $\frac{\pi}{4}\sqrt{N}, \arcsin(\frac{1}{\sqrt{N}})$, or $N\sin^2(\frac{x}{M})$, it is worth mentioning that this is not a computational bottleneck in any of the circumstances in which we use it.

All of the functions that our algorithms need to round off can be efficiently approximated with precision $\epsilon > 0$ (i.e. in time polynomial in $\log(\frac{1}{\epsilon})$ and also in the description length of x, which is logarithmic in N, M, and x in the above examples). That is, for any $\epsilon > 0$, we can efficiently compute an integer y such that $y - \epsilon \leq x \leq y + 1$ (an approximate version of $\lfloor x \rfloor$), or $|y - x| \leq \frac{1}{2} + \epsilon$ (an approximate version of $[x]$).

For simplicity, we will just use the $\lceil x \rceil$, $\lfloor x \rfloor$, or $[x]$ notation in the description of the algorithms with the understanding that if we are concerned with the efficiency of the classical part of the algorithm, then an approximate round off will suffice.

Theorem 8.1.1 *Let f be a function with exactly one solution. Let $k = \lfloor \tilde{k} \rfloor$, for $\tilde{k} = \frac{\pi}{4\theta} - \frac{1}{2}$. Running the quantum search algorithm with k applications of the Grover iteration will find a solution to $f(x) = 1$ with probability at least $1 - O\left(\frac{1}{N}\right)$.*

The assumption of having only one solution is not necessary. Before analysing how the algorithm works when there is more than one solution, we describe a more general version of quantum searching.

8.2 Amplitude Amplification

Grover's search algorithm can be generalized substantially to apply to any algorithm A for 'guessing' a solution. In the previous section we had $A = H^{\otimes n}$ which guessed the solution by setting up a uniform superposition of all possible solutions. More generally, consider any algorithm A that starts with the generic input state $|00\ldots0\rangle$, which can include additional workspace, and maps to some superposition of guesses $|\psi\rangle = \sum_x \alpha_x |x\rangle |\text{junk}(x)\rangle$ which might have some 'junk' information left in the workspace qubits. That is

$$|\psi\rangle \equiv A|00\ldots0\rangle = \sum_x \alpha_x |x\rangle |\text{junk}(x)\rangle. \tag{8.2.1}$$

Note that we can naturally split $|\psi\rangle$ into two parts:

$$|\psi\rangle = \sum_{x \in X_{\text{good}}} \alpha_x |x\rangle |\text{junk}(x)\rangle + \sum_{x \in X_{\text{bad}}} \alpha_x |x\rangle |\text{junk}(x)\rangle. \tag{8.2.2}$$

Note that

$$p_{\text{good}} = \sum_{x \in X_{\text{good}}} |\alpha_x|^2 \tag{8.2.3}$$

is the probability of measuring a good state x, and

$$p_{\text{bad}} = \sum_{x \in X_{\text{bad}}} |\alpha_x|^2 = 1 - p_{\text{good}} \tag{8.2.4}$$

is the probability of measuring a bad state x.

If $p_{\text{good}} = 1$, no amplification is necessary, and if $p_{\text{good}} = 0$, amplification will not help since there is no good amplitude to amplify. In the interesting cases that $0 < p_{\text{good}} < 1$, we can renormalize the good and the bad components into

$$|\psi_{\text{good}}\rangle = \sum_{x \in X_{\text{good}}} \frac{\alpha_x}{\sqrt{p_{\text{good}}}} |x\rangle |\text{junk}(x)\rangle \tag{8.2.5}$$

and

$$|\psi_{\text{bad}}\rangle = \sum_{x \in X_{\text{bad}}} \frac{\alpha_x}{\sqrt{p_{\text{bad}}}} |x\rangle |\text{junk}(x)\rangle. \tag{8.2.6}$$

We can then write

$$|\psi\rangle = \sqrt{p_{\text{good}}} |\psi_{\text{good}}\rangle + \sqrt{p_{\text{bad}}} |\psi_{\text{bad}}\rangle \tag{8.2.7}$$

or

$$|\psi\rangle = \sin(\theta) |\psi_{\text{good}}\rangle + \cos(\theta) |\psi_{\text{bad}}\rangle \tag{8.2.8}$$

where $\theta \in (0, \frac{\pi}{2})$ satisfies $\sin^2(\theta) = p_{\text{good}}$.

We define a more general search iterate to be $Q = AU_0^\perp A^{-1} U_f$, which one can easily verify to be equivalent to $U_\psi^\perp U_f$, where as before we define $U_\psi^\perp |\psi\rangle = |\psi\rangle$ and $U_\psi^\perp |\phi\rangle = -|\phi\rangle$ for all states $|\phi\rangle$ that are orthogonal to $|\psi\rangle$.

The state just before the first application of Q is the superposition

$$|\psi\rangle = \sin(\theta)|\psi_{\text{good}}\rangle + \cos(\theta)|\psi_{\text{bad}}\rangle. \qquad (8.2.9)$$

For convenience, let us define the state

$$|\overline{\psi}\rangle = \cos(\theta)|\psi_{\text{good}}\rangle - \sin(\theta)|\psi_{\text{bad}}\rangle \qquad (8.2.10)$$

which is orthogonal to $|\psi\rangle$. Note that

$$\{|\psi_{\text{good}}\rangle, |\psi_{\text{bad}}\rangle\} \qquad (8.2.11)$$

and

$$\{|\overline{\psi}\rangle, |\psi\rangle\} \qquad (8.2.12)$$

are orthonormal bases for the same 2-dimensional subspace.

We show that if we start with the state $|\psi\rangle$, then alternately applying U_f and $U_\psi^\perp$ leaves the system in the 2-dimensional subspace over the real numbers spanned by $|\psi_{\text{good}}\rangle$ and $|\psi_{\text{bad}}\rangle$.

Since the amplitudes will be real numbers (any complex phases are absorbed in the definitions of $|\psi_{\text{good}}\rangle$, $|\psi_{\text{bad}}\rangle$, $|\psi\rangle$, and $|\overline{\psi}\rangle$), we can conveniently draw the states on the unit circle in the plane, as seen in Figure 8.14.

Note that U_f will map

$$\sin(\theta)|\psi_{\text{good}}\rangle + \cos(\theta)|\psi_{\text{bad}}\rangle \mapsto -\sin(\theta)|\psi_{\text{good}}\rangle + \cos(\theta)|\psi_{\text{bad}}\rangle, \qquad (8.2.13)$$

as illustrated in Figure 8.15.

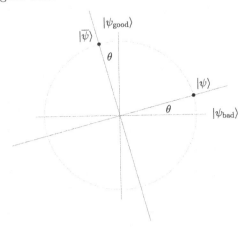

Fig. 8.14 The states $|\psi\rangle = A|00\ldots0\rangle = \sin(\theta)|\psi_{\text{good}}\rangle + \cos(\theta)|\psi_{\text{bad}}\rangle$ and $|\overline{\psi}\rangle = \cos(\theta)|\psi_{\text{good}}\rangle - \sin(\theta)|\psi_{\text{bad}}\rangle$ illustrated on the unit circle in the plane.

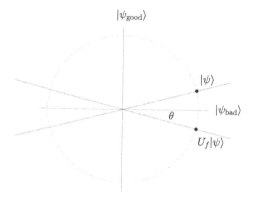

Fig. 8.15 The state $U_f|\psi\rangle = -\sin(\theta)|\psi_{\text{good}}\rangle + \cos(\theta)|\psi_{\text{bad}}\rangle$.

The action of $U_\psi^\perp$ is most easily seen in the basis

$$\{|\overline{\psi}\rangle, |\psi\rangle\}, \tag{8.2.14}$$

so it is convenient to first rewrite

$$U_f|\psi\rangle = -\sin(\theta)|\psi_{\text{good}}\rangle + \cos(\theta)|\psi_{\text{bad}}\rangle \tag{8.2.15}$$
$$= \cos(2\theta)|\psi\rangle - \sin(2\theta)|\overline{\psi}\rangle \tag{8.2.16}$$

and then it is clear that

$$U_\psi^\perp U_f|\psi\rangle = U_\psi^\perp \left(-\sin(\theta)|\psi_{\text{good}}\rangle + \cos(\theta)|\psi_{\text{bad}}\rangle\right) \tag{8.2.17}$$
$$= \cos(2\theta)|\psi\rangle + \sin(2\theta)|\overline{\psi}\rangle \tag{8.2.18}$$

and can be expressed in the $\{|\psi_{\text{good}}\rangle, |\psi_{\text{bad}}\rangle\}$ basis as

$$U_\psi^\perp U_f|\psi\rangle = \sin(3\theta)|\psi_{\text{good}}\rangle + \cos(3\theta)|\psi_{\text{bad}}\rangle. \tag{8.2.19}$$

This state is illustrated in Figure 8.16.

Notice that more generally for any real number ϕ, the operation U_f does the following:

$$U_f\left(\sin(\phi)|\psi_{\text{good}}\rangle + \cos(\phi)|\psi_{\text{bad}}\rangle\right) = -\sin(\phi)|\psi_{\text{good}}\rangle + \cos(\phi)|\psi_{\text{bad}}\rangle \tag{8.2.20}$$

and so U_f performs a reflection about the axis defined by the vector $|\psi_{\text{bad}}\rangle$.

Similarly, the operation $U_\psi^\perp$ does the following in general:

$$U_\psi^\perp\left(\sin(\phi)|\psi\rangle + \cos(\phi)|\overline{\psi}\rangle\right) = \sin(\phi)|\psi\rangle - \cos(\phi)|\overline{\psi}\rangle \tag{8.2.21}$$

and so $U_\psi^\perp$ performs a reflection about the axis defined by the $|\psi\rangle$.

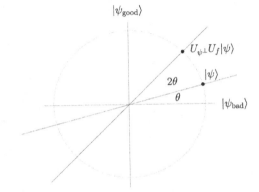

Fig. 8.16 The state $U_\psi^\perp U_f |\psi\rangle = \sin(3\theta)|\psi_{\text{good}}\rangle + \cos(3\theta)|\psi_{\text{bad}}\rangle$.

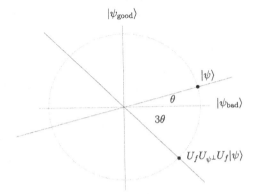

Fig. 8.17 The state $U_f U_\psi^\perp U_f |\psi\rangle = -\sin(3\theta)|\psi_{\text{good}}\rangle + \cos(3\theta)|\psi_{\text{bad}}\rangle$.

Two such refections correspond to a rotation through an angle 2θ in the 2-dimensional subspace. Thus, repeated application of $Q = U_\psi^\perp U_f$ a total of k times rotates the initial state $|\psi\rangle$ to

$$Q^k|\psi\rangle = \cos\big((2k+1)\theta\big)|\psi_{\text{bad}}\rangle + \sin\big((2k+1)\theta\big)|\psi_{\text{good}}\rangle, \qquad (8.2.22)$$

as illustrated in Figures 8.17–8.19.

Searching by amplitude amplification works by applying Q an appropriate number of times until the state is such that a measurement will yield an element of the subspace spanned by $|\psi_{\text{good}}\rangle$ with high probability. It remains to analyse how many iterations of Q are needed.

To get a high probability of measuring a good value, the smallest positive k we can choose is such that $(2k+1)\theta \approx \frac{\pi}{2}$, implying $k \in \Omega\left(\frac{1}{\theta}\right)$. Note that for small θ, $\sin(\theta) \approx \theta$ and since $\sin(\theta) = \sqrt{P_{\text{good}}}$, searching via amplitude amplification uses

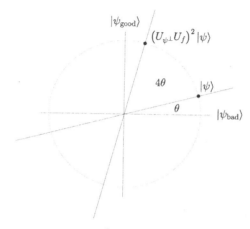

Fig. 8.18 The state $\left(U_\psi^\perp U_f\right)^2 |\psi\rangle = \sin(5\theta)|\psi_{\text{good}}\rangle + \cos(5\theta)|\psi_{\text{bad}}\rangle$.

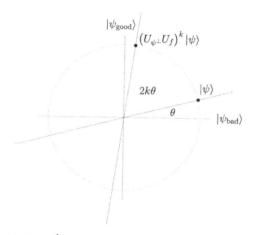

Fig. 8.19 The state $\left(U_\psi^\perp U_f\right)^k |\psi\rangle = \sin\big((2k+1)\theta\big)|\psi_{\text{good}}\rangle + \cos\big((2k+1)\theta\big)|\psi_{\text{bad}}\rangle$. We choose k so this state is close to $|\psi_{\text{good}}\rangle$.

only[2] $O\left(\sqrt{\frac{1}{p_{\text{good}}}}\right)$ queries to U_f. Assuming $p_{\text{good}} \geq \frac{1}{2^n}$, any classical algorithm would need $\Omega\left(\frac{1}{p_{\text{good}}}\right)$ queries to U_f or guesses uses the algorithm A.

Exercise 8.2.1 Suppose there are t solutions to $f(x) = 1$, with $0 < t < N$, with t known.

Show how to use amplitude amplification to find a solution with probability at least $\frac{2}{3}$ using $O\left(\sqrt{\frac{N}{t}}\right)$ applications of U_f.

---

[2]One could do better in the case that $p_{\text{good}} < \frac{1}{2^n}$ by abandoning amplitude amplification with A once K exceeds 2^n and just exhaustively searching.

You may have noticed that to apply this algorithm we have to know ahead of time how many times to apply Q. In the case that A uniformly samples the input, this requires knowing the number of solutions to the search problem. For more general A it requires knowing the probability with which A guesses a solution to $f(x) = 1$, that is, $\sin^2(\theta)$. However, in many search problems of interest we will not know in advance how many solutions there are. Later, in Section 8.4, we will address this technical problem of searching without knowing in advance how many search iterates are ideal. In the next section we will study the related question of approximating the amplitude with which A maps $|00\ldots0\rangle$ to the subspace of solutions. In other words, we study the problem of estimating the amplitude $\sin(\theta)$ (or equivalently, the probability $\sin^2(\theta)$) when $A|00\ldots0\rangle = \sin(\theta)|\psi_{\text{good}}\rangle + \cos(\theta)|\psi_{\text{bad}}\rangle$.

Exercise 8.2.2

Let U_f be a black box that implements $U_f : |x\rangle|b\rangle \mapsto |x\rangle|b \oplus f(x)\rangle$.

(a) Suppose $f : \{00, 01, 10, 11\} \rightarrow \{0, 1\}$ has the property that exactly one string x satisfies $f(x) = 1$.
Show how to find with certainty the unique x satisfying $f(x) = 1$ with only one application to U_f.

(b) Suppose $f : \{0, 1\}^n \rightarrow \{0, 1\}$, and the unitary operator A has the property that $A|00\ldots0\rangle = \sum_x \alpha_x |x\rangle|\text{junk}(x)\rangle$ with the property that the probability of measuring a good string x upon measuring $A|00\ldots0\rangle$ is $\frac{1}{4}$.
Show how to find with certainty the unique x satisfying $f(x) = 1$ with only one application to U_f.

(c) Suppose $f : \{0, 1\}^n \rightarrow \{0, 1\}$, and the unitary operator A has the property that $A|00\ldots0\rangle = \sum_x \alpha_x |x\rangle|\text{junk}(x)\rangle$ with the property that the probability of measuring a good string x upon measuring $A|00\ldots0\rangle$ is $\frac{1}{2}$.
Show how to find with certainty an x satisfying $f(x) = 1$ with only one application to U_f.

Hint: Add an extra qubit in the state $\frac{1}{2}|1\rangle + \sqrt{\frac{3}{4}}|0\rangle$, and define a new function $\tilde{f}(x, b) = b \cdot f(x)$, where $b \in \{0, 1\}$.

(d) Suppose $f : \{0, 1\}^n \rightarrow \{0, 1\}$, and the unitary operator A has the property that $A|00\ldots0\rangle = \sum_x \alpha_x |x\rangle|\text{junk}(x)\rangle$ with the property that the probability of measuring a good string x upon measuring $A|00\ldots0\rangle$ is $p > 0$.
Show that if we know p we can define a circuit that finds a solution to $f(x)$ with certainty using $O\left(\frac{1}{\sqrt{p}}\right)$ applications of U_f.

Exercise 8.2.3 Suppose we have an algorithm A that outputs a good solution with probability $\frac{1}{4} - \varepsilon$. Show how one iteration of the search iterate gives us an algorithm that succeeds with probability $1 - O(\varepsilon^2)$.

Note: There is also an algorithm that succeeds with probability $1 - O(\varepsilon^3)$.

8.3   Quantum Amplitude Estimation and Quantum Counting

Note that the material in Sections 8.1 and 8.2 on quantum searching and amplitude amplification are prerequisites to the present section on quantum amplitude
estimation and counting.

Suppose instead of being interested in *finding* a solution to a search problem
we are interested in *counting* how many solutions exist. That is, given a search
space with N elements, indexed by $\{0, 1, \ldots, N-1\}$, t of which are solutions to
$f(x) = 1$, we want to determine t. This is the *counting problem* associated with
f. We will also consider the easier problem of *approximately counting t*.

As in Section 8.1, let X_{bad} be the set of x that are *not* solutions to the search
problem, and let X_{good} be the set of x that *are* solutions to the search problem.
We again defined $|\psi_{\text{good}}\rangle$ and $|\psi_{\text{bad}}\rangle$ as in Equations (8.2.5) and (8.2.6).

The counting algorithm we describe is a special case of *amplitude estimation*,
which estimates the amplitude with which an n-qubit circuit A maps $|00\ldots0\rangle$
to the subspace of solutions to $f(x) = 1$.

Amplitude Estimation Problem

Input:

- The operator A with the property that $A|00\ldots0\rangle = \sin(\theta)|\psi_{\text{good}}\rangle + \cos(\theta)|\psi_{\text{bad}}\rangle$, $0 \leq \theta \leq \frac{\pi}{2}$.
- The operator U_f that maps $|\psi_{\text{good}}\rangle \mapsto -|\psi_{\text{good}}\rangle$ and $|\psi_{\text{bad}}\rangle \mapsto |\psi_{\text{bad}}\rangle$.

Problem: Estimate $\sin(\theta)$ (or equivalently, $\sin^2(\theta)$).

Quantum counting is a special case of quantum amplitude estimation, where we
choose A so that $A|00\ldots0\rangle = \frac{1}{\sqrt{N}}\sum_{j=0}^{N-1}|j\rangle$.[3]

So if $A|0\rangle = \frac{1}{\sqrt{N}}\sum_{j=0}^{N-1}|j\rangle$ and $0 < t < N$, then we have

$$|\psi_{\text{good}}\rangle = \sum_{j \in X_{\text{good}}} \tfrac{1}{\sqrt{t}}|j\rangle \qquad (8.3.1)$$

$$|\psi_{\text{bad}}\rangle = \sum_{j \in X_{\text{bad}}} \tfrac{1}{\sqrt{N-t}}|j\rangle \qquad (8.3.2)$$

and

$$A|00\ldots0\rangle = \sqrt{\tfrac{t}{N}}|\psi_{\text{good}}\rangle + \sqrt{\tfrac{N-t}{N}}|\psi_{\text{bad}}\rangle. \qquad (8.3.3)$$

Thus, we have $\sin^2(\theta) = \frac{t}{N}$ and thus an estimation of $\sin^2(\theta)$ gives us an estimation of t.

---

[3]In fact, it suffices that $A|00\ldots0\rangle = \frac{1}{\sqrt{N}}\sum_{j=0}^{N-1}e^{i\phi_j}|j\rangle$ for any $\phi_j \in [0, 2\pi)$.

We can consider any n-qubit circuit A so that $A|00\ldots0\rangle = \sum_{j=0}^{2^n-1} \alpha_j|j\rangle$. Define θ, $0 \le \theta \le \frac{\pi}{2}$ to satisfy

$$\sum_{j\in X_{\text{good}}} |\alpha_j|^2 = \sin^2\theta \tag{8.3.4}$$

$$\sum_{j\in X_{\text{bad}}} |\alpha_j|^2 = \cos^2\theta. \tag{8.3.5}$$

We will initially restrict attention to the cases where $0 < \sin(\theta) < 1$, and so

$$A|00\ldots0\rangle = \sin\theta|\psi_{\text{good}}\rangle + \cos\theta|\psi_{\text{bad}}\rangle. \tag{8.3.6}$$

The cases that $\sin(\theta) = 0$ and $\sin(\theta) = 1$ are easily analysed separately. Recall that in the non-trivial cases the amplitude amplification Q is a rotation in the space spanned by $|\psi_{\text{bad}}\rangle$ and $|\psi_{\text{good}}\rangle$ through an angle 2θ. So in the subspace spanned by $\{|\psi_{\text{bad}}\rangle, |\psi_{\text{good}}\rangle\}$, Q is described by the rotation matrix

$$\begin{bmatrix} \cos\theta & -\sin\theta \\ \sin\theta & \cos\theta \end{bmatrix}. \tag{8.3.7}$$

A simple calculation shows that two independent eigenvectors for this matrix are

$$\begin{pmatrix} \frac{i}{\sqrt{2}} \\ \frac{1}{\sqrt{2}} \end{pmatrix}, \quad \begin{pmatrix} -\frac{i}{\sqrt{2}} \\ \frac{1}{\sqrt{2}} \end{pmatrix} \tag{8.3.8}$$

with corresponding eigenvalues $e^{i2\theta}$ and $e^{-i2\theta}$, respectively. The above eigenvectors are expressed in the $\{|\psi_{\text{bad}}\rangle, |\psi_{\text{good}}\rangle\}$ basis, and so this means that

$$|\psi_+\rangle = \frac{1}{\sqrt{2}}|\psi_{\text{bad}}\rangle + \frac{i}{\sqrt{2}}|\psi_{\text{good}}\rangle,$$
$$|\psi_-\rangle = \frac{1}{\sqrt{2}}|\psi_{\text{bad}}\rangle - \frac{i}{\sqrt{2}}|\psi_{\text{good}}\rangle \tag{8.3.9}$$

are eigenvectors for Q with corresponding eigenvalues $e^{i2\theta}$ and $e^{-i2\theta}$, respectively. It is easy to check that

$$|\psi\rangle = \frac{1}{\sqrt{N}} \sum_{x=0}^{N-1} |x\rangle$$
$$= e^{i\theta}\frac{1}{\sqrt{2}}|\psi_+\rangle + e^{-i\theta}\frac{1}{\sqrt{2}}|\psi_-\rangle. \tag{8.3.10}$$

So $|\psi\rangle$ is an equally weighted superposition of eigenvectors for Q having eigenvalues $e^{i2\theta}$ and $e^{-i2\theta}$. The quantum amplitude estimation algorithm works by applying eigenvalue estimation (Section 7.2) with the second register in the superposition $|\psi\rangle = e^{i\theta}\frac{1}{\sqrt{2}}|\psi_+\rangle + e^{i\theta}\frac{1}{\sqrt{2}}|\psi_-\rangle$. This gives us an estimate of either 2θ or -2θ, from which we can compute an estimate of $\sin^2(\theta) = \sin^2(-\theta)$. The quantum amplitude estimation circuit is shown in Figure 8.20.

The circuit outputs an integer $y \in \{0,1,2,\ldots, M-1\}$, where $M = 2^m$, $m \ge 1$, and the estimate of $p = \sin^2(\theta)$ is $\tilde{p} = \sin^2\left(\pi\frac{y}{M}\right)$.

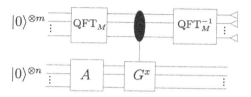

Fig. 8.20 Circuit for quantum amplitude estimation where $M = 2^m$ applications of the search iterate, and thus M applications of U_f, are used. A measurement of the top register gives a string representing an integer y. The value $\frac{2\pi y}{M}$ is an estimate of either 2θ or $2\pi - 2\theta$.

Note that if $A|00\ldots0\rangle = |\psi_{\text{good}}\rangle$, which is the case that $\theta = \frac{\pi}{2}$, then $QA|00\ldots0\rangle = -A|00\ldots0\rangle$. Thus eigenvalue estimation will be estimating the eigenvalue $-1 = e^{2\pi i \frac{1}{2}}$. Since M is even, eigenvalue estimation will output $y = \frac{M}{2}$ with certainty, and thus we will determine the correct eigenvalue $-1 = e^{i\pi}$ with certainty. So our estimate $\tilde{p} = \sin^2\left(\pi \frac{1}{2}\right) = 1$ will be exactly correct with certainty.

Similarly, if $A|00\ldots0\rangle = |\psi_{\text{bad}}\rangle$, which is the case that $\theta = 0$, then $QA|00\ldots0\rangle = |00\ldots0\rangle$, and thus eigenvalue estimation will be estimating the eigenvalue 1. Thus eigenvalue estimation will output $y = 0$ with certainty, and we will determine the correct eigenvalue $1 = e^{i0}$ with certainty. So our estimate $\tilde{p} = \sin^2(0) = 0$ will be exactly correct with certainty.

Amplitude Estimation Algorithm

1. Choose a precision parameter m. Let $M = 2^m$.
2. Let $Q = A^{-1}U_{0^\perp}AU_f$.
3. Prepare an m-qubit control register, and a second register containing the state $A|00\ldots0\rangle$.
4. Apply the QFT_M to the first register
5. Apply a controlled Q^x.
6. Apply the QFT_M^{-1} to the first register.
7. Measure the first register to obtain a string representing some integer $y \in \{0, 1, \ldots, M-1\}$.
8. Output $\sin^2(\pi \frac{y}{M})$.

Theorem 8.3.1 *For any positive integers k and m, $M = 2^m$, the amplitude estimation algorithm outputs $\tilde{p}$, $0 \leq \tilde{p} \leq 1$ such that*

$$|\tilde{p} - p| \leq 2\pi k \frac{\sqrt{p(1-p)}}{M} + k^2 \frac{\pi^2}{M^2} \tag{8.3.11}$$

with probability at least $\frac{8}{\pi^2}$ when $k = 1$ and with probability greater than $1 - \frac{1}{2(k-1)}$ for $k \geq 2$. If $p = 0$ then $\tilde{p} = 0$ with certainty, and if $p = 1$ and then $\tilde{p} = 1$ with certainty.

Counting with Error in $O(\sqrt{t})$

1. Run amplitude estimation with $M = \lceil \sqrt{N} \rceil$ iterations of the search iterate, to obtain the estimate $\tilde{p}$.
2. Let $\tilde{t} = [\tilde{p}N]$. Output $\tilde{t}$.

Corollary 8.3.2 *The above algorithm outputs a value $\tilde{t}$ such that with probability at least $\frac{8}{\pi^2}$ we have*

$$|\tilde{t} - t| < 2\pi\sqrt{\frac{t(N-t)}{N}} + 11 \in O(\sqrt{t}). \qquad (8.3.12)$$

It is also possible to vary the parameter M and get an approximate counting algorithm with the following properties. The tricky part in designing these counting algorithms that use amplitude estimation as a subroutine is to guarantee that we are very unlikely to use a value M that turns out to be much larger that was necessary. We omit the proofs of the detailed performance of these algorithms.

Counting with Accuracy ε

1. Set $l = 0$.
2. Increment l by 1.
3. Run amplitude estimation with $M = 2^l$ iterations of the search iterate, and let $\tilde{t} = [\tilde{p}N]$.
4. If $\tilde{t} = 0$ and $2^l < 2\sqrt{N}$ then go to Step 2.
5. Run the amplitude estimation algorithm with parameter $M = \lceil \frac{20\pi^2}{\varepsilon} 2^l \rceil$, to obtain the estimate $\tilde{p}$.
6. Let $\tilde{t} = [\tilde{p}N]$. Output $\tilde{t}$.

Corollary 8.3.3 *The above algorithm outputs a value $\tilde{t}$ such that $|\tilde{t} - t| \leq \varepsilon t$ with probability at least $\frac{2}{3}$. The expected number of evaluations of f is in $O\left(\frac{1}{\varepsilon}\sqrt{\frac{N}{t}}\right)$. If $t = 0$, the algorithm outputs $\tilde{t} = t = 0$ with certainty and f is evaluated a number of times in $O(\sqrt{N})$.*

Exact Counting

1. Let $\tilde{p}_1$ and $\tilde{p}_2$ be the results of two independent runs of amplitude estimation with $M = \left\lceil 14\pi\sqrt{N} \right\rceil$.
2. Let $M_1 = \left\lceil 30\sqrt{(N\tilde{p}_1 + 1)(N - N\tilde{p}_1 + 1)} \right\rceil$.
   Let $M_2 = \left\lceil 30\sqrt{(N\tilde{p}_2 + 1)(N - N\tilde{p}_2 + 1)} \right\rceil$.
   Let $M = \min\{M_1, M_2\}$.
3. Let $\tilde{p}$ be the estimate obtained by running amplitude estimation with M iterations of the search iterate.
4. Let $\tilde{t} = [\tilde{p}N]$. Output $\tilde{t}$.

Theorem 8.3.4 *The Exact Counting algorithm requires an expected number of application of U_f in $O(\sqrt{(t+1)(N-t+1)})$ and outputs the correct value of t with probability at least $\frac{2}{3}$.*

We will see in Section 9.2 that this algorithm uses an optimal number (up to a constant factor) of applications of U_f.

Exercise 8.3.1 Suppose we are promised that the number of solutions is either 0 or some integer t (that we are given).

Show how to decide whether f has a solution with certainty using $O\left(\sqrt{\frac{N}{t}}\right)$ applications of U_f.

Hint: Recall Exercise 8.2.2 (d).

Example 8.3.5 One application of counting is to compute the mean of a function $g : X \to Y$, where X is some discrete finite domain, which for convenience we assume is $\{0,1\}^n$, and Y is a subset of the real numbers, which we can assume without loss of generality is contained in the interval $[0,1)$. For convenience, we will assume $g(x) = \frac{x}{2^m}$ for some integer $x \in \{0,1,\ldots 2^m-1\}$. Note that if $g : \{0,1\}^n \mapsto \{0,1\}$ (i.e. $m = 0$), then this problem is exactly the counting problem.

One way to estimate the mean $(\sum_x g(x))/2^n$ of a function $g(x)$ is to estimate the amplitude with which an operation A that maps

$$|00\ldots0\rangle|0\rangle \mapsto \sum_x \frac{1}{\sqrt{2^n}}|x\rangle(\sqrt{1-g(x)}|0\rangle + \sqrt{g(x)}|1\rangle)$$

produces a $|1\rangle$ value in the rightmost qubit.

Exercise 8.3.2 shows how to implement this operator A given a circuit for implementing g (equivalently, for implementing $f(x)$ where $g(x) = f(x)/2^m$).

An alternative method is to express $g(x)$ as the concatentation of n binary functions $g_{n-1}(x)g_{n-2}(x)\ldots g_0(x)$. Since $g(x) = \sum_i 2^i g_i(x)$, then $\sum_x g(x) = \sum_i 2^i \sum_x g_i(x)$. Thus we can first use quantum counting to approximate each $\sum_x g_i(x)$ with $\tilde{g}_i$ and then combine the sum estimates to get an estimate of $\sum_x g(x)$ equal to $\tilde{g} = \sum_i 2^i \tilde{g}_i$.

Note: If X is continuous, like the interval $[0,1]$, then the integral of well-behaved functions g can be approximated arbitrarily well by discretizing the set X, and multiplying the mean value of g on those discrete points by the measure of the set X.

Exercise 8.3.2 Suppose you are given a circuit U_g for implementing $g : \{0,1\}^n \mapsto \{0,1,\ldots, 2^m-1\}$, where $U_f|x\rangle|y\rangle = |x\rangle|y+g(x) \bmod 2^m\rangle$.

1. Show how to implement the operation

$$|x\rangle \frac{1}{\sqrt{2}}(|0\rangle + |1\rangle) \mapsto |x\rangle \frac{1}{\sqrt{2}}(|0\rangle + e^{2\pi i \frac{g(x)}{2^m}}|1\rangle).$$

2. Show how to approximate the operation

$$|x\rangle|0\rangle \mapsto |x\rangle\sqrt{1 - \frac{g(x)}{2^m}}|0\rangle + \sqrt{\frac{g(x)}{2^m}}|1\rangle)$$

with accuracy in $O(\frac{1}{2^n})$.

Hint: Recall the $\mathrm{ARCSIN}_{n,m}$ circuit from Example 1.5.1.

8.4   Searching Without Knowing the Success Probability

Recall that the searching and amplitude amplification algorithms described in Section 8.1 required k iterations of the search iterate, where $k \approx \frac{\pi}{4\theta}$. However, if we do not know the value θ, the following procedure gives an algorithm that uses $O\left(\frac{1}{\theta}\right)$ applications of the search iterate without prior knowledge of θ.

Observe that when $0 < \sin^2(\theta) < 1$, the amplitude estimation network produces the state

$$\frac{1}{\sqrt{2}}e^{i\theta}|\widetilde{2\theta}\rangle|\psi_+\rangle + \frac{1}{\sqrt{2}}|\widetilde{2\pi - 2\theta}\rangle|\psi_-\rangle. \tag{8.4.1}$$

Since $0 < \theta < \frac{\pi}{2}$, then increasing the parameter $M = 2^m$ in the quantum amplitude estimation algorithm means that $|\widetilde{2\theta}\rangle$ and $|\widetilde{2\pi - 2\theta}\rangle$ become better estimates of 2θ and $2\pi - 2\theta$, and thus become more orthogonal (since $2\theta \neq 2\pi - 2\theta$ if $0 < \theta < \frac{\pi}{2}$).

In fact, if the eigenvalue estimation is done with an m-bit control register, it is easy to verify that the inner product between the two estimates is

$$|\langle\widetilde{2\pi - 2\theta}|\widetilde{2\theta}\rangle| \in O\left(\frac{1}{2^m\theta}\right). \tag{8.4.2}$$

Exercise 8.4.1 Prove Equation 8.4.2.

Note that once $2^m \gg \frac{1}{\theta}$, the states $|\widetilde{2\pi - 2\theta}\rangle$ and $|\widetilde{2\theta}\rangle$ are almost orthogonal.

If the states were orthogonal, then tracing out the first register leaves the second register in the state

$$\frac{1}{2}|\psi_+\rangle\langle\psi_+| + \frac{1}{2}|\psi_-\rangle\langle\psi_-| \tag{8.4.3}$$

Fig. 8.21 The circuit diagram on the left illustrates how the quantum counting circuit can be used to search by measuring the second register. Since the first register is discarded, this circuit can be simplified to a circuit, illustrated on the right, that applies the quantum search iterate Q a total of x times, where x is selected uniformly at random from $\{0, 1, \ldots, 2^m - 1\}$.

and we can easily verify that

$$\tfrac{1}{2}|\psi_+\rangle\langle\psi_+| + \tfrac{1}{2}|\psi_-\rangle\langle\psi_-| = \tfrac{1}{2}|\psi_{\text{good}}\rangle\langle\psi_{\text{good}}| + \tfrac{1}{2}|\psi_{\text{bad}}\rangle\langle\psi_{\text{bad}}|. \tag{8.4.4}$$

Note that the probability of measuring a good solution if we measure the state

$$\tfrac{1}{2}|\psi_{\text{good}}\rangle\langle\psi_{\text{good}}| + \tfrac{1}{2}|\psi_{\text{bad}}\rangle\langle\psi_{\text{bad}}| \tag{8.4.5}$$

is $\tfrac{1}{2}$.

However, since $\widetilde{|2\theta\rangle}$ and $\widetilde{|2\pi - 2\theta\rangle}$ are not perfectly orthogonal, but have inner product in $O\left(\frac{1}{2^m\theta}\right)$, we can only say that if we measure the second register of the quantum counting algorithm (as illustrated on the left side of Figure 8.21) the probability of measuring a good state is in

$$\frac{1}{2} - O\left(\frac{1}{2^m\theta}\right). \tag{8.4.6}$$

Exercise 8.4.2 Let $|\psi\rangle = \frac{1}{\sqrt{2}}|\phi_1\rangle\left(\frac{1}{\sqrt{2}}|0\rangle + \frac{1}{\sqrt{2}}|1\rangle\right) + \frac{1}{\sqrt{2}}|\phi_2\rangle\left(\frac{1}{\sqrt{2}}|0\rangle - \frac{1}{\sqrt{2}}|1\rangle\right)$ for some normalized states $|\phi_1\rangle$ and $|\phi_2\rangle$ with the property that $|\langle\phi_1|\phi_2\rangle| = \epsilon$. Find a tight upper bound on the probability that measuring the first register in the computational basis results in the outcome $|0\rangle$ in the second register.

If for a fixed m we run this quantum search routine twice,[4] then the probability of finding a solution is in $\frac{3}{4} - O\left(\frac{1}{2^m\theta}\right)$.

---

[4]Repeating twice is not of fundamental importance. This is just one way to guarantee that the probability of success p' will be strictly above $\frac{1}{r}$ once $M > \frac{1}{\sqrt{p'}}$, where r is the rate at which we increase the interval size M. We want $rp' < 1$ because the expected running time will depend on the value of the geometric series $\sum_n (rp')^n$. For simplicity, we choose $r = 2$ and thus we wish to boost the probability p' above $\frac{1}{2}$. Alternatively, we could choose any rate $r < \frac{1}{2}$.

Consider the following procedure:

Quantum Searching Without Knowing Success Probabilities I

1. Set $m = 1$.
2. Perform eigenvalue estimation with an m-qubit control register. Measure the target register to obtain a value $|y\rangle$. If $f(y) = 1$, go to Step 5.
3. Perform eigenvalue estimation with an m-qubit control register. Measure the target register to obtain a value $|y\rangle$. If $f(y) = 1$, go to Step 5. Otherwise increment m.
4. If $2^m < N$, go to Step 2. If $2^m \geq N$, do an exhaustive search to find a value y such that $f(y) = 1$. If no such y is found, output 'NO SOLUTION'.
5. Output y.

Theorem 8.4.1 *If $\theta > 0$, the above procedure will output a value y satisfying $f(y) = 1$. The expected number of queries to U_f and applications of A and A^{-1} used is in $O(\frac{1}{\theta})$ and is never greater than $O(N)$. If $\theta = 0$, the algorithm uses $\Theta(N)$ queries and applications of A and A^{-1} and outputs 'NO SOLUTION'.*

It is interesting to note that we never use the value of the first register, which means that the following algorithm is equivalent to the above algorithm (and, in the case A uniformly samples the inputs, this is equivalent to the first quantum counting algorithm invented by Brassard, Høyer, and Tapp).

Quantum Searching Without Knowing Success Probability II

1. Set $m = 1$.
2. Pick a random integer $y \in \{0, 1, 2, \ldots, 2^m - 1\}$ and compute $Q^y A|00\ldots0\rangle$. Measure the register to obtain a value $|y\rangle$. If $f(y) = 1$, go to Step 5.
3. Pick a random integer $y \in \{0, 1, 2, \ldots, 2^m - 1\}$ and compute $Q^y A|00\ldots0\rangle$. Measure the register to obtain a value $|y\rangle$. If $f(y) = 1$, go to Step 5. Otherwise increment m.
4. If $2^m < N$ go to Step 2. If $2^m \geq N$, do an exhaustive search to find a value y such that $f(y) = 1$. If no such y is found, output 'NO SOLUTION'.
5. Output y.

Exercise 8.4.3 Note that the first of the above two algorithms ('Quantum searching without knowing success probabilities I') outputs a solution with probability $\frac{1}{2} - O\left(\frac{1}{2^m\theta}\right)$ using 2^m applications of U_f. Devise a quantum algorithm using $O(2^m)$ applications of U_f that outputs a solution with probability in $1 - O\left(\left(\frac{1}{2^m\theta}\right)^2\right)$.

8.5   Related Algorithms and Techniques

We have mentioned how amplitude amplification is a very broadly applicable computational primitive. It can also be applied in more subtle ways to solve problems like *element distinctness* more efficiently than any classical algorithm. The element distinctness problem consists of deciding if there exist distinct inputs x and y so that $f(x) = f(y)$, where we are provided with a black box for implementing the function f.

It is also possible to define continuous time versions of the quantum searching algorithm which offer the same quadratic speed-up. Continuous-time computational models may or may not be practical to implement directly, but they can be simulated efficiently by the quantum circuit model we have described. Such alternative models might be a novel way to discover new quantum algorithms. One interesting continuous-time algorithmic paradigm is that of adiabatic algorithms, which are inspired by the adiabatic theorem. For example, one can naturally derive an adiabatic searching algorithm that offers the same quadratic speed-up provided by amplitude amplification. A more general notion of adiabatic computation is in fact polynomial time equivalent to the quantum circuit model.

There are also several ways to derive a quantum equivalent of a classical random walk, which we call quantum walks. Quantum walks are another interesting paradigm in which to discover new quantum algorithms. For example, the optimal quantum algorithm for element distinctness can be found using a quantum walk algorithm.

9

QUANTUM COMPUTATIONAL COMPLEXITY THEORY AND LOWER BOUNDS

We have seen in the previous chapters that quantum computers seem to be more powerful than classical computers for certain problems. There are limits on the power of quantum computers, however. Since a classical computer can simulate a quantum computer, a quantum computer can only compute the same set of functions that a classical computer can. The advantage of using a quantum computer is that the amount of resources needed by a quantum algorithm might be much less than what is needed by the best classical algorithm. In Section 9.1 we briefly define some classical and quantum complexity classes and give some relationships between them. Most of the interesting questions relating classical and quantum complexity classes remain open. For example, we do not yet know if a quantum computer is capable of efficiently solving an NP-complete problem (defined later).

One can prove upper bounds on the difficulty of a problem by providing an algorithm that solves that problem, and proving that it will work within in a given running time. But how does one prove a lower bound on the computational complexity of a problem?

For example, if we wish to find the product of two n-bit numbers, computing the answer requires outputting roughly $2n$ bits and that requires $\Omega(n)$ steps (in any computing model with finite-sized gates). The best-known upper bound for integer multiplication is $O(n \log n \log \log n)$ steps.

O, Ω, and Θ Notation

Let f and g be functions from the positive integers to the real numbers.
$O(f(n))$ denotes the set of functions $g(n)$ for which there exists a positive real c and integer N so that $g(n) \leq cf(n)$ for all $n \geq N$.
$\Omega(f(n))$ denotes the set of functions $g(n)$ for which there exists a positive real c and integer N so that $g(n) \geq cf(n)$ for all $n \geq N$.

$\Theta(f(n))$ denotes the set of functions $g(n)$ that are both in $O(f(n))$ and in $\Omega(f(n))$.

Note: One will often encounter abuses of this notation, such as '$g(n) = O(f(n))$'.

It has proved extremely difficult to derive non-trivial lower bounds on the computational complexity of a problem. Most of the known non-trivial lower bounds are in the 'black-box' model (for both classical and quantum computing), where we only query the input via a 'black-box' of a specific form. We discuss the black-box model in more detail in Section 9.2.

We then sketch several approaches for proving black-box lower bounds. The first technique has been called the 'hybrid method' and was used to prove that quantum searching requires $\Omega(\sqrt{n})$ queries to succeed with constant probability. The second technique is called the 'polynomial method'. We then describe a technique based on 'block sensitivity', and conclude with a technique known as the 'adversary method'. All of these techniques have been used to prove interesting lower bounds in the black-box model.

For concreteness, we can assume our classical computing model is the log-RAM model, and our quantum computing model that of uniform families of acyclic quantum circuits (discussed in Section 1.2 and in Chapter 4).

9.1 Computational Complexity

In an attempt to better understand the difficulty of various computational problems, computer scientists and mathematicians have organized computational problems into a variety of classes, called 'complexity classes', which capture some aspect of the computational complexity of these problems.

For example, the class P corresponds to the class of problems solvable on a deterministic classical computer running in polynomial time and PSPACE corresponds to the class of problems that can be solved using a polynomial amount of space.

For convenience, we restrict attention to 'decision' problems, where the answer is either 'yes' or 'no'. Most problems of interest can be reformulated as decision problems in a very natural way without losing their intrinsic complexity. For example, the problem of factoring any integer N into two non-trivial factors can be reduced to $O(\log N)$ decision problems of the form 'Does the integer N have a non-trivial factor less than T?', where T is an additional input we can choose.

Decision problems can be treated as the problem of recognizing elements of a *language*. This framework of language recognition problems might seem awkward at first, but much of computational complexity theory has been developed using this terminology; so it is useful to be somewhat familiar with it. Below we explain this formalism in a bit more detail and define a few of the most common complexity classes one will encounter in the quantum computing literature.

9.1.1 Language Recognition Problems and Complexity Classes

In order to compute, we need a reasonable way to represent information. Unary encoding (i.e. representing the number j by a string of 1s of length j) is exponentially less efficient than using strings of symbols from any fixed alphabet of size at least 2. Going from an alphabet of size 2 to a larger alphabet of fixed size only changes the length of the problem representation by a constant factor. So we will simply use the alphabet $\Sigma = \{0, 1\}$. The set Σ^* denotes all finite length strings over that alphabet. A language L is a subset of Σ^*. In particular, usually L is a set of strings with some property of interest.

An algorithm 'solves the language recognition problem for L' if it accepts any string $x \in L$ and rejects any string $x \notin L$.

For example, the problem of deciding whether an integer n (represented as a string of bits) is prime is rephrased as the problem of recognizing whether the string representing n is in the language PRIME = $\{10, 11, 010, 011, 101, 111, \ldots\}$ (which consists of the set of all strings representing prime numbers, according to some reasonable encoding, which in this case is standard binary encoding).

As another example, consider the problem of deciding whether a given graph x (represented by a string of bits in some reasonable way) is 3-colourable. A graph is 3-colourable if it is possible to assign each vertex v one of three colours $c(v) \in \{\text{RED, GREEN, BLUE}\}$ so that any two vertices joined by an edge are coloured with different colours. Such an assignment of colours is a proper 3-colouring. This problem is equivalent to recognizing whether the string representing x is in the language 3-COLOURABLE, which is the set of strings representing 3-colourable graphs. Note that there are only 6 possible edges on a graph with 4 vertices (let us call them v_1, v_2, v_3, v_4), namely $e_1 = \{v_1, v_2\}$, $e_2 = \{v_1, v_3\}, e_3 = \{v_1, v_4\}, e_4 = \{v_2, v_3\}, e_5 = \{v_2, v_4\}, e_6 = \{v_3, v_4\}$. Thus, we can naturally represent the graphs on 4 vertices by strings $x_1 x_2 x_3 x_4 x_5 x_6$ of length 6, by letting $x_j = 1$ if and only if x contains the edge e_j. We can easily verify that $101111 \in$ 3-COLOURABLE since the $c(v_1) = $ RED, $c(v_2) = $ BLUE, $c(v_3) = $ RED, $c(v_4) = $ GREEN is a valid 3-colouring as shown in Figure 9.1.

Now that we have shown how to phrase decision problems in terms of recognizing elements of a language, we can define various classes of languages. For example, we formally define P ('polynomial time') to be the class of languages L for which there exists a deterministic classical algorithm A running in worst-case polynomial time[1] such that for any input $x \in \Sigma^*$ the algorithm A on input x, outputs 'accept' if and only if $x \in L$. Note that this class does not capture the possible advantages of using randomness to solve problems.

---

[1]More precisely, there exists a polynomial $p(n)$ such that A runs for time at most $p(n)$ on inputs of length n.

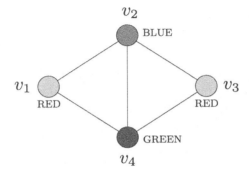

Fig. 9.1 The above graph x is represented by the string 101111. Since it is possible to colour the vertices with 3 colours so that adjacent vertices are coloured differently, we say that x is 3-colourable, or equivalently 101111 ∈ 3-COLOURABLE.

The class BPP ('bounded-error probabilistic polynomial time') consists of all languages L for which there exists a randomized classical algorithm A running with worst-case polynomial time such that for any input $x \in \Sigma^*$ we have

- if $x \in L$ then the probability that A accepts x is at least $\frac{2}{3}$
- if $x \notin L$ then the probability that A accepts x is at most $\frac{1}{3}$.

It is important to note that when we refer to 'the probability that A accepts', we are referring to the probability over random choices of paths of the computation on the fixed input $x \in L$, and not an average over all $x \in L$. It is also worth noting that there is nothing special about $\frac{2}{3}$. Any constant $\frac{1}{2} + \delta$, where $\delta > 0$ will work. For any fixed δ, we can repeat the algorithm A a total of n independent times and take the majority answer. We now get the correct answer with probability at least $1 - \epsilon^n$ for some constant ϵ, $0 < \epsilon < 1$ (see Appendix A.1).

The class BQP ('bounded-error quantum polynomial time') consists of all languages L for which there exists a quantum algorithm A running with worst-case polynomial time such that for any input $x \in \Sigma^*$ we have

- if $x \in L$ then the probability that A accepts x is at least $\frac{2}{3}$
- if $x \notin L$ then the probability that A accepts x is at most $\frac{1}{3}$.

Polynomials have the property that their sum, product, and composition are still polynomials. By only concerning ourselves with the computational complexity of an algorithm up to a polynomial factor we get a crude but very robust measure of computational complexity. Most reasonable changes in architecture one would imagine do not affect whether the computational complexity is polynomial or not (since using one architecture to simulate another only incurs a polynomial 'blow-up' in complexity). Thus distinguishing problems that can be solved with a polynomial complexity from those that cannot is a distinction that will not depend on the details of your computer architecture.

It is thus convenient to treat algorithms with polynomial complexity as 'efficient' and problems that can be solved with polynomial complexity as 'tractable', and problems without polynomial solutions as 'intractable'. Note that in any computing model where information cannot travel arbitrarily fast, and where an exponential number of operations cannot be crammed into a polynomial sized space (e.g. the Turing machine model), the space used cannot be superpolynomially more than the running time, and so in such computing models, we can equate polynomial *time* complexity with efficiency or tractability.

For practical purposes, having a polynomial complexity is (almost) necessary for being solvable in practice, but might not be sufficient. At the very least, finding a polynomial time algorithm is a good start towards finding a feasible solution.

One type of change in computational model that might drastically change the computational complexity is to change the implicit physical framework in which the computing model is based. For example, deterministic classical computation is implicitly only referring to a deterministic classical theory of physics. By adding the possibility of a randomness, we get probabilistic classical computation. By working in a quantum mechanical framework, we get quantum computation.

We traditionally view decision problems corresponding to recognizing languages in BPP as tractable on a probabilistic classical computer, and problems without such worst-case polynomial time solutions intractable on a classical computer. Analogously, we view decision problems corresponding to recognizing languages in BQP as tractable on a quantum computer, and problems without such worst-case polynomial time solutions intractable on a quantum computer.

Some problems seem to elude any efficient solution in the worst-case, such as deciding whether a given graph is 3-colourable. Note that although it might be very difficult to decide if a graph x is 3-colourable, it is very easy to check if a given colouring y is a proper 3-colouring. That is, there exists a polynomial time algorithm CHECK-3-COLOURING(a, b) such that CHECK-3-COLOURING$(x, y) = 1$ if and only if y is a valid colouring of the graph x (the algorithm simply goes through every edge of the graph x and checks that according to the colouring y the two vertices of each edge are coloured differently).

This property inspires the class NP ('non-deterministic polynomial time') which consists of all languages L for which there exists a polynomial time algorithm $A(a, b)$ such that for any input $x \in \Sigma^*$ we have

- if $x \in L$ then there exists an input y such that $A(x, y)$ outputs 'accept'
- if $x \notin L$ then $A(x, y)$ outputs 'reject' for all y

and the length of y is bounded by a polynomial in the length of x.

Another way of looking at the class NP is as the class of languages L for which for any $x \in L$ a prover can convince a verifier that x is in L by providing a short proof that the verifier can deterministically verify on a classical computer using time polynomial in the size of x (the prover's computation time is not bounded). Note that this does not imply that there is a short proof to verify some $x \notin L$. There are many variations on this class including MA ('Merlin–Arthur games') where the verifier (Arthur) uses the short proof (provided by Merlin) to *probabilistically* verify on a classical computer that $x \in L$. Clearly NP $\subseteq$ MA and BPP $\subseteq$ MA. Other complexity classes can be defined based on interactive proofs, proofs with more than one prover, and proofs using quantum computers, quantum communication, or entanglement. We will not cover this rich landscape of complexity classes in this textbook.

There is a special subclass of problems within NP that are called 'NP-complete'. These problems have the property that an efficient solution to any one of these problems implies an efficient solution to any problem in NP. More precisely, let L be any NP-complete language. Then for any language $L' \in$ NP, there exists a classical deterministic polynomial time algorithm that computes a function $f : \{0,1\}^* \to \{0,1\}^*$ with the property that $x \in L'$ if and only if $f(x) \in L$. In other words, one query to an oracle for solving L will solve any problem in NP. Well-known examples of NP-complete problems include circuit satisfiability, 3-satisfiability (defined below), 3-colouring, the traveling salesman problem (the decision version), and the subset sum problem. Integer factorization and graph isomorphism are in NP but not believed to be NP-complete.

We will refer to the NP-complete problem 3-satisfiability (3-SAT) later, so we define it here. An instance of 3-SAT is specified by a Boolean formula Φ in a particular form, called '3-conjunctive normal form' (3-CNF). A Boolean formula is in 3-CNF if it is a conjunction (logical AND) of clauses, each of which is a disjunction (logical OR) of three Boolean variables (or their negations). For example, the following is a 3-CNF formula in the variables $b_1, b_2, \ldots, b_6$:

$$\Phi = (b_1 \vee \overline{b_2} \vee b_3) \wedge (\overline{b_1} \vee b_4 \vee \overline{b_5}) \wedge (b_6 \vee b_2 \vee b_3).$$

A 'satisfying assignment' of a particular 3-CNF formula Φ is an assignment of 0 or 1 values to each of the n variables such that the formula evaluates to 1. For example, $b_1 b_2 b_3 b_4 b_5 b_6 = 110010$ is a satisfying assignment (the first clause evaluates to 1 because $b_1 = 1$, the second clause evaluates to 1 because $\overline{b_5} = 1$, and the third clause evaluates to 1 because $b_2 = 1$; therefore, the conjunction of the three clauses evaluates to 1). The language 3-SAT is the set of 3-CNF formulas (represented by some reasonable encoding) for which there exists at least one satisfying assignment. Note that given a satisfying assignment, it is easy to check if it satisfies the formula.

The class PSPACE consists of all languages L for which there exists a classical algorithm A using worst-case polynomial space such that for any input $x \in \Sigma^*$ the algorithm A accepts x if and only if $x \in L$.

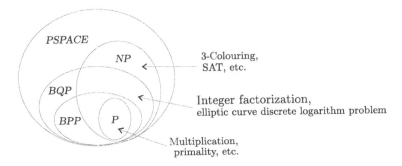

3-Colouring,
SAT, etc.

Integer factorization,
elliptic curve discrete logarithm problem

Multiplication,
primality, etc.

Fig. 9.2 This diagram illustrates the known relationships between some of the most important complexity classes. At present, none of the inclusions are known to be strict. For example, there is currently no proof that $P \neq PSPACE$.

Figure 9.2 illustrates the known relationships between the complexity classes we just defined. For example, clearly $P \subseteq BPP \subseteq BQP \subseteq PSPACE$, and $P \subseteq NP \subseteq PSPACE$. Unfortunately, to date, there is no proof that any of the containments drawn are strict. But it is widely believed that $P \neq NP$ and that $NP \neq PSPACE$. We also expect that $BPP \neq BQP$.

Note that resolving the question of whether $P = NP$ is considered one of the greatest open problems in mathematics (e.g. it is one of the million dollar 'Millennium Problems' of the Clay Mathematics Institute)

We have only sketched a very small number of complexity classes. See, for example, Aaronson's complexity 'zoo' for a listing of virtually all the complexity classes studied to date.

The biggest challenge of quantum algorithmics is to find problems that are in BQP but not in BPP; that is, to find problems that are efficiently solvable on a quantum computer but not a classical computer. The study of these complexity classes and the relationships between them can be helpful in understanding the difficulty of these problems.

Most of the interesting lower bounds have been proved in some sort of black-box model. The black-box lower bounds we describe in the next sections provide some evidence that BQP does not contain all of NP, though the possibility is not explicitly ruled out at present. The lower bound methods also prove the optimality of several of the black-box quantum algorithms we described in Chapters 6, 7 and 8.

9.2   The Black-Box Model

In the black-box model, the input to the problem is provided by a black-box (or 'oracle') $O_{\mathbf{X}}$ for accessing information about an unknown string $\mathbf{X} = X_1, \ldots, X_N$, where we will assume the N variables X_i are binary. The oracle allows us to make queries about the binary values of the individual variables. We usually assume the quantum black-box implements

$$O_{\mathbf{X}} : |j\rangle|b\rangle \rightarrow |j\rangle|b \oplus X_j\rangle. \tag{9.2.1}$$

The objective is usually to compute some function $F(\mathbf{X})$ of the string $\mathbf{X}$. Though in general the task at hand might be more complicated.[2] Solving the search problem for $\mathbf{X}$ is no easier than solving the decision problem for $\mathbf{X}$, which is to decide if there exists some j such that $X_j = 1$. This decision problem can be thought of as evaluating the OR function of the binary variables $X_1, \ldots, X_N$:

$$\mathrm{OR}(X_1 \ldots X_N) = X_1 \vee X_2 \vee \cdots \vee X_N. \tag{9.2.2}$$

A computation in the black-box model is one which computes such a function $F : \{0, 1\}^N \rightarrow \{0, 1\}$ given access to the black-box $O_{\mathbf{X}}$ for $\mathbf{X}$. The computation can perform any unitary operation (i.e. we do not worry about decomposing the unitaries into gates from a finite gate set) and makes queries to the black-box $O_{\mathbf{X}}$. Note that with no queries to $O_{\mathbf{X}}$, we cannot evaluate any non-trivial $F(\mathbf{X})$ since we have no information about the input $\mathbf{X}$. The goal of a black-box computation is to extract enough information about $\mathbf{X}$ using $O_{\mathbf{X}}$ in order to be able to reliably compute $F(\mathbf{X})$.

The 'query complexity' of an algorithm is the number of queries used by the algorithm. The query complexity of a problem is the number of queries needed in order to solve the problem. The black-box model of computation has proved useful both for algorithmic design and for understanding the limitations of algorithms for certain problems. Most of the algorithms we have seen in this textbook are essentially black-box algorithms. For example, the period-finding formulation of Shor's algorithm is a black-box algorithm, and the quantum searching and counting algorithms are black-box algorithms. In the black-box model, it can be shown that $\Omega(\sqrt{r})$ queries are required to find the period r of a periodic function f on a classical computer. A quantum algorithm finds the period with high probability using $O(1)$ queries.

Black-boxes can be replaced with 'white boxes', which are circuits that actually implement the black boxes. For example, Shor's order-finding algorithm replaces the black box for U_f by an actual circuit that computes the function $f(x) = a^x$ mod N.

When we replace black boxes by white boxes, the total complexity of the algorithm can be upper bounded by $TB + A$, where T is the query complexity of the black-box algorithm, B the computational complexity of actually implementing a query, and A the computational complexity of all the non-query operations performed by the black-box algorithm. For Shor's order-finding algorithm, T, B, and A are all polynomials in the input size, and thus the running time of the algorithm is polynomial.

---

[2]For example, in Section 8.1 we addressed the problem of outputting j such that $X_j = 1$. This corresponds to having a relation R consisting of pairs (b, j) where $X_j = b$, and wishing to sample an element with $b = 1$.

Lower bounds in the black-box model do not automatically carry over to the white-box model. However, the query lower bounds do apply to any algorithm that only probes the input to the problem in a way equivalent to a black-box query. For example, we will prove later that any quantum algorithm for searching for a solution to $f(x) = 1$, where $f : \{1, 2, \ldots, N\} \to \{0, 1\}$ must make $T \in \Omega(\sqrt{N})$ queries to the black-box for U_f. The quantum searching algorithm solves this problem with $O(\sqrt{N})$ queries, and thus any algorithm that tries to find a solution to $f(x) = 1$ and only probes the function f by implementing $f(x)$ must have complexity $TB + A$, for some $B \geq 1$ and $A \geq 0$. Thus, the computational complexity of any algorithm of this form must be in $\Omega(\sqrt{N})$.

For example, consider a 3-SAT formula (defined Section 9.1.1) Φ in n variables, $x_1, x_2, \ldots, x_n$, $N = 2^n$, and let the numbers $1, 2, \ldots, N$ encode the 2^n assignments of the variables $x_1, x_2, \ldots, x_n$. Define the function f_Φ so that $f_\Phi(y) = 1$ if setting $x_1 = y_1, x_2 = y_2, \ldots, x_n = y_n$ satisfies the formula Φ, and $f_\Phi(y) = 0$ otherwise.

We can rephrase the 3-SAT problem as follows.

Define N binary variables $X_1, \ldots, X_N$ such that $X_j = f_\Phi(j)$ and solve the search problem for $\mathbf{X} = X_1 X_2 \ldots X_N$. The function f_Φ can be evaluated in time in $O(\log^c N)$ for some positive constant c. Thus, quantum searching would find a solution in time in $O\left((\log^c N)\sqrt{N}\right)$.

Although we are actually given the formula Φ, or a circuit for evaluating f_Φ, if we restrict attention to algorithms that probe the input only by evaluating f_Φ, the query lower bound of $\Omega(\sqrt{N})$ proved later in this section applies. In order to 'beat' these lower bounds, one must exploit the structure of Φ in some clever way.

9.2.1 State Distinguishability

The general approach for proving that T queries are necessary is to show that with fewer than T queries, the algorithm cannot reliably distinguish the black-box $O_\mathbf{X}$ for an input $\mathbf{X}$ satisfying $f(\mathbf{X}) = 1$ from the black-box $O_\mathbf{Y}$ for some input $\mathbf{Y}$ satisfying $f(\mathbf{Y}) = 0$. Consider any algorithm $\mathcal{A}$ that makes T queries, and let $|\psi_\mathbf{X}\rangle$ be the state produced by the algorithm $\mathcal{A}$ with the oracle $O_\mathbf{X}$ and let $|\psi_\mathbf{Y}\rangle$ be the state produced by the algorithm $\mathcal{A}$ with the oracle $O_\mathbf{Y}$. For the algorithm to reliably compute $F(\mathbf{X})$ and $F(\mathbf{Y})$ it is necessary that the states $|\psi_\mathbf{X}\rangle$ are $|\psi_\mathbf{Y}\rangle$ are reliably distinguishable. It will be useful to state one of the earliest results in the vast literature of quantum state estimation and distinguishability.

Distinguishing Two Pure Quantum States With Minimum Error

Input: One of two known states $|\psi_\mathbf{X}\rangle$ or $|\psi_\mathbf{Y}\rangle$, with the property that $|\langle\psi_\mathbf{X}|\psi_\mathbf{Y}\rangle| = \delta$.
Output: A guess 'X' or 'Y'.
Problem: Maximize the probability $1 - \epsilon$ that the guess is correct.

The following theorem is proved in Appendix A.9, which also describes the optimal measurement.

Theorem 9.2.1 *Any procedure that on input $|\psi_\mathbf{Z}\rangle$ guesses whether $\mathbf{Z} = \mathbf{X}$ or $\mathbf{Z} = \mathbf{Y}$ will guess correctly with probability at most $1 - \epsilon = \frac{1}{2} + \frac{1}{2}\sqrt{1 - \delta^2}$, where $\delta = |\langle\psi_\mathbf{X}|\psi_\mathbf{Y}\rangle|$. This probability is achievable by an optimal measurement.*

There are many other ways of formulating the distinguishability question. For example, Helstrom originally addressed this question assuming a uniform prior distribution on $|\psi_\mathbf{X}\rangle$ and $|\psi_\mathbf{Y}\rangle$. The same procedure is optimal in order to maximize the expected probability of guessing the correct answer (averaging over the inputs).

As another example, one might want a procedure that outputs '$z = x$', '$z = y$' or 'do not know', with the guarantee that the procedure is never wrong. In this case, for example, the objective might be to minimize the probability that it will output 'do not know'. The literature on quantum state estimation and distinguishability is extensive. For the rest of this chapter, we will only need the result above.

9.3 Lower Bounds for Searching in the Black-Box Model: Hybrid Method

Given a function $f : \{1, 2, \ldots, N\} \to \{0, 1\}$, the searching problem is to find a $y \in \{1, 2, \ldots, N\}$ such that $f(y) = 1$. This framework is very general as it applies to any problem where we can *recognize* a solution and wish to actually *find* a solution.

The decision problem is to determine whether or not there exists a solution to the search problem. A solution to the searching problem yields a solution to the decision problem, so a lower bound on the difficulty of the decision problem implies a lower bound on the difficulty of the searching problem.

In Section 8.1, we saw a bounded error quantum algorithm for solving the problem of searching a solution space having N elements, making $O(\sqrt{N})$ queries to the black-box U_f. It is natural to wonder whether we could be even more clever, and get a quantum algorithm that solves this problem with even fewer oracle queries. We might even hope to get an exponential speed-up. In this section we prove a lower bound result showing that Grover's algorithm is the best possible. That is, no black-box search algorithm can solve the searching problem making fewer than $\Omega(\sqrt{N})$ queries.

Consider an algorithm making T queries. Without loss of generality it has the form shown in Figure 9.3.

Exercise 9.3.1 Show how the circuit in Figure 9.4 can be simulated by a circuit of the form in Figure 9.3 with the same number of black-box queries.

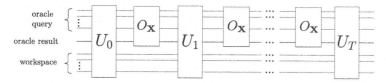

Fig. 9.3 Without loss of generality, any network which makes T black-box queries is equivalent to a network which starts with the state $|00\ldots0\rangle$, applies a unitary operator U_0, followed by a black-box query on the first $n+1$ qubits, followed by a unitary operation U_1 and so on, with a final unitary operation U_T after the last black-box call.

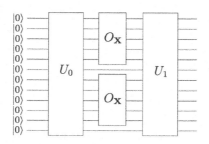

Fig. 9.4 This circuit with two queries done in parallel can be simulated by a circuit with two queries performed in series (i.e. a circuit of the same form as Figure 9.3).

Definition 9.3.1 Let $\mathbf{X}_x$ denote the string with a 1 in position x and 0 elsewhere (i.e. $X_x = 1$ and $X_y = 0$ for all $y \neq x$). Let $S = \{\mathbf{X}_x : x = 1, 2, \ldots, N\}$ be the set of all strings $\{0,1\}^N$ with exactly one 1 in the string.

We will prove the following theorem.

Theorem 9.3.2 Any bounded-error quantum algorithm that will for each $\mathbf{X} \in S \cup \{\mathbf{0}\}$ determine whether there exists a j such that $X_j = 1$ must make $\Omega(\sqrt{N})$ queries to $O_{\mathbf{X}}$.

This implies the following corollaries.

Corollary 9.3.3 Let $T \subseteq \{0,1\}^N$ satisfy $S \cup \{\mathbf{0}\} \subseteq T$. Any bounded-error quantum algorithm that will for each $\mathbf{X} \in T$ determine whether there exists j such that $X_j = 1$ must make $\Omega(\sqrt{N})$ queries to $O_{\mathbf{X}}$.

Corollary 9.3.4 Let $T \subseteq \{0,1\}^N$ satisfy $S \subseteq T$. Any bounded-error quantum algorithm that will for each $\mathbf{X} \in T$ will find a j such that $X_j = 1$ must make $\Omega(\sqrt{N})$ queries to $O_{\mathbf{X}}$.

Let us relate these results to the question of solving NP-complete problems, like 3-SAT, on a quantum computer. Note that there are $2^{O(n^3)}$ distinct 3-SAT formulas Φ, each corresponding to a string $\mathbf{X} \in \{0, 1\}^N$, $N = 2^n$ (where $X_j = f_\Phi(j)$). However, there are 2^N strings $\mathbf{X} \in \{0, 1\}^N$ (where since $N = 2^n$, we have $2^N \gg 2^{O(n^3)}$). So the relevance of a result pertaining to algorithms that succeed for all $\mathbf{X} \in \{0, 1\}^N$ to the problem of solving 3-SAT is not so clear. However, since the set of all strings $\mathbf{X} = X_1 X_2 \ldots X_N$ of the form $X_j = f_\Phi(j)$ for some 3-SAT formula Φ contains $S \cup \{\mathbf{0}\}$, this lower bound also applies to black-box algorithms for 3-SAT.

Exercise 9.3.2 Prove that the set of all strings $\mathbf{X} = X_1 X_2 \ldots X_N$ of the form $X_j = f_\Phi(j)$ for some 3-SAT formula Φ in n variables contains $S \cup \{\mathbf{0}\}$, the set of all strings of length N with at most one 1.

Corollary 9.3.5 *Any bounded-error black-box quantum algorithm that will for each 3-SAT formula Φ in n variables determine whether there exists a satisfying assignment must make $\Omega(\sqrt{N})$ queries to the black-box that evaluates f_Φ.*

The proof of Theorem 9.3.2 follows from this lemma.

Lemma 9.3.6 *Any bounded-error black-box quantum algorithm that successfully recognizes the all-zero string and also recognizes at least $\Omega(N)$ of the strings $\mathbf{X}_x \in S$ as being non-zero requires $\Omega(\sqrt{N})$ queries.*

Proof   Consider any algorithm that makes T queries. Recall $\mathbf{X}_x$ is the string with exactly one 1, located at position x.
Let

$$|\Psi_j\rangle = \sum_{y=1}^{N} \alpha_{y,j} |y\rangle |\phi_y\rangle$$

be the state of the quantum computer just before the $(j+1)^{\text{st}}$ query, assuming $\mathbf{X} = 00\ldots0$, the all-zeroes string. Let $|\psi_T\rangle$ be the final state of the computer before outputting the answer.
For the quantum algorithm to recognize that any string $\mathbf{X}$ is not equal to $\mathbf{0} = 00\ldots0$, the T queries must nudge the state of the computer to something almost orthogonal to $|\psi_T\rangle$. Let $|\psi_T^x\rangle$ be the final state of the computer querying an oracle $0_{\mathbf{X}}$.
When querying a black-box $O_{\mathbf{X}_x}$ for any non-zero $\mathbf{X}_x$, after the jth query, the total amount of nudging will be at most $\sum_{k=0}^{j-1} 2|\alpha_{x,k}|$ (see Exercise 9.3.4). For the algorithm to successfully recognize the all-zero string with probability at least $\frac{2}{3}$ and successfully distinguish a non-zero string $\mathbf{X}$ from the all-zero string with probability at least $\frac{2}{3}$, the total amount of nudging must be greater than some constant $c > 0.338$ (combine Theorem 9.2.1 and Exercise 9.3.3). In other words, for each $\mathbf{X} \neq 00\ldots0$, say $\mathbf{X}_x$,

$$\sum_{k=0}^{T-1} |\alpha_{x,k}| \geq \frac{1}{2}\||\psi_T\rangle - |\psi_T^x\rangle\| \geq \frac{c}{2} > \frac{1}{6}.$$

So for the quantum algorithm to successfully recognise M of the non-zero strings (with bounded probability) as being distinct from the all-zero string, we must have

$$\sum_{x=1}^{N} \sum_{k=0}^{T-1} |\alpha_{x,k}| > \frac{1}{6} M.$$

On the other hand, we know that $\sum_x |\alpha_{x,k}|$ can not be too big, since $\sum_x \alpha_{x,k} |x\rangle |\phi_x\rangle$ is a quantum state. Since $\sum_{x=1}^{N} |\alpha_{x,k}|^2 = 1$, the Cauchy–Schwartz inequality[3] implies $\sum_x |\alpha_{x,k}| \le \sqrt{N}$.

Thus

$$\sum_{x=1}^{N} \sum_{k=0}^{T} |\alpha_{x,k}| \le T\sqrt{N}.$$

This implies that $T \ge \frac{1}{6} \frac{M}{\sqrt{N}}$, which proves the lemma. $\square$

Exercise 9.3.3 Let $|\phi_0\rangle$ and $|\phi_1\rangle$ be any two quantum states of the same dimension. Prove that

$$\big\| |\phi_0\rangle - |\phi_1\rangle \big\| \le c$$

implies

$$|\langle \phi_0 | \phi_1 \rangle| \ge 1 - \frac{c^2}{2}.$$

Exercise 9.3.4 Let $|\psi_j^x\rangle$ be the state of the quantum computer on input X_x just before the jth query, for $j \in \{0, 1, \ldots, T-1\}$. So $|\psi_{j+1}^x\rangle = U_j O_{\mathbf{x}_x} |\psi_j^x\rangle$. Let $|\widetilde{\psi}_{j+1}^x\rangle = U_j |\psi_j^x\rangle$.

(a) Prove that

$$\big\| |\widetilde{\psi}_{j+1}^x\rangle - |\psi_{j+1}^x\rangle \big\| \le 2|\alpha_{x,j}|.$$

Note that this means $|\psi_{j+1}^x\rangle = |\widetilde{\psi}_{j+1}^x\rangle + \beta_{j+1} |E_{j+1}\rangle$ for complex β_{j+1} and normalized state $|E_{j+1}\rangle$, with $|\beta_{j+1}| \le 2|\alpha_{x,j}|$.

(b) Let $|\psi_j\rangle = \sum_y \alpha_{y,j} |y\rangle |\phi_y\rangle$ be the state of the quantum computer that is querying the black box $O_{\mathbf{X}}$ for the string $\mathbf{X} = 00\ldots0$ just before the $(j+1)^{\text{st}}$ query. Prove that

$$\big\| |\psi_j\rangle - |\psi_j^x\rangle \big\| \le 2|\alpha_{x,0}| + \cdots + 2|\alpha_{x,j-1}|.$$

9.4   General Black-Box Lower Bounds

We applied this hybrid method to one particular problem, which corresponds to computing the OR of N binary variables. We will describe the next three methods in the context of computing an arbitrary function F of N binary variables.

---

[3]The Cauchy–Schwartz inequality implies that for any real numbers $a_1, a_2, \ldots, a_N, b_1, b_2, \ldots, b_N$ we have $(a_1 b_1 + a_2 b_2 + \cdots + a_N b_N)^2 \le (a_1^2 + a_2^2 + \cdots + a_N^2)(b_1^2 + b_2^2 + \cdots + b_N^2)$.

We call a function F that is defined for all possible input values in $\{0,1\}^N$ a 'total function'. Otherwise, we say F is a 'partial function'. For example, the Deutsch-Jozsa problem of Section 6.4 evaluates the partial function F defined on strings that are either constant or 'balanced'. We can also view the problem of finding the period of a function f as evaluating a partial function. If we represent the periodic function f by a bit string of length $n2^n$ corresponding to the concatenation of $f(0)f(1)f(2)\ldots f(2^n-1)$, then the period-finding problem is only defined on strings corresponding to functions f for which $f(0), f(1), \ldots, f(r-1)$ are all distinct, and $f(x) = f(x+r)$ for $x \geq 0$. We can also call the problem of evaluating a partial function a 'promise problem', since we are promising that the input to the function has some specific form.

Before we detail the techniques for proving lower bounds in the black box model, we will show that quantum algorithms give at most a polynomial advantage over classical algorithms for total functions. Thus, in order to get a superpolynomial advantage, we need to consider promise problems.

Definition 9.4.1 *The deterministic query complexity $D(F)$ of F is the minimum number of queries to $O_\mathbf{X}$ required by a deterministic classical procedure for computing $F(\mathbf{X})$ for any $\mathbf{X} \in \{0,1\}^N$.*

Note that the jth index to be queried can depend on the outcome of the previous $j-1$ queries.

The quantum equivalent of $D(F)$ is the *exact quantum query complexity* $Q_E(F)$ of F.

Definition 9.4.2 *The exact quantum query complexity $Q_E(F)$ of F is the minimum number of queries to $O_\mathbf{X}$ required by a quantum algorithm which correctly computes $F(X)$ with probability 1 for any $\mathbf{X} \in \{0,1\}^N$.*

Exact quantum computation is not as natural a computing model as its classical counterpart, since when we translate an exact black-box algorithm into a circuit composed of gates from a finite set of gates, the probability of success will not usually be exactly one. Furthermore, as is the case with classical computation, in practice we can never implement gates exactly, and thus it makes sense for any practical purpose to focus attention on bounded-error computations. A more relevant quantity is the *2-sided error quantum query complexity* $Q_2(F)$ of F.

Definition 9.4.3 *The 2-sided error quantum query complexity $Q_2(F)$ of F is the minimum number of queries to $O_\mathbf{X}$ required by a quantum algorithm which, on any input $\mathbf{X} \in \{0,1\}^N$, outputs a $\{0,1\}$ value that with probability at least $\frac{2}{3}$ is equal to $F(\mathbf{X})$.*

Theorem 9.4.4 *If F is a total Boolean function, then $D(F) \leq 2^{12}Q_2(F)^6$.*

We say a function F is symmetric if permuting the bits of $\mathbf{X}$ does not change the value of F. In other words, F only depends on the number of 1s in the string $\mathbf{X}$.

Theorem 9.4.5 *If F is a symmetric Boolean function, then $D(F) \in O(Q_2(F)^2)$.*

What do Theorems 9.4.4 and 9.4.5 mean for the quantum complexity of computing F given a black-box for computing X_j? Suppose the best deterministic classical strategy for evaluating $F(\mathbf{X})$ requires in the worst case $T = D(F)$ queries of the bits of $\mathbf{X}$. Theorem 9.4.4 tells us that any quantum algorithm computing F requires at least $\frac{T^{\frac{1}{6}}}{4}$ queries, and if F is symmetric then $\Omega(\sqrt{T})$ queries are required.

Theorem 9.4.4 tells us that quantum query complexity is at most polynomial better than classical query complexity for total functions.

In order to get a superpolynomial advantage in the black-box model, we need to consider 'partial functions', which are only defined on a subset of $\{0,1\}^N$. For example, the black-box version of Shor's period-finding algorithm is only required to work on strings $\mathbf{X}$ that encode periodic functions. The classical bounded-error query complexity for such a partial function is in $\Theta(\sqrt{r})$ where r is the period, while the quantum query complexity is in $O(1)$. The Deutsch–Jozsa algorithm is only required to work on 'constant' or 'balanced' strings $\mathbf{X}$. The classical exact query complexity of the Deutsch–Jozsa problem is $\frac{N}{2} + 1$, while the query complexity for an exact quantum algorithm is 1 (recall that bounded-error classical algorithms only required a constant number of queries, so the gap is not so significant in that case).

All of the methods described below can be adapted to work on partial functions as well as total functions.

9.5   Polynomial Method

In this section we show how a quantum circuit which queries the string $\mathbf{X}$ a total of T times will have amplitudes that are polynomials of degree T in the variables $X_1, X_2, \ldots, X_N$. If $T = 0$, the amplitudes are independent of the variables, and the circuit computes a function that is constant. The higher T is, the more sophisticated the functions that the circuit can compute. In the subsequent section we describe several applications of this fact.

Lemma 9.5.1 *Let $\mathcal{N}$ be a quantum circuit that uses a total of m-qubits and makes T queries to a black-box $O_{\mathbf{X}}$. Then there exist complex-valued N-variate multi-linear polynomials $p_0, p_1, \ldots, p_{2^m-1}$, each of degree at most T, such that the final state of the circuit is the superposition*

$$\sum_{y=0}^{2^m-1} p_y(X)|y\rangle$$

for any oracle $O_{\mathbf{X}}$.

Proof We can assume that $N = 2^n$. We can assume that the black-box queries to $O_{\mathbf{X}}$ are done sequentially and always to the first $n + 1$ qubits (see Exercise 9.3.1). Let U_j denote the unitary transformation which we apply between the jth and $(j + 1)^{\text{th}}$ black-box query. We thus have the circuit illustrated in Figure 9.3. For the proof, it will help to consider the register in three parts: the first n-qubits, the 1 output bit, and the remaining $l = m - n - 1$ ancilla bits.

Just before the first black-box application the m-qubits will be in some state

$$\sum_{j,k} \alpha_{j0k}|j0k\rangle + \alpha_{j1k}|j1k\rangle,$$

where $0 \leq j < 2^n$, $0 \leq k < 2^l$, $b \in \{0,1\}$, and the α_{jbk}, are independent of the string $\mathbf{X}$. In other words the amplitudes α_{jbk} are polynomials of degree 0 in $X_1, X_2, \ldots, X_N$. For $b \in \{0,1\}$ we use the notation $\bar{b} = \text{NOT}(b) = 1 - b$. After the first black-box call, we have the state

$$\sum_{j,k} \alpha_{j0k}|jX_jk\rangle + \alpha_{j1k}|j\overline{X}_jk\rangle$$

$$= \sum_{j,k} [(1 - X_j)\alpha_{j0k} + X_j\alpha_{j1k}]|j0k\rangle + [(1 - X_j)\alpha_{j1k} + X_j\alpha_{j0k}]|j1k\rangle. \quad (9.5.1)$$

Therefore, the amplitudes are polynomials in the X_j of degree at most 1. The unitary operation U_1 is linear, and thus the amplitudes just after U_1 is applied are still polynomials of degree at most 1. Suppose that for some $j \geq 1$, after U_{j-1} is applied the amplitudes are polynomials of degree at most $j - 1$. Then, the jth black-box call adds at most 1 to the degree of the amplitude polynomials so they are of degree at most j. The U_j replaces the amplitude polynomials with linear combinations of amplitude polynomials, and thus the degrees remain at most j. By induction, the amplitudes are polynomials of degree T after U_T. Since $x^2 = x$ for $x \in \{0,1\}$, we can assume the polynomials are multi-linear.   □

We get the following corollary from the fact that if the amplitudes of a basis state is a polynomial $\alpha(\mathbf{X})$ of degree T in the variables $X_1, X_2, \ldots, X_N$, then the probability of measuring that basis state, $\alpha(\mathbf{X})\alpha(\mathbf{X})^*$, will be a polynomial of degree $2T$ with real coefficients.

Corollary 9.5.2 *Let $\mathcal{N}$ be a quantum circuit that makes T queries to a black-box $O_{\mathbf{X}}$, and $\mathcal{B}$ be a set of basis states. Then there exists a real-valued multi-linear polynomial P of degree at most $2T$, which equals the probability of observing a state from the set $\mathcal{B}$ after applying the circuit $\mathcal{N}$ using black-box $O_{\mathbf{X}}$.*

9.5.1 Applications to Lower Bounds

Let us start by defining the quantities $\deg(F)$ and $\widetilde{\deg}(F)$ related to the N-variate function F. Although the function F is only defined on values of 0 and 1, it is useful to extend this function to the reals.

Definition 9.5.3 *An N-variate polynomial $p \colon \mathbb{R}^N \to \mathbb{R}$ represents F if $p(X) = F(X)$ for all $X \in \{0,1\}^N$.*

Lemma 9.5.4 *Every N-variate function $F : \{X_1, \ldots, X_N\} \to \{0, 1\}$, has a unique multi-linear polynomial $p : \mathbb{R}^N \to \mathbb{R}$ which represents it.*

Proof The existence of a representing polynomial is easy: let

$$p(X) = \sum_{Y \in \{0,1\}^N} F(Y) \prod_{k=1}^{N} \left[1 - (Y_k - X_k)^2 \right].$$

To prove uniqueness, let us assume that $p_1(X) = p_2(X)$ for all $X \in \{0, 1\}^N$. Then $p(X) = p_1(X) - p_2(X)$ is a polynomial that represents the zero function. Assume that $p(X)$ is not the zero polynomial and without loss of generality, let $\alpha X_1 X_2 \ldots X_k$ be a term of minimum degree, for some $\alpha \neq 0$. Then the string X with $X_1 = X_2 = \cdots = X_k = 1$ and the remaining X_j all 0 has $p(X) = \alpha \neq 0$. This contradiction implies that $p(X)$ is indeed the zero polynomial and $p_1 = p_2$. $\square$

The degree of such a p is a useful measure of the complexity of F.

Definition 9.5.5 *The degree of the polynomial p which represents F is denoted $\deg(F)$.*

For example, the OR function is represented by the polynomial $1 - \prod_{j=1}^{N} (1 - X_j)$ which has degree N. Thus $\deg(\mathrm{OR}) = N$.

In practice, it would suffice to have a polynomial p which approximates F at every $X \in \{0, 1\}^N$. For example $\mathrm{OR}(X_1, X_2) \approx \frac{2}{3}(X_1 + X_2)$.

Definition 9.5.6 *An N-variate polynomial $p : \mathbb{R}^N \to \mathbb{R}$ approximates F if $|p(X) - F(X)| \leq \frac{1}{3}$ for all $X \in \{0, 1\}^N$.*

The minimum degree of such a polynomial p is another useful measure of the complexity of F.

Definition 9.5.7 *The minimum degree of a p approximating F is denoted $\widetilde{\deg}(F)$.*

We have the following theorems relating the quantum query complexities $Q_E(F)$ and $Q_2(F)$ to $\deg(F), \widetilde{\deg}(F)$.

Theorem 9.5.8 *If F is a Boolean function, then $Q_E(F) \geq \frac{\deg(F)}{2}$.*

Proof Consider the result of a quantum algorithm for evaluating F exactly using $Q_E(F)$ queries. By Corollary 9.5.2, the probability of observing 1 is $p_1(X)$, a polynomial of degree at most $2Q_E(F)$. We will observe 1 if and only if $F(X) = 1$. In other words $p_1(X) = F(X)$ for all $X \in \{0, 1\}^N$. This implies that $2Q_E(F) \geq \deg(F)$. $\square$

Theorem 9.5.9 *If F is a Boolean function, then $Q_2(F) \geq \frac{\widetilde{\deg}(F)}{2}$.*

Proof Consider the result of a quantum algorithm for evaluating F approximately using $Q_2(F)$ queries. By corollary 9.5.2, the probability of observing 1 is $p_1(X)$, a polynomial of degree at most $2Q_E(F)$. If $F(X) = 1$, then $p_1(X) \geq \frac{2}{3}$. Similarly, if $F(X) = 0$ then $1 - p_1(X) \geq \frac{2}{3}$. In other words $|p_1(X) - F(X)| \leq \frac{1}{3}$ for all $X \in \{0,1\}^N$, which means p_1 approximates F. This implies that $2Q_E(F) \geq \widetilde{\deg}(F)$.   □

9.5.2   Examples of Polynomial Method Lower Bounds

We have already seen that $\deg(\text{OR}) = N$, and thus $Q_E(\text{OR}) \geq \frac{N}{2}$. A more careful application of the polynomial method actually shows that $Q_E(\text{OR}) = N$.

It can be shown that $\widetilde{\deg}(\text{OR}) \in \Theta(\sqrt{N})$, and thus $Q_2(\text{OR}) \in \Omega(\sqrt{N})$. Note that this lower bound is tight (up to a constant factor), since quantum searching evaluates the OR function with bounded-error using $O(\sqrt{N})$ queries.

Consider the MAJORITY function, defined as $\text{MAJORITY}(\mathbf{X}) = 1$ if $\mathbf{X}$ has more than $\frac{N}{2}$ ones, and 0 if it has fewer or equal to $\frac{N}{2}$ ones. It can be shown that $\widetilde{\deg}(\text{MAJORITY}) \in \Theta(N)$. Thus $Q_2(\text{MAJORITY}) \in \Omega(N)$, so quantum algorithms are not very useful for computing majorities.

A generalization of MAJORITY is the THRESHOLD$_M$ function, defined as THRESHOLD$_M(\mathbf{X}) = 1$ if $\mathbf{X}$ has at least M ones, and 0 otherwise. It can be shown that $\widetilde{\deg}(\text{THRESHOLD}_M) \in \Theta(\sqrt{M(N - M + 1)})$. Note that this means that the exact quantum counting algorithm described in Section 8.3 makes an optimal number of queries (up to a constant factor).

The PARITY function is defined as $\text{PARITY}(\mathbf{X}) = 1$ if $\mathbf{X}$ has an odd number of ones, and 0 if $\mathbf{X}$ has an even number of ones. The degree of the PARITY function is $\deg(\text{PARITY}) = N$, and so $Q_E(\text{PARITY}) \geq \lceil \frac{N}{2} \rceil$. It can be shown $\widetilde{\deg}(\text{PARITY}) = N$ as well, and thus $Q_2(\text{PARITY}) \geq \lceil \frac{N}{2} \rceil$.

Exercise 9.5.1 Find a real polynomial of degree N that represents the PARITY function.

Exercise 9.5.2 Show that $Q_E(\text{PARITY}) = Q_2(\text{PARITY}) = \lceil \frac{N}{2} \rceil$ by finding an algorithm that achieves the bound.

The polynomial method can be extended to partial functions F defined on proper subsets $S \subset \{0,1\}^N$ in a very natural way by finding the minimum degree of a real polynomial P that satisfies $|F(X) - P(X)| \leq \frac{1}{3}$ on all $\mathbf{X} \in S$ and $0 \leq P(\mathbf{X}) \leq 1$ for all $\mathbf{X} \in \{0,1\}^N$.

For example, the minimum degree of a polynomial representing OR on inputs with at most one 1 is still in $\Omega(\sqrt{N})$ and thus the polynomial method provides another proof of Theorem 9.3.2.

9.6 Block Sensitivity

Intuitively, one expects functions that are very sensitive to changes of the values of almost any of the bits in the string X will require us to probe more bits of X than functions which are relatively indifferent to such changes. One way of rigorously capturing this concept of sensitivity is by the notion of the *block sensitivity* of F.

Definition 9.6.1 *Let* $F : \{0,1\}^N \to \{0,1\}$ *be a function,* $\mathbf{X} \in \{0,1\}^N$, *and* $B \subseteq \{1, 2, \ldots, N\}$ *be a set of indices.*

Let $\mathbf{X}^B$ *denote the string obtained from* $\mathbf{X}$ *by flipping the values of the variables in* B.

The function F *is sensitive to* B *on* $\mathbf{X}$ *if* $f(\mathbf{X}) \neq f(\mathbf{X}^B)$.

The block sensitivity $bs_{\mathbf{X}}(F)$ *of* F *on* $\mathbf{X}$ *is the maximum number* t *for which there exist* t *disjoint sets of indices* $B_1, \ldots, B_t$, *such that* F *is sensitive to each* B_i *on* $\mathbf{X}$.

The block sensitivity $bs(F)$ *of* F *is the maximum of* $bs_{\mathbf{X}}(F)$ *over all* $\mathbf{X} \in \{0,1\}^N$.

Theorem 9.6.2 *If* F *is a Boolean function, then* $Q_E(F) \geq \sqrt{\frac{bs(F)}{8}}$ *and* $Q_2(F) \geq \sqrt{\frac{bs(F)}{16}}$.

Intuitively, in order to distinguish a string $\mathbf{X}$ from the set of strings $\mathbf{Y}$ for which $F(\mathbf{X}) \neq F(\mathbf{Y})$ (which includes $\mathbf{X}^{B_i}$ for every block B_i to which F is sensitive on $\mathbf{X}$), we have to query each of the $bs_{\mathbf{X}}(F)$ blocks B_i to be confident that they are consistent with $\mathbf{X}$ and not $\mathbf{X}^B$. This is at least as hard as searching for a block which is not consistent with $\mathbf{X}$, which gives a $\Omega(\sqrt{bs_{\mathbf{X}}(F)})$ lower bound for any $\mathbf{X}$, which implies a lower bound of $\Omega(\sqrt{bs(F)})$ for F.

We omit a detailed proof of Theorem 9.6.2. A lower bound of $\Omega(\sqrt{bs(F)})$ can be proved by hybrid or polynomial methods, or as a special case of the technique we describe in the next section (see Exercise 9.7.4). Note that since we can never have more than N blocks, the greatest lower bound that this method can provide is $\Omega(\sqrt{N})$.

9.6.1 Examples of Block Sensitivity Lower Bounds

The block sensitivity of the OR function is N because $bs(\mathbf{0}) = N$ (each individual bit is a block). This proves that $Q_2(\text{OR}) \geq \frac{\sqrt{N}}{4}$ and leads to another proof of Theorem 9.3.2.

Exercise 9.6.1 Prove that the block sensitivity of the THRESHOLD$_M$ function is $N - M + 1$.

This method provides a lower bound of $\Omega(\sqrt{N - M + 1})$ for computing THRESHOLD$_M$. This lower bound is not tight like the one provided by the polynomial method.

The block sensitivity of the PARITY function is N, giving a lower bound of $\Omega(\sqrt{N})$ that is also not tight.

In the next section we describe a more general and powerful method for which the block sensitivity method is a special case.

9.7 Adversary Methods

Consider any algorithm A that guesses $F(\mathbf{Z})$ after t calls to a black-box for $\mathbf{Z}$. Let $|\psi_j^{\mathbf{Z}}\rangle$ be the state just after the jth call to the oracle for string $\mathbf{Z}$.

Since this algorithm is trying to compute $F(\mathbf{Z})$ for some unknown string $\mathbf{Z}$, it must try to decide whether $|\psi_t^{\mathbf{Z}}\rangle \in \mathcal{Y} = \{|\psi_t^{\mathbf{Y}}\rangle | F(\mathbf{Y}) = 1\}$ or $|\psi_t^{\mathbf{Z}}\rangle \in \mathcal{X} = \{|\psi_t^{\mathbf{X}}\rangle | F(\mathbf{X}) = 0\}$. Thus, a good algorithm will try to make these two sets as distinguishable as possible.

Our goal is to correctly guess $F(\mathbf{Z})$ for any input $\mathbf{Z}$ (recall we are interested in the worst-case performance). Suppose our algorithm A has the property that for any input $\mathbf{Z}$ the probability of guessing the correct answer is at least $1 - \epsilon$. This means that the final stage of A can correctly distinguish $|\psi_t^{\mathbf{X}}\rangle$ from $|\psi_t^{\mathbf{Y}}\rangle$ for any $\mathbf{X}, \mathbf{Y}$ with $F(\mathbf{X}) \neq F(\mathbf{Y})$ with probability at least $1 - \epsilon$. By Theorem 9.2.1, we know that we must have $|\langle \psi_t^{\mathbf{X}} | \psi_t^{\mathbf{Y}} \rangle| = \delta \leq 2\sqrt{\epsilon(1 - \epsilon)}$.

Let R be any subset of $\mathcal{X} \times \mathcal{Y}$. Notice that before any oracle queries we have $|\psi_0^{\mathbf{X}}\rangle = |\psi_0^{\mathbf{Y}}\rangle$ for all $\mathbf{X}, \mathbf{Y}$ and thus

$$\sum_{\substack{|\psi_0^{\mathbf{X}}\rangle, |\psi_0^{\mathbf{Y}}\rangle: \\ \mathbf{X}, \mathbf{Y} \in R}} |\langle \psi_0^{\mathbf{X}} | \psi_0^{\mathbf{Y}} \rangle| = |R|. \tag{9.7.1}$$

If after t oracles queries the algorithm always answers correctly with probability at least $1 - \epsilon$ we must have

$$\sum_{(x,y) \in R} |\langle \psi_t^{\mathbf{X}} | \psi_t^{\mathbf{Y}} \rangle| \leq 2\sqrt{\epsilon(1 - \epsilon)} |R|. \tag{9.7.2}$$

If we have $\epsilon < \frac{1}{2}$, then

$$2\sqrt{\epsilon(1 - \epsilon)} |R| < |R|. \tag{9.7.3}$$

In other words, if we define

$$W^j = \sum_{(x,y)\in R} \frac{1}{\sqrt{|\mathcal{X}||\mathcal{Y}|}} |\langle \psi_j^{\mathbf{X}} | \psi_j^{\mathbf{Y}} \rangle| \tag{9.7.4}$$

(we renormalize it for notational convenience later), then we know that

$$W^t - W^0 \geq |R| \frac{\left(1 - 2\sqrt{\epsilon(1-\epsilon)}\right)}{\sqrt{|\mathcal{X}||\mathcal{Y}|}} \in \Omega\left(\frac{|R|}{\sqrt{|X||Y|}}\right).$$

Thus if we can upper bound the rate at which the quantity W^j can decrease with each oracle query, we will get a lower bound on the query complexity. In other words, we wish to prove that there is some value $\Delta > 0$ so that $W^j - W^{j-1} < \Delta$. This would imply that $t \geq \frac{W^t - W^0}{\Delta}$.

We have the following lemma which is proved in Appendix A.5.

Lemma 9.7.1 *Let b and b' satisfy the following.*

- *For every $\mathbf{X} \in \mathcal{X}$ and $i \in \{1, 2, \ldots, N\}$, there are at most b different $\mathbf{Y} \in \mathcal{Y}$ such that $(\mathbf{X}, \mathbf{Y}) \in R$ and $X_i \neq Y_i$.*
- *For every $\mathbf{Y} \in \mathcal{Y}$ and $i \in \{1, 2, \ldots, N\}$, there are at most b' different $\mathbf{Y} \in \mathcal{Y}$ such that $(\mathbf{X}, \mathbf{Y}) \in R$ and $X_i \neq Y_i$.*

Then $W^k - W^{k-1} \leq \sqrt{bb'}$.

Proof See Appendix A.5. □

This implies the following lemma.

Lemma 9.7.2 *Let F be a function defined on any subset of $\{0,1\}^N$. Let $\mathcal{X} = \{\mathbf{X}|F(\mathbf{X}) = 0\}$ and $\mathcal{Y} = \{\mathbf{Y}|F(\mathbf{Y}) = 1\}$, and $R \subseteq \mathcal{X} \times \mathcal{Y}$, and b, b' satisfy the same hypotheses as in Lemma 9.7.1. Then the number of queries to $O_{\mathbf{Z}}$ required in order to compute $F(\mathbf{Z})$ with probability at least $1 - \epsilon$ (for constant $\epsilon < \frac{1}{2}$) is*

$$t \geq |R| \frac{\left(1 - 2\sqrt{\epsilon(1-\epsilon)}\right)}{\sqrt{|\mathcal{X}||\mathcal{Y}|}\sqrt{bb'}} \in \Omega\left(\frac{|R|}{\sqrt{|\mathcal{X}||\mathcal{Y}|}\sqrt{bb'}}\right). \tag{9.7.5}$$

To get some intuition behind why lower values of b and b' give a larger lower bound on the query complexity, note that to recognize that $\mathbf{X} \in \mathcal{X}$ given the black-box $O_{\mathbf{X}}$, we must rule out all the $\mathbf{Y} \in \mathcal{Y}$. A single (classical) query to $O_{\mathbf{X}}$ can rule out at most b values of $\mathbf{Y} \in \mathcal{Y}$. Similarly, if we have the black-box $O_{\mathbf{Y}}$, a single (classical) query to $O_{\mathbf{Y}}$ will rule out at most b' values of $\mathbf{X} \in \mathcal{X}$.

A further simplification to this equation is achieved with the help of the following lemma.

Lemma 9.7.3 *Let m and m' be any integers satisfying:*

- *For every $\mathbf{X} \in \mathcal{X}$ there are at least m different $\mathbf{Y} \in \mathcal{Y}$ such that $(\mathbf{X}, \mathbf{Y}) \in R$.*
- *For every $y \in Y$ there are at least m' different $\mathbf{X} \in \mathcal{X}$ such that $(\mathbf{X}, \mathbf{Y}) \in R$.*

Then $|R| \geq \sqrt{|\mathcal{X}||\mathcal{Y}|mm'}$.

Proof Note that since for each $\mathbf{X} \in \mathcal{X}$ there are at least m strings $\mathbf{Y} \in \mathcal{Y}$ such that $(\mathbf{X}, \mathbf{Y}) \in R$, we must have $|R| \geq m|\mathcal{X}|$. Similarly, we must have $|R| \geq m'|\mathcal{Y}|$, and thus $|R|$ must be at least as large as the average of these two numbers. Since the arithmetic mean of two non-negative real numbers is always greater than or equal to the geometric mean of the same two numbers we have

$$|R| \geq \frac{m|\mathcal{X}| + m'|\mathcal{Y}|}{2} \geq \sqrt{|\mathcal{X}||\mathcal{Y}|mm'}. \tag{9.7.6}$$

$\square$

This implies the following theorem.

Theorem 9.7.4 *Let F be a function defined on any subset of $\{0,1\}^N$. Let $\mathcal{X} = \{\mathbf{X}|F(\mathbf{X}) = 0\}$ and $\mathcal{Y} = \{\mathbf{Y}|F(\mathbf{Y}) = 1\}$, and $R \subset \mathcal{X} \times \mathcal{Y}$ and b, b' satisfy the same hypotheses as in Lemma 9.7.1, and m and m' satisfy the same hypotheses as in Lemma 9.7.1.*

$$Q_2(F) \in \Omega\left(\sqrt{\frac{mm'}{bb'}}\right). \tag{9.7.7}$$

9.7.1 Examples of Adversary Lower Bounds

Lower Bound for Searching

To reprove the lower bound on searching, we can let $\mathcal{X} = \{\mathbf{0}\}$, $\mathcal{Y}$ be the set of all strings with exactly one 1, and $R = \mathcal{X} \times \mathcal{Y}$. It is easy to verify that $m = N$, $m' = b = b' = 1$, which gives the $\Omega(\sqrt{N})$ lower bound.

Exercise 9.7.1 Use the adversary method to prove that $\Omega(N)$ queries are required to decide the MAJORITY function with bounded error.

Hint: Let X be the strings with $N/2$ ones, and Y be the strings with $N/2 + 1$ strings. Choose the relation R carefully.

Exercise 9.7.2 Use the adversary method to prove that $\Omega(N)$ queries are required to decide the PARITY function.

It is worth noting that all of these lower bounds were already obtained by the polynomial or block-sensitivity method. The following lower bound is one which has not yet been achieved using the previous methods.

Lower bound for AND–OR *trees*

Consider a function F consisting of the AND of ORs of the N variables $X_1, X_2, \ldots, X_N$ taken in groups of size $M = \sqrt{N}$ (for convenience we assume N is a perfect square). In other words

$$F(\mathbf{X}) = (X_1 \vee X_2 \vee \cdots \vee X_M) \wedge (X_{M+1} \vee X_{M+2} \vee \cdots \vee X_{2M}) \wedge \cdots$$
$$\cdots \wedge (X_{(M-1)M+1} \vee X_{(M-1)M+2} \vee \cdots \vee X_{M^2}).$$
$$(9.7.8)$$

A nice way of depicting this function is by a tree where the inputs are located at the leaves of the tree. Each vertex denotes the operation to apply to the inputs coming in from the edges below and are output along the edge above the vertex. Figure 9.5 illustrates the AND–OR tree that evaluates $F(\mathbf{X})$.

In order for $F(\mathbf{X})$ to equal 1, there must be at least one 1 in each OR sub-tree.

There are bounded-error quantum algorithms for solving this problem using $O(\sqrt{N})$ queries (in Exercise 9.7.3 you are asked to give an algorithm using $O(\sqrt{N} \log N)$ queries). The straightforward application of the block sensitivity or polynomial method gives a lower bound of $\Omega(N^{\frac{1}{4}})$.

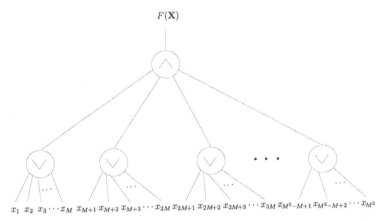

Fig. 9.5 This tree illustrates the computation of the 'AND–OR' function F. The input bits are at the leaves of the tree. Each OR vertex computes the OR of the bits along the edges below it, and outputs the answer along the edge above it. All the OR outputs are the inputs to the AND vertex, which computes the AND and outputs the answer.

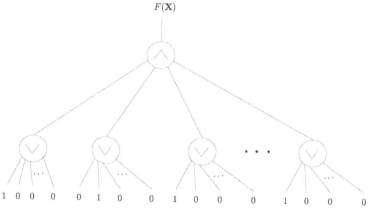

$F(\mathbf{X})$

1 0 0 0   0 1 0   0 1 0 0   0 1 0 0   0

Fig. 9.6 This diagram illustrates an input **X** to the AND–OR tree where $F(\mathbf{X}) = 1$. Note that each OR has exactly one 1 input, and thus outputs a 1. Thus the AND has all 1s as input, and outputs 1.

Exercise 9.7.3 Give a bounded-error quantum algorithm for computing the AND − OR function F on N inputs using $O(\sqrt{N}\log N)$ queries.

Using the adversary method, we get a lower bound of $\Omega(\sqrt{N})$.

Theorem 9.7.5 *Any bounded-error quantum algorithm that evaluates F on all* $\mathbf{X} \in \{0,1\}^N$ *has query complexity in* $\Omega(\sqrt{N})$.

Proof Let $\mathcal{X}$ correspond to the set of all strings with *exactly* one 1 in each of the M inputs to each OR function (see Figure 9.6 for an example). Let $\mathcal{Y}$ correspond to the set of all strings where exactly one OR function has only 0 inputs (see Figure 9.7 for an example), and the remaining ORs have exactly one 1.

Let R consist of every ordered pair $(\mathbf{X}, \mathbf{Y}) \in \mathcal{X} \times \mathcal{Y}$ where **X** and **Y** differ in exactly one bit position.

Then $m = \sqrt{N}$ since for every $\mathbf{X} \in \mathcal{X}$ there are $M = \sqrt{N}$ ones (one per OR) that could be flipped in order to give a string $\mathbf{Y} \in \mathcal{Y}$. Similarly $m' = \sqrt{N}$ since for each $\mathbf{Y} \in \mathcal{Y}$ there is one OR that has all M inputs equal to 0, and flipping any one of those M 0s to 1 gives a string in $\mathcal{X}$.

Furthermore $b = 1$ since for each $\mathbf{X} \in \mathcal{X}$ and each $i \in \{1, 2, \ldots, N\}$, there is at most one $\mathbf{Y} \in \mathcal{Y}$ that differs from **X** in the ith position. Similarly, $b' = 1$.

Theorem 9.7.4 implies that $Q_2(F) \in \Omega\left(\sqrt{\frac{mm'}{bb'}}\right) = \Omega(\sqrt{N})$. □

The bounded-error classical complexity of F is in $\Theta(N)$.

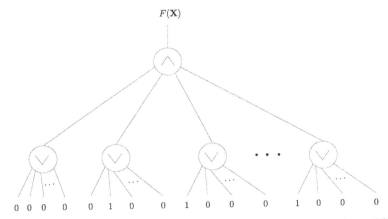

Fig. 9.7 This diagram illustrates an input **X** to the AND–OR tree where $F(\mathbf{X}) = 0$. Note that one of the ORs has no 1 inputs, and thus outputs a 0. Thus, the AND has at least one 0 input and must output a 0.

Exercise 9.7.4 Prove that the block sensitivity lower bound of $Q_2(F) \in \Omega\left(\sqrt{\mathrm{bs}(F)}\right)$ can be derived by adversary arguments.

Hint: Let $\mathcal{X}$ consist of a string that achieves $\mathrm{bs}(F)$.

9.7.2 Generalizations

There are several ways of generalizing the adversary method we have presented in order to get more powerful tools for proving lower bounds. For example, one way of looking at the definition of W^j (recall Equation (9.7.4)) is summing over all ordered pairs $(\mathbf{X}, \mathbf{Y}) \in \mathcal{X} \times \mathcal{Y}$ and weighing each pair with some weight which we took to be 1 if $(\mathbf{X}, \mathbf{Y}) \in R$, and 0 otherwise. This suggests a more general family of 'weighted' adversary methods which indeed have been defined. Other methods use spectral or Kolmogorov complexity techniques. A large class of these generalizations are in fact equivalent in that they will prove the same lower bounds.

10

QUANTUM ERROR CORRECTION

A mathematical model of computation is an idealized abstraction. We design algorithms and perform analysis on the assumption that the mathematical operations we specify will be carried out exactly, and without error. Physical devices that implement an abstract model of computation are imperfect and of limited precision. For example, when a digital circuit is implemented on a physical circuit board, unwanted electrical noise in the environment may cause components to behave differently than expected, and may cause voltage levels (bit-values) to change. These sources of error must be controlled or compensated for, or else the resulting loss of efficiency may reduce the power of the information-processing device. If individual steps in a computation succeed with probability p, then a computation involving t sequential steps will have a success probability that decreases exponentially as p^t.

Although it may be impossible to eliminate the sources of errors, we can devise schemes to allow us to recover from errors using a reasonable amount of additional resources. Many classical digital computing devices use *error-correcting codes* to perform detection of and recovery from errors. The theory of error-correcting codes is itself a mathematical abstraction, but it is one that explicitly accounts for errors introduced by the imperfection and imprecision of realistic devices. This theory has proven extremely effective in allowing engineers to build computing devices that are resilient against errors.

Quantum computers are more susceptible to errors than classical digital computers, because quantum mechanical systems are more delicate and more difficult to control. If large-scale quantum computers are to be possible, a theory of quantum error correction is needed. The discovery of quantum error correction has given researchers confidence that realistic large-scale quantum computing devices can be built despite the presence of errors.

10.1 Classical Error Correction

We begin by considering fundamental concepts for error correction in a classical setting. We will focus on three of these concepts: (a) the characterization of the error model, (b) the introduction of redundancy through encoding, and (c) an error recovery procedure. We will later see that these concepts generalize quite naturally for quantum error correction. For the remainder of this section we discuss how classical bits of information (in a classical computer, or being transmitted from one place to another) can be protected from the effects of errors.

10.1.1   The Error Model

The first step in protecting information against errors is to understand the nature of the errors we are trying to protect against. Such an understanding is expressed by an *error model*. It describes the evolution of set of bits. In analogy to the evolution or transformation that occurs on bits when they are being stored, or being moved around from one point of the computer to another, it is often called a *channel*. Ideally, we would like the state of our bits to be unaffected by the channel (i.e. we do not want a bit to change its value while it is in storage, or being moved from one place to another). We say that an error-free channel is an *identity channel*. When errors occur on the bits being stored or moved around, the channel provides a description of these errors. Ultimately, we will want to consider errors that occur *during* a computation. To understand error-correction methods, it is very useful to first consider the simpler case of just sending bits through a channel.

The simplest classical error model is the *bit-flip channel*. In this model, the state of a bit is *flipped* with probability p, and is unaffected with probability $1 - p$. The bit-flip channel is illustrated in Figure 10.1.

For the bit-flip channel, the probability p of a bit flip is independent of whether the bit is initially 0 or 1. A more complicated error model might have a different probability of error for bits in the state 0 than state 1. The bit-flip channel we consider is one where errors occur independently from bit to bit. More general error models would account for correlated errors between different bits. When errors described by a given model act on a register of bits in a circuit, we show this by a block labeled $\mathcal{E}^C$, as illustrated in Figure 10.2. The superscript C is

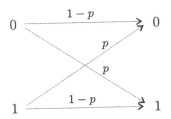

Fig. 10.1 The classical bit-flip channel.

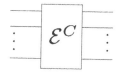

Fig. 10.2 A block representing the effect of errors on a register in a circuit diagram.

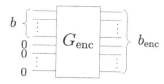

Fig. 10.3 Encoding operation taking a logical string b, and an ancilla of bits in the state 0, into the codeword b_{enc}.

used to distinguish the classical from the quantum cases, which we will discuss later.

The error model $\mathcal{E}^C$ is composed of different operations $\mathcal{E}_i^C$, where each $\mathcal{E}_i^C$ corresponds to a specific error that occurs with probability p_i.

10.1.2 Encoding

Once we have a description of an error model, we want to encode information in a way that is robust against these errors. This can be done by adding a number of extra bits to a *logical bit* that we wish to protect, and thereby transforming the resulting string into an *encoded* bit. The string of bits corresponding to an encoded bit is called a *codeword*. The set of codewords (one for each of the two possible bit values 0 and 1) is called a *code*. The codewords are designed to add some *redundancy* to the logical bits they represent. The basic idea behind the redundancy is that even when errors corrupt some of the bits in a codeword, the remaining bits contain enough information so that the logical bit can be recovered.

The above scheme can easily be generalized to encode logical strings of n bits directly (rather than by encoding each logical bit independently). A logical string b of n bits can be encoded by adding m ancillary bits (in a known state, which we will assume without loss of generality to be 0) and then transforming the resulting string into an $(n+m)$-bit codeword, which we will call b_{enc}.

The process of mapping the logical strings b to their respective codewords b_{enc} is called the *encoding* operation. In a circuit, we implement the encoding by adding some ancillary bits, initially in the 0 state, and then applying some gates. We represent this process in a circuit diagram as the G_{enc} operation, as shown in Figure 10.3.

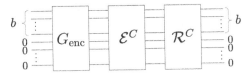

Fig. 10.4 After a codeword b_{enc} is subjected to some errors, the recovery operation $\mathcal{R}^C$ corrects these errors and recovers the logical string b.

10.1.3   Error Recovery

After a codeword b_{enc} is subjected to some errors the result is a string $\bar{b}_{\text{enc}}$. We want a procedure for *correcting* the errors in $\bar{b}_{\text{enc}}$ and for recovering the logical bit (or string) b. This is called the *recovery operation*. For convenience, we will have the recovery operation return the ancilla to the all 0's state (in general this can be achieved by discarding the old ancilla and replacing it with a freshly initialized ancilla). The recovery operation is shown in Figure 10.4.

The recovery operation must be able to unambiguously distinguish between codewords after errors have acted on them. Suppose specific errors are represented by operations $\mathcal{E}_i^C$ (where i ranges over all the possible errors that could occur on a codeword). A recovery operation will work correctly from some subset of these errors, which we call the *correctable errors*. Given a code, for a set of errors to be correctable by that code, we must have

$$\mathcal{E}_i^C\left(k_{\text{enc}}\right) \neq \mathcal{E}_j^C\left(l_{\text{enc}}\right), \qquad \forall k \neq l \tag{10.1.1}$$

where k and l are logical strings encoded into the codewords k_{enc} and l_{enc} and i, j range over the correctable errors. Equation (10.1.1) is the *condition for (classical) error correction* which says that when any errors act on two distinct codewords, the resulting strings are never equal. This means that after the errors, from the resulting strings we can unambiguously determine the original codewords. To simplify the notation, the identity transformation will always be included in the set of errors $\mathcal{E}_i^C$ (where no correction should be required).

Orthogonality conditions of the form in Equation 10.1.1 are possible because we assume the errors are described by a finite number of discrete effects and not a continuous spectrum of operations (i.e. the errors are like the discrete errors we see in digital computation and not like the continuous errors of analog computation).

The condition for error correction is illustrated in Figure 10.5 for a code with two codewords, under an error model in which there are four possible errors (including the identity).

10.2   The Classical Three-Bit Code

To make the above concepts more concrete, here we detail an example of a classical error-correcting code known as the three-bit code. The error model we

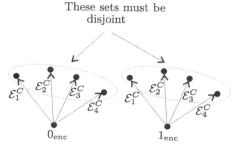

These sets must be
disjoint

Fig. 10.5 The error correction condition for a code with two codewords, under an error model in which there are four possible errors $\mathcal{E}_1^C, \mathcal{E}_2^C, \mathcal{E}_3^C, \mathcal{E}_4^C$ affecting each codeword. The condition is that when any errors act on two distinct codewords, the resulting strings are never equal.

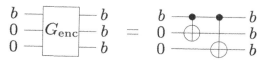

Fig. 10.6 A circuit for the encoding operation for the classical three-bit code. Recall the circuit symbol for the classical CNOT gate from Figure 1.3.

consider for this example is the bit-flip channel, described in Section 10.1.1. For the bit-flip channel the state of a (classical) bit is flipped with probability p, and is unaffected with probability $1 - p$.

A simple encoding scheme to protect information from errors introduced by the bit-flip channel is to increase the number of bits by adding two ancillary bits, and then to encode each bit b as a codeword b_{enc} of three bits, according to the rule

$$0 \mapsto 000 \mapsto 000$$
$$1 \mapsto 100 \mapsto 111. \tag{10.2.1}$$

First two ancillary bits, initially set to 0, are appended to the logical bit to be encoded. Then the value of the first bit is copied to the ancillary bits. The result is that every bit is represented as a codeword consisting of three copies of itself. A circuit for the encoding operation is shown in Figure 10.6.

After a codeword b_{enc} is subjected to the bit-flip channel, the result is a set of strings $\bar{b}_{\text{enc}}$ which occur with probability $P_{\bar{b}_{\text{enc}}}$. That is,

$$b_{\text{enc}} \to \{(\bar{b}_{\text{enc}}, P_{\bar{b}_{\text{enc}}})\} \tag{10.2.2}$$

or explicitly

$$000 \rightarrow \{ (000, (1-p)^3),$$
$$(001, p(1-p)^2), (010, p(1-p)^2), (100, p(1-p)^2),$$
$$(011, p^2(1-p)), (110, p^2(1-p)), (101, p^2(1-p)),$$
$$(111, p^3) \}. \tag{10.2.3}$$

We want to design a recovery operation that takes $\bar{b}_{enc}$ and returns the original logical bit string b. First we should verify that such a recovery operator exists, by checking that the classical error-correction condition (Equation (10.1.1)) is satisfied. For this to hold we will need to restrict the errors so that at most one bit flip occurs within each codeword (the strings given in the first two lines of (10.2.3)). This is a set of correctable errors.

Exercise 10.2.1

(a) Consider the restricted bit-flip error model where at most 1 bit flip can occur within each codeword. For the three-bit code described above, show that Equation (10.1.1) holds, and so it is possible to unambiguously correct single bit flips using this code.

(b) Show that under an error model in which 2 or more bit flips can occur within each codeword, Equation (10.1.1) does not hold, and so the three-bit code cannot correct these errors.

To recover the logical bit b from the corrupted codewords $\bar{b}_{enc}$ we need to learn which specific noise operator has been applied and undo its effect, restoring the information. A simple way to accomplish this task is to look at the value of each bit, take a majority vote of the three bits and reset all the bits to the value resulting from the majority vote. It will not be possible to generalize this procedure to the quantum case as it requires measuring all bits and that would destroy quantum information. We will instead use a different procedure. We will design the error correction procedure to restore the information in the first bit and use the last two bits to tell us on which bit the error occurred. This can be accomplished by comparing the value of the first bit to the remaining two bits in the code. In other words, we compute the *parity* (exclusive-OR) of the first and second bits, and the parity of the first and third bits. If the first bit agrees with both the other bits (i.e. both parities are 0), we conclude that no error has occurred. Similarly, if the first bit agrees with only one of the remaining two bits (and disagrees with the other remaining bit), then the first bit is correct and the bit with which the parity was 1 has flipped. In the remaining case that both the parities are 1 (i.e. the first bit disagrees with both the remaining two bits), we conclude that the first bit must have been flipped. In this last case, we can correct the first bit by flipping it back to its original value. Note that we never needed to learn the actual value of any bit, only the parities. The parities provide enough information to identify the errors that have affected the codeword. This information is called the *error syndrome*.

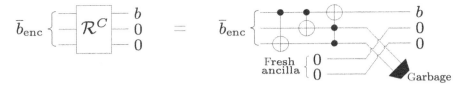

Fig. 10.7 A circuit for the recovery operation for the three-bit code.

To implement the above recovery operation in a circuit, we first need to compute the parity of the first and second bits, and the parity of the first and third bits. This can be achieved with a pair of classical CNOT gates controlled on the first bit (recall Figure 1.3 to see why this works). After each CNOT gate, the target bits equals 0 if its value (before the CNOTs) agreed with the control bit, and equals 1 otherwise. Since the first bit is only a control bit for the CNOTs, the only way in which the first bit could have been flipped is by an error applied to the first bit, in which case (assuming at most one bit flip error) both targets of the CNOT gates (parities) will have value 1. So to correct the first bit, we want to flip it if and only if the remaining two bits (after the CNOTs) both equal 1. This can be achieved with a Toffoli (controlled-controlled-CNOT) gate. After the first bit has been corrected, we must reset the two ancillary bits to their initial value of 0. Erasing bit values cannot be done reversibly, but an alternative approach is to introduce two fresh ancilla (initialized to 0) and discard (or ignore) the used ancilla. A circuit for the recovery operation for the three-bit code is shown in Figure 10.7.

There is a different way to look at the effect of encoding. Instead of looking at the behaviour of errors on the encoded state, we can think of the encoding operation as transforming the error operators as in Figure 10.8. The effect of the noise can be seen as affecting the ancilla by conjugating[1] the error $\mathcal{E}_i^C$ by the encoding operation G_{enc} and studying its effect on the input $(b, 0, 0)$. As you will see in Exercise 10.2.2, the transformed error $\mathcal{E}_i^{C'}$ flips the first bit if and only if it also flips the remaining two bits. So the first bit can be corrected by applying just a Toffoli gate. The Toffoli gate is the new recovery operation $\mathcal{R}^{C'}$, and this is equivalent to first applying the encoding operation G_{enc} for the three-bit code, and then applying the original recovery operation $\mathcal{R}^C$ for the three-bit code. This point of view tracks the bit of information itself instead of the values of the individual bits that form the code.

Exercise 10.2.2

(a) Consider the bit-flip channel, restricted to the case that at most one bit flip occurs within a block of three bits. For each of the possible errors acting on a block of three bits (no bit flip, or a bit flip on the first, second, or third qubit), conjugate the error by the encoding operation for the three-bit code (given in Figure 10.6), and compute

---

[1] To *conjugate* an operator A by another operator B means to multiply A by B^{-1} on the left, and by B on the right, forming $B^{-1}AB$.

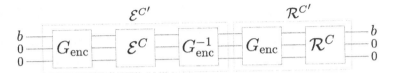

Fig. 10.8 We can insert $G_{enc}G_{enc}^{-1}$ (the identity) between the error and recovery blocks from Figure 10.4. Now we can view the error as being conjugated by the encoding operation (shown in the first dashed box on the left), and study the effect of the transformed error $\mathcal{E}^{C'}$ on the state of the three bits. The new recovery operator is $\mathcal{R}^{C'}$, shown in the dashed box at the right end of the circuit.

the effect of this transformed error $\mathcal{E}^{C'}$ on the input $(b, 0, 0)$. (Notice that $\mathcal{E}^{C'}$ flips the first bit if and only if it also flips the remaining two bits.)

(b) For the G_{enc} and $\mathcal{R}^C$ operations given for the three-bit code, show that $\mathcal{R}^{C'} = \mathcal{R}^C G_{enc}$ is the Toffoli gate.

The recovery operation for the three-bit code above will only succeed if at most 1 bit flip occurs within each codeword (correctable errors), but this suffices to reduce the *probability* of error. For the bit-flip channel, bits are flipped independently with probability p. So without error correction, this is the probability of error on a single bit. When we encode the bit using the three-bit code, the probability of two or more bits of a codeword being flipped is $3p^2(1-p)+p^3$, so the probability of an unrecoverable error changes from p to $3p^2 - 2p^3$ (a change in the exponent of the error probability). The three-bit code gives an improvement as long as $3p^2 - 2p^3 < p$, which happens whenever $p < \frac{1}{2}$ (if $p > \frac{1}{2}$, then we could modify the three-bit code accordingly by encoding 0 as 111 and 1 as 000). If $p = \frac{1}{2}$ then the error channel completely randomizes the information, and there is no hope of error correction helping.

The three-bit code is an example of a *repetition code*, since codewords are formed by simply repeating the value of each logical bit a specified number of times. We will see later that simple repetition codes do not exist for quantum error correction, but that the idea can be modified to give codes that protect quantum information.

10.3   Fault Tolerance

In the scheme described in the previous sections, the recovery operation recovers the logical string b, and so implicitly *decodes* the codeword. To protect the information from errors in later stages of the computation, we would have to re-encode the information again. However, this approach leaves the information unprotected between the decoding and re-encoding.

Another shortcoming of the above strategy is that it implicitly assumes that the encoding and error recovery operations are themselves free from errors. The

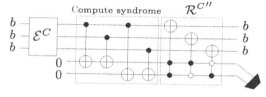

Fig. 10.9 Error correction for the three-bit code without decoding the state. A codeword $b_{enc} = bbb$ has been exposed to correctable errors, yielding the string $\bar{b}_{enc}$. The first stage of the circuit computes the error syndrome (parities) into an ancilla, and the second stage of the circuit corrects the errors in b_{enc} based on the syndrome. The hollow circles in the controlled gates in the circuit correspond to a 0-control (i.e. conditioned on that control bit being 0).

method described above will have to be modified when we take into account that all gates are prone to errors, to ensure that the correction procedure does not itself introduce more errors than it attempts to correct.

A theory of *fault-tolerant* computation gives procedures for performing computations directly on codewords (without the need for decoding), and for performing encoding and error recovery in ways that are themselves robust against errors. In this section, we describe an error correction scheme that corrects codewords directly, without decoding. We will see in Section 10.6 how this approach can be extended to realize fault-tolerant quantum computing, by performing all our computations directly on the quantum codewords themselves (so the codewords are never decoded).

Recall that for the three-bit code, the recovery operator used a classical CNOT gate to compute each of two parities. A CNOT gate computes the parity of the two bits it acts on, and puts the resulting parity on the target bit. So the recovery operator in Figure 10.7 computes the required parities *in place*, writing the resulting parities onto the last two bits of the codeword. An alternative approach is to compute these parities into two additional ancillary bits (leaving all three bits of the register initially containing the codeword unaffected). The idea is to compute the error syndrome into an ancilla, and then use this syndrome information to control a recovery operation $\mathcal{R}^{C''}$. Given a corrupted codeword $\bar{b}_{enc}$, the recovery operation $\mathcal{R}^{C''}$ returns the original codeword b_{enc}. The ancilla is then discarded, and a freshly initialized ancilla is provided for computing the syndrome in the next round of error correction. This scheme is illustrated for the three-bit code in Figure 10.9.

10.4 Quantum Error Correction

We will now turn to the quantum case and see that it is possible to generalize classical error correction despite the facts that

1. the quantum evolution is a continuous process as opposed to the classical discrete case,

2. the encoding operation cannot make multiple copies of arbitrary quantum states, and

3. the corruption of encoded quantum state cannot be detected through the complete measurement of all the qubits.

10.4.1   Error Models for Quantum Computing

When we discussed error models for classical computing, we noted that, in general, errors may not affect bits independently, and so the error models would have to account for any correlation between errors on different bits. The same is true for errors on quantum bits. It turns out to be simpler to describe codes for errors that affect qubits independently, and fortunately the important concepts for error correction can be understood under these restricted error models. For this reason, we will present the theory in the general case, but our examples will deal only with error models in which errors occur on single qubits independently.

Errors occur on a qubit when its evolution differs from the desired one. This difference can occur due to imprecise control over the qubits or by interaction of the qubits with an environment. By 'environment', we mean everything external to the qubit under consideration. A 'quantum channel' is a formal description of how qubits in a given setting are affected by their environment.

The generic evolution of a qubit in the state $|0\rangle$ interacting with an environment in the state $|E\rangle$ will yield a superposition state of the form:

$$|0\rangle|E\rangle \mapsto \beta_1|0\rangle|E_1\rangle + \beta_2|1\rangle|E_2\rangle. \qquad (10.4.1)$$

That is, with amplitude β_1 the qubit remains in the basis state $|0\rangle$ and the environment evolves to some state $|E_1\rangle$. With amplitude β_2 the qubit evolves to the basis state $|1\rangle$ and the environment evolves to some state $|E_2\rangle$. Similarly, when the qubit is initially in state $|1\rangle$ with the environment in state $|E\rangle$, we have

$$|1\rangle|E\rangle \mapsto \beta_3|1\rangle|E_3\rangle + \beta_4|0\rangle|E_4\rangle. \qquad (10.4.2)$$

More generally, when a qubit in a general pure state interacts with the environment in state $|E\rangle$, we will have

$$(\alpha_0|0\rangle + \alpha_1|1\rangle)|E\rangle \mapsto \alpha_0\beta_1|0\rangle|E_1\rangle + \alpha_0\beta_2|1\rangle|E_2\rangle + \alpha_1\beta_3|1\rangle|E_3\rangle + \alpha_1\beta_4|0\rangle|E_4\rangle. \qquad (10.4.3)$$

We can rewrite the state after the interaction as

$$\alpha_0\beta_1|0\rangle|E_1\rangle + \alpha_0\beta_2|1\rangle|E_2\rangle + \alpha_1\beta_3|1\rangle|E_3\rangle + \alpha_1\beta_4|0\rangle|E_4\rangle$$

$$= \tfrac{1}{2}\big(\alpha_0|0\rangle + \alpha_1|1\rangle\big)\big(\beta_1|E_1\rangle + \beta_3|E_3\rangle\big)$$
$$+ \tfrac{1}{2}\big(\alpha_0|0\rangle - \alpha_1|1\rangle\big)\big(\beta_1|E_1\rangle - \beta_3|E_3\rangle\big)$$
$$+ \tfrac{1}{2}\big(\alpha_0|1\rangle + \alpha_1|0\rangle\big)\big(\beta_2|E_2\rangle + \beta_4|E_4\rangle\big)$$
$$+ \tfrac{1}{2}\big(\alpha_0|1\rangle - \alpha_1|0\rangle\big)\big(\beta_2|E_2\rangle - \beta_4|E_4\rangle\big). \quad (10.4.4)$$

Let $|\psi\rangle = \alpha_0|0\rangle + \alpha_1|1\rangle$. Then we have

$$\alpha_0|0\rangle - \alpha_1|1\rangle = Z|\psi\rangle \qquad\qquad (10.4.5)$$
$$\alpha_0|1\rangle + \alpha_1|0\rangle = X|\psi\rangle \qquad\qquad (10.4.6)$$
$$\alpha_0|1\rangle - \alpha_1|0\rangle = XZ|\psi\rangle \qquad\qquad (10.4.7)$$

and the interaction between the state and the environment can be written as

$$|\psi\rangle|E\rangle \mapsto \tfrac{1}{2}|\psi\rangle\big(\beta_1|E_1\rangle + \beta_3|E_3\rangle\big) + \tfrac{1}{2}\big(Z|\psi\rangle\big)\big(\beta_1|E_1\rangle - \beta_3|E_3\rangle\big)$$
$$+ \tfrac{1}{2}\big(X|\psi\rangle\big)\big(\beta_2|E_2\rangle + \beta_4|E_4\rangle\big) + \tfrac{1}{2}\big(XZ|\psi\rangle\big)\big(\beta_2|E_2\rangle - \beta_4|E_4\rangle\big).$$
$$(10.4.8)$$

This represents the most general evolution that can occur on a single qubit, whether or not it interacts non-trivially with an environment.

The interesting point is that a generic continuous evolution has been rewritten in terms of a finite number (4 in this case) discrete transformations; with various amplitudes (which come from a continuous set) the state is either unaffected, or undergoes a phase flip Z, a bit flip X or a combination of both $XZ = -iY$. This is possible because these operators form a basis for the linear operators on a Hilbert space of a single qubit (see Exercise 10.4.1).

Exercise 10.4.1 Prove that any unitary operation U acting on a composite Hilbert space $\mathcal{H}_A \otimes \mathcal{H}_E$, where $\mathcal{H}_A$ has dimension 2 can be decomposed as $U = I \otimes E_I + X \otimes E_X + Z \otimes E_Z + Y \otimes E_Y$ for some operators E_I, E_X, E_Z, E_Y.

Specific errors can be described as special cases of the right side of expression 10.4.8. For example, suppose we know that the error is a 'bit flip', which has the effect of the NOT gate X with some amplitude and leaves the qubit unaffected (applies the identity) with possibly some other amplitude. This would correspond to states of the environment such that $\beta_1|E_1\rangle = \beta_3|E_3\rangle$ and $\beta_2|E_2\rangle = \beta_4|E_4\rangle$. Equation (10.4.8) for the general evolution thus simplifies to

$$|\psi\rangle|E\rangle \mapsto \beta_1|\psi\rangle|E_1\rangle + X\beta_2|\psi\rangle|E_2\rangle. \qquad (10.4.9)$$

Single qubit errors resulting from a lack of control leading to an imprecise rotation of the qubit about the x-axis of the Bloch sphere will have $\beta_1|E_1\rangle = c\beta_2|E_2\rangle$

for some constant c, so that the environment's state factors from the qubit's state and the operator $c\beta_2 I + \beta_2 X$ is unitary. In other words, $|\psi\rangle|E\rangle \mapsto ((c\beta_2 I + X\beta_2)|\psi\rangle) \otimes |E_2\rangle$. The error is then called *coherent*. When the environment state does not factor out, the error will be *incoherent*. The case where $\beta_1|E_1\rangle$ is orthogonal to $\beta_2|E_2\rangle$ is the quantum description of the classical bit flip error model where the operator X (bit flip) is applied with probability $|\beta_2|^2 = p$ and remains unaffected with probability $|\beta_1|^2 = 1 - p$. The generic evolution of this latter case is non-unitary.

The case of the generic evolution of a qubit can be generalized to the situation of a larger quantum system of interest (e.g. a register of qubits in a quantum computer) in some logical state $|\psi\rangle$, interacting through some error process with an environment initially in state $|E\rangle$. Suppose this process is described by a unitary operator U_{err} acting on the joint state of the system of interest and the environment. Then the state of the joint system after the interaction is $U_{\text{err}}|\psi\rangle|E\rangle$. Its density matrix is

$$\rho = U_{\text{err}}|\psi\rangle|E\rangle\langle E|\langle\psi|U_{\text{err}}^\dagger. \tag{10.4.10}$$

The density matrix of the system of interest is obtained by tracing out the environment:

$$\text{Tr}_E(\rho) = \text{Tr}_E(U_{\text{err}}|\psi\rangle|E\rangle\langle E|\langle\psi|U_{\text{err}}^\dagger) = \sum_i \mathcal{E}_i^Q|\psi\rangle\langle\psi|\mathcal{E}_i^{Q\dagger} \tag{10.4.11}$$

where the $\mathcal{E}_i^Q$ are operators acting on the system of interest (not including the environment). Recall from Section 3.5.3 that the map $\mathcal{E}^Q : |\psi\rangle\langle\psi| \mapsto \sum_i \mathcal{E}_i^Q|\psi\rangle\langle\psi| \mathcal{E}_i^{Q\dagger}$ is a superoperator, and is defined in terms of the Kraus operators $\mathcal{E}_i^Q$. The derivation of Equation (10.4.11) is the subject of Exercise 10.4.2. The error model is completely described by the $\mathcal{E}_i^Q$.

As an example, the bit-flip error discussed above can be described as the interaction between a qubit and the environment that applies the identity operator with probability $1 - p$ and the X operator with probability p. If the qubit is initially in the state $|\psi\rangle$, then the state after the error process is described by the density matrix

$$\rho_f = (1 - p)|\psi\rangle\langle\psi| + pX|\psi\rangle\langle\psi|X. \tag{10.4.12}$$

So the $\mathcal{E}_i^Q$ describing this error model are

$$\mathcal{E}_0^Q = \sqrt{1 - p}\,\mathbb{I} \tag{10.4.13}$$

$$\mathcal{E}_1^Q = \sqrt{p}\,X. \tag{10.4.14}$$

Exercise 10.4.2 Let $|\psi\rangle$ and $|E\rangle$ be the initial states of a system Q and its environment E, respectively. Derive Equation (10.4.11) by evolving $|\psi\rangle$ and $|E\rangle$ under a unitary operator U_{err} and tracing out the environment.

Hint: Define $U_{\text{err}} = \sum \alpha_{p,e} S_p \otimes E_e$, where $\{S_p\}$ and $\{E_q\}$ are bases for operators acting on the system of interest and the environment, respectively, and get $\mathcal{E}_q^Q$ in terms of S_p, E_e, $|E\rangle$, and $\alpha_{p,e}$.

Exercise 10.4.3 Show that the unitarity requirement for the evolution operator of the joint system environment state implies that

$$\sum_i \mathcal{E}_i^{Q\dagger} \mathcal{E}_i^Q = I. \tag{10.4.15}$$

10.4.2 Encoding

Once we have a description of the potential errors, we need to find a way to protect the logical states $|\psi\rangle$ of our quantum system against these errors. As in the classical case we will enlarge the system at hand by adding an ancilla to the logical states. Without loss of generality, we will assume that our ancilla is initialized to $|00\cdots0\rangle$. We then look for transformations that map the joint states $|\psi\rangle \otimes |00\cdots0\rangle$ to some encoded states $|\psi_{\text{enc}}\rangle$. The subspace spanned by the encoded states will define the *code*. We will then look for transformations of the encoded states so that the effect of the errors on the quantum information can be reversed.

As a first idea for a quantum error-correcting code, we might be tempted to do exactly what was done classically for the three-bit code and just make three copies of every qubit. The following theorem says a simple repetition code is not possible for arbitrary quantum states.

Theorem 10.4.1 *(No-cloning)*

There is no superoperator $\mathcal{F}$ that performs

$$|\psi\rangle\langle\psi| \otimes |s\rangle\langle s| \overset{\mathcal{F}}{\mapsto} |\psi\rangle\langle\psi| \otimes |\psi\rangle\langle\psi| \tag{10.4.16}$$

for arbitrary choices of $|\psi\rangle$ (where $|s\rangle$ is some fixed ancilla state). That is, there is no quantum operation which can clone an unknown arbitrary quantum state.

Theorem 10.4.1 is called the *no-cloning theorem*, and it is fundamental to quantum information (e.g. *quantum cryptography* is based on it). It essentially says that we cannot build a device that makes perfect copies of arbitrary unknown quantum states. The theorem follows from Exercise 10.4.4, and also follows directly from the fact that superoperators are linear, but the cloning map is not.

Exercise 10.4.4

(a) Suppose we have basis elements $S = \{|\psi_1\rangle, |\psi_2\rangle\}$ where $|\psi_1\rangle, |\psi_2\rangle$ are orthogonal 1-qubit states (so $\langle\psi_1|\psi_2\rangle = 0$). Describe a circuit using CNOT and 1-qubit gates that will clone both $|\psi_1\rangle$ and $|\psi_2\rangle$.

Hint: Use the basis change operator from the computational basis to the S-basis.

(b) Suppose $T = \{|\psi_3\rangle, |\psi_4\rangle\}$ where $|\psi_3\rangle, |\psi_4\rangle$ are non-orthogonal 1-qubit states (so $\langle \psi_3 | \psi_4 \rangle \neq 0$). Prove that there does not exist a unitary operator on $\mathcal{H}_1 \otimes \mathcal{H}_2$ that maps

$$|\psi\rangle|0\rangle \mapsto |\psi\rangle|\psi\rangle$$

for both $|\psi\rangle \in T$.

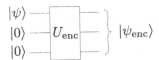

Fig. 10.10 Encoding a single qubit $|\psi\rangle$ by a three-qubit codeword $|\psi_{\text{enc}}\rangle$.

In light of the no-cloning theorem, we will have to use a different principle to devise an encoding scheme for quantum error correction. Encoding for quantum error correction must be implemented via a unitary operator U_{enc} that acts on the state we wish to encode, tensored with an ancilla of some fixed number of qubits in some specified initial state. If the state we wish to encode is a qubit state $|\psi\rangle$ and the ancilla is initially in the state $|00\cdots0\rangle$, then the result of the encoding is the codeword state:

$$|\psi_{\text{enc}}\rangle = U_{\text{enc}}|\psi\rangle|00\cdots0\rangle. \qquad (10.4.17)$$

As an example, we can define a quantum version of the 3-bit code, that encodes a 1-qubit state $|\psi\rangle$ by a codeword of three qubits. The encoding operation U_{enc} will take the qubit $|\psi\rangle$ along with two ancillary qubits initially in state $|0\rangle|0\rangle$ and output a three-qubit encoded state $|\psi_{\text{enc}}\rangle$, as shown in Figure 10.10.

In a more formal way, a code $\mathcal{C}$ is defined as a subspace of a Hilbert space. An encoded qubit is a 2-dimensional subspace.

A possible choice for the unitary U_{enc} for a three-qubit code could be that which maps

$$(\alpha_0|0\rangle + \alpha_1|1\rangle)\underbrace{|0\rangle|0\rangle}_{\text{ancilla}} \mapsto \alpha_0|0\rangle|0\rangle|0\rangle + \alpha_1|1\rangle|1\rangle|1\rangle. \qquad (10.4.18)$$

Later, we will see that this three-qubit code can be used for correcting a certain restricted class of single-qubit errors. In the next section, we will see conditions that the encoding operator U_{enc} must satisfy for this to be possible.

10.4.3   Error Recovery

As we saw in Section 10.4.1, when a quantum system initially in a state $|\psi\rangle$ is exposed to errors through unwanted interaction with the environment, the result is the noisy state with density matrix

$$\sum_i \mathcal{E}_i^Q |\psi\rangle\langle\psi| \mathcal{E}_i^{Q\dagger} \qquad (10.4.19)$$

where the $\mathcal{E}_i^Q$ are operators that define the error model. The goal of error correction is to find a way to invert the effect of the noise on the quantum information. Suppose we encode the state $|\psi\rangle$ as described in Section 10.4.2,

$$|\psi_{\text{enc}}\rangle = U_{\text{enc}}|\psi\rangle|00\cdots0\rangle. \qquad (10.4.20)$$

Errors transform $|\psi_{\text{enc}}\rangle$ to a state with density matrix

$$\sum_i \hat{\mathcal{E}}_i^Q |\psi_{\text{enc}}\rangle\langle\psi_{\text{enc}}| \hat{\mathcal{E}}_i^{Q\dagger} \qquad (10.4.21)$$

where we write $\hat{\mathcal{E}}_i^Q$ to emphasize that the noise operators $\mathcal{E}_i^Q$ must be modified to correspond to the noise acting on a quantum codeword $|\psi_{\text{enc}}\rangle$ which has higher dimension than the original quantum state $|\psi\rangle$.

Exercise 10.4.5 Suppose the states $|\psi\rangle$ are 1-qubit states. Consider the error model for independent bit flips given by the $\mathcal{E}_i^Q$ defined in Equations (10.4.13) and (10.4.14). Suppose we encode each qubit of information by adding two ancillary qubits. Give error operators $\hat{\mathcal{E}}_i^Q$ that describe the effect of this error model on this three-qubit system. Hint: There are $2^3 = 8$ different $\hat{\mathcal{E}}_i^Q$.

In general, if we encode the quantum information, subject it to the noise and decode (using the inverse of the encoding operation, $U_{\text{enc}}^\dagger$) we will not always recover original state $|\psi\rangle$. That is, in some cases

$$\text{Tr}_{\text{anc}}\left[U_{\text{enc}}^\dagger \left(\sum_i \hat{\mathcal{E}}_i^Q |\psi_{\text{enc}}\rangle\langle\psi_{\text{enc}}| \hat{\mathcal{E}}_i^{Q\dagger} \right) U_{\text{enc}} \right] \neq |\psi\rangle\langle\psi|. \qquad (10.4.22)$$

To recover the quantum information we need a quantum operation $\mathcal{R}^Q$, called the *recovery operation*, that has the effect of undoing enough of the noise on the encoded state so that after decoding and tracing out the ancilla we are left with the original state $|\psi\rangle$, as shown in Figure 10.11.

In general the recovery operation $\mathcal{R}^Q$ will be a superoperator defined in terms of a sum over some operators $\mathcal{R}_j^Q$. To define an error-correcting recovery operation, we first need a notion of error which can be introduced through the notion of *fidelity*. For given code subject to noise described by $\mathcal{E}_i^Q$, we define the fidelity of a recovery operation $\mathcal{R}$ by

$$F(\mathcal{R}, \mathcal{C}, \mathcal{E}) = \min_{|\psi\rangle}\langle\psi|\rho_\psi|\psi\rangle \qquad (10.4.23)$$

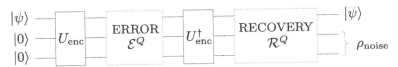

Fig. 10.11 We want to define our code so that we can find a recovery operation $\mathcal{R}^Q$ such that applying $\mathcal{R}^Q$ to the state after decoding recovers the original state $|\psi\rangle$, with the noise transferred to the ancilla. Note that in comparison with Figure 10.8, $\mathcal{R}^Q$ is the analogue of $\mathcal{R}^{C'}$ and $\mathcal{E}^Q$ is the analogue of $\mathcal{E}^C$.

where

$$\rho_\psi = \mathrm{Tr}_{\mathrm{anc}} \left(\sum_j \mathcal{R}_j^Q U_e^\dagger \left(\sum_i \mathcal{E}_i^Q U_{\mathrm{enc}} |\psi\rangle |00\cdots 0\rangle \langle 00\cdots 0| \langle\psi| U_{\mathrm{enc}}^\dagger \mathcal{E}_i^{Q\dagger} \right) U_e \mathcal{R}_j^{Q\dagger} \right)$$

$$(10.4.24)$$

and the corresponding worst-case *error probability parameter* p is

$$p = 1 - F(\mathcal{R}, \mathcal{C}, \mathcal{E}).$$

$$(10.4.25)$$

It is worth explaining the meaning of the above definition. Suppose some state $|\psi\rangle$ is encoded into the state $U_{\mathrm{enc}}|\psi\rangle|00\ldots0\rangle$, then subjected to some noise (corresponding to the $\mathcal{E}_i^Q$ operators), then subjected to a recovery operation (corresponding to the $\mathcal{R}_j^Q$ operators), and then the ancilla workspace is discarded giving back some state ρ_ψ on the original Hilbert space. We are interested in how close ρ is to the original state $|\psi\rangle\langle\psi|$. The probability $p_\psi = \langle\psi|\rho_\psi|\psi\rangle$ can be regarded as the probability of no error on the encoded state. The quantity $F(\mathcal{R}, \mathcal{C}, \mathcal{E})$ is the minimum of all such probabilities p_ψ over all encoded states $|\psi\rangle$. Thus the error probability parameter defined in Equation 10.4.25 gives us an upper bound on the probability with which a generic encoded state will end up at the wrong state (strictly speaking, its square root is the probability amplitude with which an error has occurred; this will be the more relevant quantity when consider 'coherent errors').

A recovery operation $\mathcal{R}^Q$ is *error correcting* with respect to a set of error operators if the error probability parameter p equals zero when $\mathcal{R}^Q$ is applied to a codeword that was exposed only to those error operators. This implies that

$$\mathrm{Tr}_{\mathrm{anc}} \left[\sum_j \mathcal{R}_j^Q \left(U_{\mathrm{enc}}^\dagger \left(\sum_i \hat{\mathcal{E}}_i^Q |\psi_{\mathrm{enc}}\rangle \langle\psi_{\mathrm{enc}}| \hat{\mathcal{E}}_i^{Q\dagger} \right) U_{\mathrm{enc}} \right) \mathcal{R}_j^{Q\dagger} \right] = |\psi\rangle\langle\psi|.$$

$$(10.4.26)$$

One way of thinking about the action of the recovery operation $\mathcal{R}^Q$ is that it pushes all the noise into the ancilla, so that the errors are eliminated when the ancilla are traced out. The encoding operation can be seen as a way of transforming the errors so that their action on the encoded states is recoverable.

Inserting $|\psi_{\text{enc}}\rangle = U_{\text{enc}}|\psi\rangle|00\cdots0\rangle$ into the expression on the left hand side of Equation (10.4.26) (not showing the trace step), we have

$$\sum_j \mathcal{R}_j^Q \left(U_{\text{enc}}^\dagger \left(\sum_i \hat{\mathcal{E}}_i^Q U_{\text{enc}}|\psi\rangle|00\cdots0\rangle\langle00\cdots0|\langle\psi|U_{\text{enc}}^\dagger\hat{\mathcal{E}}_i^{Q\dagger} \right) U_{\text{enc}} \right) \mathcal{R}_j^{Q\dagger}.$$

(10.4.27)

The above state can be rewritten as

$$\sum_j \mathcal{R}_j^Q \left(\sum_i \left(U_{\text{enc}}^\dagger\hat{\mathcal{E}}_i^Q U_{\text{enc}} \right) |\psi\rangle|00\cdots0\rangle\langle00\cdots0|\langle\psi| \left(U_{\text{enc}}^\dagger\hat{\mathcal{E}}_i^{Q\dagger} U_{\text{enc}} \right) \right) \mathcal{R}_j^{Q\dagger}.$$

(10.4.28)

We can think of the operators $\left(U_{\text{enc}}^\dagger\hat{\mathcal{E}}_i^Q U_{\text{enc}} \right)$ as representing transformed errors acting on $|\psi\rangle|00\cdots0\rangle$. The goal is to choose U_{enc} in such a way that the behaviour of these transformed errors allows us to find a recovery operation $\mathcal{R}^Q$ that gives back $|\psi\rangle\langle\psi| \otimes \rho_{\text{noise}}$ (notice that the noise will in general be a mixed state, so we have written the final state with a density matrix).

For a code with two logical codewords, applying U_{enc} to the computational basis states $|0\rangle$ and $|1\rangle$ produces the codewords $|0_{\text{enc}}\rangle$ and $|1_{\text{enc}}\rangle$, respectively. If the code is to be useful, there must exist a recovery operation $\mathcal{R}^Q$ satisfying Equation (10.4.26) for both $|0_{\text{enc}}\rangle$ and $|1_{\text{enc}}\rangle$. It can be shown (by a lengthy calculation) that for such an $\mathcal{R}^Q$ to exist, we must have

$$\langle l_{\text{enc}}|\hat{\mathcal{E}}_i^{Q\dagger}\hat{\mathcal{E}}_j^Q|m_{\text{enc}}\rangle = c_{ij}\delta_{lm}$$

(10.4.29)

for $l, m \in \{0, 1\}$, where the c_{ij} are constants. Equation (10.4.29) gives the *conditions for quantum error correction*. It implies that after being subjected to errors, the different encoded states ($l \neq m$) remain orthogonal. This condition is necessary as otherwise we would be unable to reliably determine which codeword a given corrupted state came from.

Equation (10.4.29) also implies that the noise scales all the encoded states $|l_{\text{enc}}\rangle$ by the same amount. This ensures that when encoded states in quantum superposition are exposed to errors, the relative coefficients are undisturbed.

If Equation (10.4.29) is satisfied by some set of correctable errors $\{\hat{\mathcal{E}}_j^Q\}$, then it is also satisfied for any linear combinations $\hat{\mathcal{E}}_j^{\prime Q}$ of errors from $\{\hat{\mathcal{E}}_j^Q\}$. This means that if a set of errors is correctable for a given code, then any linear combination of those errors is correctable for the same code. Furthermore, the same recovery operation that corrects the errors $\{\hat{\mathcal{E}}_j^Q\}$ will correct the errors $\{\hat{\mathcal{E}}_j^{\prime Q}\}$.

In particular, it is useful to note the following. Any single-qubit unitary operator can be written as a linear combination of the Pauli operators I, X, Y, Z. So if we can devise a quantum error-correcting code for which $I, X, Y,$ and Z are correctable errors on a qubit, then *any* single-qubit unitary (with identity on the remaining qubits) is a correctable error. This is a *discretization of errors*, and it implies that when we design quantum error-correcting codes, it suffices to consider errors from a finite set.

Exercise 10.4.6 Prove that if the error operators $\{\hat{\mathcal{E}}_j^Q\}$ satisfy Equation (10.4.29), then so do the error operators $\{\hat{\mathcal{E}}_j'^Q\}$, where $\hat{\mathcal{E}}_j'^Q = \sum_k c'_{jk}\hat{\mathcal{E}}_k^Q$ for some constants c'_{jk}.

Exercise 10.4.7 Prove that if the recovery operator $\mathcal{R}^Q$ defined by Kraus operators $\{\mathcal{R}_j^Q\}$ corrects an error model described by the error operators $\{\hat{\mathcal{E}}_j^Q\}$, which satisfy Equation (10.4.29), then $\mathcal{R}^Q$ will also correct an error model described by the error operators $\{\hat{\mathcal{E}}_j'^Q\}$, where $\hat{\mathcal{E}}_j'^Q = \sum_k c'_{jk}\hat{\mathcal{E}}_k'^Q$ for some constants c'_{jk}.

Example 10.4.2 Recall from Section 4.2.1 the operator $R_x(\theta)$, which corresponds to a rotation about the x-axis of the Bloch sphere by mapping

$$|0\rangle \mapsto \cos\left(\tfrac{\theta}{2}\right)|0\rangle - i\sin\left(\tfrac{\theta}{2}\right)|1\rangle \tag{10.4.30}$$

$$|1\rangle \mapsto \cos\left(\tfrac{\theta}{2}\right)|1\rangle - i\sin\left(\tfrac{\theta}{2}\right)|0\rangle. \tag{10.4.31}$$

Consider the error model that randomly selects one qubit out of a block of three qubits and applies $R_x(\theta)$ to it (and does nothing to the other three qubits). Recalling from Section 4.2.1 that

$$R_x(\theta) = \cos\left(\tfrac{\theta}{2}\right)I - i\sin\left(\tfrac{\theta}{2}\right)X \tag{10.4.32}$$

we see that this error model corresponds to the error model with Kraus operators

$$\mathcal{E}_1' = \tfrac{1}{\sqrt{3}}\left(\left(\cos\left(\tfrac{\theta}{2}\right)I - i\sin\left(\tfrac{\theta}{2}\right)X\right)\otimes I \otimes I\right)$$

$$\mathcal{E}_{2'} = \tfrac{1}{\sqrt{3}}\left(I \otimes \left(\cos\left(\tfrac{\theta}{2}\right)I - i\sin\left(\tfrac{\theta}{2}\right)X\right)\otimes I\right)$$

$$\mathcal{E}_3' = \tfrac{1}{\sqrt{3}}\left(I \otimes I \otimes \left(\cos\left(\tfrac{\theta}{2}\right)I - i\sin\left(\tfrac{\theta}{2}\right)X\right)\right)$$

So we have expressed error operators in the error model as a linear combination of

$$
\begin{aligned}
\mathcal{E}_0 &= I \otimes I \otimes I \,, \\
\mathcal{E}_1 &= X \otimes I \otimes I \,, \\
\mathcal{E}_2 &= I \otimes X \otimes I \,, \\
\mathcal{E}_3 &= I \otimes I \otimes X \,.
\end{aligned}
\tag{10.4.33}
$$

This implies that if there is a recovery procedure for correcting the errors $\mathcal{E}_j$, then there is a recover procedure for correcting an $R_x(\theta)$ error to at most one of the three qubits.

Example 10.4.3 In the previous example, we showed that the error operators of the given error model can be expressed as linear combinations of $I \otimes I \otimes I, X \otimes I \otimes I, I \otimes X \otimes I$, and $I \otimes I \otimes X$.

Let us assume that there is an error recovery procedure $\mathcal{R}^Q$ (for simplicity, we will assume it is unitary, which means there is only one Kraus term) that will correct up to one bit flip on the three qubits.

This means that, for any codeword $|\psi_{\text{enc}}\rangle = U_{\text{enc}}|\psi\rangle|00\rangle$, encoding a single qubit $|\psi\rangle$ there exists a $\mathcal{R}^Q$ such that

$$\mathcal{R}^Q U_{\text{enc}}^\dagger \mathcal{E}_j^Q |\psi_{\text{enc}}\rangle\langle\psi_{\text{enc}}| \mathcal{E}_j^{Q\dagger} U_{\text{enc}} \mathcal{R}^{Q\dagger} = |\psi\rangle\langle\psi| \otimes |\phi_j\rangle\langle\phi_j| \qquad (10.4.34)$$

for some normalized state vector $|\phi_j\rangle$, which means that (up to a global phase) we have

$$\mathcal{R}^Q U_{\text{enc}}^\dagger \mathcal{E}_j^Q |\psi_{\text{enc}}\rangle = |\psi\rangle|\phi_j\rangle. \qquad (10.4.35)$$

Suppose the error operator $\mathcal{E}_1'$, as expressed in the previous example in terms of the correctable operators $\{\mathcal{E}_j\}$, is applied to the codeword. Then it evolves to the state

$$\begin{aligned}
\mathcal{E}_1'|\psi_{\text{enc}}\rangle\langle\psi_{\text{enc}}|\mathcal{E}_1'^\dagger = {} & \cos^2\left(\tfrac{\theta}{2}\right)\left(I \otimes I \otimes I\right)|\psi_{\text{enc}}\rangle\langle\psi_{\text{enc}}|\left(I \otimes I \otimes I\right) \\
& -\sin^2\left(\tfrac{\theta}{2}\right)\left(X \otimes I \otimes I\right)|\psi_{\text{enc}}\rangle\langle\psi_{\text{enc}}|\left(X \otimes I \otimes I\right) \\
& +i\sin\left(\tfrac{\theta}{2}\right)\cos\left(\tfrac{\theta}{2}\right)\left(I \otimes I \otimes I\right)|\psi_{\text{enc}}\rangle\langle\psi_{\text{enc}}|\left(X \otimes I \otimes I\right) \\
& -i\sin\left(\tfrac{\theta}{2}\right)\cos\left(\tfrac{\theta}{2}\right)\left(X \otimes I \otimes I\right)|\psi_{\text{enc}}\rangle\langle\psi_{\text{enc}}|\left(I \otimes I \otimes I\right).
\end{aligned}$$

After we apply $U_{\text{enc}}^\dagger$ followed by $\mathcal{R}^Q$, we get (using Equation 10.4.35)

$$\begin{aligned}
\mathcal{R}^Q U_{\text{enc}}^\dagger \mathcal{E}_1'|\psi_{\text{enc}}\rangle\langle\psi_{\text{enc}}|\mathcal{E}_1'^\dagger U_{\text{enc}}\mathcal{R}^{Q\dagger} = {} & \cos^2\left(\tfrac{\theta}{2}\right)|\psi\rangle\langle\psi| \otimes |\phi_0\rangle\langle\phi_0| \\
& -\sin^2\left(\tfrac{\theta}{2}\right)|\psi\rangle\langle\psi| \otimes |\phi_1\rangle\langle\phi_1| \\
& +i\sin\left(\tfrac{\theta}{2}\right)\cos\left(\tfrac{\theta}{2}\right)|\psi\rangle\langle\psi| \otimes |\phi_0\rangle\langle\phi_1| \\
& -i\sin\left(\tfrac{\theta}{2}\right)\cos\left(\tfrac{\theta}{2}\right)|\psi\rangle\langle\psi| \otimes |\phi_1\rangle\langle\phi_0| \\
= {} & |\psi\rangle\langle\psi| \otimes |\phi'\rangle\langle\phi'| \qquad (10.4.36)
\end{aligned}$$

where $|\phi'\rangle = \cos\left(\tfrac{\theta}{2}\right)|\phi_0\rangle - i\sin\left(\tfrac{\theta}{2}\right)|\phi_1\rangle$.

Thus after tracing out the ancilla, we are left with $|\psi\rangle\langle\psi|$.

Given an error model corresponding to a specified set of error operators $\hat{\mathcal{E}}_i^Q$, designing a quantum error-correcting code reduces to finding an encoding operator U_{enc} and a recovery operation $\mathcal{R}^Q$ so that Equation (10.4.26) is satisfied.

Exercise 10.4.8 Consider again the case of single qubits subject to independent bit flip errors. Suppose we encode each qubit with a codeword of three qubits according to Equation (10.4.18).

(a) Simplify the error model obtained in Exercise 10.4.5 assuming that at most 1 bit flip occurs on each codeword. Give the corresponding error operators $\hat{\mathcal{E}}_0^Q, \hat{\mathcal{E}}_1^Q, \hat{\mathcal{E}}_2^Q$ and $\hat{\mathcal{E}}_3^Q$.

(b) Show that the four error operators obtained above, together with the encoded states $|0_{\text{enc}}\rangle = |000\rangle$ and $|1_{\text{enc}}\rangle = |111\rangle$, satisfy Equation (10.4.29). (This shows that there exists a recovery operation $\mathcal{R}^Q$ so that using the three-qubit code described in the next section we can correct single bit flip errors within a codeword).

(c) Show that if we allow more than one bit flip within a codeword (so that we have all 8 of the $\hat{\mathcal{E}}_i^Q$ obtained in Exercise 10.4.5), Equation (10.4.29) is no longer satisfied.

10.5 Three- and Nine-Qubit Quantum Codes

10.5.1 The Three-Qubit Code for Bit-Flip Errors

The no-cloning theorem prevents us from implementing a quantum three-qubit repetition code that encodes a qubit by a codeword consisting of three copies of that qubit. However, the idea can be modified slightly giving a three-qubit code that can be used to correct bit flip errors.

The error model we are initially interested in is the *bit-flip channel* as described in Section 10.4.1:

$$\rho = |\psi\rangle\langle\psi| \mapsto \rho_f = (1 - p)|\psi\rangle\langle\psi| + p\, X|\psi\rangle\langle\psi|X. \qquad (10.5.1)$$

The *three-qubit bit-flip code* is obtained by introducing ancillary qubits and encoding each logical qubit by a codeword of three physical qubits according to Equation (10.5.2).

$$\alpha_0|0\rangle + \alpha_1|1\rangle \mapsto \alpha_0|000\rangle + \alpha_1|100\rangle \mapsto \alpha_0|000\rangle + \alpha_1|111\rangle. \qquad (10.5.2)$$

In other words, the encoding works by mapping the basis state $|0\rangle$ to $|000\rangle$, and mapping the basis state $|1\rangle$ to $|111\rangle$. We can think of this encoding operation as *embedding* the state into a 2-dimensional subspace of a larger 8-dimensional space. Note that this procedure is *not* a simple repetition rule. The encoding of the basis states $|0\rangle$ and $|1\rangle$ is achieved by simple repetition, but consider for example the encoding of a uniform superposition:

$$\frac{1}{\sqrt{2}}(|0\rangle + |1\rangle) \mapsto \frac{1}{\sqrt{2}}(|000\rangle + |100\rangle) \mapsto \frac{1}{\sqrt{2}}(|000\rangle + |111\rangle)$$

$$\neq \frac{1}{\sqrt{2}}(|0\rangle + |1\rangle)^{\otimes 3}. \qquad (10.5.3)$$

A circuit that performs the encoding procedure for the three-qubit code is shown in Figure 10.12.

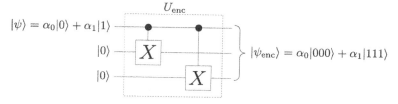

Fig. 10.12 A circuit for performing the encoding given by Equation (10.4.18).

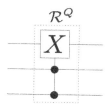

Fig. 10.13 The recovery operation $\mathcal{R}^Q$ for the three-qubit bit flip code is the quantum Toffoli gate. Providing at most one bit flip error occurred on the codeword, the Toffoli gate will recover the original state $|\psi\rangle$, leaving some 'noise' in the ancillary qubits.

In Exercise 10.4.8 (b), the objective was to prove that if at most one bit flip error occurs in a codeword, then there exists a recovery operation $\mathcal{R}^Q$ that works for the encoding given by Equation (10.5.2). This recovery operation $\mathcal{R}^Q$ is the quantum Toffoli (controlled-controlled-NOT) gate, as shown in Figure 10.13.

Providing at most one bit flip error occurred in the codeword $|\psi_{\text{enc}}\rangle$, the Toffoli gate, after a decoding operation, which is the inverse of the encoding operation, will recover the original state $|\psi\rangle$ in the first qubit, leaving some 'noise' in the ancillary qubits.

Exercise 10.5.1 Show that if at most 1-qubit error occurs on a codeword for the 3-qubit bit flip code, then, after decoding using the inverse of the encoding operation, the Toffoli gate will recover the original state $|\psi\rangle$, transferring the 'noise' to the ancillary qubits.

When the error is independent, there is some chance of having more than one bit flip operator acting on the encoded state. Exercise 10.4.8 (c) shows that when this happens the error is not in general correctable. After the independent errors act on the encoded state, the resulting state will be a linear combination of the encoded state with correctable errors applied to it and of the encoded state with uncorrectable errors applied to it. The component with correctable errors operators will be corrected by the recovery procedure, but the component with uncorrectable in general will not return to the original state. The worst-case error probability parameter (or 'error probability') as defined in Equation 10.4.25 after error correction will be of order p^2 in analogy to the classical discussion at the end of Section 10.2.

Exercise 10.5.2 Prove that the error operation $\rho \mapsto U_\theta \otimes U_\theta \otimes U_\theta \rho U_\theta^\dagger \otimes U_\theta^\dagger \otimes U_\theta^\dagger$, with $\sin^2(\theta) = p$ has worst-case error probability parameter in $O(p^2)$.

10.5.2 The Three-Qubit Code for Phase-Flip Errors

Qubits can undergo errors other than bit flip (X) errors; they could also undergo phase flip (Z) errors. In the case where only phase errors are induced, Equation (10.4.8) reduces to

$$|\psi\rangle|E\rangle \mapsto \tfrac{1}{2}|\psi\rangle\big(\beta_1|E_1\rangle + \beta_3|E_3\rangle\big) + \tfrac{1}{2}Z|\psi\rangle\big(\beta_1|E_1\rangle - \beta_3|E_3\rangle\big). \tag{10.5.4}$$

The above equation describes the evolution of the qubit when the amplitudes evolve either through an identity operator or a phase flip operator (Z). This behaviour can result from mis-calibration of single qubit gates (an under- or over-rotation on the Bloch sphere) leading to a coherent phase error, (when $|E_1\rangle = e^{i\phi}|E_3\rangle$ for some ϕ) or more generally from an undesired interaction with neighbouring qubits or the environment (when $|E_1\rangle \neq e^{i\phi}|E_3\rangle$). Both error models contain the operators I and Z and thus if we find an error correcting code for one set of operators, it will also be error correcting for the other one as discussed in Section 10.4.3.

In the case where $\big(\langle E_1|\beta_1^* - \langle E_3|\beta_3^*\big)\big(\beta_1|E_1\rangle + \beta_3|E_3\rangle\big) = 0$ this evolution can be thought as a qubit that undergoes a Z error with probability p, and no error with probability $1 - p$ where

$$p = \tfrac{1}{4}\big\|\beta_1|E_1\rangle - \beta_3|E_3\rangle\big\|^2 \tag{10.5.5}$$

$$1 - p = \tfrac{1}{4}\big\|\beta_1|E_1\rangle + \beta_3|E_3\rangle\big\|^2. \tag{10.5.6}$$

We will call this error model the *phase-flip channel* in analogy to the bit flip error model we have seen previously.

There are no phase errors in classical digital information, but fortunately it is easy to transform a phase-flip error into a bit-flip error, which means we can adapt the three-qubit bit-flip code to correct phase-flip errors. Specifically, consider the Hadamard basis states

$$|+\rangle \equiv \tfrac{1}{\sqrt{2}}\big(|0\rangle + |1\rangle\big),$$

$$|-\rangle \equiv \tfrac{1}{\sqrt{2}}\big(|0\rangle - |1\rangle\big). \tag{10.5.7}$$

The effect of a phase flip is to take the state $|+\rangle$ to the state $|-\rangle$, and vice versa. So if we work in the Hadamard basis, phase flip errors are just like bit flip errors.

So we encode $|0\rangle$ as $|+\rangle|+\rangle|+\rangle$ and $|1\rangle$ as $|-\rangle|-\rangle|-\rangle$. According to this rule, a general 1-qubit state is encoded as:

$$\alpha_0|0\rangle + \alpha_1|1\rangle \mapsto \alpha_0|000\rangle + \alpha_1|100\rangle \mapsto \alpha_0|+++\rangle + \alpha_1|---\rangle. \qquad (10.5.8)$$

The operations needed for encoding, error detection, and recovery are performed exactly as they were for the three-qubit bit-flip code, only now with respect to the $\{|+\rangle, |-\rangle\}$-basis.

Recall that the Hadamard gate performs a basis change from the computational basis to the Hadamard basis, and vice versa (since H is its own inverse). Therefore, we see that the encoding for the three-qubit phase-flip code is accomplished by the circuit shown in Figure 10.14.

Just as phase flip error model is equivalent to the bit-flip error conjugated by Hadamard gates model, we can see that the phase-flip recovery and the bit-flip recovery operation are also the same up to a conjugation by Hadamard gates.

It will be useful to introduce the notion of the 'phase parity' of a product of $|+\rangle$ and $|-\rangle$ states as the parity of the number of $|-\rangle$ factors in the product. Let parity '-1' correspond to states with an odd number of $|-\rangle$s, and let parity '$+1$' correspond to an states with an even number of $|-\rangle$s.

Exercise 10.5.3 Give the unitary operator for error recovery for the three-qubit phase flip code.

10.5.3   Quantum Error Correction Without Decoding

In Section 10.3 we briefly discussed the need for an error correction scheme that corrects codewords directly, without decoding the state. We saw such a scheme that made use of an ancilla of bits, into which the error *syndrome* was computed. The recovery operation was controlled by this syndrome. In this section we recast the three-qubit quantum code in this framework. In general, quantum error-correcting codes that are used to implement *fault-tolerant quantum computing* (see Section 10.6) are usually formulated in this way.

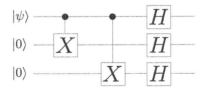

Fig. 10.14 Encoding circuit for the three-qubit phase flip code.

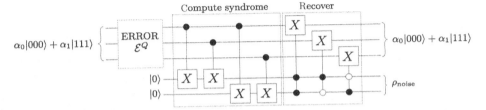

Fig. 10.15 The recovery operation for the three-qubit bit flip code by computing the error syndrome into an ancilla, and then controlling the recovery operation by the syndrome. The hollow circles in the controlled gates in the circuit correspond to a 0-control (i.e. conditioned on that control qubit being $|0\rangle$).

Fig. 10.16 The CNOT gate is equivalent to a controlled-Z gate, interchanging the roles of the control and target qubits, and conjugating the new control qubit by the Hadamard.

The recovery operation for the three-qubit bit-flip code by computing the error syndrome into an ancilla, and then controlling the recovery operation by the syndrome, is shown in Figure 10.15.

As illustrated in Figure 10.16, the CNOT gate is equivalent to a controlled-Z gate, interchanging the roles of the control and target qubits, and conjugating the new control qubit by the Hadamard gate. Note that if in Figure 10.16 we initialize the second qubit to $|0\rangle$ and then measure the second qubit in the computational basis, this realizes a measurement of the Z-observable on the first qubit (recall Section 3.4, Example 3.4.1). The result of the measurement indicates whether the first qubit is in the eigenstate $|0\rangle$ of Z corresponding to eigenvalue $+1$, or the eigenstate $|1\rangle$ corresponding to eigenvalue -1.

Exercise 10.5.4 Show the identity between the circuits depicted in Figure 10.16. Note that $Z = HXH$, and the controlled-Z operation is symmetric with respect to which qubit is the target and which is the control qubit.

Instead of quantumly controlling the recovery operation on the syndrome as shown in Figure 10.15, we could perform a measurement of the syndrome and then classically control the recovery operation on the measurement result (recall Exercise 4.2.8), as illustrated in Figure 10.17.

Since a CNOT gate is equivalent to a controlled-Z gate, then the parity measurements composed of CNOTs in Figure 10.15 can equivalently be realized by

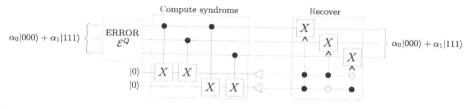

Fig. 10.17 The recovery operation could also be performed by measuring the syndrome in the ancilla qubits and classically controlling which correction operator to apply depending on the syndrome bits.

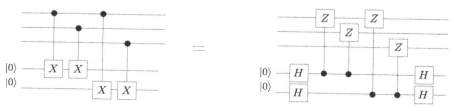

Fig. 10.18 An equivalent circuit for the computation of the syndrome for the three-qubit bit flip code.

controlled-Z gates, as shown in Figure 10.18. This syndrome measurement is thus equivalent (recall Exercise 7.2.2 which shows a similar equivalence) to measuring the observables

$$Z \otimes Z \otimes I \,,$$
$$Z \otimes I \otimes Z \qquad \qquad (10.5.9)$$

Since these operators are tensor products of Pauli matrices, their eigenvectors have eigenvalues ± 1. The code, which consists of all states of the form $\alpha|000\rangle + \beta|111\rangle$, is the subspace of eigenvectors with eigenvalue $+1$. When this set of states undergoes any product of X-errors, the resulting states are still eigenvectors of products of Z-operators, but the eigenvalues are modified as follows:

	$Z \otimes Z \otimes I$	$Z \otimes I \otimes Z$
$I \otimes I \otimes I(\alpha|000\rangle + \beta|111\rangle)$	$+1$	$+1$
$X \otimes I \otimes I(\alpha|000\rangle + \beta|111\rangle)$	-1	-1
$I \otimes X \otimes I(\alpha|000\rangle + \beta|111\rangle)$	-1	$+1$
$I \otimes I \otimes X(\alpha|000\rangle + \beta|111\rangle)$	$+1$	$-1.$

$$(10.5.10)$$

For example, the eigenvalue of $Z \otimes Z \otimes I$ on state $I \otimes I \otimes X(\alpha|000\rangle + \beta|111\rangle)$ is -1.

There is a one-to-one correspondence between the eigenvalues and how the code is mapped under the errors. When we learn the parities, we know which error has occurred and we can undo it using a recovery operation that, here, corresponds to the error operator itself.

There is a short cut to evaluating the table of parities when the parity operators are tensor products of Pauli operators and the error operators are also tensor product of Pauli operators. In this case, the parity operators (i.e. $Z \otimes Z \otimes I$ and $Z \otimes I \otimes Z$) and the error operators either commute or *anti-commute*.[2] The commutation or anti-commutation relation corresponds to the parities $+1$ or -1 we get when we measure the parity operator A on the state $B|\psi\rangle$ where $|\psi\rangle$ was a $+1$ eigenstate of A. For example, the bit flip error operator acting on the second qubit, $I \otimes X \otimes I$, anti-commutes with $Z \otimes Z \otimes I$ but commutes with $Z \otimes I \otimes Z$, and thus we obtain the parities in the third row of Equation (10.5.10). This is a short cut in the sense that we can compute the parities (equivalently, measure the parity operators) by simply computing whether the error operator and parity operator commute or anti-commute.

Just as a bit parity measurement of 2 qubits corresponds to measuring the observable $Z \otimes Z$, we can see that evaluating the phase parity of 2 qubits corresponds to measuring the observable $X \otimes X$.

In particular, the phase-flip error correcting code on three qubits can similarly be defined by the set of phase parity measurements corresponding to the observables

$$X \otimes X \otimes I \,, \qquad\qquad (10.5.11)$$
$$X \otimes I \otimes X$$

which will have corresponding commutation and anti-commutation relations with the associated (product of Pauli operators) error operators.

When the error operators are described by tensor products of Pauli operators (i.e. suffices that the Kraus operators of the error model are linear combinations of such error operators), it is possible to define a large class of quantum error-correcting codes as the subspace spanned by the eigenstates with eigenvalue $+1$ of a set of operators that are generalizations of classical parities that we have encountered in the classical setting. The three-qubit code that we have seen indeed defines a subspace spanned by states of eigenvalue $+1$ of the operators $Z \otimes Z \otimes I$ and $Z \otimes I \otimes Z$. These operators generate a group, called the *stabilizer*. Measuring the generators[3] of the stabilizer gives the syndromes.

The stabilizer leads to a formalism based on the group-theoretic properties of the set formed from tensor products of Pauli operators (e.g. their commutation relations). When the error operators are also tensor products of Pauli operators, such as in the case here, it is possible to find the syndrome by learning how these generators commute or anticommute with each error operator. In other

---

[2] Two operators A and B *anti-commute* if $AB = -BA$.

[3] Recall that the generators of the stabilizer are products of Pauli operators, which are Hermitean and thus can be regarded as observables.

words, when a code corresponds to the $+1$ eigenspace of a stabilizer, it suffices to study the effect of the error operators on the generators of the stabilizer and not on the codewords themselves. This turns out to be simpler than looking at the encoding, error, and decoding procedures that we have seen. The stabilizer formalism is also useful for designing gates that have fault-tolerant properties.

10.5.4   The Nine-Qubit Shor Code

The three-qubit bit-flip and phase-flip codes can be combined to give a nine-qubit code which corrects bit flip or phase flip errors on one of the nine qubits. It also allows us to correct for a simultaneous bit and phase flip on the same qubit, as we explain in more detail below. These errors, with the identity error operator, provide a basis for a generic one-qubit operator. Thus, this code allows to correct for a generic one-qubit error.

Encoding for the Shor code works in two stages. First each qubit is encoded as in the three-qubit phase-flip code:

$$\begin{aligned} |0\rangle &\mapsto |+++\rangle, \\ |1\rangle &\mapsto |---\rangle. \end{aligned} \qquad (10.5.12)$$

Second, each of the three qubits in the phase-flip codeword are encoded in a set of triplets as in the three-qubit bit-flip code:

$$\begin{aligned} |+\rangle &\mapsto \tfrac{1}{\sqrt{2}}\left(|000\rangle + |111\rangle\right), \\ |-\rangle &\mapsto \tfrac{1}{\sqrt{2}}\left(|000\rangle - |111\rangle\right). \end{aligned} \qquad (10.5.13)$$

This results in codewords of nine qubits:

$$\begin{aligned} |0\rangle &\mapsto \tfrac{1}{2\sqrt{2}}\left(|000\rangle + |111\rangle\right)\left(|000\rangle + |111\rangle\right)\left(|000\rangle + |111\rangle\right), \\ |1\rangle &\mapsto \tfrac{1}{2\sqrt{2}}\left(|000\rangle - |111\rangle\right)\left(|000\rangle - |111\rangle\right)\left(|000\rangle - |111\rangle\right). \end{aligned} \qquad (10.5.14)$$

Suppose we subject these codewords to both the bit-flip and the phase-flip channels, with the restriction that there is at most one bit flip and at most one phase flip. We can view the combined effect as a single channel, whose effect is a bit flip with some amplitude, and a phase flip with some other amplitude, and a combination of both.

In a way analogous to the bit-flip channel seen previously, we can see that bit flip (X operator) on any of the nine qubits will move the code described by 10.5.14 to an orthogonal subspace. A phase flip (Z operator) on any of the qubit will also move the code to an orthogonal subspace through a sign change between the triplets of qubits. A peculiarity of this code not encountered in the three-bit codes is that applying the Z error on any member of the triplet will move the code to the same subspace. This will not prevent error correction as we only need to know where the code has moved to undo the error, as we show in Example 10.5.1.

A product of X and Z will give rise to a Y error which also moves the code to another orthogonal subspace. This shows that the error correction conditions 10.1.1 are satisfied and that an error-correcting recovery operation can be found (as illustrated in Example 10.5.1).

Note that the syndrome for the bit-flip code measures parities of bits values of a subset of the qubits, and the syndrome for the phase-flip code measures the phase parities of a subset of the qubits.

We can use a generalization of the syndromes for the bit-flip and phase-flip codes from the previous section to compare the bit or phase values of various qubits and make a table relating them to the corresponding error. A way to do this is to use the stabilizer formalism introduced in the previous subsection. We see that the bit-flip errors will be identified by two parities for each triplet of the qubits. The parity operators, which are also just sometimes referred to as 'parities' in this context, are given by

$$
\begin{aligned}
Z \otimes Z \otimes I \otimes I \otimes I \otimes I \otimes I \otimes I \otimes I \,, \\
Z \otimes I \otimes Z \otimes I \otimes I \otimes I \otimes I \otimes I \otimes I \,, \\
I \otimes I \otimes I \otimes Z \otimes Z \otimes I \otimes I \otimes I \otimes I \,, \\
I \otimes I \otimes I \otimes Z \otimes I \otimes Z \otimes I \otimes I \otimes I \,, \\
I \otimes I \otimes I \otimes I \otimes I \otimes I \otimes Z \otimes Z \otimes I \,, \\
I \otimes I \otimes I \otimes I \otimes I \otimes I \otimes Z \otimes I \otimes Z \,.
\end{aligned}
\tag{10.5.15}
$$

Measuring these operators through a generalization of Figure 10.18 will reveal which qubit, if any, has undergone a bit flip.

The phase-flip errors will be identified by the parities of the signs that appear in each triplet. Note that the logical bit encoded in states $|000\rangle \pm |111\rangle$ can be extracted by measuring the eigenvalue of the $X \otimes X \otimes X$ operator on the encoded state. Thus the parity of the first two logical bits encoded by $|000\rangle \pm |111\rangle$ can be extracted by measuring the observable $X \otimes X \otimes X \otimes X \otimes X \otimes X$ on the first six qubits. Furthermore, note that applying any combination of X errors to the states $|000\rangle \pm |111\rangle$ does not change the phase parity of those states. Thus the relevant phase-flip errors on the nine-qubit state can be determined by measuring the parities

$$
\begin{aligned}
X \otimes X \otimes X \otimes X \otimes X \otimes X \otimes I \otimes I \otimes I \,, \\
I \otimes I \otimes I \otimes X \otimes X \otimes X \otimes X \otimes X \otimes X \,.
\end{aligned}
\tag{10.5.16}
$$

Exercise 10.5.5 Make a table analogous to the one in Equation 10.5.10 that calculates the parities in Equation 10.5.15 for bit flip errors acting each qubit. Do the same for the parities in Equation 10.5.16 for phase flip errors. The recovery operation becomes the error operators themselves (as they are their own inverse). Which operator to apply is conditioned on the values of the parities.

These two parities will reveal which qubit, if any, has undergone a phase flip. A $ZX = iY$ error will be revealed by a obtaining '-1' parities when measuring operators in each of Equations 10.5.15 and 10.5.16

The Shor code can be defined as the 2-dimensional subspace spanned by eigenvectors with $+1$ eigenvalue of the eight operators in Equations (10.5.15) and (10.5.16).

Example 10.5.1 The nine-qubit code will, for example, correct a Y error on the first qubit of the encoded state

$$\alpha(|000\rangle + |111\rangle)(|000\rangle + |111\rangle)(|000\rangle + |111\rangle),$$
$$+\beta(|000\rangle - |111\rangle)(|000\rangle - |111\rangle)(|000\rangle - |111\rangle).$$

Note if a Y error occurs to this state, it will transform to (we can factor out and ignore the global phase of i) the state

$$\alpha(|100\rangle - |011\rangle)(|000\rangle + |111\rangle)(|000\rangle + |111\rangle),$$
$$+\beta(|100\rangle + |011\rangle)(|000\rangle - |111\rangle)(|000\rangle - |111\rangle).$$

The parity measurement corresponding to the operator

$$Z \otimes Z \otimes I \otimes I \otimes I \otimes I \otimes I \otimes I \otimes I$$

will give us the outcome '-1' indicating that the first two bits do not agree. The parity measurement corresponding to the operator

$$Z \otimes I \otimes Z \otimes I \otimes I \otimes I \otimes I \otimes I \otimes I$$

will also give us the outcome '-1' indicated that the first and third bits do not agree. Therefore, we know (assuming there was at most one bit flip on the first three qubits) that there was a bit flip on the first qubit.

The remaining four bit parity measurements will all give values of '$+1$', giving no indication of any other bit flips.

The phase parity measurement corresponding to the operator

$$X \otimes X \otimes X \otimes X \otimes X \otimes X \otimes I \otimes I \otimes I$$

would give an outcome of '-1' indicating that (assuming there was at most one phase flip on the nine qubits), there was a phase flip somewhere on one of the first six qubits.

The phase parity measurement corresponding to the operator

$$I \otimes I \otimes I \otimes X \otimes X \otimes X \otimes X \otimes X \otimes X$$

would give an outcome of $+1$ indicating that there was no phase flip on the last six qubits. Thus the phase flip must have occurred on one of the first three qubits.

Thus the 8 parity measurements will tell us that there was an X error on the first qubit and a Z error on one of the first three qubits. Note that the overall effect of a Z error is the same regardless of which of the first three qubits it acted on. Therefore, we can correct the codeword by applying an X gate on the first qubit and a Z gate on any one of the first three qubits.

This peculiar feature of not knowing or caring which qubit was affected by a Z error and which qubit should be corrected by a Z gate is due to a property of this code called *degeneracy*. A code is degenerate if more than one error operator have the same effect on the codewords.

If we assume the Z error occurred on the first qubit, then we know that the first qubit experience both an X and a Z error, and thus the effective error operator on the first qubit was a Y gate (note that up to global phase, Y, XZ, and ZX are all equal).

Exercise 10.5.6 The error recovery operations for the bit flip and phase flip codes can be adapted and combined to give a recovery operation for the nine-qubit Shor code.

Give the error recovery operation for the nine-qubit code.

The above Example 10.5.1 conveniently only had one error operator acting on the codeword. In general, as we saw in previous examples, if the error operation is described by a combination of correctable Pauli errors, then the syndrome measurement will 'collapse' the system into the component of the state corresponding to the encoded state affected by the Pauli error operators with that particular syndrome. In other words, as we discussed at the end of Section 10.4.3, if we can correct some discrete set of errors, we will also be able to correct a generic linear combination of these errors due to the linearity of quantum mechanics. Since the Shor code corrects all of the four Pauli errors (acting on one qubit, with the identity acting on the rest), it will also correct any linear combination of those four. Therefore, the Shor code will correct an arbitrary error on a single qubit. This basic idea is a vital aspect of why quantum error correction works, despite the apparently daunting task of having to correct for a continuum of possible quantum errors.

There are some quantum error correcting codes that are more efficient than Shor's code which uses 9 qubits to encode 1 qubit of quantum information and protects for one (but only one) generic single-qubit error within each codeword. Steane has discovered a code which uses only 7 qubits as the subspace with eigenvalue $+1$ of the operators:

$$
\begin{aligned}
Z \otimes Z \otimes Z \otimes Z \otimes I \otimes I \otimes I \,, \\
Z \otimes Z \otimes I \otimes I \otimes Z \otimes Z \otimes I \,, \\
Z \otimes I \otimes Z \otimes I \otimes Z \otimes I \otimes Z \,, \\
X \otimes X \otimes X \otimes X \otimes I \otimes I \otimes I \,, \\
X \otimes X \otimes I \otimes I \otimes X \otimes X \otimes I \,, \\
X \otimes I \otimes X \otimes I \otimes X \otimes I \otimes X \,.
\end{aligned}
\tag{10.5.17}
$$

There is an even more compact code which uses only 5 qubits and is defined through the operators:

$$X \otimes Z \otimes Z \otimes X \otimes I \,,$$
$$I \otimes X \otimes Z \otimes Z \otimes X \,,$$
$$X \otimes I \otimes X \otimes Z \otimes Z \,,$$
$$Z \otimes X \otimes I \otimes X \otimes Z \,,$$
$$Z \otimes Z \otimes X \otimes I \otimes X \,.$$

(10.5.18)

It is possible to show that it is not possible to use fewer than 5 qubits to protect against a generic single qubit error.

10.6   Fault-Tolerant Quantum Computation

Consider a circuit having S gates. If individual gates in the circuit introduce incoherent errors independently with probability p, then the expected number of errors at the output of the circuit is Sp. The probability of there being at least one error in the output of the circuit is at most Sp (Exercise 10.6.1). If the errors were all coherent, this probability would be $S^2 p$. In what follows, we will assume for convenience that errors are incoherent, but a very similar analysis can be done taking into account the possibility of coherent errors by keeping track of the probability *amplitude* of errors, instead of the probabilities.

Exercise 10.6.1 For a circuit having S gates, if individual gates introduce incoherent errors independently with some error probability p (recall Definition 10.4.25), show that the probability of there being at least one error in the output of the circuit is at most Sp. Also show that if the errors are fully coherent the probability is at most $S^2 p$.

Suppose we want to use a quantum error-correcting code to protect our quantum information from errors as it propagates through the circuit (for some quantum algorithm or protocol). A first approach would be to encode the information at the beginning of the circuit, and then just before each gate, decode the state, apply the gate, and then re-encode the state. Of course, between the decoding and re-encoding, the gate still may produce an error with probability p. This approach only protects the information from errors that occur *between* gates. As we mentioned in Section 10.3, a better approach is to design gates that act directly on encoded states. Furthermore, we want to be able to do this *fault-tolerantly*. This means we want to implement the gates on encoded states in such a way that if one (unencoded) gate in the implementation produces an error, the quantum information is not lost. For a given error-correcting code, a fault-tolerant implementation of a gate would restrict the evolution so that correctable errors do not propagate leading to uncorrectable errors.

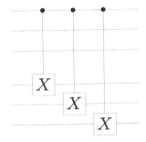

Fig. 10.19 A non-fault-tolerant implementation of CNOT for the three-qubit code.

Definition 10.6.1 *Suppose individual quantum gates produce errors in their output independently with probability p. For a given error-correcting code that corrects one error, an implementation of a gate acting directly on encoded states is considered to be* fault-tolerant *if the probability that the implementation introduces an unrecoverable error is bounded above by* cp^2 *for some constant c.*

Note that the upper bound cp^2 on the error probability for a fault-tolerant gate is an improvement over the error probability p for the physical gates as long as $p < \frac{1}{c}$. This condition is called the *threshold condition* and the value $\frac{1}{c}$ is called the *threshold* error probability.

Suppose we are given an error-correcting code capable of correcting an arbitrary error on a single qubits within a codeword. Then an implementation of a gate acting directly on codewords is considered to be fault-tolerant if the probability that the implementation introduces two or more errors on the encoded output is cp^2 for some constant c. As an example, consider the 3-qubit code, and suppose you want to implement an encoded version of the CNOT gate:

$$\text{CNOT}_{\text{enc}} : \begin{cases} |000\rangle|000\rangle & \mapsto |000\rangle|000\rangle \\ |000\rangle|111\rangle & \mapsto |000\rangle|111\rangle \\ |111\rangle|000\rangle & \mapsto |111\rangle|111\rangle \\ |111\rangle|111\rangle & \mapsto |111\rangle|000\rangle. \end{cases}$$

One way of implementing the encoded CNOT using 3 un-encoded-CNOT gates is shown in Figure 10.19. Note the gate acts on 2 *encoded blocks* of three qubits each.

The implementation shown in Figure 10.19 is not fault-tolerant. Suppose an error occurs in the first (un-encoded) CNOT gate in the implementation, and that the error occurs on the control bit for this gate. Then, it is easy to see that the resulting error will propagate to the second and third qubits of the second block, by the next two (un-encoded) CNOT gates in the implementation. So a single physical gate error, which occurs with probability p, results in multiple errors in the output of the encoded CNOT. The idea behind fault-tolerance is to design gates that avoid such bad error propagation.

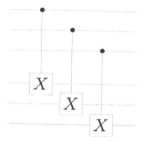

Fig. 10.20 A fault-tolerant implementation of CNOT for the three-qubit code.

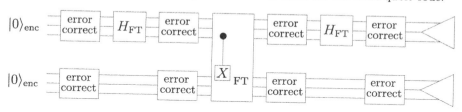

Fig. 10.21 Each encoded gate introduces an unrecoverable error with probability cp^2 for some constant c. The expected number of errors at the output of the circuit is Scp^2, and so the probability of an error at the output of the circuit is at most Scp^2.

An example of a fault-tolerant implementation of CNOT is shown in Figure 10.20.

To implement a circuit fault-tolerantly, we should choose a quantum code suitable for the error model (e.g. the 3-qubit code as shown in the example, or perhaps the 7-qubit Steane code), and then design fault-tolerant implementations, appropriate for that code, of a universal set of gates.

For a gate U, denote its fault-tolerant implementation by U_{FT}. Suppose we implement the circuit of Figure 10.19 using fault-tolerant gates for the 3-qubit code. Also, suppose we do error correction between every pair of gates in the circuit. Then, the resulting circuit would look like Figure 10.21. Suppose that we can do encoding and error correction perfectly (i.e. assume there is no chance of a gate producing an error during the encoding or error correction procedures). The 3-qubit code corrects bit flip errors on 1 qubit, and we have implemented our encoded gates in a fault-tolerant manner. So the only way that the error correction could fail is, if at least two bit flip errors occurred in the fault-tolerant implementation of the gate just before the error correction. This happens with probability $3p^2(1-p)$. So the probability of error (after error correction) for each fault-tolerant gate is now less than cp^2, for $c = 2$ (since $p^2 < p^3$). Note that the threshold condition for $c = 2$ is $p < \frac{1}{2}$, which is a condition that we have already seen to be necessary for the three-qubit code to be effective. Consider a circuit containing S such fault-tolerant gates. The probability of an unrecoverable error in the (encoded) output of the fault-tolerant circuit is at most cSp^2.

The bound cSp^2 for the error probability of the fault-tolerant circuit is an improvement over the bound Sp for the error probability of the original circuit as long as the threshold condition $p < \frac{1}{c}$ is satisified.

Of course, we cannot assume that the (un-encoded) gates used in the error correction and encoding procedures are themselves immune to the errors. These gates may also introduce errors with probability p. So we would like to devise a way to perform these procedures in such a way that the probability of error is at most cp^2 for some constant c. Fortunately, there are techniques for doing this. Recall that for stabilizer codes, error correction can be achieved by performing a measurement of the stabilizer generators. There are techniques for performing such measurements fault-tolerantly (i.e. in such a way that the probability of error is cp^2 for some constant c).

In summary, the plan of fault-tolerant quantum computing is as follows. We assume that our individual (un-encoded) gates introduce errors with probability p. If we do not use error correction, the probability of an error at the output of a circuit with S gates is at most Sp. To implement the circuit fault-tolerantly, we first choose a suitable quantum code and then devise implementations for:

1. *a fault-tolerant universal set of gates.* This is a set of gates implemented to act directly on encoded states, such that the probability of an unrecoverable error in the encoded output is at most cp^2 for some constant c.

2. *a fault-tolerant measurement procedure.* This is a procedure for performing measurements such that that the probability the measurement introduces an error is at most cp^2 for some constant c. Notice that if we have chosen a stabilizer code, then a fault-tolerant method for performing measurements of stabilizer generators will give us a fault-tolerant technique for performing error correction. Fault-tolerant measurements also provide a means to prepare the initial state for the computation fault-tolerantly.

Given a circuit with S gates, if we encode the qubits in the circuit with a suitable quantum error-correcting code, and then replace the gates and measurements in the given circuit with fault-tolerant implementations, the probability of an error in the output of the circuit is at most Scp^2 for some constant c. This is an improvement over the bound Sp for the probability that the original circuit produces an error, as long as $p < p_{\text{th}} = \frac{1}{c}$.

The error probability can be reduced even further (in fact, *arbitrarily* low) by *concatenating* quantum error-correcting codes to obtain new, larger codes.

10.6.1 Concatenation of Codes and the Threshold Theorem

For a circuit with S gates, where individual gate errors occur independently with probability p, the techniques described above can be used to produce an encoded version of the circuit whose overall probability of error is at most cSp^2, for some constant c. This is an improvement, as long as p is below the threshold value $p_{th} = \frac{1}{c}$. In this section we show how codes can be combined, or *concatenated*, to get even better improvement. Using this idea, we get a bound on the number of gates required to implement a circuit if we require the error be reduced to at most ε. We find that the size of the circuit grows polynomially with $\log \varepsilon$. It is an important result called the *threshold theorem*.

The idea of concatenating quantum codes is quite simple. In a *first-level encoding*, we encode each qubit using an appropriate code. Then, for each of the codewords we encode each of the qubits in the codeword again, using the same code. This is called the *second-level encoding*. Note that after two levels of encoding using an n-qubit code, each qubit is ultimately encoded by n^2 qubits. Concatenation is illustrated in Figure 10.22. This is a good strategy as long as the error model at each encoding level has the same form, that is, the same Kraus operators with possibly different amplitude.

Suppose we use a two-level encoding, and individual errors occur at the lowest level (on a physical qubit) with probability p. Through one level of encoding, the probability for unrecoverable errors on fault-tolerant versions of the gates at the middle layer is reduced to cp^2 for some constant c. Then the second level of encoding reduces the probability of unrecoverable errors on fault-tolerant gates at the top layer to $c(cp^2)^2 = c^3p^4$. So concatenation improves the error rate exponentially as long as $p < \frac{1}{c}$. If we use k levels of encoding, then the probability of an error at the highest level is reduced to $\frac{(cp)^{2^k}}{c}$. The number of physical gates

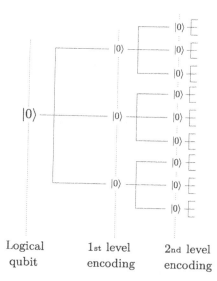

Fig. 10.22 Concatenation of error-correcting codes.

required to implement each fault-tolerant gate (for k levels of concatenation) is d^k for some constant d. We seek to obtain a bound on this number d^k, to show that the error rate decreases faster than the size of the circuit grows.

Suppose that we wish to give a fault-tolerant implementation of a quantum circuit having S gates and we wish to make the overall error probability for the circuit less than ε. To do so, the fault-tolerant implementation of each gate must be made to have an error probability less than $\frac{\varepsilon}{S}$. Using the observations about concatenation, we must concatenate our codes a number of times k such that

$$\frac{(cp)^{2^k}}{c} \leq \frac{\varepsilon}{S}. \tag{10.6.1}$$

Provided that p is below the threshold $\frac{1}{c}$, such a k can be found. To find a bound on d^k, begin with (10.6.1), and take the logarithm of both sides:

$$2^k \leq \frac{\log\left(\frac{S}{c\varepsilon}\right)}{\log\left(\frac{1}{cp}\right)}. \tag{10.6.2}$$

Now using the fact that $2 = d^{1/\log_2 d}$ we get:

$$d^k \leq \left(\frac{\log\left(\frac{S}{c\varepsilon}\right)}{\log\left(\frac{1}{cp}\right)}\right)^{\log_2 d}$$

$$\in O\left(\log^m\left(\frac{S}{\varepsilon}\right)\right), \tag{10.6.3}$$

for some positive constant $m \geq 1$. Therefore, fault-tolerant circuit consisting of S gates concatenated to k levels has its size (number of gates) bounded by

$$Sd^k = O\left(S\left(\log^m\left(\frac{S}{\varepsilon}\right)\right)\right) \tag{10.6.4}$$

gates. Summarizing, we have the following *threshold theorem for quantum computation*.

Theorem 10.6.2 *A quantum circuit containing S gates may be simulated with a probability of error at most ε using*

$$O\left(S\left(\log^m\left(\frac{S}{\varepsilon}\right)\right)\right) \tag{10.6.5}$$

gates on hardware whose components introduce errors with probability p, provided p is below some constant threshold, $p < p_{th}$, and given reasonable assumptions about the noise in the underlying hardware.

The threshold theorem tells us that, in principle, we will be able to construct devices to perform arbitrarily long quantum computations using a polynomial amount of resources, so long as we can build components such that the per-gate error is below a fixed threshold value. In other words, noise and imprecision of physical devices should not pose a fundamental obstacle to realizing large-scale quantum computers. This shows that the model of quantum information processing is robust and corroborates the suggestion that quantum information is more powerful than its classical counterpart. Although the threshold value calculated today is demanding from the experimental point of view, by designing better quantum error correcting codes, the numerical value of the threshold continues to be improved. The techniques and methods for quantum error correction also provide guides and requirements for the physical implementation of quantum information-processing devices. The theorem has given confidence that they can be built.

APPENDIX A

A.1 Tools for Analysing Probabilistic Algorithms

Markov's inequality is a simple but powerful tool in probability theory. We will state it here in the case of discrete random variables, but it has a straightforward continuous analogue.

A *discrete random variable* X is a variable whose values come from a finite or countable subset S of the real numbers and that correspond to the outcome of some random event.

For example, if we consider a random coin flip, we can let $X = 0$ if the coin comes up 'heads' and $X = 1$ if the coin comes up 'tails'.

As another example, we could toss a coin n times and let X equal the number of times the coin comes up 'heads'.

The expected value of a random variable X is

$$E(X) = \sum_{x \in S} x Pr(X = x)$$

which we will also denote by μ_X.

Theorem A.1.1 (*Markov's Inequality*) *Let X be a discrete random variable that takes on non-negative values. Then*

$$Pr(X \geq c\mu_X)) \leq \frac{1}{c}. \qquad \text{(A.1.1)}$$

The proof follows from the simple observation that if with probability at least p, X will be greater than or equal to some threshold value t, then the expected value of X must be at least pt.

Proof Let Y be the random variable satisfying $Y = 0$ if $0 \leq X < cE(X)$ and $Y = cE(X)$ if $X \geq cE(X)$. Thus $Pr(Y = 1) = Pr(X \geq cE(X))$. Since $X \geq Y$, then

$$E(X) \geq E(Y) = 0 Pr(Y = 0) + cE(X)Pr(Y = 1)$$
$$= cE(X)Pr(Y = 1)$$
$$= cE(X)Pr(X \geq cE(X))$$

and the result follows.

□

Example A.1.2 We can use Markov's Inequality to show how to turn a randomized algorithm A that correctly solves a problem with some expected running time at most T into a zero-error algorithm with bounded running time and bounded probability of outputting the answer.

Let X be a random variable corresponding to the running time of A on a particular input, and suppose we know the expected running time is at most T. Markov's Inequality implies that for any constant c, the probability that the running time of the algorithm A exceeds $cE(X)$ is at most $\frac{1}{c}$. Thus, if we know the expected running time of A, we can derive an algorithm with bounded running time by simply running A, and if does not find the answer within time $3T$, then stop and output 'FAIL'. With probability at least $\frac{2}{3}$ the modified algorithm will have successfully solved the problem.

Markov's inequality can be used to derive more powerful inequalities including Chebyshev's Inequality and Chernoff's Inequality.

Define a new random variable $Y = (X - \mu_X)^2$. Let $\sigma_X = \sqrt{E(Y)}$. Applying Markov's inequality to the random variable Y gives Chebyshev's Inequality:

$$Pr[|X - \mu_X| \geq c\sigma_X] \leq \frac{1}{c^2}.$$

We can get stronger bounds when the random variable X is the sum of several independent random variables with outcomes 0 or 1.

Let $X_1, X_2, \ldots, X_n$ be random variables corresponding to the result of n independent coin-tosses with outcomes 0 or 1, where $Pr[X_i = 1] = p_i$. The random variables X_i are also known as 'Poisson' trials. If the p_i are all equal, they are known as 'Bernoulli' trials.

Let $X = \sum_{i=1}^{n} X_i$, and $\mu_X = E(X) = \sum_i p_i$.

By applying the Markov Inequality to the random variable $Y = e^{cX}$, for an appropriately chosen positive real value c, we can derive what are known as Chernoff bounds.

For example, one can bound the probability that X is much less than its expected value:

Theorem A.1.3 For any real value δ, $0 < \delta \leq 1$, we have

$$Pr[X < (1 - \delta)\mu_X] < e^{-\frac{\mu_X \delta^2}{2}}.$$

One can also bound the probability that X is much greater than its expected value:

Theorem A.1.4 *For any real value $\delta > 0$, we have*

$$Pr[X > (1+\delta)\mu_X] < \left(\frac{e^\delta}{(1+\delta)^{(1+\delta)}} \right)^{\mu_X}.$$

Example A.1.5 One application of the Chernoff bound is to amplify the success probability of a bounded-error algorithm. Suppose we have a bounded-error algorithm for a decision problem that outputs the correct answer with probability $\frac{1}{2} + \beta$, where $0 < \beta < 1$.

If we repeat the algorithm n independent times (with the same input), and output the majority answer, then the probability of error reduces to γ^n for some constant γ.

Let $X_i = 1$ if the ith run of the algorithm outputs the correct answer, and let $X = \sum_i X_i$.

Then $E(X) = \frac{n}{2} + \frac{n\beta}{2}$.

Letting $\delta = \frac{\beta}{1-\beta}$ we get

$$Pr[X < \frac{n}{2}] < e^{-\frac{n\beta^2}{4(1+\beta)}} = \gamma^n,$$

where $\gamma = e^{-\frac{\beta^2}{4(1+\beta)}}$.

This means that if we would like the majority answer to be the correct value with probability at least $1 - \epsilon$, it suffices to repeat n times where $n \geq 4\frac{1+\beta}{\beta^2} \log \frac{1}{\epsilon}$.

A.2   Solving the Discrete Logarithm Problem When the Order of a Is Composite

There are several methods for reducing the problem of finding the discrete logarithm of b to the base a where a has composite order $r = r_1 r_2 \ldots r_n$ to finding several discrete logarithms to some other bases a_j with order r_j.

One method requires that the r_j be pairwise coprime. Thus if we want to reduce the discrete logarithm problem to a series of discrete logarithm problems in groups of prime order (and not just prime-power order), this method (which uses the Chinese Remainder Theorem) will not suffice in general.

So we will sketch some other methods that do not require that the r_j are pairwise coprime. The first such method requires a factorization of r into its prime factors. In light of the efficient quantum algorithm for factoring integers, this is not an unreasonable assumption. The last two methods, which we sketch more briefly, do not assume we have a prime factorization of r.

Assuming a Prime Factorization of r

For simplicity, we will give the proof for the case that $r = r_1 r_2$, since the method generalizes in a straightforward way.

Theorem A.2.1 *Consider an element a with order $r = r_1 r_2$, for integers $r_1 > 1, r_2 > 1$.*

The logarithm of any element b to the base a can be computed by evaluating one discrete logarithm with respect to the base $a_1 = a^{r_1}$ (which has order r_2) and one discrete logarithm with respect to the base $a_2 = a^{r_2}$ (which has order r_1), and $O(\log^2 r)$ other group operations.

Proof   Suppose $b = a^k$ and a has order $r = r_1 r_2$. Note that for each k satisfying $0 \le k < r$ there are unique integers c_1, c_2 satisfying $0 \le c_1 < r_2, 0 \le c_2 < r_1$ such that $k = c_2 r_2 + c_1$. Let $b_1 = b^{r_1}$ and $a_1 = a^{r_1}$. Note that this means $b_1 = a_1^{c_1}$, where the order of a_1 is r_2. Thus by computing the discrete logarithm of b_1 to the base a_1, we obtain c_1. Once we know c_1, we can compute $b_2 = ba^{-c_1} = a^{r_2 c_2}$. Let $a_2 = a^{r_2}$. Note that a_2 has order r_1 and that $b_2 = a_2^{c_2}$. Thus we can find c_2 by computing a logarithm to the base a_2. From c_1 and c_2 we can easily compute k. □

Corollary A.2.2 *Consider an element a with order r. Let $r = p_1 p_2 \ldots p_k$ be the factorization of r into primes (the p_i are not necessarily distinct). For $i = 1, 2, \ldots, k$, define $a_i = a^{\frac{r}{p_i}}$. Note that a_i has order p_i.*

The logarithm of any element b to the base a can be computed by evaluating k discrete logarithms with respect to the bases $a_1, a_2, \ldots, a_k$, and $O(\log^2 r)$ other group operations.

No Assumption of a Prime Factorization of r. Method 1.

The basic idea behind this method to simply run the discrete logarithm algorithm and not worry about r not being prime, and just proceed as usual. Recall that with high probability[1] the algorithm will sample a pair of integers k and $kt \bmod r$, where t is the logarithm of b to the base a. One of three things will happen:

1. we will get lucky and the sampled k will be coprime with r, and we can directly find $t = (k^{-1} \bmod r)(kt \bmod r) \bmod r$.
2. we will be somewhat unlucky, and k will have a non-trivial common factor $d = \text{GCD}(k, r)$ with r. In this case, we will be able to split $r = r_1 d$. We will also be able to determine $t \bmod r_1$, and reduce the problem to a discrete logarithm problem in a group of order d. We elaborate on this possibility below.

---

[1]If QFT_r and QFT_r^{-1} are used, the probability is 1.

3. we will be very unlucky and sample $k = 0$. This only happens with probability $1 - \frac{1}{r}$, so we can simply keep trying until we get a non-zero k.[2]

In the case that $d = \mathrm{GCD}(k, r) > 1$, we know that $r = r_1 d$, $k = k_1 d$, and $kt = k_1 dt \bmod r$ for some integers r_1, k_1. We can compute the value of $t_1 = t \bmod r_1$ by computing $(k_1^{-1} \bmod r_1)(k_1 t \bmod r_1) \bmod r_1$. Then we know that $t = t_2 r_1 + t_1$ for some non-negative integer $t_2 < d$. If we define $b_1 = b^{r_1}$ and $a_1 = a^{r_1}$ then we can see that $b_1 = a_1^{t_2}$, and a_1 has order d. We can then apply the discrete logarithm algorithm to find $t_2 \bmod d$ or t_2 modulo some non-trivial factor of d. The expected number of recursive applications of the generalized discrete logarithm algorithm is at most $O(\log r)$.

No Assumption of a Prime Factorization of r. Method 2.

If r is not prime, we can proceed with the general analysis given in Section 7.5 for the Hidden Subgroup Problem. This method consists of repeating the discrete logarithm algorithm $O(\log r)$ times to generate pairs $(k_1 t, k_1), (k_2 t, k_2) \ldots (k_m t, k_m)$. We then solve the linear system

$$
\begin{bmatrix}
k_1 t & k_1 \\
k_2 t & k_2 \\
\vdots & \\
k_m t & k_m
\end{bmatrix}
\begin{pmatrix} x_1 \\ x_2 \end{pmatrix}
= \begin{pmatrix} 0 \\ 0 \end{pmatrix}.
$$

With high probability the solution space will be the 1-dimensional vector space spanned by

$$
\begin{pmatrix} 1 \\ -t \end{pmatrix}.
$$

A.3 How Many Random Samples Are Needed to Generate a Group?

Consider any group G of order $N = p_1^{n_1} p_2^{n_2} \ldots p_l^{n_l}$, where the p_j are prime and $n_j > 0$.

Let $n = \sum_j n_j$.

Suppose we have a means for sampling elements from G independently and uniformly at random. How many samples do we need so that with probability at least $\frac{2}{3}$ the sampled elements generate G?

A similar argument as in Exercise 6.5.3 shows that the expected number of uniformly random samples from G that are needed in order to generate G is less than $n + 1$.

---

[2]Note that Exercise 8.2.2 shows how to eliminate this third possibility using Amplitude Amplification.

Thus, $3n + 3$ samples from G suffice in order to generate G with probability at least $\frac{2}{3}$.

However, much fewer samples are actually necessary in order to generate G with high probability. Upper bounds of $n + O(1)$ could be shown using Chernoff bound methods (Appendix A.1).

However, we will give an alternative proof in the case that G is the additive Abelian group $G = Z_2^n$ (in which case, we can treat it as vector space over Z_2, and avoid group theory language), as is needed for analysing Simon's algorithm. In general, it can be shown that the number of samples needed for a group G of order $N = p_1^{n_1} p_2^{n_2} \ldots p_l^{n_l}$ with $n = \sum_j n_j$ is no more than is needed in the case of $G = Z_2^n$.

Theorem A.3.1 *Let* $t_1, t_2, \ldots$ *be a sequence of elements selected independently and uniformly at random from a subspace* $H \leq Z_2^n$, *where* $|H| = 2^m$.

Then the probability that $\langle t_1, t_2, \ldots, t_{m+4} \rangle$ *generates* H *is at least* $\frac{2}{3}$.

Proof Let $S_j = \langle t_1, t_2, \ldots, t_j \rangle$ for $j \geq 1$, and $S_0 = \{0\}$.

With probability $1 - \frac{|S_0|}{|H|} = 1 - \frac{1}{2^m}$, we have $t_1 \notin S_0$ and thus $|S_1| = 2$. Assuming this is the case, then with probability at least $1 - \frac{|S_1|}{|H|} = 1 - \frac{1}{2^{m-1}}$ we have $t_2 \notin S_1$, and thus $|S_2| = 4$. And so on, so that with probability at least $1 - \frac{1}{2^2}$ we have $t_{m-1} \notin S_{m-2}$ and $|S_{m-1}| = 2^{m-1}$, and finally with probability at least $1 - \frac{1}{2}$ we have $t_m \notin S_m$, and so $|S_m| = 2^m$; since S_m is subspace of H (which has size 2^m), then $S_m = H$.

Note that[3]

$$\left(1 - \frac{1}{2^m}\right)\left(1 - \frac{1}{2^{m-1}}\right) \cdots \left(1 - \frac{1}{2^k}\right) > 1 - \sum_{j=k}^{m} \frac{1}{2^j} > 1 - \frac{1}{2^{k-1}}.$$

This means that

$$\left(1 - \frac{1}{2^m}\right)\left(1 - \frac{1}{2^{m-1}}\right) \cdots \left(1 - \frac{1}{4}\right) > \frac{1}{2}$$

and thus

$$\left(1 - \frac{1}{2^m}\right)\left(1 - \frac{1}{2^{m-1}}\right) \cdots \left(1 - \frac{1}{4}\right)\left(1 - \frac{1}{2}\right) > \frac{1}{4}.$$

Note that this means that the probability that we get 'lucky' and the first m samples $t_1, t_2, \ldots, t_m$ from H are independent (and thus generate all of H) is at least $\frac{1}{4}$. However, we would like to boost this probability to be greater than $\frac{2}{3}$.

---

[3]This follows by inductively applying the fact that for non-negative real values x_1, x_2, the following always holds $(1 - x_1)(1 - x_2) \geq 1 - x_1 - x_2$.

Note that

$$\left(1 - \frac{1}{2^m}\right)\left(1 - \frac{1}{2^{m-1}}\right)\cdots\left(1 - \frac{1}{16}\right) > \frac{7}{8}$$

so that with probability at least $\frac{7}{8}$, the first $m - 3$ samples will be independent, and thus generate a subgroup S_{m-3} of H of size 2^{m-3}.

The probability that the next two samples $\mathbf{t}_{m-2}$ and $\mathbf{t}_{m-1}$ are both in S_{m-3} is $\left(\frac{1}{2^3}\right)^2 = \frac{1}{2^6}$, thus the probability that S_{m-1} is strictly greater than S_{m-3} is at least $1 - \frac{1}{64}$. In this case, for convenience [4] let S'_{m-1} be a subgroup of size 2^{m-2} satisfying $S_{m-3} \subset S'_{m-1} \subseteq S_{m-1}$. In this case, the probability that $\mathbf{t}_m, \mathbf{t}_{m+1}$ are both in S'_{m-1} is $\left(\frac{1}{4}\right)^2 = \frac{1}{16}$, and thus the probability that S_{m+1} is strictly greater than S'_{m-1} is at least $1 - \frac{1}{16}$.

In this case, again for convenience, let S'_{m+1} be a subgroup of size 2^{m-1} satisfying $S'_{m-1} \subset S'_{m+1} \subseteq S_{m+1}$.

Lastly, the probability that $\mathbf{t}_{m+2}, \mathbf{t}_{m+3}, \mathbf{t}_{m+4}$ are all in S'_{m+1} is $\left(\frac{1}{2}\right)^3 = \frac{1}{8}$, and thus the probability that S_{m+3} is strictly greater than S'_{m+1} is at least $1 - \frac{1}{8}$. In this case, S_{m+4} must have at least 2^m elements, and since it is a subspace of H (which only has 2^m elements), then $S_{m+4} = H$.

The probability of this occurring is at least

$$\frac{7}{8} \times \frac{63}{64} \times \frac{15}{16} \times \frac{7}{8} > \frac{2}{3}.$$

□

A.4   Finding r Given $\frac{k}{r}$ for Random k

Theorem A.4.1 *Suppose the integers k_1, k_2 are selected independently and uniformly at random from $\{0, 1, \ldots, r - 1\}$. Let r_1, r_2, c_1, c_2 be integers satisfying $GCD(r_1, c_1) = GCD(r_2, c_2) = 1$ and $\frac{k_1}{r} = \frac{c_1}{r_1}$ and $\frac{k_2}{r} = \frac{c_2}{r_2}$. Then $Pr(LCM(r_1, r_2) = r) > \frac{6}{\pi^2}$.*

Proof Since r is a common multiple of r_1 and r_2, we must have the least common multiple $LCM(r_1, r_2)$ divides r. Thus to prove $r = LCM(r_1, r_2)$, it suffices to show that $r|LCM(r_1, r_2)$.

For convenience, note that we can equivalently assume k_1, k_2 were selected independently and uniformly at random from $\{1, 2, \ldots, r\}$ (since whether $k_1 = 0$ or r, we always get $r_1 = 1$). Note that $r_1 = \frac{r}{GCD(r, k_1)}$ and $r_2 = \frac{r}{GCD(r, k_2)}$. If $GCD(r, k_1)$ and $GCD(r, k_2)$ are coprime, then whichever factors were 'removed' from r to produce r_1 will remain in r_2 and vice versa. In this case, r will divide $LCM(r_1, r_2)$, which implies that $r = LCM(r_1, r_2)$. The probability that $GCD(r, k_1)$ and $GCD(r, k_2)$ are coprime is $\prod_{p|r}(1 - \frac{1}{p^2})$, where the product is

---

[4]This might seem awkward, but it makes the analysis easier.

over the prime factors of r (without repeating multiple factors). This probability is strictly larger than $\prod_p(1 - \frac{1}{p^2})$, where the product is over all primes p. It can be shown that this series equals the reciprocal of the Riemann zeta function evaluated at the integer 2, $\zeta(2) = \sum_{n=1}^{\infty} \frac{1}{n^2}$, which is known to equal $\frac{\pi^2}{6}$. □

A.5 Adversary Method Lemma

Here we prove the following lemma, based on definitions given in Section 9.7. Recall that for $j \in \{0, 1, \ldots, T\}$, we define

$$W^j = \sum_{(\mathbf{X},\mathbf{Y}) \in R} \frac{1}{\sqrt{|\mathcal{X}||\mathcal{Y}|}} |\langle \psi_\mathbf{X}^j | \psi_\mathbf{Y}^j \rangle|. \tag{A.5.1}$$

The state $|\psi_\mathbf{Z}^j\rangle$ denotes the state of the quantum computer just after the jth query to the black box $O_\mathbf{Z}$, and U_j denotes the unitary operation performed after the jth query to $O_\mathbf{Z}$ and before any other queries.

Lemma A.5.1 *Let b and b' satisfy the following.*

- *for every $\mathbf{X} \in \mathcal{X}$ and $i \in \{1, 2, \ldots, N\}$, there are at most b different $\mathbf{Y} \in \mathcal{Y}$ such that $(\mathbf{X}, \mathbf{Y}) \in R$ and $X_i \neq Y_i$.*
- *for every $\mathbf{Y} \in \mathcal{Y}$ and $i \in \{1, 2, \ldots, N\}$, there are at most b' different $\mathbf{X} \in \mathcal{X}$ such that $(\mathbf{X}, \mathbf{Y}) \in R$ and $X_i \neq Y_i$.*

Then, for any each integer $k \in \{0, 1, \ldots, T-1\}$, we have $W^{k+1} - W^k \leq 2\sqrt{bb'}$.

Before we give the proof, let us note that for convenience we will assume that we are given the phase-shift version of the black-box for f, in particular, one that maps $|x\rangle \mapsto (-1)^{f(x)}|x\rangle$. This might appear to be a weaker black-box. For example, up to a global phase, the phase shift oracle for $f(x)$ is the same as the phase shift oracle for the complement of f, $\overline{f}(x) = \overline{f(x)}$. However by adding one additional input, z, to the domain of f and fixing $f(z) = 0$, we can easily show (see Exercise 8.1.1) that the two types of oracles are equivalent. (It also suffices to know the value of f on any of the existing inputs, or to be given a controlled-U_f.)

Proof From the definition of W^j, we know that

$$W^{k+1} - W^k = \frac{1}{\sqrt{|\mathcal{X}||\mathcal{Y}|}} \sum_{(\mathbf{X},\mathbf{Y}) \in R} |\langle \psi_\mathbf{X}^{k+1} | \psi_\mathbf{Y}^{k+1} \rangle| - |\langle \psi_\mathbf{X}^k | \psi_\mathbf{Y}^k \rangle| \tag{A.5.2}$$

and by the triangle inequality we have

$$W^{k+1} - W^k \leq \frac{1}{\sqrt{|\mathcal{X}||\mathcal{Y}|}} \sum_{(\mathbf{X},\mathbf{Y}) \in R} |\langle \psi_\mathbf{X}^{k+1} | \psi_\mathbf{Y}^{k+1} \rangle - \langle \psi_\mathbf{X}^k | \psi_\mathbf{Y}^k \rangle|. \tag{A.5.3}$$

Define $\alpha_{i,j,\mathbf{X}}$ so that

$$U_j|\psi_{\mathbf{X}}^j\rangle = \sum_{i=1}^{N} \alpha_{i,j,\mathbf{X}}|i\rangle|\phi_{i,j,\mathbf{X}}\rangle$$

for some normalized state $|\phi_{i,j,\mathbf{X}}\rangle$. Similarly, define $\alpha_{i,j,\mathbf{Y}}$ so that

$$U_j|\psi_{\mathbf{Y}}^j\rangle = \sum_{i=1}^{N} \alpha_{i,j,\mathbf{Y}}|i\rangle|\phi_{i,j,\mathbf{Y}}\rangle$$

for some normalized state $|\phi_{i,j,\mathbf{Y}}\rangle$.

It follows that

$$|\psi_{\mathbf{X}}^{k+1}\rangle = O_{\mathbf{X}}U_k|\psi_{\mathbf{X}}^k\rangle = U_k|\psi_{\mathbf{X}}^k\rangle - 2\sum_{i:X_i=1} \alpha_{i,k,\mathbf{X}}|i\rangle|\phi_{i,k,\mathbf{X}}\rangle \tag{A.5.4}$$

and

$$|\psi_{\mathbf{Y}}^{k+1}\rangle = O_{\mathbf{Y}}U_k|\psi_{\mathbf{Y}}^k\rangle = U_k|\psi_{\mathbf{Y}}^k\rangle - 2\sum_{i:Y_i=1} \alpha_{i,k,\mathbf{Y}}|i\rangle|\phi_{i,k,\mathbf{Y}}\rangle \tag{A.5.5}$$

and therefore[5]

$$\langle\psi_{\mathbf{X}}^{k+1}|\psi_{\mathbf{Y}}^{k+1}\rangle - \langle\psi_{\mathbf{X}}^k|\psi_{\mathbf{Y}}^k\rangle = -2\sum_{i:X_i=1} \alpha_{i,k,\mathbf{X}}\alpha_{i,k,\mathbf{Y}}^*\langle\phi_{i,\mathbf{X}}^k|\phi_{i,\mathbf{Y}}^k\rangle \tag{A.5.6}$$

$$-2\sum_{i:Y_i=1} \alpha_{i,k,\mathbf{X}}\alpha_{i,k,\mathbf{Y}}^*\langle\phi_{i,\mathbf{X}}^k|\phi_{i,\mathbf{Y}}^k\rangle \tag{A.5.7}$$

$$+4\sum_{i:X_i=Y_i=1} \alpha_{i,k,\mathbf{X}}\alpha_{i,k,\mathbf{Y}}^*\langle\phi_{i,\mathbf{X}}^k|\phi_{i,\mathbf{Y}}^k\rangle \tag{A.5.8}$$

$$= -2\sum_{i:X_i\neq Y_i} \alpha_{i,k,\mathbf{X}}\alpha_{i,k,\mathbf{Y}}^*\langle\phi_{i,\mathbf{X}}^k|\phi_{i,\mathbf{Y}}^k\rangle. \tag{A.5.9}$$

It follows that

$$W^k - W^{k-1} \leq \frac{1}{\sqrt{|\mathcal{X}||\mathcal{Y}|}}\sum_{(\mathbf{X},\mathbf{Y})\in R}\sum_{i:X_i\neq Y_i} |2\alpha_{i,k,\mathbf{X}}\alpha_{i,k,\mathbf{Y}}^*\langle\phi_{i,k,\mathbf{X}}|\phi_{i,k,\mathbf{Y}}\rangle|$$

$$\leq \sum_{(\mathbf{X},\mathbf{Y})\in R}\sum_{i:X_i\neq Y_i} 2\frac{|\alpha_{i,k,\mathbf{X}}|}{\sqrt{|\mathcal{X}|}}\frac{|\alpha_{i,k,\mathbf{Y}}|}{\sqrt{|\mathcal{Y}|}}.$$

---

[5]Note that $\langle\psi_{\mathbf{X}}^k|\psi_{\mathbf{Y}}^k\rangle = \langle\psi_{\mathbf{X}}^k|U_k^\dagger U_k|\psi_{\mathbf{Y}}^k\rangle$.

Note that for any non-negative real number r and real numbers a, b, it follows that[6] $2ab \leq \frac{1}{r}a^2 + rb^2$. Letting $r = \sqrt{\frac{b'}{b}}$ we get

$$W^{k+1} - W^k \leq \sum_{(\mathbf{X},\mathbf{Y}) \in R} \sum_{i:X_i \neq Y_i} \sqrt{\frac{b'}{b}} \frac{|\alpha_{i,k,\mathbf{X}}|^2}{|\mathcal{X}|} + \sqrt{\frac{b}{b'}} \frac{|\alpha_{i,k,\mathbf{Y}}|^2}{|\mathcal{Y}|}$$

$$= \sum_{(\mathbf{X},\mathbf{Y}) \in R} \sum_{i:X_i \neq Y_i} \sqrt{\frac{b'}{b}} \frac{|\alpha_{i,k,\mathbf{X}}|^2}{|\mathcal{X}|} + \sum_{(\mathbf{X},\mathbf{Y}) \in R} \sum_{i:X_i \neq Y_i} \sqrt{\frac{b}{b'}} \frac{|\alpha_{i,k,\mathbf{Y}}|^2}{|\mathcal{Y}|}.$$

We can reorder the summations to get

$$W^{k+1} - W^k \leq \sum_i \sum_{\mathbf{X} \in \mathcal{X}} \sum_{\mathbf{Y} \in \mathcal{Y}:(\mathbf{X},\mathbf{Y}) \in R, X_i \neq Y_i} \sqrt{\frac{b'}{b}} \frac{|\alpha_{i,k,\mathbf{X}}|^2}{|\mathcal{X}|}$$

$$+ \sum_i \sum_{\mathbf{X} \in \mathcal{X}} \sum_{\mathbf{Y} \in \mathcal{Y}:(\mathbf{X},\mathbf{Y}) \in R, X_i \neq Y_i} \sqrt{\frac{b}{b'}} \frac{|\alpha_{i,k,\mathbf{Y}}|^2}{|\mathcal{Y}|}.$$

Using the hypotheses of the lemma we get

$$W^k - W^{k-1} \leq \sum_i \sum_{\mathbf{X} \in \mathcal{X}} b\sqrt{\frac{b'}{b}} \frac{|\alpha_{i,k,\mathbf{X}}|^2}{|\mathcal{X}|} + \sum_i \sum_{\mathbf{Y} \in \mathcal{Y}} b'\sqrt{\frac{b}{b'}} \frac{|\alpha_{i,k,\mathbf{Y}}|^2}{|\mathcal{Y}|}$$

$$= \frac{\sqrt{b'b}}{|\mathcal{X}|} \sum_{\mathbf{X} \in \mathcal{X}} \sum_i |\alpha_{i,k,\mathbf{X}}|^2 + \frac{\sqrt{b'b}}{|\mathcal{Y}|} \sum_{\mathbf{Y} \in \mathcal{Y}} \sum_i |\alpha_{i,k,\mathbf{Y}}|^2$$

$$= \frac{\sqrt{b'b}}{|\mathcal{X}|} \sum_{\mathbf{X} \in \mathcal{X}} 1 + \frac{\sqrt{b'b}}{|\mathcal{Y}|} \sum_{\mathbf{Y} \in \mathcal{Y}} 1$$

$$\leq 2\sqrt{bb'}.$$

$\square$

A.6   Black-Boxes for Group Computations

We mentioned in Sections 7.3 and 7.4 that the order-finding and discrete logarithm algorithms would also work with 'black-box groups' (with unique encodings).

One natural quantum version of the black-box group model is to assume we have a black-box that implements the unitary map U_M that implements the group multiplication $|a\rangle|c\rangle \mapsto |a\rangle|ca\rangle$, where for any group element g, we let $|g\rangle$ denote the unique quantum encoding of the group element g. We assume we can also implement U_M^{-1}, which maps $|a\rangle|c\rangle \mapsto |a\rangle|ca^{-1}\rangle$. Thus $U_M^{-1}|a\rangle|a\rangle = |a\rangle|1\rangle$, which

---

[6] Note that $(\frac{a}{r} - rb)^2 \geq 0$.

means we have a means for computing the identity element, given two copies of a given group element. Further, $U_M^{-1}|a\rangle|1\rangle = |a\rangle|a^{-1}\rangle$, so we can compute inverses if we have the identity element.

If the unique encodings are unique strings of some fixed length n (which we will assume here), then the black-box U_M is all we need to perform the standard black-box group operations (multiplication, inverse, and recognizing the identity). Otherwise, we would need an explicit black-box for computing inverses and recognizing the identity.

Another natural quantum version of the black-box group model is to assume we have a black-box that implements the unitary map U_M' that implements the group multiplication $|a\rangle|c\rangle|y\rangle \mapsto |a\rangle|c\rangle|y \oplus ca\rangle$ by XOR-ing the string representing the product ac into the 3rd register. Such a black-box can be derived by standard methods (see Section 1.5 on reversible computing) from a classical circuit that maps inputs a and c to the output ac, without any understanding of the inner workings of the circuit. The previous black-box cannot in general be efficiently derived from a classical circuit for computing ac by such generic methods. So in some sense U_M' is a weaker black-box than U_M. For example, given U_M' one cannot in general efficiently derive a circuit that multiplies by a^{-1}. This also means that it will in general be no harder (and sometimes easier) to find situations where we can construct a black-box for U_M', than for U_M.

In Sections 7.3 and 7.4, we discuss two such types of black-boxes that perform the group operations. Note that in the following black-boxes we 'hard-wire' the group element a into the definition of the black-boxes:

- The first type of black-box for exponentiation was derived from a multiplication black-box that maps $|c\rangle \mapsto |ca\rangle$, for any group element c, and assuming we are given the identity element. The analogous exponentiation circuit implements the map c-$U_a^x : |x\rangle|c\rangle \mapsto |x\rangle|ca^x\rangle$. The algorithm in Section 7.3.3 uses this exponentiation circuit as a black-box.
- The second type of black-box for exponentiation can be derived from a multiplication black-box that maps $|c\rangle|y\rangle \mapsto |c\rangle|y \oplus ca\rangle$, where c is any group element, and y is any bit-string of length n. The analogous exponentiation circuits implement the maps $V_a : |x\rangle|y\rangle \mapsto |x\rangle|y \oplus a^x\rangle$ and $V_{a,b} : |x\rangle|y\rangle|z\rangle \mapsto |x\rangle|y\rangle|z \oplus a^x b^y\rangle$. We noted in Sections 7.3.4 and 7.4 that the states in Equation 7.3.15 (equivalently Equation 7.3.14) and Equation 7.4.4 could alternatively have been created using V_a and $V_{a,b}$, respectively.

The black-boxes c-U_a^x and c-U_b^x together with the identity element are at least as strong as V_a and $V_{a,b}$, since we can implement V_a using two queries of c-U_a^x, and we can implement $V_{a,b}$ using two queries of c-U_a^x and two queries of c-U_b^x. However, c-U_a^x and c-U_b^x cannot in general be simulated by the black-boxes V_a and $V_{a,b}$.

Exercise A.6.1

(a) Show how to simulate V_a using two applications of c-U_a^x and one copy of the identity element.

(b) Show how to simulate $V_{a,b}$ using two applications of c-U_a^x and two applications of c-U_b^x and one copy of the identity element.

In Exercise 7.3.7, we see that order finding is a special case of the more general problem of finding the period of a periodic function. In the exercise, we introduced a black-box U_f that maps $|x\rangle|0\rangle \mapsto |x\rangle|f(x)\rangle$. Note that any black-box that allows us to create the state $\sum |x\rangle|f(x)\rangle$ will work.

In analogy with the two exponentiation black-boxes above, we could define two types of black-boxes for computing f.

- The black-box for f that is analogous with c-U_a^x is one that maps $|x\rangle|f(y)\rangle \mapsto |x\rangle|f(y+x)\rangle$. Such a black-box for f is natural to implement when $f(x) = a^x \bmod N$. However, for other periodic functions it might not be so straightforward. In such cases, it might still be useful to talk about such a black-box for the purposes of analysing the algorithm.
- The black-box for f that is analogous with V_a is one that maps $|x\rangle|y\rangle \mapsto |x\rangle|y \oplus f(x)\rangle$. Such a black-box is easy to implement given a classical circuit for computing $f(x)$ (using standard techniques for making a circuit reversible; see Section 1.5).

Just as the order-finding problem is a special case of the period-finding problem, we can treat the discrete logarithm algorithm as a special case of the following problem.

Generalization of Discrete Logarithm Problem

Input: A black-box U_f that computes a function $f : Z_r \times Z_r \to X$ with the following property:

$$f(x_1, y_1) = f(x_2, y_2) \Leftrightarrow y_1 - y_2 = t(x_1 - x_2) \bmod r \qquad \text{(A.6.1)}$$

for some fixed integer t.
Problem: Find t.

Note that Equation A.6.1 is equivalent to

$$f(x_1, y_1) = f(x_2, y_2) \leftrightarrow (x_1, y_1) - (x_2, y_2) \in \langle(1, -t)\rangle.$$

We can assume the black-box U_f maps $|x\rangle|y\rangle|z\rangle \mapsto |x\rangle|y\rangle|z \oplus f(x, y)\rangle$, which would be easy to implement if $f(x, y) = a^x b^y$ for elements a and b in some group

G with unique encodings and in which we can multiply efficiently. We would apply this black-box to the state $\sum |x\rangle|y\rangle|0\rangle$ to create the state $\sum |x\rangle|y\rangle|f(x,y)\rangle$, and then apply $\text{QFT}_r^{-1} \otimes \text{QFT}_r^{-1}$ (or approximations of them) to the control registers, followed by measurements of the control registers. The measured values will be of the form k and $kt \bmod r$ for a random integer k.

However, a black-box U'_f that maps $|x_1, y_1\rangle|f(x_2, y_2)\rangle \mapsto |x_1, y_1\rangle|f(x_2+x_1, y_2+y_1)\rangle$ would also work (if we are given $|f(0,0)\rangle$, and we apply the black box to the state $\sum |x\rangle|y\rangle|f(0,0)\rangle$). The black-box U'_f can be implemented efficiently in the case that $f(x,y) = a^x b^y$ for elements a and b in some group G with unique encodings in which we can multiply efficiently.

The generalized discrete logarithm algorithm described above will output a pair of integers $(kt \bmod r, k \bmod r)$ for $k \in \{0, 1, \ldots, r-1\}$ distributed uniformly at random. In order to find r, we can proceed with an analysis analogous to any of those detailed in Appendix A.2, which deals with the special case that $f(x,y) = a^x b^y$ for elements a, b from some group. In order to see how to apply those techniques to the generalized discrete logarithm problem, note that running the discrete logarithm algorithm with new values $a_1 = a^c$ and $b_1 = b^c$ for some integer c corresponds to running the generalized discrete logarithm algorithm for the function $f_1(x,y) = f(cx, cy)$. Also note that running the discrete logarithm algorithm with new values $b_2 = ba^{-c}$ and $a_2 = a^r$ corresponds to running the generalized discrete logarithm algorithm for the function $f_2(x,y) = f(rx - cy, y)$.

A.7 Computing Schmidt Decompositions

We present a simple method for computing Schmidt decompositions, based on the observation at the end of Section 3.5.2 that the reduced density operators are diagonal in the Schmidt bases. The approach is to compute the partial trace for either one of the subsystems, and diagonalize it in order to find a Schmidt basis for that subsystem. We illustrate this process through an example. Consider the two-qubit state

$$|\psi\rangle = \left(\tfrac{\sqrt{3}-\sqrt{2}}{2\sqrt{6}}\right)|00\rangle + \left(\tfrac{\sqrt{6}+1}{2\sqrt{6}}\right)|01\rangle + \left(\tfrac{\sqrt{3}+\sqrt{2}}{2\sqrt{6}}\right)|10\rangle + \left(\tfrac{\sqrt{6}-1}{2\sqrt{6}}\right)|11\rangle. \quad \text{(A.7.1)}$$

Tracing the second qubit out of the density operator, we get the reduced density operator for the first qubit

$$\text{Tr}_2|\psi\rangle\langle\psi| = \tfrac{1}{2}|0\rangle\langle0| + \tfrac{1}{4}|0\rangle\langle1| + \tfrac{1}{4}|1\rangle\langle0| + \tfrac{1}{2}|1\rangle\langle1|. \quad \text{(A.7.2)}$$

In terms of the matrix representation, this looks like

$$\begin{bmatrix} \tfrac{1}{2} & \tfrac{1}{4} \\ \tfrac{1}{4} & \tfrac{1}{2} \end{bmatrix}. \quad \text{(A.7.3)}$$

To diagonalize this matrix, we find the characteristic polynomial

$$\left(\tfrac{1}{2} - \lambda\right)^2 - \tfrac{1}{16} = \lambda^2 - \lambda + \tfrac{3}{16} \tag{A.7.4}$$

and see that its roots are $\tfrac{1}{4}$ and $\tfrac{3}{4}$. These are the eigenvalues of the reduced density matrix. The eigenvectors are computed as follows. The eigenvalue equation corresponding to the eigenvalue $\tfrac{1}{4}$ is

$$\begin{bmatrix} \tfrac{1}{2} & \tfrac{1}{4} \\ \tfrac{1}{4} & \tfrac{1}{2} \end{bmatrix} \begin{pmatrix} x_1 \\ y_1 \end{pmatrix} = \tfrac{1}{4} \begin{pmatrix} x_1 \\ y_1 \end{pmatrix}. \tag{A.7.5}$$

Solving gives $x = -y$. We want the normalized eigenvector (since it is to represent a quantum state vector), so we solve $x = -y$ together with $x^2 + y^2 = 1$, obtaining the eigenvector

$$\begin{pmatrix} x_1 \\ y_1 \end{pmatrix} = \begin{pmatrix} \tfrac{1}{\sqrt{2}} \\ -\tfrac{1}{\sqrt{2}} \end{pmatrix}. \tag{A.7.6}$$

Similarly, the normalized eigenvector corresponding to eigenvalue $\tfrac{3}{4}$ is

$$\begin{pmatrix} x_2 \\ y_2 \end{pmatrix} = \begin{pmatrix} \tfrac{1}{\sqrt{2}} \\ \tfrac{1}{\sqrt{2}} \end{pmatrix}. \tag{A.7.7}$$

In terms of the Dirac notation, these are

$$|-\rangle = \tfrac{1}{\sqrt{2}}\left(|0\rangle - |1\rangle\right) \tag{A.7.8}$$

and

$$|+\rangle = \tfrac{1}{\sqrt{2}}\left(|0\rangle + |1\rangle\right). \tag{A.7.9}$$

Recall our earlier observation that density operators are normal operators. Therefore, the spectral theorem of Section 2.4 applies, and the eigenvectors form an orthonormal basis. We take the eigenvectors computed above to be the Schmidt basis vectors for the first subsystem.

The state $|\psi\rangle$ was originally given to us in the 2-qubit computational basis. To write $|\psi\rangle$ in Schmidt form, we simply perform a change of basis on the first system from the computational basis to the Schmidt basis we just found. The Schmidt basis for the second system will become apparent once we have a Schmidt basis for the first system. The state written in Schmidt form is

$$|\psi\rangle = \tfrac{\sqrt{3}}{2}|+\rangle \left(\tfrac{1}{\sqrt{3}}|0\rangle + \sqrt{\tfrac{2}{3}}|1\rangle\right) + \tfrac{1}{2}|-\rangle \left(-\sqrt{\tfrac{2}{3}}|0\rangle + \tfrac{1}{\sqrt{3}}|1\rangle\right). \tag{A.7.10}$$

Exercise A.7.1 Verify Equation (A.7.10).

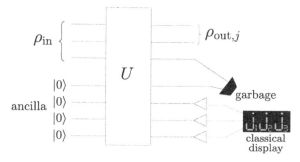

Fig. A.8.1 A very general kind of quantum map that involves adding an ancilla system, unitarily evolving the joint system, extracting some classical information, keeping part of the joint system as a quantum output of the map, and discarding the rest of the system. Such a general quantum map can be derived by combining the operations described in Chapter 3.

A.8   General Measurements

In this section we describe more general notions of measurement that can be derived from the Measurement Postulate. We will explain the notions using circuit diagrams, which are introduced in Chapter 4. We will also use the notions of mixed states, density matrices, and partial trace that are introduced in Section 3.5.

In Section 3.5.3 we characterize the most general kind of quantum operation possible that do not involve extracting information via a measurement.[7] Of course, one could describe an even more general type of quantum map (depicted in Figure A.8.1) that does include measurements, which output non-trivial 'classical' information and therefore involves some renormalization[8] of the remaining quantum state that depends on the classical measurement outcome. There is a variety of literature on these kinds of general quantum operations, which are often referred to as 'quantum channels' or 'quantum instruments', depending on the precise details of the operations. For this introductory textbook, we do not need to delve into the many possible ways of characterizing and categorizing such very general quantum operations. Instead we will focus on creating familiarity with more simple but universal[9] quantum operations.

We give an example of a more general measurement operation. This kind of measurement can be referred to as a 'pure' measurement, since if a pure state is

---

[7]It is worth noting that sometimes we might refer to a measurement where one discards or ignores or is not told the (classical) measurement outcome. In such a case one usually describes the state of the quantum system as a weighted mixture of the possible post-measurement outcomes. This type of measurement *does* fall under this category of general quantum operations since we are not actually extracting information about the state of the system.

[8]Alternatively, some mathematical treatments of general quantum operations will leave the state unnormalized.

[9]These simple operations are 'universal' in the sense that the more general quantum operations can be constructed by composing the simple operations in a natural way.

measured, the resulting state, after renormalization depending on the classical measurement outcome, is again a pure state.

Suppose we want to measure some property of a quantum system of dimension N (e.g. a register of n-qubits with $N = 2^n$). We can add an ancilla of arbitrary dimension, say $L = 2^l$, initialized to

$$|0\rangle^l \equiv \underbrace{|0\rangle|0\rangle \dots |0\rangle}_{l}, \tag{A.8.1}$$

and apply *any* unitary U to the joint (NL-dimensional) state $|0\rangle^l|\psi\rangle$ and then perform a Von Neumann measurement on the ancilla system obtain a label 'i'.

In order to derive the standard mathematical formulation of this kind of measurement, notice that the matrix U can be decomposed in block form as

$$\begin{bmatrix} M_{0,0} & M_{0,1} & \cdots & M_{0,L-1} \\ M_{1,0} & M_{1,1} & \cdots & M_{1,L-1} \\ \vdots & \vdots & \ddots & \vdots \\ M_{L-1,0} & M_{L-1,1} & \cdots & M_{L-1,L-1} \end{bmatrix} \tag{A.8.2}$$

where each submatrix $M_{i,j}$ has dimension $N \times N$. Recalling how to take tensor products for matrices from Section 2.6, we can write $|0\rangle^l|\psi\rangle$ as a column matrix in block form as

$$\begin{bmatrix} [|\psi\rangle] \\ [0^N] \\ \vdots \\ [0^N] \end{bmatrix} \tag{A.8.3}$$

where $[|\psi\rangle]$ denotes the N-dimensional column vector representation of the state $|\psi\rangle$ and $[0^N]$ is an N-dimensional column vector of all 0's.

Considering the action of U on the state $|0\rangle^l|\psi\rangle$ as a matrix multiplication of the matrix in Equation (A.8.2) by the vector in Equation (A.8.3), it can be seen that only the first column of matrix (A.8.2) is significant. The matrix multiplication gives

$$U|0\rangle^l|\psi\rangle = \sum_{j=0}^{L-1} |j\rangle M_{j,0}|\psi\rangle. \tag{A.8.4}$$

When we write $|j\rangle$ as above, the label j refers to the l-bit binary representation of the index j (so $|j\rangle$ is an l-qubit state). Renormalizing[10] the $M_{j,0}|\psi\rangle$ terms[11]

$$U|0\rangle^l|\psi\rangle = \sum_{j=0}^{L-1} \sqrt{p(j)}|j\rangle \frac{M_{j,0}|\psi\rangle}{\sqrt{p(j)}} \tag{A.8.5}$$

---

[10] By *renormalizing* a non-zero vector $|\phi\rangle$ which might not have norm 1, we mean multiplying $|\phi\rangle$ by $\frac{1}{\sqrt{\langle\phi|\phi\rangle}}$ so that it is a state vector with norm 1.

[11] If any of the terms $M_{j,0}|\psi\rangle$ have norm 0, then $p(j) = 0$, which means we never measure j. We can thus just exclude those j from the summation.

where

$$p(j) = \langle\psi|M_{j,0}^\dagger M_{j,0}|\psi\rangle. \qquad (A.8.6)$$

Notice that the unitarity of U guarantees that

$$\sum_{j=0}^{L-1} M_{j,0}^\dagger M_{j,0} = I. \qquad (A.8.7)$$

Now if we measure the first register, we get the result 'j' with probability $p(j)$, and are left with the state

$$|j\rangle \otimes \frac{M_{j,0}|\psi\rangle}{\sqrt{p(j)}}. \qquad (A.8.8)$$

We can discard the quantum state $|j\rangle$ of the system we measured, and be left with $\frac{M_{j,0}|\psi\rangle}{\sqrt{p(j)}}$.

We could in general measure any subsystem of the joint system, and remove the restriction that the $M_{j,0}$ are square. If we measure a subsystem of dimension $\frac{NL}{D}$ (we assume NL is divisible by D), then the $M_{j,0}$ have dimension $D \times N$, and the resulting quantum state will have dimension D (after we discard the register we measured). We can summarize this more general measurement procedure in the following way.

General (Pure) Measurements

Consider a set of operators $\{M_i\}$, mapping a state space $\mathcal{H}$ of dimension N to a state space $\mathcal{H}'$ of dimension D, that satisfy the completeness equation,

$$\sum_i M_i^\dagger M_i = I. \qquad (A.8.9)$$

The indices 'i' label the possible measurement outcomes. For any such set of measurement operators $\{M_i\}$ it is possible to perform a quantum measurement that takes input state $|\psi\rangle$ and with probability

$$p(i) = \langle\psi|M_i^\dagger M_i|\psi\rangle, \qquad (A.8.10)$$

outputs outcome 'i' and leaves the system in state

$$\frac{M_i|\psi\rangle}{\sqrt{p(i)}}. \qquad (A.8.11)$$

Note that the completeness equation (A.8.9) guarantees that the probabilities $p(i)$ always sum to one. If $p(i) = 0$, we never get the outcome 'i' and we do not need to worry about renormalizing the state $M_i|\psi\rangle$.

A projective measurement with respect to the decomposition $I = \sum_i P_i$ is a special case of a projective measurement where $M_i = P_i$, and thus $M_i^\dagger M_i = P_i$.

As we mentioned at the beginning of this appendix, one could discard some or all of the remaining quantum state after a measurement. When we discard the entire remaining quantum state, this corresponds to a 'POVM measurement'. Note that such a measurement would be characterized solely by the positive operators[12] $E_i = M_i^\dagger M_i$. Conversely, for any positive operators E_i (not necessarily orthogonal projections) that sum to the identity, there exists operators M_i satisfying $E_i = M_i^\dagger M_i$. Thus a POVM measurement with respect to the operators $\{E_i\}$ is realizable by a general pure measurement described above.

A.9   Optimal Distinguishing of Two States

In this Appendix, we detail an optimal procedure for solving the following state distinguishability problem.

Distinguishing Two Pure Quantum States with Minimum Error

Input: One of two known states $|\psi_\mathbf{X}\rangle$ or $|\psi_\mathbf{Y}\rangle$, with the property that $|\langle\psi_\mathbf{X}|\psi_\mathbf{Y}\rangle| = \delta$.
Output: A guess '$\mathbf{X}$' or '$\mathbf{Y}$'.
Problem: Maximize the probability $1 - \epsilon$ that the guess is correct.

A.9.1   A Simple Procedure

We can first implement a unitary operation that maps $|\psi_\mathbf{X}\rangle \mapsto |\phi_x\rangle = \cos(\theta)|0\rangle + \sin(\theta)|1\rangle$ and $|\psi_\mathbf{Y}\rangle \mapsto |\phi_y\rangle = \sin(\theta)|0\rangle + \cos(\theta)|1\rangle$, where θ is chosen so that $0 \leq \theta \leq \frac{\pi}{4}$ and $\sin(2\theta) = \delta = \langle\phi_x|\phi_y\rangle$.

Since $\cos(\theta) \geq \frac{1}{2}$, a natural procedure (illustrated in Figure A.9.1) is to measure the state in the computational basis, and output '$\mathbf{X}$' if the measured value is 0 and output '$\mathbf{Y}$' if the measured value is 1. Such a procedure will output the correct answer, regardless of the input, with probability $\cos^2(\theta)$. Setting $1 - \epsilon = \cos^2(\theta)$ gives us $\epsilon = \sin^2(\theta)$. This relationship between ϵ and δ can be rewritten as $\epsilon = \frac{1}{2} - \frac{1}{2}\sqrt{1 - \delta^2}$, which implies that $\delta = 2\sqrt{\epsilon(1 - \epsilon)}$.

A.9.2   Optimality of This Simple Procedure

We now show that we cannot do any better than the above simple procedure. In other words, the best estimation procedure can guess correctly in the worst case with probability no higher than the $\frac{1}{2} + \frac{1}{2}\sqrt{1 - \delta^2}$.

Any measurement can be realized by adding an ancilla to the input state, performing a unitary operation U on the whole system, and measuring the first qubit of the whole system. If the output is 0 guess '$\mathbf{X}$' and if the output is 1 guess '$\mathbf{Y}$'.

---

[12]Since the operators sum to the identity, they correspond to a measure (called a 'Positive Operator Valued Measure') on the space of density matrices. A measurement corresponding to this measure is thus traditionally called a POVM measurement.

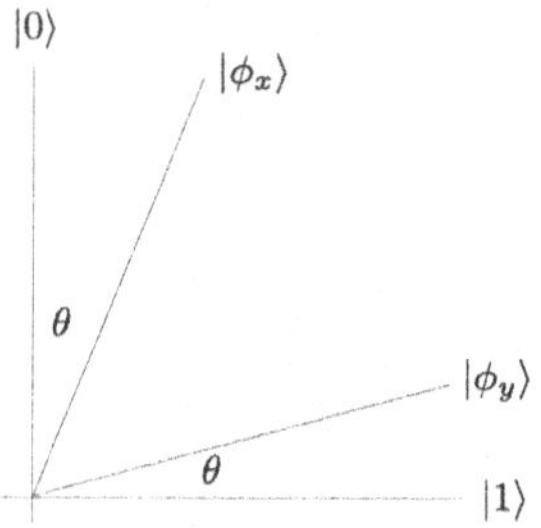

Fig. A.9.1 This diagram illustrates a simple Von Neumann measurement for distinguishing $|\phi_x\rangle$ and $|\phi_y\rangle$. The probability of guessing correctly is $\cos^2(\theta)$ where $\langle\phi_x|\phi_y\rangle = \sin(2\theta)$. No other procedure can achieve a higher correctness probability.

Suppose

$$U|\psi_{\mathbf{X}}\rangle|00\ldots0\rangle = \sqrt{1-\epsilon_x}|0\rangle|\text{junk}(x,0)\rangle + \sqrt{\epsilon_x}|1\rangle|\text{junk}(x,1)\rangle$$

and

$$U|\psi_{\mathbf{Y}}\rangle|00\ldots0\rangle = \sqrt{\epsilon_y}|0\rangle|\text{junk}(y,0)\rangle + \sqrt{1-\epsilon_y}|1\rangle|\text{junk}(y,1)\rangle.$$

In other words, the algorithm correctly recognizes $|\psi_{\mathbf{X}}\rangle$ with probability $1-\epsilon_x$ and correctly recognizes $|\psi_{\mathbf{Y}}\rangle$ with probability $1-\epsilon_y$. The worst-case success probability is $1-\epsilon$ where $\epsilon = \max(\epsilon_x, \epsilon_y)$.

We also have the property that

$$\delta = |\langle\psi_{\mathbf{X}}|\psi_{\mathbf{Y}}\rangle| = |\langle\psi_{\mathbf{X}}|\langle00\ldots0|U^\dagger U|\psi_{\mathbf{Y}}\rangle|00\ldots0\rangle| \qquad (A.9.1)$$

$$= \left|\sqrt{(1-\epsilon_x)\epsilon_y}\langle\text{junk}(x,0)|\text{junk}(y,0)\rangle + \sqrt{(1-\epsilon_y)\epsilon_x}\langle\text{junk}(x,1)|\text{junk}(y,1)\rangle\right|.$$

$$(A.9.2)$$

This implies that

$$\delta \leq \sqrt{(1-\epsilon_x)\epsilon_y} + \sqrt{(1-\epsilon_y)\epsilon_x}.$$

We wish to find the smallest value of $\epsilon = \max(\epsilon_x, \epsilon_y)$ allowed by the above inequality. It is easy to show that the optimum is achieved when $\epsilon = \epsilon_x = \epsilon_y = \frac{1}{2} - \frac{1}{2}\sqrt{1-\delta^2}$.

Theorem A.9.1 *Any procedure that on input $|\psi_{\mathbf{Z}}\rangle$ guesses whether $\mathbf{Z} = \mathbf{X}$ or $\mathbf{Z} = \mathbf{Y}$ will guess correctly with probability at most $1-\epsilon = \frac{1}{2} + \frac{1}{2}\sqrt{1-\delta^2}$, where $\delta = |\langle\psi_{\mathbf{X}}|\psi_{\mathbf{Y}}\rangle|$. This probability is achievable by an optimal measurement.*

Bibliography

[] **Note:** *'arXiv e-print' refers to the electronic archive of papers, available at http://www.arxiv.org/.*

[Aar] S. Aaronson. 'Complexity Zoo'. `http://qwiki.caltech.edu/wiki/Complexity_Zoo`

[Aar05] S. Aaronson. 'Quantum Computing, Postselection, and Probabilistic Polynomial-Time'. *Proceedings of the Royal Society of London A*, 461:3473–3482, 2005.

[AAKV01] D. Aharonov, A. Ambainis, J. Kempe, and U. Vazirani. 'Quantum Walks On Graphs'. *Proceedings of ACM Symposium on Theory of Computation (STOC'01)*, 50–59, 2001.

[ABNVW01] A. Ambainis, E. Bach, A. Nayak, A. Vishwanath, and J. Watrous. 'One-Dimensional Quantum Walks'. *Proceedings of the 33rd ACM Symposium on Theory of Computing*, 37-49, 2001.

[ABO97] D. Aharonov, and M. Ben-Or. 'Fault Tolerant Quantum Computation with Constant Error'. *Proceedings of the 29th Annual ACM Symposium on the Theory of Computing (STOC'97)*, 1997. *Also arXiv e-print quant-ph/9611025.*

[ADH97] L. Adleman, J, Demarrais, and M.D. Huang. 'Quantum Computability'. *SIAM Journal on Computing*, 26(5):1524–1540, 1997.

[ADKLLR04] D. Aharonov, W. van Dam, J. Kempe, Z. Landau, S. Lloyd, and O. Regev. 'Adiabatic Quantum Computation Is Equivalent to Standard Quantum Computation.' *Proceedings of the 45th Annual IEEE Symposium on Foundations of Computer Science (FOCS'04)*, 42–51, 2004.

[AHU74] Alfred V. Aho, John E. Hopcroft, and Jeffrey D. Ullman. '*The Design and Analysis of Computer Algorithms*'. (Addison-Wesley, Reading, MA, 1974).

[AKN98] D. Aharonov, A. Kitaev, and N. Nisan. 'Quantum Circuits with Mixed States'. *Proceedings of the 31st Annual ACM Symposium on the Theory of Computation (STOC'98)*, 20–30, 1998.

[Amb02] A. Ambainis. 'Quantum Lower Bounds by Quantum Arguments'. *J. Comput. Syst. Sci.* 64:750–767, 2002.

[Amb04] A. Ambainis. 'Quantum Walk Algorithm for Element Distinctness'. *Proceedings of the 45th Annual IEEE Symposium on Foundations of Computer Science (FOCS'04)*, 22–31, 2004.

[AR05] D. Aharonov and O. Regev. 'Lattice Problems in NP Intersect coNP'. *Journal of the ACM* 52:749–765, 2005.

[AVZ05] Dorit Aharonov, Vaughan Jones, and Zeph Landau. 'A Polynomial Quantum Algorithm for Approximating the Jones Polynomial'. *Proceedings of the thirty-eighth annual ACM symposium on Theory of computing (STOC'06)*, 427–436, 2006.

[BBBV97] Charles H. Bennett, Ethan Bernstein, Gilles Brassard, and Umesh Vazirani. 'Strengths and Weaknesses of Quantum Computing'. *SIAM Journal on Computing*, 26:1510–1523, 1997.

[BBC+95] Adriano Barenco, Charles H. Bennett, Richard Cleve, David P. DiVincenzo, Norman Margolus, Peter Shor, Tycho Sleator, John Smolin, and Harald Weinfurter. 'Elementary Gates for Quantum Computation'. *Physical Review A*, 52(5):3457–3467, 1995.

[BBC+98] Robert Beals, Harry Buhrman, Richard Cleve, Michele Mosca, and Ronald de Wolf. 'Quantum Lower Bounds by Polynomials'. *Journal of the ACM (2001)*, 48(4): 778–797.

[BBCJPW93] Charles Bennett, Gilles Brassard, Claude Crepeau, Richard Josza, Asher Peres, and William Wootters. 'Teleporting an Unknown Quantum State via Dual Classical and Einstein-Podolsky-Rosen Channels'. *Physical Review Letters*, 70:1895–1898, 1993.

[BBD+97] A. Barenco, A. Berthiaume, D. Deutsch, A. Ekert, R. Jozsa, and C. Macchiavello. 'Stabilization of Quantum Computations by Symmetrization'. *SIAM Journal on Computing*, 26(5):1541–1557, 1997.

[BBHT98] Michel Boyer, Gilles Brassard, Peter Høyer, and Alain Tapp, 'Tight Bounds on Quantum Searching'. *Fortschritte der Physik* 56(5–5):493–505, 1988.

[BBPS95] Charles Bennett, Herbert Bernstein, Sandu Popescu, and Benjamin Schumacher. 'Concentrating Partial Entanglement by Local Operations'. *Phys. Rev. A*, 53:2046, 1996.

[BCD05] D. Bacon, A. Childs, and W. van Dam. 'From Optimal Measurement to Efficient Quantum Algorithms for the Hidden Subgroup Problem over Semidirect Product Groups'. *Proc. 46th IEEE Symposium on Foundations of Computer Science (FOCS 2005)*, 469–478, 2005.

[BCW98] Harry Buhrman, Richard Cleve, and Avi Wigderson. 'Quantum vs. Classical Communication and Computation'. *Proceedings of the 30th Annual ACM Symposium on Theory of Computing (STOC 1998)*, 63–68, 1998.

[BDEJ95] Adriano Barenco, David Deutsch, Artur Ekert, and Richard Jozsa. 'Conditional Quantum Dynamics and Quantum Gates'. *Physical Review Letters*, 74:4083–4086, 1995.

[BDHHMSW05] H. Buhrman, C. Durr, M. Heiligman, P. Høyer, F. Magniez, M. Santha, and R. de Wolf. 'Quantum Algorithms for Element Distinctness'. *SIAM J. Comput.*, 34:1324–1330, 2005.

[Bea97] Robert Beals. 'Quantum Computation of Fourier Transforms over Symmetric Groups'. *Proceedings of the 29th Annual ACM Symposium on Theory of Computing (STOC'97)*, 48–53, 1997.

[Ben73]   Charles H. Bennett. 'Logical Reversibility of Computation'. *IBM Journal of Research and Development*, 17:525–532, November 1973.

[Ben89]   Charles H. Bennett. 'Time/Space Trade-offs for Reversible Computing'. *SIAM Journal on Computing*, 18(4):766–776, 1989.

[Beth87a]   Thomas Beth., 'On the Computational Complexity of the General Discrete Fourier Transform'. *Theoretical Computer Science*, 51:331–339, 1987.

[Beth87b]   Thomas Beth. 'Generalized Fourier Transforms'. *Trends in Computer Algebra*, 92–118, 1987.

[BH97]   Gilles Brassard and Peter Høyer. 'An Exact Quantum Polynomial-Time Algorithm for Simon's Problem'. *Proceedings of Fifth Israeli Symposium on Theory of Computing and Systems*, IEEE Computer Society Press, 12–23, 1997.

[BHMT00]   Gilles Brassard, Peter Høyer, Michele Mosca, and Alain Tapp. 'Quantum Amplitude Amplification and Estimation'. In S.J. Lomonaco, Jr., H.E. Randt, editors, *Quantum Computation and Information, Contemporary Mathematics 305* (Providence, RI: AMS 2002), pp. 53–74.

[BHT97]   G. Brassard, P. Høyer, and Alain Tapp. 'Cryptology Column—Quantum Algorithm for the Collision Problem'. *ACM SIGACT News*, 28: 14–19, 1997.

[BHT98]   Gilles Brassard, Peter Høyer, and Alain Tapp. 'Quantum Counting'. *Proceedings of the ICALP'98 Lecture Notes in Computer Science*, 1820–1831, 1988.

[BL95]   D. Boneh and R.J. Lipton. 'Quantum Cryptanalysis of Hidden Linear Functions' (Extended Abstract). *Lecture Notes in Computer Science*, 1443:820–831, Springer-Verlag, 1998.

[BMP+99]   P. Boykin, T. Mor, M. Pulver, V. Roychowdhury, and F. Vatan. 'On Universal and fault-tolerant quantum computing: a novel basis and a new constructive proof of universality for Shor's basis'. *Proceedings of the 40th Annual Symposium on Foundations of the Computer Science*, 486–494, 1999.

[Br03]   Michael Brown. 'Classical Cryptosystems in a Quantum Setting'. *MMath Thesis*. University of Waterloo, 2003.

[Buh96]   H. Buhrman. 'A Short Note on Shor's Factoring Algorithm'. *SIGACT News*, 27(1):89–90, 1996.

[BV97]   Ethan Bernstein and Umesh Vazirani. 'Quantum Complexity Theory'. *SIAM Journal on Computing*, 26(5):1411–1473, October 1997.

[CDV96]   Richard Cleve and David P. DiVincenzo. 'Schumacher's Quantum Data Compression As a Quantum Computation'. *Physical Review A*, 54(4):2636–2650, 1996.

[CEG95]   Ran Canetti, Guy Even, and Oded Goldreich. 'Lower Bounds for Sampling Algorithms for Estimating the Average'. *Information Processing Letters*, 53:17–25,1995.

[CEH+99]   Richard Cleve, Artur Ekert, Leah Henderson, Chiara Macchiavello, and Michele Mosca. 'On Quantum Algorithms'. *Complexity*, 4:33–42, 1999.

[CEMM98] Richard Cleve, Artur Ekert, Chiara Macchiavello, and Michele Mosca. 'Quantum Algorithms Revisited'. *Proceedings of the Royal Society of London A*, 454:339–354, 1998.

[Che02] Donny Cheung. 'Using Generalized Quantum Fourier Transforms in Quantum Phase Estimation Algorithms'. *MMath Thesis*. University of Waterloo, 2002.

[Chu36] A. Church. 'An unsolvable Problem of Elementary Number Theory'. *Am. J. Math.*, 58:345, 1936.

[Cla] http://www.claymath.org/millennium/P_ vs _ NP/

[Cle00] Richard Cleve, "The Query Complexity of Order-Finding". *IEEE Conference of Computational Complexity*, 54–, 2000.

[Cle99] Richard Cleve. 'An Introduction to Quantum Complexity Theory'. In C. Macchiavello, G.M. Palma, and A. Zeilinger, editors, *Collected Papers on Quantum Computation and Quantum Information Theory* (World Scientific, 1999).

[CM01] K.K.H. Cheung and M. Mosca. 'Decomposing Finite Abelian Groups'. *Quantum Information and Computation*, 1(3):2632, 2001.

[Coc73] C. Cocks. 'A Note on Non-Secret Encryption'. *Technical report, Communications-Electronics Security Group*, U.K., 1973. *Available at http://www.cesg.gov.uk/downlds/nsecret/notense.pdf*

[Coh93] Henry Cohen. '*A Course in Computational Algebraic Number Theory*' (Springer-Verlag, 1993).

[Coo71] S.A. Cook. 'The Complexity of Theorem Proving Procedures'. *Proceedings of the 3rd Annual ACM Symposium on the Theory of Computing (STOC'71)*, 151–158, 1971.

[Cop94] Don Coppersmith. 'An Approximate Fourier Transform Useful in Quantum Factoring'. Research report, IBM, 1994.

[CRR054] Sourav Chakraborty, Jaikumar Radhakrishnan, and Nandakumar Raghunathan. 'Bounds for Error Reduction with Few Quantum Queries'. *APPROX-RANDOM 2005*, 245–256, 2005.

[CS96] A.R.Calderbank and P.W. Shor. 'Good Quantum Error-Correcting Codes Exist'. *Physical Review A*, 54:1098–1105, 1996.

[CTDL77] Claude Cohen-Tannoudji, Bernard Diu, and Franck Laloe. *Quantum Mechanics*, Volume 1 (John Wiley and Sons, 1977).

[Dav82] Martin Davis. *Computability and Unsolvability* (Dover Publications Inc., New York, 1982).

[Deu85] David Deutsch. 'Quantum Theory, the Church-Turing Principle and the Universal Quantum Computer'. *Proceedings of the Royal Society of London A*, 400:97–117, 1985.

[Deu89] David Deutsch. 'Quantum Computational Networks'. *Proceedings of the Royal Society of London A*, 425:73–90,1989.

[DH76a] W. Diffie and M.E. Hellman. 'Multiuser Cryptographic Techniques'. *Proceedings of AFIPS National Computer Conference*, 109–112, 1976.

[DH76b] W. Diffie and M.E. Hellman. 'New Directions in Cryptography'. *IEEE Transactions on Information Theory*, 22:644–654, 1976.

[DH00] W. van Dam and S. Hallgren. 'Efficient Quantum Algorithms for Shifted Quadratic Character Problems'. *Proceedings of the Fourteenth Annual ACM-SIAM Symposium on Discrete Algorithms*, 489–498, 2003.

[DHHM04] C. Durr, M. Heiligman, P. Høyer, and M. Mhalla. 'Quantum Query Complexity of Some Graph Problems'. *Proc. of 31st International Colloquium on Automata, Languages, and Programming (ICALP'04)*, 481–493, 2004.

[DHI03] W. van Dam, S. Hallgren, and L. Ip. 'Quantum Algorithms for Some Hidden Shift Problems'. *Proceedings of the ACM-SIAM Symposium on Discrete Algorithms (SODA'03)*, 489–498, 2003.

[Dir58] Paul A.M. Dirac. *'The Principles of Quantum Mechanics* (Clarendon Press, Oxford, 4th edition, 1958).

[DiV95] David DiVincenzo. 'Two-Bit Gates Are Universal for Quantum Computation'. *Physical Review A*, 51(2):1015–1022,1995.

[DJ92] David Deutsch and Richard Josza. 'Rapid Solution of Problems by Quantum Computation'. *Proceedings of the Royal Society of London A*, 439:553–558, 1992.

[DMV01] W. van Dam, M. Mosca, and U. Vazirani. 'How Powerful Is Adiabatic Quantum Computation?'. *Proc. 46th IEEE Symposium on Foundations of Computer Science (FOCS'01)*, 279–287, 2001.

[EH98] Mark Ettinger and Peter Høyer. 'On Quantum Algorithms for Noncommutative Hidden Subgroups'. *arXiv e-print quant-ph/9807029*, 1998.

[EHK04] M. Ettinger, P. Høyer, and E. Knill. 'The Quantum Query Complexity of the Hidden Subgroup Problem Is Polynomial'. *Inf. Process. Lett.*, 91:43–48, 2004.

[Ell70] J.H. Ellis. 'The Possibility of Non-Secret Encryption'. *Technical Report, Communications-Electronics Security Group*, U.K., 1970.
Available at *http://www.cesg.gov.uk/downloads/nsecret/possnse.pdf*

[Ell87] J.H. Ellis. 'The Story of Non-Secret Encryption'.
Technical report, Communications-Electronics Security Group, U.K., 1987.
Avialable at *http://www.cesg.gov.uk/downloads/nsecret/ellis.pdf*

[EPR35] A. Einstein, B. Podolsky, and N. Rosen. 'Can Quantum-Mechanical Description of Reality Be Considered Complete?' *Physical Review* 47:777–780, 1935.

[Fey65] Richard P. Feynman. *The Feynman Lectures on Physics, Volume III: Quantum Mechanics* (Addison-Wesley, 1965).

[Fey82] Richard Feynman. 'Simulating Physics with Computers'. *International Journal of Theortical Physics*, 21(6,7):467–488, 1982.

[FGGS98] E. Farhi, J. Goldstone, S. Gutmann, and M. Sipser. 'A Limit on the Speed of Quantum Computation in Determining Parity'. *Technical Report 9802045*, Los Alamos Archive, 1998.

[FGGS00] E. Farhi, J. Goldstone, S. Gutmann, and M. Sipser. 'Quantum Computation by Adiabatic Evolution'. *e-print arXiv: quant-ph/0001106*, 2000.

[FIMSS03] K. Friedl, G. Ivanyos, F. Magniez, M. Santha, and P. Sen. 'Hidden Translation and Orbit Coset in Quantum Computing'. *Proceedings of the*

Thirty-Fifth Annual ACM Symposium on Theory of Computing (STOC'03), 1–9, 2003.

[GGJ76] Garey, Graham and Johnson. 'Some NP-Complete Geometric Problems'. *Proceedings of the 8th Annual ACM Symposium on the Theory of Computing (STOC'76)*, 10–22, 1976.

[GJ79] Michael R. Garey and David S. Johnson. *Computers and Intractibility A Guide to the Theory of NP-Completeness* (W.H. Freeman and Company, New York, 1979).

[GJS76] M.R. Garey, D.S. Johnson, and L. Stockmeyer. 'Some Simplified NP-Complete Graph Problems'. *Theoretical Computer Science*, 1:237–267, 1976.

[GN96] R.B. Griffiths and C.S. Niu. 'Semi-Classical Fourier Transform for Quantum Computation'. *Physical Review Letters*, 3228–3231, 1996.

[Got98] Daniel Gottesman. 'A Theory of Fault-Tolerant Quantum Computation'. *Physical Review A*, 57:127–137, 1998.

[Gri97] D.Y. Grigoriev. 'Testing the Shift-Equivalence of Polynomials by Deterministic, Probablistic and Quantum Machines'. *Theoretical Computer Science*, 180:217–228, 1997.

[Gro96] Lov Grover. 'A Fast Quantum Mechanical Algorithm for Database Search'. *Proceedings of the 28th Annual ACM Symposium on the Theory of Computing (STOC 1996)*, 212–219.

[Gro98] Lov K. Grover. 'Quantum Computers Can Search Rapidly by Using Almost Any Transformation'. *Physical Review Letters*, 80:4329–4332, 1998.

[Gro05] L. Grover. 'Quantum Searching Amidst Uncertainty'. *Unconventional Computation, 4th International Conference*, Sevilla, Spain, 11–18, 2005.

[GSVV01] M. Grigni, L. Schulman, M. Vazirani, and U. Vazirani. 'Quantum Mechanical Algorithms for the Nonabelian Hidden Subgroup Problem'. *Proceedings of the Thirty-Third Annual ACM Symposium on Theory of Computing (SODA'03)*, 68–74, 2001.

[Hal05] S. Hallgren. 'Fast Quantum Algorithms for Computing the Unit Group and Class Group of a Number Field'. *Proceedings of the 37th ACM Symposium on Theory of Computing (STOC 2005)*, 468–474, 2005.

[HMW03] P. Høyer, M. Mosca, and R. de Wolf. 'Quantum Search on Bounded-Error Inputs'. *Proceedings of the Thirtieth International Colloquium on Automata, Languages and Programming (ICALP03)*, Eindhoven, The Netherlands, 291–299, 2003.

[Hoy97] Peter Høyer. 'Conjugated Operators in Quantum Algorithms'. *Physical Review A*, 59(5):3280–3289, 1999.

[HR90] Torben Hagerup and Christine Rub. 'Guided Tour of Chernoff Bounds'. *Information Processing Letters*, 33(6):305–308, 1990.

[HRS05] S. Hallgren, M. Roetteler, and P. Sen. 'Limitations of Quantum Coset States for Graph Isomorphism'. *arXiv e-print quant-ph/0511148*, 2005.

[HW79] G.H. Hardy and E.M. Wright. *An Introduction to the Theory of Numbers* (Oxford University Press, Oxford, 5th edition, 1979).

[IW97] R. Impagliazzo and A. Wigderson. 'P=BPP if E Requires Exponential Circuits: Derandomizing the XOR Lemma'. *Proceedings of the Twenty-*

Ninth Annual ACM Symposium on Theory of Computing, 220-229, 1997.

[JL02] R. Jozsa and N. Linden. 'On the Role of Entanglement in Quantum Computational Speed-ups'. *arXiv e-print quant-ph/0201143*, 2002.

[Jos99] Richard Jozsa. 'Searching in Grover's Algorithm'. *arXiv e-print quant-ph/9901021*.

[Kar72] R. Karp. 'Reducibility Among Combinatorial Problems'. *Complexity of Computer Computations*, 85–103, 1972.

[Kit96] A. Kitaev. 'Quantum Measurements and the Abelian Stabilizer Problem'. *Electronic Colloquium on Computational Complexity (ECCC)*, 3, 1996.

[Kit97] A.Y. Kitaev. 'Quantum Computations: Algorithms and Error Correction'. *Russ. Math. Surv.*, 52(6):1191–1249, 1998.

[KLZ97] Emanuel Knill, Raymond Laflamme, and Wojciech, Zurek. 'Resilient Quantum Computation: Error Models and Thresholds'. Technical Report, 1997. *Also arXiv e-print quant-ph/9702058*.

[KM01] P. Kaye and M. Mosca. 'Quantum Networks for Concentrating Entanglement'. *Journal of Physics A: Mathematical and General*, 34(35):6939–6948, 2001.

[KM02] P. Kaye and M. Mosca. 'Quantum Networks for Generating Arbitrary Quantum States'. *Proceedings of the International Conference on Quantum Information, OSA CD-ROM (Optical Society of America, Washington, D.C., 2002)*, PB28.

[Knu98] Donald E. Knuth. *Seminumerical Algorithms*, Volume 2 (Addison-Wesley, 3rd edition, 1998).

[Kob94] Neil Koblitz. *A Course in Number Theory and Cryptography* (Springer-Verlag, New York, 2nd edition, 1994).

[KS05] J. Kempe and A. Shalev. 'The Hidden Subgroup Problem and Permutation Group Theory'. *Proceedings of the Sixteenth Annual ACM-SIAM Symposium on Discrete Algorithms (SODA'05)*, 1118–1125, 2005.

[Kup05] G. Kuperberg. 'A Subexponential-Time Quantum Algorithm for the Dihedral Hidden Subgroup Problem'. *SIAM Journal on Computing*, 35: 170–188, 2005.

[KW03] I. Kerenidis and R. de Wolf. 'Exponential Lower Bound for 2-Query Locally Decodable Codes via a Quantum Argument'. *STOC '03: Proceedings of the Thirty-Fifth Annual ACM Symposium on Theory of Computing (STOC 2003)*, 106–115, 2003.

[Lev73] L.A. Levin. 'Universal Sorting Problems'. *Problems of Information Transmission*, 9:265–266, 1973.

[Llo95] Seth Lloyd. 'Almost Any Quantum Logic Gate Is Universal'. *Physical Review Letters*, 75:346–349, 1995.

[Llo96] S. Lloyd. 'Universal Quantum Simulators'. *Science*, 273:1073–1078, 1996.

[LTV98] M. Li, J. Tromp, and P. Vitanyi. 'Reversible Simulation of Irreversible Computation'. *Physica D*, 120:168–176, 1998.

[ME99] Michele Mosca and Artur Ekert. 'The Hidden Subgroup Problem and Eigenvalue Estimation on a Quantum Computer'. *Lecture Notes in Computer Science*, Volume 1509, 1999.

[Mil75] J.C.P. Miller. 'On factorisation, with a suggested new approach'. *Mathematics of Computation*, 29(129):155–172, 1975.

[Mos98] Michele Mosca. 'Quantum Searching and Counting by Eigenvector Analysis'. *Proceedings of Randomized Algorithms, Workshop of MFCS98, Brno, Czech Republic*, 1998.

[Mos99] Michele Mosca. *Quantum Computer Algorithms*. D.Phil. Dissertation, Wolfson College, University of Oxford, 1999.

[Mos01] M. Mosca. 'Counting by Quantum Eigenvalue Estimation'. *Theoretical Computer Science*, 264:139–153, 2001.

[MR95] Rajeev Motwani and Prabhakar Raghavan. *Randomized Algorithms* (Cambridge University Press, 1995).

[MRRS04] C. Moore, D. Rockmore, A. Russell and L. Schulman. 'The Power of Basis Selection in Fourier Sampling: Hidden Subgroup Problems in Affine Groups'. *Proceedings of the Fifteenth Annual ACM-SIAM Symposium on Discrete Algorithms (SODA'04)*, 1113–1122, 2004.

[MSS05] F. Magniez, M. Santha, and M. Szegedy. 'Quantum Algorithms for the Triangle Problem'. *Proceedings of the Sixteenth Annual ACM-SIAM Symposium on Discrete Algorithms (SODA'05)*, 1109–1117, 2005.

[MvOV97] Alfred J. Menezes, Paul C. Van Oorschot, and Scott A. Vanstone. *Handbook of Applied Cryptography* (CRC Press, London, 1997).

[MZ04] M. Mosca and C. Zalka. 'Exact Quantum Fourier Transforms and Discrete Logarithm Algorithms'. *International Journal of Quantum Information*, 2(1):91–100, 2004.

[NC00] Michael Nielson and Isaac Chuang. *Quantum Computation and Quantum Information* (Cambridge University Press, 2000).

[Neu56] John von Neumann. 'Probabilistic Logics and Synthesis of Reliable Organisms From Unreliable Components'. In C.E. Shannon and J. McCarthy, editors, *Automata Studies* (Princeton University Press, 1956).

[NS94] N. Nisan and M. Szegedy. 'On the Degree of Boolean Functions As Real Polynomials'. *Computational Complexity*, 4(4):301–313, 1994.

[NW99] Ashwin Nayak and Felix Wu. 'On the Quantum Black-Box Complexity of Approximating the Mean and Related Statistics'. *Proceedings of the 21st Annual ACM Symposium on Theory of Computing (STOC'99)*, 1999.

[Pap94] C. Papadimitriou. *Computational Complexity* (Addison-Wesley, 1994).

[Pat92] R. Paturi. 'On the Degree of Polynomials that Approximate Symmetric Boolean Functions'. *Proceedings of the 24th Annual Symposium on Theory of Computing*, 468–474, 1992.

[Pra75] Vaughan R. Pratt. 'Every Prime Has a Succinct Certificate'. *SIAM Journal on Computing*, 4(3):214–220, 1975.

[PRB99] Markus Püschel, Martin Rötteler, and Thomas Beth. 'Fast Quantum Fourier Transforms for a Class of Non-Abelian Groups'. *AAECC 1999*, 148–159.

[Pre] John Preskill. *Lecture notes. Available at http://www.theory.caltech.edu/% 7Epreskill/ph219/index.html# lecture*

[Raz99] Ran Raz. 'Exponential Separation of Quantum and Classical Communication Complexity'. *Proceedings of the 31st Annual ACM Symposium on the Theory of Computing (STOC 1999)*, 358–367.

[RB98] Martin Rötteler and Thomas Beth. 'Polynomial-Time Solution to the Hidden Subgroup Problem for a Class of Non-Abelian Groups'. *arXiv e-print quant-ph/9812070*, 1998.

[Reg04] O. Regev. 'Quantum Computation and Lattice Problems'. *SIAM Journal on Computing*, 33:738–760, 2004.

[Rog87] Hartley Rogers. 'Theory of Recursive Functions and Effective Computability' (MIT Press, 1987).

[RRS05] J. Radhakrishnan, M. Rötteler, and P. Sen. 'On the Power of Random Bases in Fourier Sampling: Hidden Subgroup Problem in the Heisenberg Group'. *In Proceedings of the 32nd International Colloquium on Automata, Languages and Programming (ICALP)*, 1399–1411, 2005.

[RSA78] R.L. Rivest, A. Shamir, and L.M. Adleman. 'A Method for Obtaining Digital Signatures and Public-Key Cryptosystems'. *Communications of the ACM*, 21:120–126, 1978.

[Sch95] Benjamin Schumacher. 'Quantum Coding'. *Phys. Rev. A* 51, 2738–2747, 1995.

[Sch98] R. Schack. 'Using a Quantum Computer to Investigate Quantum Chaos'. *Physical Review A*, 57:1634–1635, 1998.

[Sho94] Peter Shor. 'Algorithms for Quantum Computation: Discrete Logarithms and Factoring'. *Proceedings of the 35th Annual Symposium on Foundations of Computer Science*, 124–134, 1994.

[Sho95a] Peter Shor. 'Scheme for Reducing Decoherence in Quantum Computer Memory'. *Phys. Rev. A*, 52:2493, 1995.

[Sho96] Peter Shor. 'Fault-Tolerant Quantum Computation'. *Proceedings of the 37th Annual Symposium on Fundamentals of Computer Science*, 56–65, (IEEE Press, Los Alimitos, CA, 1996).

[Sho97] P. Shor. 'Polynomial-Time Algorithms for Prime Factorization and Discrete Logarithms on a Quantum Computer'. *SIAM J. Computing*, 26:1484–1509, 1997.

[Sim94] Daniel R. Simon. 'On the Power of Quantum Computation'. In Shafi Goldwasser, editor, *Proceedings of the 35th Annual Symposium on Foundations of Computer Science*, pp. 116–123 (IEEE Computer Society Press, November 1994).

[Sim97] D. Simon. 'On the Power of Quantum Computation'. *SIAM J. Computing*, 26:1474–1483, 1997.

[Sip83] M. Sipser. 'A Complexity Theoretic Approach to Randomness'. *Proc. 15th ACM Symp. on the Theory of Computing*, 330–335, 1983.

[Sip96] M. Sipser. 'Introduction to the Theory of Computation' (Brooks-Cole, 1996).

[SS71] A. Schönhage and V. Strassen. 'Schnelle Multiplikation grosser Zahlen'. *Computing*, 7:281–292, 1971.

[Ste96] A.M. Steane. 'Error Correcting Codes in Quantum Theory'. *Physical Review Letters*, 77:793–797, 1996.

[Ste97] A.M. Steane. 'Active Stabilization, Quantum Computation, and Quantum State Synthesis'. *Physical Review Letters*, 78:2252–2255, 1997.

[TDV04] Barbara Terhal and David DiVincenzo. 'Classical Simulation of Noninteracting-Fermion Quantum Circuits'. *Physical Review A*, 65:32325–32334, 2004.

[Ter99] Barbara Terhal. *Quantum Algorithms and Quantum Entanglement*. Ph.D. thesis, University of Amsterdam, 1999.

[Tur36] A.M. Turing. 'On Computable Numbers, with an Application to Entscheid-ungsproblem'. *Proc. London Math Society*, 42:230–265, 1936. Also, 43:544–546, 1937.

[Val02] L.G. Valiant. 'Quantum Circuits That Can Be Simulated Classically in Polynomial Time'. *SIAM Journal on Computing*, 31(4):1229–1254, 2002.

[Vaz98] U. Vazirani. 'On the Power of Quantum Computation'. *Philosophical Transactions of the Royal Society of London, Series A*, 356:1759–1768, 1998.

[Vid03] G. Vidal. 'On the Role of Entanglement in Quantum Computational Speedup.' *Physical Review Letters*, 91:147902, 2003.

[Wel88] Dominic Welsh. *Codes and Cryptography* (Oxford University Press, Oxford, 1998).

[Yao93] Andrew Chi-Chih Yao. 'Quantum Circuit Complexity'. *Proceedings of the 34th IEEE Symposium on Foundations of Computer Science*, pp. 352–361. (Institute of Electrical and Electronic Engineers Computer Society Press, Los Alamitos, CA, 1993).

[Zal98a] Christof Zalka. 'Fast Versions of Shor's Quantum Factoring Algorithm'. *Technical report 9806084, Los Alamos Archive*, 1998.

[Zal98b] Ch. Zalka. 'Efficient Simulation of Quantum Systems by Quantum Computers'. *Proc. Roy. Soc. Lond. A*, 454:313–322, 1998.

Index

Note: The italic page numbers indicate where terms are defined.

2-sided error quantum query complexity *192*

3-COLOURABLE, *see* 'problem—3-COLOURABLE'

3-CNF (3-conjunctive normal form) *184*

3-SAT (3-satisfiability), *see* 'problem—3-SAT'

Aaronson 185

Abelian stabilizer problem, *see* 'problem—Abelian stabilizer'

adiabatic algorithm, *see* 'algorithm—adiabatic'

adjoint *28*

adversary methods 180, *198*, 248

Alan Turing *3*

algorithm *1*, 4
  adiabatic 178
  amplitude estimation *172*
  continued fractions 123
  counting with accuracy ε *173*
  counting with error in $O(\sqrt{t})$ *173*
  Deutsch 94–8
  Deutsch–Jozsa 99–103
  discrete logarithm *144*
  eigenvalue estimation *129*
  estimating a random integer multiple of $\frac{1}{r}$ *139*
  exact counting *173*
  extended Euclidean *124*
  finding the period of a periodic state *122*
  finite Abelian hidden subgroup problem *149*
  searching 152–6, *157*, 158–63
  order-finding *137*
  order-finding, Shor's approach *139*
  probabilistic 86, 241
  quantum 88
  searching without knowing success probabilities I *177*
  searching without knowing success probabilities II *177*
  Simon's 103, 104, *105*, 109
  zero-error 107

amplitude *39*, 50, 87, 88

amplitude amplification 163–9

amplitude estimation 170–2

amplitude estimation algorithm, *see* 'algorithm—amplitude estimation'

amplitude estimation problem, *see* 'problem—amplitude estimation'

ancilla *50*, 75

AND-OR tree *201*

anti-commute *229*

approximating unitary transformations 71–3

balanced function *95*, 99

basis
  Bell *75*
  change of *30*, 74–6
  computational 22, *39*
  dual *27*
  orthonormal *25*
  vectors 22

beam splitter *15*, 18

Bell basis, *see* 'basis—Bell'

Bell measurement, *see* 'measurement—Bell'

Bell state *75*, 78

Bernoulli trials *242*

bit
  deterministic classical 39, 41, 43
  probabilistic classical 41, 42, 43
  quantum, *see* 'qubit'
  flip 205, 214

black box 94, 138, *180*, 185

black-box model *185*

black-box group *250*

Bloch sphere *42*, 43, 63, 65, 70

block sensitivity 180, *197*

Bohr 19

Boolean formula 184

bounded-error probabilistic polynomial time, *see* 'BPP'

bounded-error quantum polynomial time, *see* 'BQP'

BPP *182*, 183

BQP *182*, 183

bra *21*

Cauchy–Schwartz inequality *191*
change of basis *30*
channel *205*
    communication *78*, 79
    quantum *213*
character (of a group) 148
Chebyshev's inequality 242
Chernoff bound (inequality) 103, *242*, 246
Church–Turing thesis *3*
circuit
    acyclic *6*
    diagram *61*
    model of computation *6*, 61
    probabilistic *7*
    quantum 20, 61
    reversible *6*
    satisfiability 184
    uniform families of 6, *7*, 77, 180
Clay Mathematics Institute 185
Clifford group *91*
coherent error *215*
coin-flipper *4*, 5
communication channel, *see*
        'channel—communication'
communication protocol *78*
commute *229*
complete measurement, *see*
        'measurement—complete'
completely positive map 60
complex conjugate 23
complexity *2*, 7
    computational complexity theory *179*
    of discrete logarithm problem *145*
    of order finding 139
composite system 45, 46, 47, 57
Composition of Systems Postulate *46*
computational basis, *see*
        'basis—computational'
computational complexity theory, *see*
        'complexity—computational
        complexity theory'
computer *1*
condition for error correction *207*, 208
conditions for quantum error correction
    220
conjugate commutativity 23
constant function *94*, 99
continued fractions algorithm, *see*
        'algorithm—continued fractions'
control bit *10*
controlled-NOT gate (CNOT), *see*
        'gate—controlled-NOT
controlled-*U* gate (CNOT), *see*
        'gate—controlled-*U*
convergents *123*
correctable errors *206*
counting 170, 173, 174

de Broglie 19

decision problem *180*
density operator (density matrix) 27, *53*,
    54–7
depth *7*
discretization of errors *221*
deterministic *8*
deterministic query complexity *192*
Deutsch algorithm, *see*
        'algorithm—Deutsch'
Deutsch problem, *see* 'problem—Deutsch'
Deutsch–Jozsa algorithm, *see*
        'algorithm—Deutsch–Jozsa'
Deutsch–Jozsa problem, *see*
        'problem—Deutsch–Jozsa'
Dirac delta function $\delta_{i,j}$ *32*
Dirac notation *21*, 22, 24, 37
discrete Fourier transform 116
discrete logarithm algorithm, *see*
        'algorithm—discrete logarithm'
discrete logarithm problem, *see*
        'problem—discrete logarithm'
discrete random variable 241
dot product 23
dual vector space 24, 27

efficiency 2, 4, *183*
eigenspace 51
eigenstate, *see* 'eigenvector'
eigenvalue *29*, 30, 31, 51, 94
eigenvalue estimation 125–30
eigenvector *29*, 30, 31, 92, 94, 98
electromagnetism 19
electron 40
element distinctness problem, *see*
        'problem—element distinctness'
elliptic curve 142, 145
encoding *206*, 216
ensemble of pure states *53*
entanglement *46*, 56, 82
environment *213*
EPR-pair, *see* 'Bell state'
error-correcting code 5
error correction 5, 212–23
error model *205*, 213
error probability parameter *219*
error syndrome *209*
estimating a random integer multiple of
    $\frac{1}{r}$, *see* 'algorithm—estimating a
        random integer multiple of $\frac{1}{r}$'
Euclidean norm *25*
Evolution Postulate *44*, 45
exact quantum query complexity *192*
excited state 40
exclusive-OR operation *10*
exponential *2*
exponential function 32
extended Euclidean algorithm, *see*
        'algorithm—extended Euclidean'

factoring 110, 130, 132, *see also*
        'problem—integer factorization'
fault tolerance 5, *212*, 226, 234–8
fidelity *218*
finite Abelian hidden subgroup problem,
        see 'algorithm—finite Abelian
        hidden subgroup problem'
Feynman 20

gate *6*, 9
    1-qubit *44*, 47, 63, 66
    3-bit *7*
    AND 11
    controlled-NOT (CNOT) *10*, 47, 66–7, 82,
        91–2, 212
    controlled-*U* 66, *67*
    entangling *69*
    Hadamard, *see* 'Hadamard'
    NOT *9*, 44
    Pauli *44*, 64
    phase *71*
    rotation *63*, *64*, 70, 114
    square root of NOT *91*
    Toffoli *7*, 68, 210
    unitary 44, 61
    universal set *69*, 70, 71
    X *44*
    Y *44*
    Z *44*
general measurement, *see*
        'measurement—general'
general quantum operations 59–60
general search iterate 164
generalized Simon's algorithm, *see*
        'algorithm—generalized Simon's'
generalized Simon's problem, *see*
        'problem—generalized Simon's'
Gottesman–Knill theorem 91
graph automorphism problem, *see*
        'problem—graph automorphism'
greatest common divisor (GCD) *124*
ground state *40*
group representation theory 148
Grover's algorithm, *see*
        'algorithm—search'
Grover iterate *156*

Hadamard *70*, *71*, 100, 111
Hamiltonian 29, *45*
Heisenberg 19
Hermitean 29, *45*
Hermitean conjugate 24, *28*
hidden linear functions, *see*
        'problem—hidden linear functions'
hidden string 103, 107
hidden subgroup 109
hidden subgroup problem, *see*
        'problem—hidden subgroup'
Hilbert space *21*, 39, 50

hybrid method 180, 188

incoherent error *215*
information 19
information processing 1
inner product 21, *23*, 24, 25, 27, 37
integer factorization problem, *see*
        'problem—integer factorization'
integers mod *N 131*
interactive proofs 184
interference 16, 19, 88, 89, 94, 96
interval of convergence 32
intractable *183*
inversion about the mean 158
irreversible 12

ket *21*
Kraus operators *59*, *60*, 215, 221, 222,
        229, 238
Kronecker delta function, $\delta_{i,j}$ *25*
Kronecker product (left) *34*

language *180*
language recognition problem *180*
linear operator *27*
log-RAM model *4*, 180
logarithmic *2*
lower bounds *179*
lower bounds for searching 188
lowest common multiple (LCM) *124*

MA *184*
MAJORITY function *196*, 200
Markov's inequality 107, 241
matrix representation 8, 9, 24, 28, 34, 44,
        47, 71
Maxwell 19
measurement 19, 48, 49, 54
    Bell 75–6, 79, 82
    circuit diagram symbol 61
    complete 51, 77
    general 255
    implementing 73–7
    parity 51, 76, 130
    POVM 258
    projective 50, 76, 257
    pure *255*
    von Neumann 50–2, 77
Measurement Postulate 40, 41, 48, *49*, 50
Merlin–Arthur games, *see* 'MA'
Millennium Problems 185
mixed state *53*, 56
mixture *53*
modular arithmetic 131

network *6*
Newton 19
nine-qubit code, *see* 'Shor code'
no-cloning theorem 82, *216*

non-deterministic polynomial time, *see*
    'NP'
normalization constraint *40*
NP *183*
NP-complete *184*

O-notation 2, *179*
observable 51, 52, 130
Ω-notation *179*
operator 9, 21
  1-qubit unitary 45
  function of 32, 33
  Krauss 60
  normal 30
  Pauli, *see* 'gate—Pauli'
OR function *186*, 195, 196, 197
oracle, *see* 'black box'
order finding algorithm, *see*
    'algorithm—order finding'
order finding problem, *see*
    'problem—order finding'
orthogonal *25*
orthogonal complement *104*
orthonormal *25*
outer product 27

P *180*
P = NP question 185
parallel(ism) *8*, 94
parity 76, 77, 209, 212
PARITY function *196*, 200
parity measurement, *see*
    'measurement—parity'
partial function *192*
partial trace 56
period-finding algorithm, *see*
    'algorithm—finding the period of a
    periodic state'
period-finding problem, *see*
    'problem—period-finding'
periodic states *120*, 122
phase *40*
  estimation 112–20
  estimation problem, *see*
    'problem—phase estimation'
  flip *225*
  gate, *see* 'gate—phase'
  global 41
  kick-back 91–4
  parity 229
  relative 40
photon *15*, 38, 39
Planck 19
Poisson trials *242*
polynomial 2, 4, 72, *182*
polynomial method 180
polynomial time, *see* 'P'
positive operator valued measure 258
POVM, *see* 'measurement—POVM'

probabilistic algorithm, *see*
    'algorithm—probabilistic'
probabilistic Turing machine 4, 7, 20
probability amplitude, *see* 'amplitude'
problem
  3-COLOURABLE *181*, 183
  3-SAT 184, 190
  Abelian stabilizer *147*
  amplitude estimation *170*
  Deutsch *95*, 146
  Deutsch–Jozsa *99*, 192
  discrete logarithm *142*, 243
  discrete logarithms in any group *146*
  eigenvalue estimation *126*
  element distinctness 178
  generalized Simon's *108*, 146
  graph automorphism *147*
  graph isomorphism 184
  hidden linear functions *146*
  hidden subgroup *146*
  integer factorization *132*, 184
  order-finding 130, *133*, 146
  period-finding *146*, 192
  phase estimation *112*
  sampling estimates to an almost
    uniformly random integer multiple
    of $\frac{1}{r}$ *134*
  search *153*
  self-shift-equivalent polynomials *147*
  Simon's *104*
  splitting an odd non-prime-power
    integer *132*
  subset sum 184
  traveling salesman 184
projective measurement, *see*
    'measurement—projective'
projector 27, *29*, 50, 51
promise problem *192*
PSPACE *180*, 184
pure measurement, *see*
    'measurement—pure'
pure state *53*

quantize 40
quantum
  bit, *see* 'qubit'
  channel, *see* 'channel—quantum'
  computer *1*, 20
  electrodynamics 38
  error correction, *see* 'error correction'
  field theory 38
  Fourier transform (QFT) 94, 110, *116*,
    117
  information processing *1*, 38
  instrument *255*
  mechanics *19*, 38
  physics 15, 19, 38
  strong Church–Turing thesis *6*
  Turing machine 7

qubit *38*, 39
query complexity *186*

randomness *4*
  random access machine (RAM) *4*
  realistic model of computation *5*
  recovery operation *206*, 217–9
reduced density operator *56*
repetition code *211*
resolution of the identity *28*
reversible *12*, 13, 14
rounding off 163
RSA cryptosystem 130

sampling estimates to an almost
    uniformly random integer multiple
    of $\frac{1}{r}$, *see* 'problem—sampling
    estimates to an almost uniformly
    random integer multiple of $\frac{1}{r}$'
Schmidt
  basis 36, 59
  coefficients 35
  decomposition *35*, 37, 58, 253
Schrödinger 19
Schrödinger equation *45*
search algorithm, *see* 'algorithm—search'
search problem, *see* 'problem—search'
searching without knowing the success
    probability 175–7
self-shift-equivalent polynomials, *see*
    'problem—self-shift-equivalent
    polynomials'
Shor, Peter 130
Shor code *230*
Shor's algorithm, *see*
    'algorithm—order-finding, Shor's
    approach'
Simon's algorithm, *see*
    'algorithm—Simon's'
Simon's problem, *see* 'problem—Simon's'
simulation *3*, 4, 20, 91
Solovay–Kitaev theorem 72, 73
space *2*, 7, 8
spectral theorem 30, *31*, 32
spin 40
splitting an odd non-prime-power integer,
    see 'problem—splitting an odd
    non-prime-power integer'
stabilizer *229*
state 8, 39
state distinguishability *187*, 258
State Space Postulate *39*
stochastic matrix 89
strong Church–Turing thesis 2, *5*, 20
subset sum problem, *see*
    'problem—subset sum'
subsystem 10, 46, 56

superdense coding 78–80
superoperator *57*, 59, 61, 215
superpolynomial *2*
superposition 16, 18
symmetric function *192*

target bit *10*
Taylor series 32, 33
teleportation 80–5
tensor product 10, *33*, *34*, 46
Θ-notation *179*
threshold
  condition *235*, 236
  error probability *235*
  theorem 237, *239*
THRESHOLD$_M$ function *196*
time *2*, 7
time evolution 43
total function *192*
trace *29*, 54
tracing-out *57*
tractable *183*
traveling salesman problem, *see*
    'problem—traveling salesman'
Turing machine *3*
two-level system 39, 40

unary encoding *181*
uncompute 14
uniform *7*
unitary operator *29*, 44, 45, 48, *see also*
    'gate—unitary'
universal *7*, 69
  for 1-qubit gates *70*
  for classical computation *7*
  set of quantum gates, *see*
    'gate—universal set'

vector 8, 18, 21
  column 22, 23
  dual 21, 23, *24*
  norm of 25
  sparse 23
  state 39, 42, 53
  unit 25, 39, 40
verifier *184*
von Neumann measurement, *see*
    'measurement—von Neumann'

white box *186*
width *8*
wire *6*

XOR 102

zero-error algorithm, *see* 'algorithm—zero
    error'